Habeas Corpus after 9/11

Habeas Corpus after 9/11

Confronting America's
New Global Detention System

Jonathan Hafetz

NEW YORK UNIVERSITY PRESS
New York and London

NEW YORK UNIVERSITY PRESS
New York and London
www.nyupress.org

© 2011 by New York University
All rights reserved
First published in paperback in 2012.

Library of Congress Cataloging-in-Publication Data

Hafetz, Jonathan.
Habeas corpus after 9/11 : confronting America's
new global detention system / Jonathan Hafetz.
p. cm.
Includes bibliographical references and index.
ISBN 978-0-8147-3703-3 (cl : alk. paper) — ISBN 978-0-8147-2440-8 (pb : alk. paper) —
ISBN 978-0-8147-7343-7 (ebook)
1. Habeas corpus—United States. 2. Detention of persons—United States.
3. Terrorism—United States—Prevention. 4. Combatants and noncombatants
(International law) 5. Detention of persons—Cuba—Guantánamo Bay Naval
Base. 6. Prisoners of war—Legal status, laws, etc.—Cuba—Guantánamo Bay
Naval Base. 7. Guantánamo Bay Detention Camp. I. Title.
KF9011.H34   2010
345.73'056—dc22   2010026424

New York University Press books are printed on acid-free paper,
and their binding materials are chosen for strength and durability.
We strive to use environmentally responsible suppliers and materials
to the greatest extent possible in publishing our books.

Manufactured in the United States of America
10 9 8 7 6 5 4 3 2 1

To Martha, Ben, and Sam

Contents

Acknowledgments   ix

Introduction   1

PART 1

1   Laying the Foundation for the "War on Terror"   11

2   Guantánamo: Microcosm of a Prison beyond the Law   31

3   Guantánamo beyond Guantánamo: 46
    Toward a Global Detention System

4   Crossing a Constitutional Rubicon: 68
    The Domestic "Enemy Combatant" Cases

PART 2

5   Habeas Corpus and the Right to Challenge   81
    Unlawful Imprisonment

6   The Seeds of a Global Constitution   101

PART 3

7   A Modest Judicial Intervention: 117
    The First Supreme Court "Enemy Combatant" Decisions

8   The Battle for Habeas Corpus Continues   129

9   Tackling Prisons beyond the Law: Guantánamo Revisited   150

PART 4

10 Toward a Better Understanding of Habeas Corpus: 175
    Individual Rights and the Role of the Judiciary during Wartime

11 The Elusive Custodian: Some Potential Limits of Habeas Corpus   191

12 Terrorism as Crime: 205
    Toward a Lawful and Sustainable Detention Policy

13 Continuity and Change: 238
    The Detention Policy of a New Administration

    Notes   259

    Index   313

    About the Author   323

Acknowledgments

First I would like to thank the Brennan Center for Justice at New York University School of Law, my professional home for three years, which generously provided me with the opportunity and the support to write this book.

My thanks also to Baher Azmy, Emily Berman, Mark Denbeaux, Eric Freedman, Frederick Hafetz, Aziz Huq, Joe Margulies, Gabor Rona, and David Udell for their thoughtful comments and suggestions on draft versions of the book; to Margaret Rocco for her wonderful assistance with research; to Zak Shirley for all his help in the last stages; and to all my former colleagues at the ACLU's National Security Project for their inspiration, ideas, and support in challenging the illegal network of prisons beyond the law that are this book's subject. All errors, of course, remain my own.

In addition, I want to extend my gratitude to my editor, Debbie Gershenowitz, as well as to Gabrielle Begue, Despina Gimbel, and everyone else at NYU Press whose commitment and assistance made this book possible.

Finally, my deepest appreciation to my wife, Martha, and sons, Ben and Sam, to my parents, Fred and Myra, and to Jerry and Risa Pollack for their love and support.

Introduction

The U.S. detention center at the Guantánamo Bay Naval Base in Cuba has long been synonymous with torture, secrecy, and the abuse of executive power. It has come to epitomize lawlessness in the eyes of the world. Created in the name of protecting the country, Guantánamo has weakened it, undermining America's security as well as well as its values.

For too long, however, Guantánamo has been viewed in isolation, overshadowing other abuses and concealing broader shifts in America's national security policy since September 11, 2001. Guantánamo was never simply a prison, nor was it hermetically sealed. Rather, Guantánamo was part of a larger, interconnected global detention system that included other military prisons such as the Bagram Air Base in Afghanistan, secret CIA jails, and the transfer of prisoners to other countries for torture. This system encompassed even the military detention of individuals arrested inside the United States, whom President George W. Bush claimed he could hold indefinitely without charge as part of a "war on terrorism" without geographic or temporal bounds. Guantánamo, in short, was like an island in an archipelago of U.S. detention operations: the most visible example of a larger prison system designed to operate outside the law.

This system grew out of a series of decisions by Bush administration officials following the terrorist attacks of September 11. The Bush administration wanted to treat terrorism as an armed conflict rather than criminal activity and yet also wanted to avoid the limits that the law imposes on the detention and treatment of prisoners during wartime. In addition, the administration tried to create a category of prisoners without legal protections in order to justify a state-sanctioned policy of torture and other cruel and inhuman treatment. In this newly envisioned detention system, prisoners could be held indefinitely, potentially forever, without charge and without a meaningful hearing. The only trials were to be held in jerry-rigged military commissions that fell far short of constitutional and international standards. This system was intended to exist not only beyond the law but also beyond the reach of any court, as the Bush administration took every possible measure to prevent judges from examining its detention and treatment of prisoners held as "enemy combatants." Its goal was to imprison and interrogate without constraint or scrutiny.

The U.S. government's detention policies sparked intense legal battles. At the center of many of them was habeas corpus. Habeas corpus has long served as the preeminent safeguard of individual liberty and check against arbitrary government power by mandating that the state justify a prisoner's detention before a judge. The use of habeas, however, had changed over time, becoming principally a remedy for prisoners challenging their convictions based on constitutional defects at trial. After 9/11, habeas resumed its historic function as a remedy for executive imprisonment without trial. In three decisions since 9/11, the United States Supreme Court vindicated the importance of habeas by upholding the right of Guantánamo detainees to access U.S. courts, including two cases in which Congress had tried to strip the detainees of that right. In these rulings, the Court rejected the president's claim that he could detain prisoners without legal protections or hold them indefinitely without judicial review simply by imprisoning them outside the United States.

These victories, however, were both limited and incomplete. Although the Supreme Court rejected the notion that the Constitution necessarily stops at America's shores and upheld the right of Guantánamo detainees to habeas corpus, it did not guarantee judicial review of detention operations at other overseas prisons. The Court also did not grapple with other important questions in these cases or in its other "war on terror" decisions. It did not, for example, address who could be detained as an "enemy combatant" other than someone who was captured in Afghanistan while engaging in hostilities against U.S. or allied troops on behalf of Taliban forces. The Court thus failed to take on the president's claim that the entire world was a battlefield and that even individuals who were arrested in civilian settings in the United States and who never took part in hostilities on a battlefield (or anywhere else), could be treated as "combatants" and thereby denied the right to a criminal trial.

Other limits were inherent in the nature of habeas corpus itself. Habeas had proved its resilience in securing court review for prisoners at Guantánamo, where the fact of U.S. detention was clear and undisputed. But it was less effective where the United States sought to conceal its custody of or control over prisoners, whether by holding them in secret or enlisting another nation to detain them on its behalf. Similarly, habeas had shown a limited capacity to obtain judicial review over the rendition of prisoners to other countries for torture and continued detention. Habeas had also proved vulnerable in cases in which a court had found the detention by the United States to be illegal but believed that it lacked the authority to order the prisoner's release where release in the United States was the only available remedy since the detainee could not be safely returned home or repatriated to a third country.

The arrival of a new administration offered hope and the promise of change. President Barack Obama began with bold strokes, banning torture and ordering the closure of the prison at Guantánamo within a year. But the decisions in the following months suggested that most of these changes were small, if not cosmetic, and left the outgoing administration's policies intact in important respects. For example, Obama revived military commission trials and continued the indefinite detention of suspected terrorists without charge, two centerpieces of the Bush administration's "war on terror." Obama also resisted transparency in many cases and sought to deny torture victims access to U.S. courts based on exaggerated claims of government secrecy that served to conceal government misconduct and abuse. The Supreme Court had left Obama no choice but to accept habeas corpus jurisdiction at Guantánamo. But Obama tried to defend the executive's power to hold prisoners elsewhere without judicial review and continued to do so at Bagram, which had replaced Guantánamo as the United States' principal offshore detention center. In short, even as Obama spoke about the need to restore the rule of law and to return to constitutional principles, he preserved many of his predecessor's policies, tinkering at the edges but leaving the core intact. By the close of his first year in office, Obama had not only delayed the closing of Guantánamo. He had moved to adopt and institutionalize many of Guantánamo's key features.

This book describes the rise of the U.S.-run global detention system that emerged after 9/11 and the efforts to challenge it through habeas corpus. It examines both the achievements and the shortcomings of these legal challenges and confronts and repudiates arguments for limiting habeas. Finally, it advocates other measures necessary to prevent lawless detentions in the future and to create a rights-respecting national security policy that keeps America both safe and free.

The book is divided into four parts. The first part (chapters 1 through 4) examines the rise of the interconnected global detention system. Chapter 1 traces the origins of this system to a series of executive branch decisions and legal opinions that opened the door to arbitrary detention, sham military trials, and torture, all without court review. The system was intended to establish a new paradigm—the "war on terrorism"—in the name of meeting new threats facing the nation. This paradigm gave the president unprecedented powers to detain and interrogate without any restriction, rules, or accountability.

Chapter 2 examines how this new paradigm took shape at Guantánamo. It charts how Guantánamo grew to embody a prison beyond the law, pervaded by illegal detention, abuse, and secrecy. Then chapter 3 describes other off-shore U.S. prisons, from the military detention centers in Afghanistan and Iraq to secret CIA jails or "black sites." The chapter also details the use of extraordinary rendition, in which the United States outsourced torture by sending prisoners to other countries for brutal interrogations that U.S. officials did not want to conduct themselves. Chapter 4 looks at military detentions in the United States, examining three seminal cases in which the Bush administration sought to create a lawless enclave—a new Guantánamo—on American soil. Although few in number, these domestic "enemy combatant" cases represented the most far-reaching assertions of executive detention power in the "war on terrorism."

The second part (chapters 5 and 6) travels back in time to examine the origins of habeas corpus and its development over the centuries. Chapter 5 explains how habeas corpus came to protect individuals against unlawful imprisonment by the executive. It also discusses the role of habeas during wartime and how habeas helps police the line between civilian and military authority and prevent arbitrary government action. Chapter 6 examines how habeas corpus challenged detentions overseas before 9/11 as well as the principles that governed the extraterritorial application of constitutional rights more generally. It concludes by describing the gradual erosion of the idea that the Constitution's protections were strictly confined to the United States or to American citizens, a development with significant consequences for post-9/11 habeas cases.

Part 3 (chapters 7 through 9) turns to these cases, highlighting several themes and an enduring tension. The chapters illustrate, on the one hand, how habeas corpus has provided an important check against illegal detention and interrogation in U.S. counterterrorism operations. They also show, on the other hand, how habeas's checking function has led to continual efforts to undermine it, from congressional court-stripping measures to eleventh-hour machinations by the executive to avoid judicial review.

Chapter 7 discusses the trio of "enemy combatant" cases that reached the Supreme Court in 2004: *Rasul v. Bush*, *Hamdi v. Rumsfeld*, and *Rumsfeld v. Padilla*. These decisions established important principles, including the right of Guantánamo detainees to seek habeas corpus review in federal court and the right of American citizens to a fair hearing when they are detained by their government, even in time of war. They indicated that the executive would not be able to exclude the judiciary from the "war on terrorism." But the cases also left open important questions, including who exactly could be detained as an "enemy combatant" and what protections such persons could invoke.

The response by the president and Congress to these rulings is discussed in chapter 8. The Bush administration immediately moved to nullify the Supreme Court's ruling in *Rasul* by creating a rigged system of military status tribunals intended to ratify prior determinations that prisoners were "enemy combatants" and to prevent habeas hearings from going forward in federal courts, where the administration's allegations might be carefully scrutinized. Then Congress, at the administration's urging, passed legislation, the Detainee Treatment Act of 2005, which purportedly stripped federal courts of habeas jurisdiction over Guantánamo detentions altogether. Chapter 8 also describes the landmark Supreme Court ruling that followed, *Hamdan v. Rumsfeld*, which rejected this court-stripping measure, invalidated the president's military commissions, and concluded that no prisoner could be held without the baseline protections contained in Common Article 3 of the Geneva Conventions.

Chapter 9 examines the political backlash to *Hamdan* that resulted in new court-stripping legislation, the Military Commissions Act of 2006. This legislation purported to deny habeas corpus to any noncitizen held as an "enemy combatant," not just those held at Guantánamo. It also undermined the Geneva Conventions, sought to immunize U.S. officials for past abuse of detainees, and revived military commissions. The chapter then examines the Supreme Court's ruling in *Boumediene v. Bush*, decided near the end of the Bush administration. In affirming the right of Guantánamo detainees to habeas corpus, the Court decisively rejected the executive's claim that the Constitution was limited to the United States or to American citizens. Yet the Court left open important questions about whether habeas corpus reached other offshore prisons. The Court also suggested some limits on the relief that a habeas judge could order in a decision involving two American citizens detained in Iraq that it issued on the same day as *Boumediene*.

The fourth and final part (chapters 10 through 13) provides the broad outline of a legal and sustainable detention policy. As its starting point, it takes the singular importance of habeas corpus as a constraint against the growth of prisons beyond the law. It also explains why habeas alone is insufficient, its potential constrained by a combination of practical limits on its availability and the government's proclivity to seek new ways to detain and interrogate without judicial oversight.

Chapter 10 argues why habeas corpus should be available to any prisoner in U.S. custody, regardless of his or her citizenship or location. The chapter explains why this review is necessary to help prevent the growth of prisons beyond the law. It also explains why this review, properly understood, does not interfere with the government's ability to wage war or fight terrorism but instead provides a safeguard against illegal detention and other abuses.

Chapter 11 explores some of the potential limits of habeas corpus. For example, it describes the difficulties of challenging more covert forms of executive action, such as proxy detention and rendition, in which the U.S. role is either concealed or outsourced, and offers some possible solutions. Chapter 12 continues this discussion. It focuses not on where habeas corpus may extend (as chapter 11 does) but on the questions that habeas courts may consider in adjudicating petitions. While habeas corpus provides the opportunity for meaningful judicial review of executive action, the mere availability of that review does not by itself resolve the underlying legal and constitutional questions surrounding the scope of the executive's legal authority to detain in counterterrorism operations or to hold individuals without criminal trial in the regular federal courts. Chapter 12 argues for restricting that detention authority by returning to the long-standing practice of prosecuting suspected terrorists in civilian courts. The chapter thus argues against indefinite military detention, military commissions, and hybrid proposals like national security courts that sanction imprisonment without trial and the use of adjudicatory tribunals with fewer protections of individual rights.

Chapter 13 summarizes national security policy during President Obama's first year in office. It contrasts the new president's initial moves, like ordering Guantánamo's closure and banning torture, with his subsequent adoption of military commissions and indefinite detention. Chapter 13 shows that despite some positive steps, the Obama administration has largely embraced continuity over change and that key components of the post-9/11 detention system are threatening to become permanent features of America's legal fabric and political discourse.

The book concludes that the United States' counterterrorism policy since 9/11 underscores the continued importance of habeas corpus as a safeguard of individual liberty against illegal government action. Despite its limitations, habeas remains the single most important check against arbitrary and unlawful detention, torture, and other abuses. As it did centuries ago for those jailed without trial, habeas today still promises "the water of life to revive from the death of imprisonment."[1] The threat of terrorism, some people believe, makes the United States' historic commitment to habeas unnecessary and unwise. But precisely the opposite is true. The pressure that terrorism puts on government officials to avoid legal limits and to find new ways to imprison allegedly dangerous or suspicious people without charge, due process, or meaningful scrutiny, makes habeas corpus all the more important, both now and in the future.

— Part 1 —

1

Laying the Foundation for
the "War on Terror"

On the morning of September 11, 2001, the United States suffered the most devastating attacks on American soil in the nation's history. Nineteen men hijacked four commercial jet airliners and attempted to fly them into several U.S. targets. Two planes crashed into New York City's World Trade Center, destroying both towers. A third plane hit the Pentagon. The fourth plane was diverted by the passengers and crashed in a field in Pennsylvania. Nearly three thousand people died in the attacks, and the United States suffered untold trauma and billions of dollars in damages. Within days, responsibility had been attributed to al Qaeda and its leader, Osama bin Laden.[1] Al Qaeda's ability to orchestrate a complicated attack within the United States shocked the country and seared into its collective conscience the fact that the oceans separating it from the rest of the world would not protect it from those who sought its destruction.[2]

Vice President Dick Cheney declared that "9/11 changed everything."[3] But it was the decisions made after that fateful day that had the most far-reaching consequences. On September 18, President George W. Bush signed into law the Authorization for Use of Military Force (AUMF), a congressional resolution authorizing him to "use all necessary and appropriate force against those nations, organizations, or persons he determines planned, authorized, committed, or aided the terrorist attacks that occurred on September 11, 2001, or harbored such organizations or persons."[4] Two days later, President Bush addressed a joint session of Congress, condemning the attacks as "an act of war against our country" and promising to bring the perpetrators—the terrorist organization al Qaeda—to justice. He also made clear that the Taliban, the government of Afghanistan, would be subject to retaliation for sheltering and harboring al Qaeda. Bush, however, did not stop there. He also described a military conflict of an apocalyptic nature that extended beyond any nation or single terrorist group. "Americans," he said, "should not expect one battle, but a lengthy campaign, unlike any other we have ever seen." That battle would be waged against enemies wherever they were and would "not end until every terrorist group of global reach has been found, stopped, and defeated."[5]

Meanwhile, a coterie of high-level administration officials began laying the foundation for sweeping presidential powers in this new global "war on terrorism." The group included the then White House counsel Alberto R. Gonzales, Cheney's legal adviser and longtime aide David S. Addington, Pentagon general counsel William J. Haynes II, and John Yoo, a thirty-four-year-old lawyer in the Department of Justice's Office of Legal Counsel (OLC), the office that provides legal advice to the executive branch and whose opinions bind executive agencies.[6] Together, these men would help create the conceptual and legal architecture for this "new type of war."[7]

Yoo became one of the most important—and vocal—proponents of sweeping executive power. In a September 25, 2001, memo, Yoo described the president's paramount role in protecting the nation through the use of military force. The decision whether to use armed force abroad, as well as the amount of force to be used, Yoo insisted, fell within the president's "sole constitutional authority." He claimed his theories were grounded in the tradition of a strong executive that dated back to Alexander Hamilton. Yoo also pointed to more recent precedents in which presidents had ordered military strikes in response to terrorist attacks: President Bill Clinton in Afghanistan and Sudan in 1998 and President Ronald Reagan in Libya in 1986. Besides maintaining that Congress had given President Bush power to wage war against terrorism under the AUMF, Yoo also claimed that the president inherently possessed this power by virtue of his role as commander in chief under Article II of the U.S. Constitution. He further asserted that Congress could not impose any limits on the president's power to use military force to defend the nation.[8]

In another OLC memo, Yoo wrote that the president could deploy the military against suspected terrorists within the United States, with or without congressional approval.[9] In doing so, Yoo said, the president would not be bound by the Fourth Amendment to the Constitution, which prohibits searches and seizures without a warrant or probable cause, since that amendment does not apply to the military during wartime. The president would thus have unfettered discretion to set up checkpoints in an American city, raid or attack dwellings, use deadly force against individuals, and suspend First Amendment freedoms of speech and press. The Posse Comitatus Act, on the books since 1878, prohibited the military from engaging in domestic law enforcement.[10] But Yoo's memo sought to emasculate that act and circumvent limits on using the armed forces inside the United States by redefining terrorism broadly as a "military matter."

Notwithstanding these assertions of virtually limitless presidential power, U.S. detention policy remained largely unchanged during the first months after September 11. Two high-profile federal cases suggested that the Bush administration might continue to treat terrorism as a crime subject to prosecution in civilian court rather than through the president's war powers. The first case involved John Walker Lindh, an American citizen who had been captured in a military raid in Afghanistan in December 2001. Lindh was charged three months later in federal court in Virginia for his alleged role in the death of a CIA officer killed during fighting in Afghanistan. The second involved Zacarias Moussaoui, initially believed to be the replacement for the "twentieth hijacker"—the person who failed to board the plane that crashed in Pennsylvania on 9/11. Moussaoui had been arrested by immigration officials in Minnesota in August 2001 and was indicted on terrorism charges in Virginia four months later.

Congress, meanwhile, had enacted new counterterrorism legislation, commonly known as the "Patriot Act."[11] Passing by wide margins in both houses six weeks after 9/11, the Patriot Act expanded law enforcement's authority to investigate and prosecute suspected terrorists. For example, the act loosened restrictions on electronic surveillance and on the use of pen register or trap-and-trace devices that identify the source and destination of telephone and Internet communications.[12] It also broadened the use of "national security letters," an administrative subpoena that permits the FBI to compel the disclosure of telephone, e-mail, and financial records without a court order. Another provision authorized officials to conduct secret "sneak and peak" searches of suspects' homes without notifying them.[13] In addition, the Patriot Act increased the government's authority to obtain personal records, including lists of books that people borrow from libraries or purchase at bookstores, by certifying it was conducting an investigation to obtain foreign intelligence information or to protect against international terrorism.[14] Besides enhancing the government's investigative powers, the Patriot Act strengthened existing criminal statutes, including expanding the reach of existing laws against providing material support to terrorists and widening the definition of "domestic terrorism" to apply to groups targeting the United States or attempting to influence U.S. policy through threats and coercion.[15] Although the Patriot Act has been rightly criticized for curtailing civil liberties, it still operated within a legal framework that subjected the government to some limitations and oversight and continued to treat terrorism predominantly as a law enforcement problem.

Nonetheless, a different approach was taking shape beyond the public's view. After John Walker Lindh's capture, his parents retained defense attorney James Brosnahan to represent him. Brosnahan immediately contacted high-level U.S. officials to inform them that he was representing Lindh and wanted to meet with him. For the next two months, Brosnahan's requests were refused, even though Lindh repeatedly asked to speak to a lawyer. All this while, Lindh was held incommunicado and interrogated by U.S. officials. Letters from Lindh's parents to their son were blocked. Lindh was blindfolded, tied to a stretcher with duct tape, held in a freezing dark cell while naked, and deprived of sleep and food. In an effort to extract a confession through force, top Pentagon officials instructed interrogators to "take the gloves off."[16] Ultimately, the confession extracted from Lindh through brutal interrogation sessions served as the basis for his prosecution. Meanwhile, Justice Department attorneys who raised concerns about Lindh's treatment were ignored or discredited.[17] When Lindh's lawyers prepared to challenge the validity of his confession in open court, prosecutors offered a last-minute deal that would shield Lindh's abuse from scrutiny by allowing Lindh to plead guilty to one of ten charges and serve a twenty-year sentence rather than face the death penalty.[18] Lindh accepted, fearful of a jury's response in the emotionally charged atmosphere after 9/11.

Some administration officials believed that Lindh's case showed why the criminal justice system should not be used to handle suspected terrorists. In their view, the problem was that criminal prosecutions were incompatible with secrecy, incommunicado detention, and coercive interrogation and thus were ill suited for the challenges presented by the current terrorist threat. Involving lawyers and courts made it more difficult to engage in harsh interrogations, to justify detention without evidence, and to conceal mistakes. A new approach—or "new paradigm," as President Bush called it—was needed. That paradigm substituted indefinite military detention and possible prosecution in military tribunals for the requirement that individuals suspected of terrorism or other wrongdoing be charged and tried in the regular criminal courts. It also embraced torture and other abusive interrogation methods and spurned the rules that had long governed the conduct of war, including the Geneva Conventions, U.S. military regulations, and customary international law. In late 2001 and early 2002, the Bush administration made a series of decisions laying the legal groundwork for this new paradigm. These decisions helped define the post-9/11 era and pave the way for an unprecedented global detention system outside the law.

• • •

On October 7, 2001, the United States commenced Operation Enduring Freedom, launching its first military strikes against Afghanistan. This military campaign sought to target al Qaeda and to punish the Taliban for supporting and harboring it. The United States was aided by other members of NATO and by the Afghan Northern Alliance, an umbrella group of mujahideen, who provided the bulk of the armed forces on the ground. At first, the U.S.-led military invasion of Afghanistan resembled past armed conflicts more than the new kind of war that President Bush had described in speeches. It began with air strikes against cities, al Qaeda training camps, and Taliban air defenses and was followed by a ground offensive by U.S. and allied troops. Soon, however, the intervention in Afghanistan departed from these earlier military campaigns when the Bush administration jettisoned the legal rules that applied to armed conflict in order to evade any restrictions on the detention and treatment of those it captured.

These rules commonly known as "international humanitarian law" (or the "law of war"), are divided into two branches. The first branch, known as *jus ad bellum*, is concerned with the legitimacy of the resort to armed force. The second, *jus in bello*, provides a legal framework for an armed conflict already in progress. It is derived from international treaties ratified by individual countries as well as binding customary law. This branch includes the Hague Conventions of 1899 and 1907, which address the methods and means of warfare and seek to mitigate the harm and violence beyond that necessary to achieve the military goal by, for example, codifying the principle that military organizations may lawfully attack only targets of military value.[19] It also includes the Geneva Conventions. First drafted in Geneva, Switzerland, in 1864 and last revised in 1949, the Conventions have been ratified by every country in the world and thus enjoy universal acceptance. The Conventions together set forth rules governing the detention, interrogation, and release of prisoners by individual states. Each of the four Conventions provides rules for a different category of prisoners. The two best known are the Third Geneva Convention, which regulates the treatment of enemy prisoners of war, and the Fourth Geneva Convention, which applies to civilians (or noncombatants).[20] Under the Geneva Conventions, a nation can hold enemy soldiers for the duration of the conflict, but prisoners cannot be mistreated under any circumstances. To the contrary, prisoners of war "must at all times be treated humanely" and "protected . . . against acts of violence or intimidation."[21] They also must be "released and repatriated without delay after the cessation of active hostilities."[22] Civilians enjoy similar protections against abuse and mistreatment as well as restrictions on their continued detention and the guarantee of a fair trial if they are prosecuted for any crimes they commit during the armed conflict.

The Geneva Conventions recognize that some individuals will not qualify for prisoner-of-war status because, for example, they are not members of the armed forces of a party to the conflict, or they are part of a militia or volunteer corps that does not operate under an organized command structure, carry its weapons openly, have a fixed sign of identification, or adhere to the laws of war.[23] Article 5 of the Third Geneva Convention, however, requires that individuals be treated as prisoners of war until a determination is made by a competent tribunal, should any doubt arise as to their status.[24] In addition, Common Article 3—so named because it is common to all four Geneva Conventions— provides a baseline of treatment for all individuals denied prisoner-of-war status. It prohibits trials that do not meet internationally recognized standards and bars torture, cruel, humiliating or degrading treatment, and other abuse. Common Article 3 is widely understood to have attained the status of customary international law, making it binding on the United States even against an enemy that has not signed the Geneva Conventions. In short, the Geneva Conventions ensure that "nobody in enemy hands can be outside the law."[25]

Before the attacks on September 11, the United States had followed the Geneva Conventions, even in those conflicts in which the enemy did not.[26] It also had implemented the Geneva Conventions through internal regulations. The United States' decades-long adherence to the Geneva Conventions was not simply the product of idealism; it also reflected a pragmatic assessment by military leaders that the arbitrary detention and mistreatment of prisoners would place U.S. service members at greater risk if they fell into enemy hands and that abusive interrogation methods were counterproductive as well as immoral.[27]

The Bush administration, however, deliberately scuttled this legal framework. An ominous sign came on November 13, 2001, when Bush issued an order calling for the establishment of military commissions to try prisoners captured in the "war on terror."[28] The order stated that the commissions could prosecute any foreign national if the president had "reason to believe" he "is or was a member of . . . al Qaeda" or had "engaged in, aided or abetted, or conspired to commit" a terrorist act.[29] The order empowered the commissions to impose sentences of up to life imprisonment or death.

Military commissions historically were ad hoc trials conducted by military officers to fill a gap in criminal jurisdiction created when the ordinary courts were not open and functioning. Commissions were used, for example, in battlefield situations in which martial law had been declared because no civilian authority existed or in occupied enemy territory. In fact, the first American military commissions were used by General Winfield Scott in occupied parts of Mexico to punish undisciplined action and other miscon-duct by American troops during the Mexican-American War.[30]

The United States had not used military commissions since World War II, and those commissions had come under attack as unprincipled and unfair.[31] Moreover, those military commissions were of limited scope, as they were used against only a handful of individuals in a declared war among nations. By contrast, the new commissions could assert jurisdiction over any person suspected of supporting, aiding, or committing terrorism in a loosely defined war without geographic or temporal limits.

U.S. military law also had evolved significantly since the establishment of the Uniform Code of Military Justice (UCMJ) in 1951. The UCMJ applies to all members of the armed services of the United States. By 2001, the UCMJ's courts-martial system could plausibly boast that it provided more robust protections to defendants than did the civilian justice system. But President Bush's order threatened to take military justice backward, undermining the integrity and reputation it had gained through years of reforms dedicated to providing fair trials for defendants.

The Bush administration's creation of military commissions was largely carried out in secret, driven by "a small core of conservative administra-tion officials" wielding "remarkable power."[32] These officials excluded other executive branch agencies and Congress. They also refused to consult with the military's lawyers, the Judge Advocate General's (JAG) Corps, who would eventually become some of the commissions' harshest critics.[33] "There was great concern that we were setting up a process that was contrary to our own ideals," commented John A. Gordon, a retired air force general and for-mer deputy CIA director who served on President Bush's National Security Council staff.[34] Officials from the Justice Department's criminal division also criticized the use of military commissions, arguing that federal courts could more capably prosecute terrorism suspects without compromising constitu-tional principles.[35]

Although Bush's November 13, 2001, order promised defendants "a full and fair trial," that promise was illusory. The commissions lacked critical safeguards, including the presumption of innocence, the right to see the government's evidence and cross-examine its witnesses, and any right of appeal to civilian court. The order also did not guarantee that trials would adhere to the Geneva Conventions, the customary laws of war, or U.S. military law. The Defense Department tried to quell the criticism that sur-rounded announcement of the president's order by tweaking the commis-sions' procedures. But those reforms failed to address critical shortcomings.

The commissions still allowed evidence obtained through coercion, denied defendants the right to be present during their trial, and lacked impartiality. The commissions also claimed the authority to try offenses, such as conspiracy, that had never been recognized as war crimes. Furthermore, only foreign citizens could be tried by the commissions, presaging the creation of a permanent second-class justice system for noncitizens that openly discriminated based on nationality.

President Bush's military commissions, however, formed only one part of the emerging detention regime. The administration also began classifying prisoners as "enemy combatants" and claiming that it could hold them indefinitely without trial (whether military or civilian) if it chose to.[36] Even though the power to detain enemy soldiers for the duration of a conflict is grounded in the law of war, the administration's concept of "enemy soldier" was entirely novel. Most prisoners seized after 9/11 bore little, if any, resemblance to the legal definition or traditional understanding of a combatant. They were not members of an enemy government's armed forces. They also had never been on a battlefield nor had they taken part in hostilities against the United States or its allies. In time, imprisonment without trial would become the central feature of the post-9/11 detention system, condemning prisoners to what one Pentagon official called a "Kafkaesque sort of purgatory."[37]

A series of secret legal memos issued in early 2002 addressed the treatment of prisoners held in the "war on terror," and over time, many of these memos became public. They tell a disturbing story of a concerted attempt by top Bush administration lawyers and officials to create a category of prisoners outside the law.

On January 9, 2002, John Yoo and Robert J. Delahunty, a special counsel in the Department of Justice, advised William Haynes about the potential applicability of international humanitarian law to the "war on terrorism."[38] Yoo and Delahunty concluded that the Geneva Conventions did not apply to al Qaeda or the Taliban and thus would not constrain the long-term detention of prisoners or use of military commissions. Yoo and Delahunty also defined the conflict with al Qaeda separately from the conflict with the Taliban in Afghanistan, thus claiming legitimacy for a global war against a terrorist organization whose members were not entitled to the protections afforded prisoners of war or civilians under the Geneva Conventions. Even the minimal protections of Common Article 3, they argued, did not cover al Qaeda or associated organizations because it applied only to civil wars within nations, not "international" conflicts with terrorist groups.

Yoo and Delahunty reached a similar conclusion about the Taliban, even though Afghanistan had been a party to all four Geneva Conventions since 1956. They contended that Afghanistan was a "failed state" whose territory had been overrun and was under the control of a violent militia or faction rather than a central government. They claimed that the Taliban and its leadership were dominated by, and could not be distinguished from, al Qaeda. As a result, Afghanistan had ceased to be a party to the Geneva Conventions, so Taliban members were not entitled to any of the Conventions' protections. Nor could Taliban members invoke the protections of customary international law, since those rules did not bind the president, thus placing those individuals entirely outside any protections provided under the law of war.

Jay S. Bybee, then the OLC's top lawyer and now a federal appeals court judge, reached a similar conclusion.[39] The Geneva Conventions, Bybee pointed out in a memo to both Haynes and White House counsel Alberto Gonzales, did not apply to the detention of al Qaeda prisoners. In addition, the president could unilaterally "suspend" America's Geneva Convention obligations toward Afghanistan or, alternatively, conclude that members of the Taliban failed to qualify as prisoners of war under the treaty. Either way, the decision whether to afford prisoners protection under the Geneva Conventions was the president's alone to make.

These memos helped provide the building blocks for a detention regime subject to no restriction other than executive say-so. In what became a hallmark of U.S. policy after 9/11, the president would invoke the language and imagery of war to justify extraordinary powers while at the same time defining the war in such a way as to avoid any limits on the exercise of those powers. The memos also served a darker purpose: insulating U.S. officials from potential criminal liability. A 1996 law known as the War Crimes Act had made it a federal felony to commit a grave breach of the Geneva Conventions (which included any violation of Common Article 3).[40] The Geneva Conventions required state parties to enact penal legislation to punish any person who committed or ordered a grave breach of the Conventions.[41] The War Crimes Act, passed by an overwhelming majority in Congress, was intended to ensure that the United States could prosecute war criminals, such as the North Vietnamese who tortured American soldiers during the Vietnam War. After 9/11, however, White House officials were concerned about exposing American military as well as CIA officials to liability for violating the Geneva Conventions in their treatment and interrogation of detainees. The determination that the Geneva Conventions did not apply to al Qaeda or the Taliban thus provided a shield against future criminal liability, since liability attached only if an abused prisoner fell within the Conventions' zone of protection.

Alberto Gonzales summarized these views in a memo to the president dated January 25, 2002.[42] The "war against terrorism," Gonzales stated, "is a new kind of war," one that placed "a high premium" on obtaining information quickly from detainees to prevent a future attack. It made "obsolete" the Geneva Conventions' restrictions on interrogating detainees and rendered "quaint" the various privileges and protections afforded to prisoners of war. Gonzales thus urged the president to make a blanket determination that the Geneva Conventions did not apply to al Qaeda or the Taliban. Such a determination would not only free interrogators to use harsh methods; it also would create "a reasonable basis in law" that the War Crimes Act did not apply and thus "provide a solid defense to any future prosecution." The potential harm to America's credibility caused by skirting the Geneva Conventions, Gonzales said, could be minimized by promising to treat detainees "humanely."[43]

Not everyone in the administration agreed. Secretary of State Colin L. Powell urged the president to follow the Geneva Conventions.[44] Powell explained that denying detainees the protections of the Geneva Conventions would carry significant costs, reversing "over a century of U.S. policy and practice" and "undermin[ing] the protections of the law of war for our troops." It would also deprive the United States of the strongest legal foundation for detaining individuals and could weaken public support among critical allies. William H. Taft IV, Powell's top legal adviser, echoed these concerns.[45]

But Bush rejected their advice. Instead, on February 7, 2002, the president concluded that the Geneva Conventions did not apply to the conflict with al Qaeda in Afghanistan "or elsewhere throughout the world."[46] He also determined that although the Geneva Conventions applied to the conflict with the Taliban in Afghanistan, all Taliban detainees were "unlawful combatants." As such, Bush said, they failed to qualify not only for prisoner-of-war status but also for the baseline protections of Common Article 3. Furthermore, Bush asserted his authority to suspend the Geneva Conventions as he deemed necessary.[47] To be sure, Bush said that as a matter of policy, U.S. forces should "treat detainees humanely and, to the extent appropriate and consistent with military necessity, in a manner consistent with the principles of Geneva."[48] But "humane" treatment was a malleable term and, once severed from any legal obligation, this weak instruction would do nothing to prevent the pervasive and wholesale abuse of prisoners, especially when pressure to produce actionable intelligence mounted. In addition, the promise of "humane treatment" never included the CIA, which remained free from even this minimal constraint.

The themes that Bush had sounded in the first days after 9/11 thus started to assume a tangible form. In the following months, the administration sought legal cover for interrogation methods designed to sanction the torture and abuse of prisoners by the United States. Supporters of these methods claimed they were necessary to prevent future terrorist acts and that the United States was not obligated—morally or legally—to afford suspected terrorists any protections.

An important step in the descent into lawlessness was an August 1, 2002, OLC memo signed by Bybee but reportedly drafted by Yoo, with contributions from Addington and White House counsel Timothy E. Flanigan.[49] The memo assessed the permissible standards of conduct under a 1994 federal statute criminalizing torture.[50] Congress had enacted this law to implement the United States' obligations under the Convention against Torture and other Cruel, Inhuman or Degrading Treatment or Punishment.[51] By signing the treaty in 1988, the United States recognized that the ban on torture was absolute and could not be excused even under exigent circumstances. Under the federal statute, any person who "specifically intended to inflict severe mental pain or suffering," other than pain administered pursuant to lawful sanctions, on a person in his custody or control could be prosecuted and sentenced to up to twenty years in prison or to death, if death of the prisoner resulted.[52] Thus, even if U.S. officials could not be prosecuted under the War Crimes Act because the Geneva Conventions did not apply to the conflict with al Qaeda and the Taliban, as Bush claimed, they still could be held criminally liable under the federal antitorture statute.

The "torture memo," as it is became known, helped create what Georgetown Law School professor David Luban called a "torture culture" within the executive branch of the U.S. government.[53] The memo interpreted the phrase "specifically intended" in the antitorture statute to mean that infliction of severe pain must be the interrogator's "precise objective." Thus, if the interrogator's intent were obtaining information to prevent some future harm, rather than inflicting pain (which could almost always said to be the case), the interrogator would not be liable. The memo also narrowly defined "severe pain" to mean pain causing "death, organ failure, or permanent damage resulting in the loss of significant bodily functions" and asserted that mental suffering must be prolonged to be severe.[54] The source for the definition was an irrelevant medical benefits statute that had no relationship to established domestic or international understandings of torture but that conveniently suited the authors' needs. Under this twisted logic, although a technique such as waterboarding—in which water is poured over a bound prisoner's cloth-covered face to induce the sensation of drowning—might induce extraordinary suffering, it would not constitute torture.

The "torture memo" was not an academic exercise, nor was it penned in a vacuum. Rather, as a second classified OLC memo from the same day shows, it was drafted in response to a request for permission to apply a series of "enhanced interrogation techniques" to Abu Zubaydah, a recently captured terrorist suspect.[55] Following his seizure in Pakistan in March 2002, Zubaydah was taken to a secret CIA prison in Thailand. The CIA insisted that Zubaydah was a high-ranking al Qaeda official with valuable and time-sensitive information that could prevent another attack, information the CIA believed Zubaydah was not providing.[56] In mid-May, attorneys from the CIA's Office of General Counsel met with top administration officials, including the attorney general, the national security adviser, and the White House counsel, to discuss the use of "alternative" interrogation methods. Another meeting took place two months later to discuss using these methods against Zubaydah. The OLC was asked to prepare a memo assessing the methods' legality and subsequently informed the CIA of its conclusions.[57]

Bybee's classified August 1, 2002, memo (later made public) applied the OLC's legal interpretation of the federal antitorture law to specific interrogation methods. Set forth in painstaking and mind-numbing detail, those methods not only included waterboarding but also extreme sleep deprivation; stuffing detainees in dark, constricted boxes; repeatedly slamming detainees into walls; and dousing detainees with cold water for up to twenty minutes while they were clothed in only a diaper.[58] The methods were intended for use in combination and over long periods of time to instill helplessness, fear, and desperation. Medical and psychological personnel would be on hand to monitor the interrogations and ensure that the suffering did not leave a trace. As one medical official later told a detainee, "I look after your body only because we need you for information."[59]

The memo described the interrogation methods in sterile, almost clinical terms:

> In this procedure [waterboarding], the individual is bound securely to an inclined bench, which is approximately four feet by seven feet. The individual's feet are gently elevated. A cloth is placed over the forehead and eyes. Water is then applied to the cloth in a controlled manner. As this is

done, the cloth is lowered until it covers both the nose and mouth. Once the cloth is saturated and completely covers the mouth and nose, air flow is slightly restricted for 20 to 40 seconds due to the presence of the cloth. This causes an increase in carbon dioxide level in the individual's blood. This increase in the carbon dioxide level stimulates increased effort to breathe. This effort plus the cloth produces the perception of "suffocation and incipient panic," i.e., the perception of drowning. The individual does not breathe any water into his lungs. During those 20 to 40 seconds, water is continuously applied from a height of twelve to twenty-four inches. After this period, the cloth is lifted, and the individual is allowed to breathe unimpeded for three or four full breaths. The sensation of drowning is immediately relieved by the removal of the cloth. The procedure may then be repeated.[60]

Arbitrary lines were drawn in an effort to defend the techniques' legality: waterboarding could be practiced, but only with a saline solution to keep blood sodium levels within a safe range; detainees could be shackled to floors or ceilings to keep them awake, but not for more than seven days; detainees could be stuffed in cramped, dark containers, but not for more than eight hours at a time. The memo's language, the New York Times later wrote, was "the precise bureaucratese favored by dungeon masters throughout history," detailing

> how to fashion a collar for slamming a prisoner against the wall, exactly how many days he can be kept without sleep (11), and what, specifically, he should be told before being locked in a box with an insect—all to stop just short of having a jury decide that these acts violate the laws against torture and abusive treatment of prisoners.[61]

Language was distorted, logic twisted, and morality abandoned in order to provide legal impunity—a "golden shield," as one former CIA official dubbed it—for state-sanctioned torture.[62] The torture memos were approved by the White House counsel's office, attorneys at the National Security Council, and the vice president's office.[63] All of President Bush's top national security advisers—Vice President Cheney, National Security Adviser Condoleezza Rice, Secretary of Defense Donald Rumsfeld, Secretary of State Powell, CIA Director George Tenet, and Attorney General John Ashcroft—met and discussed the CIA's use of these "enhanced interrogation techniques."[64] ("Why are we talking about this in the White House? History will not judge this kindly,"

Ashcroft reportedly warned at the time.)[65] The Republican and Democratic heads of the Senate and House intelligence committees—the so-called Gang of Four—also were briefed on the techniques, although the details of what and how much they were told remains unknown.[66]

In a subsequent March 2003 memo, Yoo sought to extend the logic and conclusions of his August 2001 "torture memo" from the CIA to the Defense Department, which had already been resorting to harsh interrogation methods.[67] Although Yoo later described the legal advice as "near boilerplate," the memo reiterated his extraordinary and unprecedented vision of executive power.[68] The March 2003 memo not only asserted that foreign nationals outside the United States had no constitutional rights, but it also questioned the applicability of constitutional protections to individuals inside the United States in the "war on terror."[69] According to Yoo, the president could order the military to seize people living in the United States, interrogate them without restriction, and imprison them without charges, trial, or a hearing if he believed they presented a threat to the country.

Yoo also said that criminal prohibitions against abuse in the UCMJ should not be applied to the military during wartime and would interfere with the president's constitutional power as commander in chief to detain and interrogate terrorist suspects.[70] Yoo thus directly questioned Congress's prerogative to legislate on national security issues, suggesting that the executive branch's constitutional authority to protect the country from attack would justify any interrogation method. "Congress," Yoo wrote, "may no more regulate the president's ability to detain and interrogate enemy combatants than it may regulate his ability to direct troop movements on the battlefield."[71] Furthermore, any military official accused of violating criminal prohibitions against prisoner abuse could properly assert a claim of necessity or self-defense as long as he said he was trying to protect the country against further terrorist attacks. In other words, any action was legal if taken in the name of national security.[72]

U.S. officials had condoned, encouraged, and engaged in torture before September 11. American soldiers waterboarded Filipinos in attempting to quash the insurgency that arose after the United States seized the Philippines from Spain during the Spanish-American War.[73] During the 1980s, the U.S. government trained and funded paramilitary groups in Central America that tortured and brutalized their own people. And police officers across America routinely beat and mistreated criminal suspects by giving them the "third degree" before legal and judicial reforms started to curb these practices in the mid-twentieth century.[74] But the U.S. government had never before sought to legalize torture nor to make torture official U.S. policy in all but name. Nor had any president previously claimed the authority to ignore explicit domestic and international prohibitions against torture or to set up an alternative, extrajudicial detention regime to engage in the practice.

The Bush administration maintained that its actions were justified by the global terrorist threat, which 9/11 had shown was unprecedented in its nature and ability to inflict damage on the United States and its citizens. The administration's approach was shaped by the "One Percent Doctrine" articulated by Vice President Cheney: "even if there's just a one percent chance of the unimaginable coming due, act as if it is a certainty."[75] In the name of preventing another terrorist attack at all cost, the doctrine sanctioned action without evidence and analysis, licensed circumventing the law, and fueled excessive secrecy to hide bad conduct and mistakes. The One Percent Doctrine lay behind major military and foreign policy decisions, including the U.S. invasion of Iraq. It also helped create and sustain an interrogation policy without limits. It excused torturing even those who likely were innocent or did not have any relevant information. And it condoned torture without regard for whether the desired information could be obtained through lawful means.

The Bush administration's policies sparked sharp criticism from across the legal and political spectrum. Harold H. Koh, the former dean of Yale Law School, called the torture memo "perhaps the most clearly erroneous legal opinion" he had ever read.[76] Ruth Wedgwood, who initially had defended using military commissions, and former CIA director James R. Woolsey condemned the memo in an op-ed in the *Wall Street Journal*.[77] Thomas J. Romig, the army's judge advocate general, called Yoo's conclusions "downright offensive."[78] And Harvard Law School professor Jack Goldsmith, who headed the OLC from October 2003 until resigning the following July, criticized the August 2002 and March 2003 memos for an "unusual lack of care and sobriety in their legal analysis" and recommended that officials stop relying on them.[79]

A Justice Department internal ethics report ultimately concluded that both Yoo and Bybee had committed professional misconduct through their slipshod reasoning and by disregarding their duty to exercise independent legal judgment and render thorough, candid, and objective legal advice.[80] Long before that, in early 2004, the CIA inspector general raised questions about the agency's interrogation program. Subsequently, in December 2004, the Department of Justice withdrew the OLC's unclassified August 2002 memo setting out the legal defense of "enhanced interrogation techniques" under the antitorture statute. But the December 2004 OLC opinion that replaced it continued to define torture narrowly and did not question the legality of the various tactics described in the separate, classified August 2002 memo.[81] Then, in May 2005, the OLC issued three more memos aimed at shoring up the CIA's torture program. One explained why the techniques in the classified August 2002 memo were still legal;[82] another explained why those techniques were legal even if used in combination;[83] and a third described why the CIA's interrogation methods did not contravene even the lower threshold of cruel, inhuman, or degrading treatment (sometimes called "torture lite").[84]

Like the earlier OLC memos, the May 2005 memos cloaked the harsh and brutal treatment of prisoners in a veil of legality even as they discussed the intricacies of throwing detainees into walls, manipulating their sleep cycles, and changing their soiled diapers. The memos acknowledged that these interrogation methods might be impermissible under the rules for ordinary criminal investigations or traditional wars governed by the Geneva Conventions and U.S. military regulations. But, the memos explained, these were national security interrogations. The normal rules therefore did not apply, and virtually anything could be justified based on the theory that the government was protecting the country from another terrorist attack.[85] The "war on terrorism" had become a license for torture.

The Bush administration's response to 9/11 flouted both America's legal obligations and its constitutional heritage. Those who founded the country viewed the separation of powers between the three branches of government as essential to preserving both liberty and security. As James Madison warned, the "accumulation of all powers, legislative, executive, and judiciary, in the same hands . . . may justly be pronounced the very definition of tyranny."[86] Consequently, Madison and others who framed the Constitution created a system of checks and balances to prevent any one branch, including the executive, from becoming too powerful. Even though the Constitution made the president the commander in chief of the nation's armed forces, it sought to limit this power. Alexander Hamilton, no foe of executive authority, recognized that the commander in chief's power "amount[s] to nothing more than the supreme command and direction of the military and naval forces."[87] The Constitution also vested significant control over war powers in Congress, including the power to declare war, to raise and support the armed forces, to define and punish offenses against the law of nations, and to make rules concerning the capture and treatment of enemy prisoners.[88] As Supreme Court Justice Robert Jackson wrote in a seminal case invalidating President Harry Truman's seizure of privately owned steel mills during the

Korean War, the Constitution did not make the president "Commander in chief of the country" or give him a "monopoly of 'war powers.'"[89]

Nonetheless, President Bush claimed exclusive executive control over the war power, at least insofar as the "war on terrorism" was concerned. Bush did so under the premise that he had constitutional authority not merely to interpret statutes but to do so independently and unilaterally. The torture memos contained perhaps the most chilling articulations of this theory, with their assertion that even federal laws prohibiting torture would be unconstitutional if read to limit the president's authority to conduct interrogations as he saw fit.[90]

This conception of presidential power is sometimes associated with the theory of the "unitary executive." In its initial incarnation, the unitary executive theory maintained that the other two branches of government could not constitutionally infringe on the distinct powers of the executive, such as the executive's control over administrative agencies through firing and hiring procedures. But the theory took on a more extreme form during the Reagan administration's battles with Congress during the 1980s. In a key development, Dick Cheney, then the ranking Republican on a House select committee investigating the Iran-Contra scandal, commissioned a report (later known as the "Minority Report") that argued that Congress had exceeded its constitutional authority by prohibiting President Reagan from supporting the Contras in Nicaragua.[91] Cheney criticized various post-Watergate reforms restricting executive power and advocated virtually unlimited presidential prerogatives in the area of foreign policy and national security.[92] After 9/11, Cheney, along with David Addington (who had served on the minority committee's staff), sought to implement their expansive vision of executive power by claiming that Congress could not regulate the president's authority to do what he deemed necessary to protect the country, from imprisoning and interrogating prisoners to listening to the private conversations of American citizens without a warrant. In their view, only a strong executive, unchecked by Congress and the courts and free to act without public scrutiny, could safeguard the nation from terrorism and other threats to its security.

The linchpin in the Bush administration's detention and interrogation policy was its effort to avoid all court review. The policy's architects viewed America's commitment to judicial process and the rule of law as a weakness that undermined its ability to confront the current terrorist threat. Courts, they believed, might impose constraints on executive action in a realm where there should be none if the country were to be optimally protected. Ironically, many of these architects were themselves lawyers.

The desire to avoid judicial review quickly gained momentum because of the growing number of prisoners seized by the United States in Afghanistan and elsewhere. By December 2001, the United States had forty-five prisoners in its custody: thirty-seven were being held at the Kandahar airport in Afghanistan, and the rest were on an amphibious assault ship in the northern Arabian Sea. In addition, more than three thousand prisoners were being held by the Northern Alliance and other anti-Taliban forces elsewhere in Afghanistan.[93] The United States wanted to bring the prisoners to a secure location for continued detention and interrogation.[94] On December 27, 2001, the Defense Department disclosed that location: al Qaeda and Taliban prisoners, it announced, were being transferred to the U.S. Naval Base at Guantánamo Bay, Cuba.[95] The administration's choice of Guantánamo spoke volumes about the aims—and contradictions—of its emerging detention policy.

Located in Cuba's southeast corner, Guantánamo Bay is approximately four hundred air miles from Miami, Florida. Guantánamo Bay's forty-five square miles (thirty-one of them on land) make it larger than Manhattan and almost half as big as the District of Columbia. After acquiring Guantánamo Bay during the Spanish-American War, the United States established a naval base and coaling station there. A 1903 treaty between Cuba and the United States created a lease agreement that gave the United States "complete jurisdiction and control" over the base while recognizing Cuba's "ultimate sovereignty" over the territory.[96] A 1934 treaty stipulated that this lease agreement would continue until both parties agreed to modify or abrogate it.[97] The lease agreement made Guantánamo unique in that all other overseas American military bases are leased for a specific term and when that term expires, the base must be closed or the agreement renegotiated.[98] Guantánamo, by contrast, would remain under U.S. control for as long as the United States desired.

Over time, Guantánamo became part of the United States in all but name. In 1953, Guantánamo's commander announced that the naval base "for all practical purposes, is American territory."[99] Guantánamo also became entirely self-sufficient, with its own water plant, schools, transportation system, entertainment facilities, and franchise outlets and chains, from Starbucks to McDonalds.[100] Also, unlike every other U.S. overseas military base, there is no Status of Forces Agreement at Guantánamo to define the assignment of civil and criminal jurisdiction over military and other personnel there. Instead, U.S. law applies at Guantánamo not only to U.S. military personnel but also to the third-party nationals employed there in various civilian capacities.[101] Thus at Guantánamo, the United States remains accountable only to itself.[102]

So why make Guantánamo the flagship prison in the "war on terrorism"? A secret December 28, 2001 memo by Yoo and fellow OLC attorney Patrick F. Philbin suggests the answer.[103] Leaked to the press in 2004, the memo shows that the Bush administration chose Guantánamo because it believed Guantánamo would be beyond the jurisdiction of the federal courts and thus immune from judicial review. Without jurisdiction, a court could not examine the basis for any prisoner's confinement. It could not, therefore, consider whether the prisoners were entitled to any legal protections (contrary to the president's determination) or examine the allegations against them. It could not order that the prisoners be provided access to attorneys, to family members, or to anyone else from the outside world. A court also could not inquire into the prisoners' treatment, thus insulating torture and other abuse from judicial scrutiny.

By bringing prisoners to Guantánamo, the Bush administration sought to evade one of the most fundamental protections in the Constitution and Anglo-American legal tradition: the writ of habeas corpus. Derived from Latin words meaning "you shall produce the body," habeas corpus is the most celebrated of the English writs that became part of America's legal system. Habeas corpus, whose history and development are described more fully in chapters 5 and 6, safeguards individual liberty by guaranteeing that those detained by the state have the opportunity to challenge the lawfulness of their imprisonment before a judge. As Supreme Court Justice Robert Jackson explained:

> Executive imprisonment has been considered oppressive and lawless since John, at Runnymede, pledged that no free man should be imprisoned, dispossessed, outlawed, or exiled save by the judgment of his peers or by the law of the land. The judges of England developed the writ of habeas corpus largely to preserve these immunities from executive restraint.[104]

Habeas corpus not only helped prevent imprisonment by the executive without charge or trial, but it was precisely in this context that its protections were strongest and most important.

The Bush administration nevertheless calculated that federal courts would refuse to hear any habeas corpus challenges brought by or on behalf of prisoners at Guantánamo. This calculation rested primarily on two related factors: that the prisoners were foreign nationals and that they had been captured and were being held outside the sovereign territory of the United States. Thus, the administration believed, courts would deny habeas corpus review despite the United States' total and exclusive control over Guantánamo. This was, after all, the same the argument that the U.S. government had made with some success during the 1990s to try to stave off court review when it brought tens of thousands of Haitian and Cuban refugees intercepted on the high seas to Guantánamo and detained them behind barbed wire in hastily erected tent cities.[105]

Yoo and Philbin did acknowledge that bringing prisoners to Guantánamo involved "some litigation risk" from detainee lawsuits. But they concluded that courts would be "reluctant" to interfere with the president's decisions in the area of military and foreign affairs. The same thinking would underlie the administration's effort to create other offshore detention centers at the Bagram Air Base in Afghanistan and at secret CIA "black sites" in Europe and Asia, which together helped create a new global network of prisons outside the law. The belief that habeas corpus could provide some resistance to sweeping claims of executive power to detain without charge or a hearing, to try by military commission, and to interrogate without restriction proved prescient, while the administration's gamble that the courts would decline to exercise their habeas powers, at least over Guantánamo, failed.

Guantánamo

Microcosm of a Prison beyond the Law

On January 11, 2002, the first twenty prisoners arrived at Guantánamo after twenty-seven hours on an air force cargo plane that had departed the previous day from the U.S. Marine Corps base in Kandahar, Afghanistan. The prisoners were hooded, wore orange jumpsuits, and were shackled at the arms and legs. They had been chained to their seats during the flight and were given only urinal spittoons to relieve themselves. At least one prisoner was forcibly sedated. More flights into Guantánamo followed, transporting prisoners with surgical masks over their faces, black-out goggles over their eyes, and a "three-piece suit" restraint that consisted of handcuffs, leg restraints, and a chain around their waists.[1]

Guantánamo's prison population rose rapidly, and within a month, the number of detainees had swelled to 300. In time, approximately 775 prisoners would be detained at Guantánamo.[2] Conditions were initially primitive and brutal. The first prisoners were housed at Camp X-Ray, so named because it was possible to see right through its six-by-eight-foot, makeshift, open-air cells. Prisoners were given only the barest essentials: a bucket to relieve themselves; a thin mat to sleep on, but no blanket; and two towels (one to use as a prayer mat and the other for washing). Halogen floodlights remained on throughout the night, and detainees were confined to their cells twenty-four hours a day, except for two fifteen-minute breaks each week when they were taken alone, in shackles, to a small pen to exercise.[3]

In late April 2002, the United States moved the detainees to Camp Delta, a new and more permanent facility constructed to house Guantánamo's expanding prison population. A sprawling complex, Camp Delta initially contained three detention camps (three more were added later) as well as guard towers, interrogation trailers, and a hospital, all surrounded by six concentric rings of barbed wire. Camps 1, 2, and 3 consisted of eight hundred individual steel-and-mesh cells in boxcar-style arrangements. Prisoners were typically confined to their six-foot-eight-inch by eight-foot cells twenty-four hours a day, except for twenty to thirty minutes of exercise five days per week followed by a five-minute shower. They were given only a T-shirt and boxer shorts and "comfort items" such as a toothbrush, toothpaste, washcloth, prayer cap, and Qur'an, all of which could be taken away for "noncompliant" behavior or at the discretion of the interrogators. No air conditioning was provided, even though summer temperatures routinely soared to more than 100 degrees Fahrenheit.[4]

As Guantánamo's prison population continued to increase, the United States constructed new facilities, each more modern and permanent than the last. Opened in February 2003, Camp 4 provided a dormitory-style facility for more "cooperative" prisoners who could eat and exercise together. The prisoners there wore white instead of orange jumpsuits and could be outside for up to ten hours a day.[5] They also were given access to a small library for books and movies.[6] The military, however, soon began shifting prisoners from Camp 4 to newer, higher-security facilities at Camps 5 and 6.[7]

The Defense Department described Camp 5 as a "state-of-the-art prison that many states [in America] would envy." Modeled after a state prison in Bunker Hill, Indiana, this two-story maximum-security facility was intended for "higher-level" detainees, considered to be of greater intelligence value. Prisoners in Camp 5 were confined alone in solid-wall cells, their every movement monitored through touch-screen computers in a control center. Camp 5 also contained special interrogation cells "outfitted with faux Persian carpets, blue velour reclining chairs with an ankle shackle point, monitors, panic buttons, and open-air, cage-like recreation areas" to create a false sense of security during long interrogation sessions.[8]

Camp 6, which opened in 2006, is a $39 million, two hundred–cell prison modeled on maximum security prisons in the United States. Camp 6 was originally intended to give prisoners greater freedom and opportunities to interact during recreation and mealtime, but the military soon abandoned that plan.[9] Prisoners at Camp 6 instead were confined to solid-metal cells without windows or natural light or air for at least twenty-two hours a day, during which time they had no contact with anyone except guards. Their only opportunity for socialization took place during recreation when they were placed alone in twelve-by-nine-foot pens for two hours and were permitted to talk to prisoners in adjacent pens. By 2007, most of the prisoners were held in Camps 5 and 6.[10]

U.S. officials have described Guantánamo as a "world-class" detention facility,[11] pointing out that Guantánamo has "mature[d] over time" and highlighting various "perks" that the detainees receive, such as nutritious meals of "honey-glazed chicken and rice pilaf."[12] But these superficial comparisons obscure and distort the underlying reality, for Guantánamo remains sui generis, no matter how modern or state-of-the-art its facilities have become. Guantánamo's essence does not lie in bricks and mortar. It is not simply another prison but the physical embodiment of a new type of prison, one that was created to justify prolonged detention without charge, due process, or judicial review.

Bush administration officials compared the Guantánamo detainees with enemy soldiers from prior wars: men "captured on the battlefield" held merely to prevent them from taking up arms against U.S. or allied forces.[13] As the then White House counsel Alberto R. Gonzales explained, "Captured enemy combatants, whether soldiers or saboteurs, may be detained for the duration of hostilities. They need not be 'guilty' of anything; they are detained simply by virtue of their status as enemy combatants in war."[14] Or as Guantánamo's former commander Rear Admiral Harry B. Harris put it, "What we're trying to do here in Guantánamo is simply keep [the prisoners] off the battlefield" and prevent them from "go[ing] back to the fight."[15] Holding detainees at Guantánamo was thus characterized as a "simple war measure," much like the detention of thousands of German or Japanese prisoners during World War II and other enemy soldiers during prior conflicts. These comparisons were intended to make Guantánamo seem normal, acceptable, and consistent with long-standing practice.

But Bush administration officials also repeatedly described the Guantánamo detainees as terrorists. Former Defense Secretary Donald Rumsfeld labeled them as "among the most dangerous, best trained, vicious killers on the face of the earth."[16] Other high-ranking military officials followed suit, calling the detainees "the worst of the worst" and claiming that Guantánamo held many senior al Qaeda operatives involved in terrorist plots against Americans.[17] President Bush continued to assert that Guantánamo detainees "are killers," even though only a handful had been charged with any offense.[18] These comparisons painted a very different picture of the Guantánamo detainees, one of hardened criminals who should be punished for their terrorist activities rather than soldiers detained for the nonpunitive purpose of preventing their return to the battlefield.

The administration attempted to paper over the contradictions between the concepts of "soldier" and "criminal" by classifying the Guantánamo detainees as "enemy combatants" or "unlawful combatants." (It used the two terms interchangeably.) As combatants, Guantánamo detainees were subject to military detention and did not have to be charged and tried, as suspected terrorists and other criminals did. But unlike soldiers in past conflicts, they were not entitled to any protections under the Geneva Conventions or customary laws of war. In short, the prisoners at Guantánamo were being held in a legal black hole—without the protections afforded to prisoners of war, on the one hand, or to accused criminals, on the other hand. And given the nature of the "war on terrorism"—a conflict with no discernable end—they could be detained for decades, if not for life.

At the same time, the administration defined "enemy combatant" in broad and elastic terms. An important study by Seton Hall Law School in 2006 found that only 8 percent of the detainees at Guantánamo were characterized as al Qaeda fighters and 40 percent had no definitive connection with al Qaeda. The study, which was based solely on government data, found that 55 percent of the detainees had never committed a hostile act against the United States or its coalition allies. It further determined that only 5 percent of Guantánamo detainees were captured by the United States, while 86 percent had been turned over to the United States by Pakistani or Northern Alliance forces.[19] A subsequent Seton Hall study found that one-third of the detainees at Guantánamo were identified based on links to organizations other than al Qaeda. Also, in many of those cases, neither Congress nor the State Department had identified the organizations as a terrorist group. This meant that a person could be detained at Guantánamo as an "enemy combatant" based on an alleged association with an organization that would not bar him from entering the United States if he sought admission at the country's borders.[20]

Guantánamo soon became a collection point for an unprecedented global dragnet. In total, Guantánamo held citizens of forty-four different countries.[21] Although some prisoners were seized in or near the war in Afghanistan, few were captured on a battlefield.[22] Some, moreover, were picked up thousands of miles from any conflict zone. For example, Lakhdar Boumediene and five other Guantánamo detainees were initially seized by Bosnian police—acting at the request of U.S. officials—as they were being released from prison in Sarajevo after being cleared of any involvement in a plot to blow up the U.S. embassy there. Shackled and hooded, the men were taken to an unknown location before being transferred to Guantánamo.[23] Two British residents, Bisher al-Rawi and Jamil el-Banna, were arrested in the Gambia, where they had traveled on business to set up a mobile peanut-processing plant, before they were taken to Guantánamo based on their alleged association with Abu Qatada, a radical Islamic cleric from England.[24]

The Bush administration did not merely define "enemy combatant" in sweeping terms; it also denied Guantánamo detainees any fair process to show that they did not fall into that category. It did so, moreover, precisely in circumstances that made the need for such a process critical.

When the United States invaded Afghanistan in October 2001, Afghanistan was still in the throes of a humanitarian crisis, the result of more than two decades of civil war and three consecutive years of severe drought.[25] Factions and rivalries plagued the country. Meanwhile, charitable groups and individuals poured in to provide humanitarian assistance.[26]

U.S. and allied forces in Afghanistan thus encountered a situation of considerable confusion, increasing the chance that people could be swept up by mistake. The United States exacerbated the problem by offering significant financial rewards for the capture of individuals in Afghanistan and surrounding areas of Pakistan. It went so far as to drop thousands of flyers over Afghanistan and the border area advertising its money-for-capture program. A typical flyer stated:

> Get wealth and power beyond your dreams. . . . You can receive millions of dollars helping the anti-Taliban forces catch al-Qaida and Taliban murders. This is enough money to take care of your family, your village, your tribe for the rest of your life. Pay for livestock and doctors and school books and housing for your people.[27]

Defense Secretary Donald Rumsfeld later boasted that such leaflets fell over Afghanistan "like snowflakes in December in Chicago."[28] Given the deep factionalism in this impoverished and war-torn region, the money-for-capture program provided an incentive for people to fulfill personal or tribal vendettas or simply to turn over someone for money to feed their family. Under the program, many of the individuals eventually turned over to the United States had been swept up and sold for bounty.[29] Indeed, Pakistani President General Pervez Musharraf boasted that Pakistanis had handed over hundreds of individuals to the CIA for reward money after 9/11.[30]

Army Regulation 190-8 (AR 190-8), which implements the United States' obligations under the Third Geneva Convention, requires hearings to prevent erroneous detentions during military operations. These hearings must be held promptly after capture if there is any doubt about a prisoner's status. A military panel then determines whether the individual should be held as a prisoner of war, detained as a civilian internee (for security concerns or incident to a criminal investigation), or "immediately returned to his home or released."[31]

The United States introduced AR 190-8 hearings during the Vietnam War precisely because the nature of the conflict—one against insurgent groups whose members often fought without uniform—made it more difficult to identify the enemy and distinguish friend from foe. The United States also held AR 190-8 hearings in subsequent armed conflicts to help ensure accurate detention decisions. During Operation Desert Storm, for example, the United States processed 69,822 Iraqi detainees under AR 190-8.[32] During the conflict with Panama in 1989/1990, the United States held tribunal hearings to determine the status of 4,100 captured individuals, promptly releasing 4,000 and granting prisoner-of-war status to the rest.[33] And during the first Gulf War, 1,196 hearings were held, and 886 of the detainees were released as innocent civilians.[34]

Military officials proposed conducting AR 190-8 hearings in Afghanistan following the U.S. invasion in October 2001. But civilian officials in Washington overruled them.[35] Instead, the United States provided a "screening process" that lacked the basic protections provided by existing military regulations, including the opportunity for a detainee to testify and present available evidence before a tribunal promptly after his capture.[36] The process used in Afghanistan also allowed for detention based on a person's suspected "intelligence value"—that is, indefinite imprisonment for purposes of interrogation—without any indication that he had engaged in hostilities, posed a threat to the United States, or met the definition of a combatant under the law of war. As former Justice Department official Viet D. Dinh acknowledged, there "was not a real process for determining who was an enemy combatant."[37]

Prisoners captured in or around Afghanistan after September 11 soon disappeared into a legal void without any opportunity to verify the facts surrounding their capture.[38] Many of those taken to Guantánamo were "victims of incompetent battlefield vetting" and should never have been detained in the first place, said a former senior Bush administration official.[39] Like Faiz Muhammad, a "partially deaf, shriveled old man" who was unable to answer basic questions and was nicknamed "al Qaeda Claus."[40] Or Shakhrukh Hamiduva, an eighteen-year-old Uzbek refugee who had fled his country after the government killed one of his uncles and jailed his other relatives and who was captured by a tribal leader and sold to the United States for bounty while trying to cross the border from Afghanistan after the U.S. bombing there had started.[41] Or Hozaifa Parhat and other Uighurs who fled persecution in northwestern China for Afghanistan, where they were captured, sold to the United States for reward money, and detained for years, even though they never had taken up arms against or presented any threat to the United States.[42] Or Abdul Rahim al-Ginco, a college student from the United Arab Emirates who went to Afghanistan in 2000 to escape his strict Muslim father, was captured by the Taliban, and was tortured with electric shocks to his ears and toes and almost drowned in a water tank until he falsely confessed to being a spy for Israel and the United States.[43] Or Gholam Ruhani, an Afghani shopkeeper who was seized near his hometown and conscripted into the Taliban by force and who agreed to do menial cleaning and clerical jobs at a nearby police office rather than fight on the front lines.[44] AR 190-8 hearings had helped avoid these kinds of mistakes before. But the United States refused to provide them in Afghanistan because the priority was to gather information at all costs, not to find out whether prisoners were combatants, terrorists, or innocent civilians.

From the beginning, military and intelligence officials expressed misgivings about who the United States was holding at Guantánamo. Major General Michael Dunlavey, who came to Guantánamo in February 2002 to supervise interrogations, soon discovered that as many as half the prisoners had little or no intelligence value. Dunlavey subsequently traveled to Afghanistan to complain that too many "Mickey Mouse" prisoners were being brought to Guantánamo.[45] A confidential report sent by the CIA to Washington in October 2002, and ignored by White House officials, reported that most Guantánamo detainees did not belong there.[46] In October 2004, Brigadier General Martin Lucenti Jr., the deputy commander at Guantánamo, stated that most of the prisoners "will either be released or transferred to their own countries" and "weren't fighting" but rather "were running."[47] As former Guantánamo commander Major General Jay Hood acknowledged, "Sometimes we just didn't get the right folks." Nonetheless, detainees continued to languish at Guantánamo, Hood said, because "nobody wants to be the one to sign the release papers."[48] Errors became "institutionalized" as government officials became unwilling or unable to correct them, and Guantánamo took on "a life of its own."[49]

The Bush administration had originally planned to try most Guantánamo detainees quickly through the military commissions established under President Bush's November 13, 2001, order.[50] Those trials, however, never took place because the administration did not have enough evidence to charge, let alone convict, most of the prisoners, even under the commissions' lax standards and flawed rules. Early on, Defense Department lawyers asked intelligence officers at Guantánamo to complete a one-page form for each prisoner, certifying the basis for suspecting that they were involved in terrorism. This request was made in January 2002. Within weeks, intelligence officers indicated that they did not have sufficient evidence to complete the forms. As one member of the original military team slated to work on the prosecutions put it, "It became obvious to us as we reviewed the evidence that, in many cases, we had simply gotten the slowest guys on the battlefield. We literally found guys who had been shot in the butt."[51] So the administration switched gears, claiming that it could hold prisoners at Guantánamo indefinitely without trial as "enemy combatants" in the global "war on terrorism."[52] For the United States, "enemy combatant" detention would serve the same purpose as a trial—incarceration—but since that detention was in theory intended to be only "temporary" and "nonpunitive," it could be achieved with fewer legal protections and public attention. Military commissions, meanwhile, would target a handful of minor figures and pressure them to plead guilty, thereby creating the illusion of a functioning system and perpetuating the myth that Guantánamo held "the worst of the worst."[53]

Guantánamo's overriding purpose, however, was not detention but intelligence gathering. America's flagship prison in the "war on terrorism," in other words, was created and maintained not to imprison suspected terrorists but to interrogate without restraint. The desire to extract information through torture and other illegal methods shaped virtually every aspect of Guantánamo, from the creation of a category of prisoners without legal protection to the effort to avoid habeas corpus review by federal courts.

The government's effort to squeeze every drop of available information from detainees at all costs—even though most detainees had no intelligence value and without regard for whether the information obtained was reliable—quickly descended into gross and systematic abuse. With no rules to apply, military personnel on the ground had initially tried to fill the vacuum by adhering to the Geneva Conventions and even arranged for the International Committee of the Red Cross (ICRC) to visit Guantánamo. But Rumsfeld, frustrated by what he considered a failure to obtain valuable intelligence from the detainees, scuttled these efforts.[54] By mid-2002, interrogators were under increasing pressure to use more aggressive measures.[55] One of the first subjects was a detainee named Mohammed al-Qahtani, suspected by some to be the "twentieth hijacker." On September 25, 2002, vice presidential adviser David Addington, Pentagon general counsel William J. Haynes II, CIA acting general counsel John Rizzo, and other high-level officials traveled to Guantánamo to discuss the interrogation of detainees. The following week, those officials met with the CIA's associate general counsel, Jonathan Fredman, to discuss the use of "enhanced interrogation methods," which the CIA had already begun using in its secret jails on so-called high-value detainees. Fredman reportedly gave them the green light. He stated that interrogators had a great deal of latitude and could engage in cruel, inhuman, and degrading treatment as long as it did not rise to the level of torture—a term, he noted, that was "written vaguely" in federal statutes and treaties. Torture is "basically subject to perception," Fredman said. "If the detainee dies, you're doing it wrong."[56] Diane Beaver, a military judge advocate general (JAG) who attended the meeting, noted that interrogators could use sleep deprivation and other highly coercive interrogation methods as long as they had approval—that is, as long as the president had authorized it. Beaver also cautioned that interrogators might need to "curb" the "harsher operations while the ICRC is around."[57] Sleep deprivation, she said, was already being used at Bagram in Afghanistan. But "it is not happening" because "it is not being reported officially."[58]

On October 11, 2002, Dunlavey, Guantánamo's commander, sent a formal plan for al-Qahtani's interrogation up the chain of command. Dunlavey sought approval for nineteen "counterresistance techniques" not in *Army Field Manual* 34-52, which governed military interrogations and prohibited "acts of violence or intimidation, including physical or mental torture, threats, insults, or exposure to unpleasant and inhumane treatment as a means of or aid to interrogation."[59]

In a memo, Beaver recommended using enhanced interrogation measures to increase psychological manipulation. The techniques were divided into three categories. They included permitting interrogators to identify themselves as citizens of foreign countries known to use torture (category I); isolation for up to thirty days, stress positions such as standing for four hours straight, removal of clothing, putting prisoners in hoods for up to twenty hours, and depriving prisoners of light and auditory stimuli (category II); using scenarios to convince a prisoner that death or severe pain was imminent for him and his family; exposing prisoners to cold weather or freezing water; and using a wet towel and dripping water to induce a sensation of suffocation (category III).[60] A fourth category would have permitted the military to render prisoners to Egypt, Jordan, and other countries for torture, but was dropped following protests by FBI agents that those renditions would constitute crimes.[61] Beaver explained that the ambiguity of existing guidelines prevented interrogators from doing "anything that could be considered 'controversial.'"[62] She therefore gave blanket approval for all category I techniques and approval for all category II and III techniques as long as there was a "legitimate governmental objective" and the techniques were not imposed for the "specific purpose" of inflicting severe pain or suffering.[63] Beaver suggested that even the most brutal techniques, such as waterboarding, would pass muster as long as they were applied "in a good faith effort and not maliciously or sadistically for the very purpose of causing harm."[64] For good measure, she added that "permission" or "immunity" could be obtained "in advance" via executive branch approval.[65]

General James T. Hill of the U.S. Southern Command, which oversaw Guantánamo, questioned Beaver's analysis and conclusions. Hill sent a memo to General Richard B. Meyers, the chairman of the Joint Chiefs of Staff, expressing his concern that some of the interrogation techniques might violate both the federal antitorture statute and the Uniform Code of Military Justice (UCMJ), which prohibited physical assault, cruelty, and other mistreatment.[66] Hill recommended seeking additional legal advice. The JAGs said the techniques would likely constitute crimes and advised against them.[67] Officials from the Naval Criminal Investigative Services (NCIS), which was working with the FBI to elicit incriminating evidence from detainees, proposed an alternative plan using traditional, nonaggressive interrogation techniques. But their advice and warnings were ignored.[68]

On November 23, 2002, Major General Geoffrey D. Miller received a verbal command authorizing the use of "enhanced interrogation techniques" on al-Qahtani. The interrogation log for that day reflects the change: "The detainee arrives at the interrogation booth at Camp X-Ray. His hood is removed and he is bolted to the floor."[69] Four days later, on November 27, Haynes sent a memo to Rumsfeld stating that all the proposed techniques in categories I, II, and III "may be legally available" and recommending approval of fifteen of the eighteen techniques.[70] Less than one week later, on December 2, Rumsfeld approved the fifteen techniques, including stress positions, forced nudity, the use of dogs, and extreme sensory deprivation—all of which were prohibited by the *Army Field Manual*. Commenting on one approved technique, Rumsfeld added, "I stand for 8–10 hours a day. Why is standing limited to 4 hours?" Although he did not give advance approval to the remaining three techniques, Rumsfeld indicated that they were still "legally available."[71]

Interrogations of al-Qahtani continued until January 16, 2003. During this almost two-month period, al-Qahtani was interrogated for eighteen to twenty hours per day. If he fell asleep, interrogators doused al-Qahtani with water. Military dogs were used to frighten and intimidate him. One interrogator tied a leash around al-Qahtani's neck and made him perform dog tricks. Al-Qahtani was forced to wear a bra and thong underwear on his head. After al-Qahtani started refusing food and water, he was forcibly administered fluids by an intravenous drip. When al-Qahtani asked to go to the bathroom, he was told he could go only if he answered additional questions. After repeating his request, al-Qahtani was told to urinate in his pants. On another occasion, the government drugged al-Qahtani and simulated a flight to the Middle East to increase his fear of further torture. At one point, al-Qahtani had to be taken to the hospital and revived after his heart rate fell to thirty-five beats per minute.[72] His condition was so critical that a neurological specialist was brought in from off the island. According to an army medical expert, al-Qahtani's interrogation "contributed to significant physical and metabolic symptoms such that he required close cardiac monitoring" and put him "in danger of dying."[73] When al-Qahtani was revived, the interrogation resumed. "We tortured [al-] Qahtani," a Bush administration official overseeing military commission prosecutions later admitted.[74]

Navy General Counsel Alberto J. Mora was one of the career military officers to protest the methods used to interrogate al-Qahtani. Mora sent a draft memorandum to Haynes expressing his strong opposition and his view that the methods were illegal. Haynes assured Mora that Rumsfeld would stop the harsh measures. On January 15, 2003, Rumsfeld rescinded his December 2 order, withdrawing support for all category II techniques and the one approved category III technique. To appease Mora and other JAGs, Rumsfeld established a working group to evaluate the armed forces' interrogation of prisoners in the "war on terrorism." On March 14, 2003, Department of Justice lawyer John Yoo gave Haynes a memo that was intended to provide the Defense Department with the same legal cover that his earlier August 2002 "torture memo" had given the CIA and to quash internal opposition from Mora and others. In essence, the memo argued that if the president approved of a particular interrogation measure, it must be legal, and, moreover, that the interrogation of prisoners was within the president's sole discretion as commander-in-chief, akin to his power to "direct troop movements on a battlefield."[75]

The working group was forced to accept Yoo's analysis, which then supplied the "controlling authority" for its final April 3, 2003, report.[76] That report approved thirty-five possible interrogation methods, including extreme isolation, prolonged standing, sleep deprivation, and slaps to the face and stomach.[77]

On April 16, 2003, Rumsfeld issued a memo to the U.S. Southern Command to govern interrogations at Guantánamo. The memo authorized a number of the techniques from the working group's April 3 report, including prolonged isolation, dietary and environment manipulation, and other tactics designed to exploit a detainee's fears and desperation. The report was accompanied by Pentagon briefings to Guantánamo's commander premised on the Justice Department's earlier conclusion that the president and his agents could override any legal restrictions in the name of national security.

Al-Qahtani's interrogation became emblematic of a larger pattern of torture and abuse at Guantánamo.[78] FBI documents obtained by the American Civil Liberties Union and other organizations through the Freedom of Information Act detail the type of practices commonly used at the prison during its first years. The documents describe detainees chained hand and foot in a fetal position on the floor for twenty hours or more, without food or water. They also show prisoners being forced to endure extreme temperatures: one was found shivering on the floor naked because the air condition had been turned up so high; another was discovered almost unconscious on the floor, sweltering in more than 100-degree heat after the air condition had been turned off. Detainees were kept in rooms continually flooded with light, causing severe trauma. One detainee was found crouched in a corner of a cell with a sheet over his head for hours at a time, talking to nonexistent people and hearing voices. Interrogators also used dogs to terrify detainees, wrapped detainees in Israeli flags as a form of religious harassment, sexually humiliated detainees, and engaged in wholesale physical abuse, including grabbing detainees' genitals and burning detainees with lit cigarettes.[79] Several detainees reported that they were forcibly given drugs during interrogations, causing them to experience physical effects ranging from extreme drowsiness to hallucinations.[80]

Some FBI agents and Justice Department officials warned that these interrogation methods were both illegal and counterproductive. Bruce C. Swartz, a criminal division deputy at the Justice Department, repeatedly questioned their effectiveness at White House meetings, cautioning that the abuse of detainees would do "grave damage" to the country's reputation and law enforcement record.[81] The NCIS expressed similar concerns.[82] In 2004, the ICRC complained (in a report leaked to the press) that the U.S. military had purposefully used psychological and physical coercion "tantamount to torture."[83] The warnings, however, were largely ignored, ultimately prompting the FBI and NCIS to withdraw their agents from interrogation rooms in protest.[84]

Ironically, these interrogation methods grew out of a program designed to help American soldiers resist torture. The Survival, Evasion, Resistance and Escape (SERE) program had previously helped train U.S. Special Forces and other military personnel to withstand torture and other abuse at the hands of enemy forces. The SERE program was a response to the brutal interrogation methods used by the Chinese Communists against American soldiers during the Korean War to obtain false confessions. The CIA had collected information about psychological torture in the 1963 *KUBARK Manual* and its companion, the 1983 *Human Resources Exploitation Training Manual*, formerly secret documents that became public during the 1990s following extensive litigation.[85] The *KUBARK Manual* described psychological torture's devastating effects:

> The circumstances of detention are arranged to enhance within the subject his feelings of being cut off from the known and the reassuring, and of being plunged into the strange. . . . Control of the source's environment permits the interrogator to determine his diet, sleep pattern and other fundamentals. Manipulating these into irregularities, so that the subject becomes disorientated, is very likely to create feelings of fear and helplessness.[86]

The SERE program was designed to prepare American service members in the event they again faced an enemy that resorted to such methods. The program tried to simulate acute anxiety by creating an environment of extreme uncertainty during harsh interrogations by mock interrogators. Trainees, for example, would be hooded, stripped of clothing, exposed to extreme temperatures, and sexually humiliated. Their sleep patterns would be disrupted and their religious faith desecrated.

The SERE program had never before been used to elicit information, and neither its personnel nor anyone in the Joint Personnel Recovery Agency (JPRA), which oversaw the program, had any experience in conducting interrogations or gathering intelligence. After 9/11, however, the Bush administration decided to "reverse-engineer" SERE, transforming the program into a template for the interrogation of terrorist suspects. One of the leading proponents and architects of this reverse-engineering was SERE's chief psychologist, Bruce Jessen, who was hired by the military as a private contractor. In April 2002, Jessen created the Guantánamo Bay "Exploitation Draft Plan" to instruct inexperienced Guantánamo interrogators under his direction. He also proposed an "exploitation facility' at the detention center that would remain "off limits to non-essential personnel," including the ICRC: a secret prison within the prison.[87] Two months later, Jessen began advising the CIA in its interrogation of Abu Zubaydah, the first detainee tortured at a CIA black site, while a JPRA team that included James Mitchell, another

SERE psychologist working as a private contractor, was dispatched to assist in Zubaydah's interrogation.[88] The Justice Department's Office of Legal Counsel, in turn, attempted to provide legal cover for the CIA's interrogation of Zubaydah and other detainees in its classified August 1, 2002, torture memo.[89]

The SERE program was soon reverse-engineered for interrogations at Guantánamo. In June 2002, the Behavioral Science Consultation Team (BSCT) was formed to help maximize the collection of intelligence by enlisting the assistance of mental health professionals.[90] In September 2002, military intelligence personnel from Guantánamo, including at least one medical adviser, traveled to Fort Bragg, North Carolina, which housed the Army's flagship SERE program. The interrogation plans for Guantánamo developed by the BSCT and sent up the chain of command relied heavily on the SERE program and the input of key SERE personnel, including Mitchell and Jessen. In December 2002, after Rumsfeld had signed off on the memo approving harsh interrogation techniques, military trainers traveled to Guantánamo to provide instruction in SERE methods. An entire interrogation class was based on a chart showing the effects of sleep deprivation, prolonged standing, and exposure to extreme cold that had been copied verbatim from a 1957 air force study of the techniques used by the Chinese Communists to obtain false confessions from American prisoners.[91] SERE techniques were subsequently documented in the interrogations of Guantánamo detainees, including al-Qahtani and Mohamedou Ould Slahi, for whom a brutal interrogation plan modeled on al-Qahtani's was personally approved by Rumsfeld. Internal warnings about the use of SERE methods to interrogate detainees, including from several SERE trainers, were ignored.[92]

Although these techniques originally may have been intended for a limited number of detainees, they quickly spread "like a germ," with nothing to check their growth and no court available to scrutinize why prisoners were being detained or how they were being treated.[93] The techniques not only led to the gross mistreatment of prisoners at Guantánamo but soon migrated to Afghanistan and Iraq as pressure mounted "to get tougher" with detainee interrogations.[94] Rumsfeld's approval of physical and psychologically abusive interrogation techniques, for example, was submitted "virtually unchanged" to the interrogation officer in charge at Abu Ghraib and led ultimately to the Defense Department's approval of stress positions, sleep deprivation, the use of military dogs to exploit detainees' fears, and other brutal tactics in Iraq.[95]

These interrogation methods were supported by medical officials who cooperated with the government, an eerie reminder of the medical profession's role in the commission of atrocities in the past, including in Nazi

Germany. Major General Miller, who commanded Guantánamo from November 2002 to March 2004, called the work of these medical personnel "essential in developing integrated interrogation strategies and assessing interrogation intelligence production."[96] Doctors consulted detainee medical records to help facilitate interrogations, a practice denounced as an ethical breach by the American Medical Association and as a "flagrant violation of medical ethics" by the ICRC.[97] Although the Defense Department eventually released a new set of formal ethical guidelines stressing the need for "the humane treatment of detainees," those guidelines allowed scientific and medical personnel not directly responsible for a patient's care to participate in his interrogations and failed to curb the abuses.[98]

Not surprisingly, there was a concerted effort to shroud these interrogations in secrecy. Guantánamo remained a virtual black hole for more than the first two years of its operation. Even the names of the Guantánamo detainees remained largely hidden from the world. The Bush administration not only denied the detainees contact with their families and with lawyers but also refused all outside requests to interview the detainees (except by the ICRC, whose reports remained confidential). Above all, the administration sought to resist court review, which it realized could shed light on, if not halt, its harsh interrogations and invalidate its illegal detention of hundreds of men. Creating a prison beyond the law at Guantánamo thus depended on avoiding the judicial scrutiny provided by habeas corpus.

Guantánamo beyond Guantánamo

Toward a Global Detention System

On April 10, 2002, Binyam Mohamed was arrested while boarding a flight to Zurich from Karachi Airport in Pakistan. Born in Ethiopia in 1978, Mohamed had been residing in London, England, before traveling to Afghanistan in the spring of 2001. Mohamed says he went to Afghanistan to escape the London street culture and to experience living in a Muslim country. The U.S. government had a different story: that Mohamed received weapons training at an al Qaeda camp in the summer of 2001 and additional training in bomb making before he and American citizen Jose Padilla were tapped by al Qaeda's leadership to travel to the United States to set off a "dirty bomb," a device containing radioactive materials.[1] The government based these suspicions largely on statements obtained from Abu Zubaydah, the suspected al Qaeda agent who was captured in March 2002 and rendered to a secret CIA prison for waterboarding and other torture.[2]

Following his arrest, Binyam Mohamed was taken to a series of local prisons, where he was questioned by Pakistani intelligence, British intelligence, and the FBI. During those interrogations, Mohamed was repeatedly threatened. As one FBI agent told him the first day, "If you don't talk to me, you're going to Jordan. We can't do what we want here; the Pakistanis can't do exactly what we want them to. The Arabs will deal with you."[3] And sure enough, in July 2002 Mohamed was taken by masked CIA agents and flown to Morocco on a CIA-operated Gulfstream jet plane. In Morocco, Mohamed was imprisoned for eighteen months and tortured by a team of eight men and women, who, among other things, beat him, cut his penis with a razor, and threatened him with rape and electrocution. Mohamed never saw a judge or a lawyer. As he later recalled, "I never saw the sun, not even once. I never saw any human being except the guards and my tormentors."[4] Mohamed's captors forced him to repeat information they fed him, including making him admit under threat of torture that he had met

Osama bin Laden and had volunteered to serve as an operations man for al Qaeda.[5]

Binyam Mohamed's journey did not end in Morocco. In January 2004, he was flown on another CIA plane to a secret CIA-run prison in Kabul, Afghanistan, known as the "Dark Prison" because captives there were kept in total blackness for twenty-four hours a day while made to listen to music loud enough to perforate an eardrum. From the Dark Prison, Mohamed was taken in May 2004 to Bagram in Afghanistan, where he was forced to sign a false confession.[6] Three months later, he was flown to Guantánamo and charged before a military commission. He was then held at Guantánamo for more than four years without a trial or a hearing. Finally, after seven years of illegal detention, the government abandoned the allegations that Mohamed was involved in a bomb plot, dropped all charges against him, and returned him to England, where he was released.[7]

The case of Binyam Mohamed's alleged accomplice, American citizen Jose Padilla, took a different path. On May 8, 2002, the FBI arrested Padilla as he was entering the United States at Chicago's O'Hare International Airport. Padilla was initially detained as a material witness in connection with the government's criminal investigation of the 9/11 attacks. Padilla's court-appointed attorney, Donna R. Newman, filed a motion in the district court challenging the warrant and seeking Padilla's release. The district judge, Michael B. Mukasey, scheduled a hearing for the following week. But before the hearing took place, President Bush issued a one-page order on June 9, 2002, declaring Padilla an "enemy combatant" and directing the secretary of defense to take him into custody.[8] The order alleged that Padilla was "closely associated with al Qaeda," had "engaged in conduct that constituted hostile and war-like acts," and represented "a continuing, present, and grave danger" to the United States.[9] Attorney General John Ashcroft publicly announced that Padilla—who the government said had previously met and trained with al Qaeda in Afghanistan—was planning to explode a "dirty bomb" in the United States and that his designation as an "enemy combatant" had "disrupted an unfolding terrorist plot."[10] Ashcroft did not mention that the allegations against Padilla—like those against Binyam Mohamed—were based on statements extracted through torture at a secret U.S. prison. Ashcroft also neglected to mention why Padilla's military detention was necessary to prevent a terrorist attack, since Padilla was already in federal custody and could have been prosecuted under any number of criminal statutes based on what the government alleged. The following day, the lower court proceedings were terminated at the government's request, and Padilla was transferred to the Consolidated Naval Brig in Charleston, South Carolina, where he would languish in military custody for the next three-and-one-half years in defiance of the Constitution's guarantee of due process and a speedy trial.

Abu Zubaydah, meanwhile, remained in secret CIA detention where he was waterboarded, shackled by his hands and feet for weeks while naked, denied food and water, exposed to extremely cold temperatures, subjected to prolonged sleep deprivation, and threatened with disappearance and death.[11] The CIA later destroyed video recordings of those interrogations, covering up criminal activity by U.S. officials and eliminating evidence that could have helped exonerate the numerous prisoners who were being held based on Zubaydah's coerced statements.[12] Finally, in September 2006, President Bush transferred Zubaydah from secret CIA detention to Guantánamo, along with thirteen other "high-value detainees." Bush, however, not only continued to restrict Zubaydah's access to the courts but even sought to prevent Zubaydah from telling his own lawyers how he had been tortured on the ground that it would reveal classified "sources and methods."

These three cases illustrate how Guantánamo is part of a larger network of prisons that emerged after the attacks of September 11, 2001, an interconnected global detention system used by the United States to facilitate torture and other abusive interrogation methods and to hold individuals without charge, due process, or access to any court. That network included both military detention centers such as Bagram and secret CIA jails or "black sites." It also encompassed practices like "extraordinary rendition," in which prisoners were secretly handed over to other governments for continued imprisonment and torture. These detentions beyond Guantánamo became the breeding ground for some of the worst abuses of the post-9/11 era and underscored the importance of habeas corpus.

Located on a 6.5-square-mile plot in the countryside forty miles north of Kabul, the Bagram Theater Internment Facility at the Bagram Air Base reflects Afghanistan's recent turbulent history. The Soviet Union built Bagram as a base of operations for troops and supplies following its invasion of Afghanistan in 1979. Control of Bagram then changed hands several times during the decades of civil war that followed the Soviets' withdrawal from Afghanistan in 1989. When the United States took over the base in 2001, it remodeled its once cavernous machine shop into a detention center.[13]

After its military invasion of Afghanistan in October 2001, the United States began using Bagram as a temporary center to screen individuals before taking them to other prisons for further detention and interrogation. The prisoners' journeys to and from Bagram varied: some were taken from Bagram to Guantánamo; others were brought from Guantánamo to Bagram; some came to Bagram from CIA "black sites"; and others were taken from Bagram to CIA custody or rendered to third countries for further interrogation.[14] Over time, Bagram became a permanent facility. Its population rose from about 100 prisoners at the start of 2004 to as many as 600 by the end of 2005.[15] More recent estimates put the number at approximately 700.[16]

Bagram remained a stark and forsaken place under the Bush administration. For years after 9/11, the prison contained an open-plan detention area on the first floor, with six large sixty-foot-long cages separated by wire that held between fifteen and twenty detainees each, and six nine-foot-by-seven-foot isolation cells on the second floor made of plywood walls and chicken wire ceilings. Most of the windows at Bagram were broken and boarded up. Former detainees described sharing cages, which often contained nothing more than a bucket to serve as a toilet for dozens of prisoners. One detainee compared Bagram to a zoo, "where they put animals,"[17] and a former interrogator called it a dungeon, full of "medieval sounds" such as the dragging of leg shackles and shouts of military police.[18]

The ICRC has reported that prisoners held at Bagram were subjected to gross mistreatment in violation of the Geneva Conventions.[19] Former prisoners have described abuses similar to those approved for use at Guantánamo, including being held in solitary confinement for up to eleven months at a time while continuously shackled, subjected to prolonged sleep deprivation, and forced to kneel or stand in painful positions for extended periods. One former Bagram prisoner who later was taken to Guantánamo described his time at Bagram as "the longest days of [his] life."[20]

The most notorious cases of abuse at Bagram occurred in December 2002. Two detainees—a twenty-two-year-old taxi driver known as Dilawar and the brother of a Taliban commander—were both found dead, hanging from the wrists by shackles in isolation cells. (Their stories were later depicted in the Oscar award-winning documentary *Taxi to the Dark Side.*) An Army investigation revealed that the two men had been brutalized by interrogators, deprived of sleep for days, and struck so often in the legs by guards that a coroner compared their injuries to those from being run over by a bus.[21] Army investigators later learned that Dilawar was an innocent man who was in the wrong place at the wrong time.[22] Both deaths were eventually ruled homicides, contradicting the military's initial assertion that the men had died of natural causes.[23]

The Bush administration labeled the detainees at Bagram "enemy combatants," just as it did at Guantánamo. It also defined "enemy combatant" in sweeping terms. While some prisoners at Bagram were allegedly seized in connection with hostilities in Afghanistan, others were captured in places as distant as Central Africa and Southeast Asia and brought to Bagram.[24] The United States also denied Bagram detainees any legal protections, whether those afforded by the Geneva Conventions or those provided under domestic and human rights law to individuals accused of terrorism or other crimes. Bagram detainees were simultaneously denied access to any U.S. or Afghan court. They were thus imprisoned for years without charge, without trial, and without any meaningful opportunity to challenge the allegations against them.

The sham military process that the Bush administration instituted at Bagram worked as follows: After an initial determination made "at the place of capture," the detainees' cases were reviewed after ninety days and then again every year by a panel of five military officers known as an Enemy Combatant Review Board (ECRB).[25] The ECRB suffered from multiple flaws and lacked the safeguards necessary to achieve accurate results. For example, it denied detainees the opportunity to be present at the hearings, to see the evidence against them, and to have the assistance of a lawyer. As one official familiar with the process explained, "The detainee is not involved at all."[26] In addition, in making its assessments, the ECRB could use statements gained through torture or other coercion. Although the United States claimed that the average length of detention at Bagram was about fifteen months, many detainees were held there for several years and, in some cases, for six years or more.[27]

The United States structured its operations at Bagram to create an American enclave without accountability, much like Guantánamo. Since 2003, the United States has operated Bagram under a series of lease agreements with Afghanistan. The current lease grants the United States complete, exclusive, and permanent control over Bagram, allowing it to occupy the land, rent free, for as long as it wishes and without interference by Afghanistan. The lease even allows the United States to assign possession of Bagram to another nation or organization, a power that even the Guantánamo lease does not provide.[28] By disclaiming formal sovereignty over the base, however, the United States has sought to preserve the fiction that Bagram is not U.S.-controlled territory. Therefore, the United States says, it is not obligated to give detainees there the protections of its laws or Constitution or provide them any access to its courts. At the same time, the detainees at Bagram have no rights under Afghan law and no access to Afghan courts. The result is a U.S.-run legal black hole.

Despite the similarities between Guantánamo and Bagram, there are differences between the two prisons. As we shall see, over time Guantánamo was subjected to some judicial process. Through federal habeas corpus litigation, attorneys gained the right to visit the detainees there and to seek relief in court. These legal challenges helped undercut the U.S. government's effort to maintain a system of unchecked executive detention at Guantánamo. Ironically, they also caused the government to imprison more people at Bagram, where for a long time detainees remained largely "out of sight" and "out of mind."[29] As a Defense Department official who has visited both facilities put it, "Anyone who has been to Bagram would tell you it's worse."[30]

If overseas military prisons like Guantánamo and Bagram represent one facet of the post-9/11 global detention system, "extraordinary rendition" illustrates another. Extraordinary rendition generally describes the transfer of prisoners to another country for possible torture. Like U.S.-run detention facilities designated to operate outside the law, extraordinary rendition is driven by a desire to incarcerate and interrogate individuals without legal constraint. It also places a premium on secrecy that makes it both more difficult to challenge and more vulnerable to the worst human rights abuses.

The origins of extraordinary rendition date back several decades. The U.S. Marshals Service first coined the phrase to describe the process of kidnapping fugitives abroad and bringing them to the United States.[31] This practice enabled U.S. officials to apprehend wanted individuals in "lawless" states or countries that lacked an extradition treaty with the United States.[32] In 1987, for example, FBI and CIA agents lured a terrorism suspect named Fawaz Yunis into international waters off the coast of Cyprus and arrested him. Yunis was then transferred to the United States, where he was tried and convicted for his role in the hijacking of a Jordanian airliner.[33] This form of rendition became known as "rendition to justice." Rendition to justice has generally been upheld by the courts, which ordinarily focus on whether defendants are provided due process at trial and not what happened to them beforehand.[34]

By mid-1980s, the United States was increasingly using "rendition to justice" for national security purposes. In 1986, President Ronald Reagan reportedly authorized U.S. law enforcement personnel to covertly apprehend suspected terrorists in places where it was thought that the traditional extradition process would not work.[35] President George H. W. Bush authorized specific rendition procedures, and President Bill Clinton expanded the program, making the return of wanted terrorists "a matter of the highest priority."[36] Former FBI Director Louis J. Freeh stated that during the 1990s, the United States "successfully returned" thirteen suspected international terrorists to face trial in the United States for plotting or carrying out acts of terrorism against U.S. citizens.[37] Despite these changes, "rendition to justice" remained a law enforcement matter, and suspects were ultimately brought to trial within the civilian justice system, with its guarantees of due process.

By the mid-1990s, however, "rendition to justice" had started to drift further from its original focus of bringing suspects to trial in U.S. courts. Michael Scheuer, the former head of the CIA's bin Laden unit, estimated that the agency had identified and located al Qaeda leaders but "couldn't capture them because [it] had nowhere to take them."[38] The CIA established a rendition branch in its Counter-Terrorism Center and assigned case officers to track down wanted individuals.[39] Several secret orders issued in the late 1990s gave the CIA greater leeway to deal with Osama bin Laden, including the "authority to use foreign proxies to detain Bin Laden lieutenants, without having to transfer them to U.S. custody."[40]

The 9/11 Commission's interim staff report on diplomacy described the shift: "If extradition procedures were unavailable or put aside, the United States could seek the local country's assistance in a rendition, secretly putting the fugitive in a plane back to America or some third country for trial."[41] The main alternative destination was Egypt, a country known for torturing prisoners and one that had outstanding warrants against several suspected terrorists. The United States rendered at least nine individuals to Egypt, including Talaat Fouad Qassem, who had been sentenced to death in absentia there for his involvement in the plot to assassinate Egypt's former president, Anwar Sadat. Qassem was arrested in Croatia, where he was questioned by U.S. agents for two days on a ship in the Adriatic Sea before he was sent to Egypt. Qassem has never been seen again.[42] His case illustrates that even before 9/11 the United States had started moving away from "rendition to justice" and toward a new form of rendition, in which a suspect's transfer and imprisonment occurred entirely outside the U.S. legal system and the focus was not on bringing a suspect to trial in U.S. courts.

But these changes were relatively small compared with those made after 9/11 when, as a former FBI agent put it, the rendition program "really went out of control."[43] The program not only expanded dramatically in size and scope but also began operating without any legal or bureaucratic constraints. The concept of "rendition to justice" disappeared entirely, as individuals were placed beyond any form of judicial or legal process. The program became what we know today as "extraordinary rendition."

Vice President Dick Cheney set the tone five days after September 11, explaining on *Meet the Press* that the United States needed to "work . . . the dark side," doing things "quietly, without any discussion, using sources and methods that are available to our intelligence agencies."[44] A classified presidential directive issued on September 17 increased the CIA's power, including the power to kill, capture, or detain members of al Qaeda anywhere in the world. The directive also dispensed with the previous practice of requiring the CIA's legal counsel to approve every proposed operation. The focus expanded from a discrete category of individuals—alleged terrorists against whom there were already outstanding arrest warrants—to a broad and vaguely defined class of people suspected of plotting terrorist acts, associating with suspected terrorists, or simply having useful intelligence.[45] The program's purpose changed, too, from bringing wanted suspects to trial to imprisoning people only to question them and extract information by whatever means deemed necessary. In the process, the outsourcing of torture became the rendition program's raison d'être and driving force.

The documented accounts of extraordinary rendition read like lurid tales from a cold war spy novel: hooded detainees being spirited away in the night and sent in CIA-owned or chartered jets to secret destinations for imprisonment and torture. One of the first known cases involved Muhammad al-Zery and Ahmed Agiza, two Egyptians seeking political asylum in Sweden. The Swedish government bypassed its legally required procedures and ordered both men deported without a hearing at the urging of its security police. The security police were acting at the behest of U.S. officials, who had been planning the men's clandestine transfer to Egypt. Swedish security officers, accompanied by masked CIA agents, took al-Zery and Agiza into a changing room at Stockholm's Bromma Airport for what they said was a routine "security check." The two men's clothes were cut into pieces, and they were forcibly administered sedatives by suppository, swaddled in diapers, and dressed in orange jumpsuits. Al-Zery and Agiza were then blindfolded, placed in handcuffs and leg irons, and flown to Cairo aboard a Gulfstream jet registered to a front company for the CIA, whose agents operated and manned the flight. Once in Egypt, both men were tortured, including through the application of electric charges to their naked bodies in cold underground rooms.[46]

Agiza was later convicted on terrorism charges and sentenced to twenty-five years in prison. Al-Zery was released after two years without any charges. It turned out that he had been rendered based on the flimsiest of evidence:

his name had been found on the computer of an Egyptian dissident arrested in London two months earlier for his suspected involvement in a suicide bomb attack but subsequently cleared of all charges. Al-Zery and Agiza were just two of the estimated sixty prisoners rendered to Egypt after 9/11.[47]

One of the most infamous rendition cases was that of thirty-six-year-old Canadian citizen Maher Arar. Arar's ordeal began on September 22, 2002, when he was detained and questioned by U.S. officials at New York's John F. Kennedy International Airport during a layover while returning to Montreal from a family vacation in Tunisia. After two days, Arar, a computer engineer by trade, was taken in chains and shackles to a federal jail in Brooklyn, where he was held in solitary confinement and subjected to further interrogation without an attorney. Meanwhile, the Immigration and Naturalization Service commenced removal proceedings based on Arar's alleged ties to al Qaeda. Arar maintained his innocence and asked to be sent to Canada, telling U.S. officials that he would be tortured if he were sent to Syria, a country he had fled as a teenager two decades earlier. The government, however, continued to block Arar's access to his lawyer, thus preventing him from seeking judicial redress and enforcing legal safeguards designed to prevent transfers to likely torture. An immigration judge subsequently ordered Arar's removal to Syria based on secret evidence. On October 8, Arar was flown to Jordan, where local authorities chained and beat him before stuffing him in a van and driving him across the border to Syria.

For the next ten months, Arar was kept in a dark, rat-infested cell resembling a grave. He was beaten on his palms, hips, and lower back with a two-inch-thick electric cable, and was told he would be placed in a spine-breaking "chair," hung upside down in a "tire" for beatings, and given electric shocks. In a desperate effort to end the suffering, Arar falsely confessed to having trained with terrorists in Afghanistan, a country he had never even visited.[48]

Syria released Arar in October 2003 after Canada finally intervened on his behalf. In September 2006, a Canadian commission of inquiry released a three-volume report finding "no evidence to indicate Mr. Arar has committed any offense or that his activities constitute a threat to the security of Canada."[49] The commission also determined that the United States had likely relied on inaccurate and misleading information about Arar's supposed terrorist connections provided by Canadian officials and confirmed that Arar was tortured while in Syria. The Canadian government subsequently issued Arar a formal apology and awarded him more than $9 million to compensate him for his pain and suffering.[50] The United States, however, refused to apologize for its role in Arar's rendition and sought to block Arar's civil lawsuit against the responsible U.S. officials, claiming that the suit would jeopardize national security if allowed to go forward. In the face of mounting criticism over the United States' handling of the case, former attorney general Alberto Gonzales admitted that he had not bothered to read the Canadian commission's report and was "not aware" that Arar had been tortured.[51] Meanwhile, the United States—unwilling to admit that it had made a mistake, let alone give Arar any compensation—kept Arar on a terrorist watch-list that prevented him from entering the country.[52]

The renditions of Arar, al-Zery, and Agiza all occurred under the guise of immigration law, which was manipulated and subverted for illegal ends. The rendition of Osama Mustafa Hassan Nasr, also known as "Abu Omar," by contrast, occurred entirely outside any legal framework. The Egyptian-born Abu Omar was living with his family in Milan, Italy, and had been granted political asylum based on his fear of persecution for his membership in a radial Islamic organization. On February 17, 2003, Abu Omar was walking to his local mosque for midday prayers when masked CIA agents kidnapped him less than a mile from his home.

As Abu Omar later related, Italian-speaking men claiming to be police officers sprayed an unknown substance on his mouth and nose before pushing him into a van and driving him to a U.S. air base five hours away. In the van, English- and Italian-speaking individuals gagged Abu Omar and beat him repeatedly while questioning him about his relation to radical Islamists and about recruiting terrorist volunteers to fight in Iraq. Abu Omar's captors then flew him to another military base in Europe before taking him to Egypt. On arrival in Egypt, Abu Omar was immediately brought to the headquarters of the secret police. When Abu Omar refused to work as an informer, Egyptian officials took him to an underground prison and tortured him, including by hanging him upside down and applying electric shocks to his genitals.

The details of Abu Omar's kidnapping were uncovered only by chance. At the time of his abduction, Abu Omar was under investigation for terrorism-related crimes as part of a broader inquiry into Islamic militancy based in Milan. Italian prosecutors, who had originally tapped Abu Omar's phone as part of their investigation, intercepted a call that Abu Omar had made from Egypt to his wife in Italy after fourteen months of captivity there. Egypt had by that time released Abu Omar because of his failing health. During the call, Abu Omar recounted his abduction and rendition to his wife. Egypt subsequently rearrested Abu Omar and continued to hold him under an emergency detention law until February 2007, when it finally released him.[53]

Revelation of Abu Omar's abduction prompted an outcry in Italy and across Europe. Italian prosecutors brought criminal charges against twenty-six CIA agents, including the two top CIA officials in Italy and five Italian secret service agents.[54] An Italian court ultimately convicted more than twenty CIA officers in absentia for their role in Abu Omar's kidnapping. (The United States refused to extradite the defendants, who had fled Italy in advance of the investigation.)[55] In addition to creating political controversy, the abduction undermined the original criminal investigation against Abu Omar and a cell of alleged terrorists in Italy and around Europe while damaging relations with the Muslim community.[56]

These are just a few of the numerous U.S.-directed extraordinary renditions that took place after the September 11 attacks. Logs obtained by the *Sunday Times* of London showed that one Gulfstream jet used in rendition operations flew to forty-nine destinations, including Afghanistan, Egypt, Iraq, Jordan, Libya, Morocco, and Uzbekistan.[57] Estimates of the number of people subjected to "extraordinary rendition" vary from as few as seventy to as many as several thousand.[58] And these estimates cover only the CIA-related renditions. If the Defense Department renditions to Guantánamo and Bagram are included, that number would be significantly higher.

Extraordinary rendition violates the United States' legal obligation not to send people to places where their lives or freedom could be threatened, an obligation known as *non-refoulement* (or non-return). This obligation is set forth in the Convention against Torture and Other Cruel, Inhuman or Degrading Treatment or Punishment (Convention against Torture), a treaty signed by the United States and more than 145 other countries. The Convention against Torture categorically prohibits states from expelling, returning, or extraditing a person to another state "where there are substantial grounds for believing that he would be in danger of being subjected to torture."[59] The treaty's *non-refoulement* obligation is one of a number of measures designed to prohibit and prevent torture worldwide.[60] The International Covenant on Civil and Political Rights (ICCPR), another human rights treaty to which the United States is also a party, contains an even broader *non-refoulement* obligation. It prohibits exposing individuals to the risk not only of torture but also of cruel, inhuman, or degrading treatment or punishment. While the ICCPR's *non-refoulement* obligation is not explicit, the Human Rights Committee, which monitors the treaty's implementation, has determined that this obligation falls within the treaty's prohibition against torture and other mistreatment and is binding under the treaty's general legal obligations.[61] Furthermore, human rights law supports construing the *non-refoule-*

ment obligation broadly to encompass territories and persons under a state's authority or control.[62]

The Bush administration tried to defend extraordinary rendition as both necessary and legal. To protect the American people, Bush asserted, the United States had "to find those who would do harm to us and get them out of [the] way."[63] Secretary of State Condoleezza Rice similarly remarked, "Renditions take terrorists out of action, and save lives." Echoing the administration's earlier refusal to apply the Geneva Conventions to "enemy combatants," Rice noted that the "war on terrorism" is a "new kind of conflict" that requires new approaches for dealing with "captured terrorists . . . [who] do not fit easily into traditional systems of criminal or military justice."[64]

The Bush administration sought to justify extraordinary rendition based on the same theories of unchecked executive power that it invoked to justify the detention of prisoners at Guantánamo and Bagram. It argued that the Convention against Torture's *non-refoulement* obligation did not apply extraterritorially and therefore excluded transfers outside the United States. It insisted that the ICCPR also did not apply extraterritorially and that human rights law more generally did not apply to extraordinary renditions because the "war on terrorism" was subject only to the law of war.[65] And the law of war, the administration maintained, did not restrict the transfer of "enemy combatants" to another government, even if that transfer would likely result in their torture.[66]

The Bush administration, however, also tried to have it both ways: to defend the legality of extraordinary rendition while maintaining that U.S. policy was not to transfer prisoners to countries where they faced torture. In January 2005, President Bush told the *New York Times* that "torture is never acceptable, nor do we hand people over to countries that do torture."[67] But three months later, after more details of the administration's extraordinary rendition program had emerged, Bush explained that the United States only "send[s] people to countries where *they say* they're not going to torture the people."[68] The administration defended this practice by relying on guarantees from the receiving state—known as "diplomatic assurances"—that those transferred would not be tortured.[69]

Diplomatic assurances were first used in death penalty cases in response to demands by some countries that the United States not execute a fugitive if extradited to the United States to face trial. They translated poorly to the rendition context where compliance is difficult to monitor and where most transfers are to countries with records of official torture.[70] Diplomatic assurances also are not subject to any regulations but are completely informal and ad hoc. One CIA agent went so far as to call them "a farce."[71] "No one was kidding anyone here," Michael Scheuer said of diplomatic assurances. "We knew exactly what that kind of promise was worth."[72] Or as another official explained, "We don't kick the [expletive] out of them. We send them to other countries so they can kick the [expletive] out of them."[73]

But not all torture was outsourced. In addition to authorizing the CIA to kill or capture al Qaeda members anywhere in the world, the classified presidential directive that jump-started the post-9/11 extraordinary rendition program also approved the creation of a network of secret CIA-run prisons or "black sites."[74] These prisons offered something even Guantánamo and Bagram could not: total invisibility. After 9/11, hundreds of prisoners were rendered to these "black sites," which were located in various countries, including Afghanistan, Thailand, Poland, Romania, and Lithuania.[75] The goal in selecting prisons, one CIA official said, was researching "how to make people disappear."[76]

Prisoners in CIA custody came to be referred to as "ghost detainees."[77] Even the ICRC was denied access to them.[78] The CIA "loved that these guys would just disappear off the books, and never be heard of again," said a former FBI agent. "They were proud of it."[79] Although more secret than military detentions at Guantánamo and Bagram, CIA "black sites" were predicated on a similar concept: that the detainees were unlawful combatants in the global "war on terrorism" and therefore had no rights or legal protection under domestic or international law.

The Bush administration authorized secret CIA prisons primarily to extract information. The prisons, in turn, served as laboratories for the administration's most abusive interrogation methods—the "enhanced interrogation techniques" sanctioned by executive branch decisions and legal memoranda gutting the definition of torture and justifying any action taken by the president or his agents in the name of national security. The use of these techniques was closely monitored by CIA lawyers and supervised at the highest levels of the U.S. government. One outside expert familiar with the interrogation protocol described it as "one of the most sophisticated, refined programs of torture ever."[80]

Cases like Khaled el-Masri's show how easily people could be mistakenly ensnared in this new, law-free detention system. A German citizen and car salesman, el-Masri was traveling to Macedonia for vacation during the Christmas holiday in 2003. On December 31, his bus stopped at the main border crossing between Serbia and Macedonia. El-Masri was singled out from other tourists. His passport was confiscated, and he was taken to a windowless room where his captors accused him of terrorism. That evening, el-

Masri was brought to a hotel room in Skopje where he was beaten, drugged, and interrogated at gunpoint. After twenty-three days of incommunicado captivity, el-Masri was brought to the airport and turned over to masked CIA agents. Shackled, diapered, and blindfolded, el-Masri was then flown to Afghanistan. Upon arrival, el-Masri was driven to the Salt Pit, the code name for a secret CIA-run interrogation facility located in an abandoned brick factory outside Kabul. There, el-Masri was again held incommunicado and deprived of basic necessities. El-Masri's conditions did not improve until he commenced a hunger strike that caused his captors to fear that he might die. Despite evidence that el-Masri was not a terrorist, the head of the CIA's al Qaeda unit insisted that el-Masri continue to be held based on her "gut feeling" that he was bad.[81] Finally, on May 28, 2004, CIA agents took el-Masri to a roadside hilltop in Albania and deposited him without explanation. When el-Masri returned home after five months' of captivity, his appearance had changed so much that the German border guard who checked his documents could not recognize him from the picture in his passport.[82]

The ordeal of Marwan Jabour provides another chilling account of secret detention. Following his arrest in Lahore, Pakistan, in May 2004, Jabour was taken initially to the local station of Pakistan's Inter-Services Intelligence. Four days later, he was brought to a clandestine prison in Islamabad operated jointly by Pakistanis and Americans. During his detention, Jabour was beaten, denied sleep for days, and kept naked and chained to a wall in a cell while his penis was tied with a string so that he could not urinate. American officials participated in Jabour's interrogations and warned him that he could "be taken away somewhere and would never see his children again." After a month, Jabour was blindfolded, shackled, and taken to an airport along with three other prisoners. The men were then put on a plane by Americans and flown to a secret facility in Afghanistan, where more than thirty other prisoners were being held. All the individuals operating and working at the prison were Americans, with the possible exception of the Arab-speaking translators. Jabour was chained in painful positions, held in prolonged solitary confinement, and prevented from seeing sunlight for a year-and-a-half. Jabour was also denied all contact with the outside world, including the ICRC and his family. Finally, after two years, Jabour was sent to Jordan and then to Israel, which released him to his family in Gaza. During his entire confinement, Jabour was never brought before a judge, charged with a crime, or allowed to see a lawyer.[83]

The U.S. has never acknowledged how many people it detained in secret jails around the world. But that number likely exceeds several hundred,[84] and the location of some of these prisoners still remains unknown.[85]

Guantánamo, Bagram, CIA "black sites," and extraordinary rendition together demonstrate the emergence of an interconnected global detention system designed to circumvent legal protections and avoid accountability. U.S. detentions in Iraq illustrate a different but related phenomenon. They show how the ideas and impulses behind that system could warp what began as a more traditional military operation, pushing it to operate outside the law by defining it as another front in the global "war on terrorism."

On March 18, 2003, the United States and United Kingdom invaded Iraq, with the support of smaller contingents from other nations that formed the "Coalition of the Willing." The invasion's stated goals were to rid Iraq of weapons of mass destruction, to end Saddam Hussein's support for terrorism, and to liberate the Iraqi people. Both President Bush and British Prime Minister Tony Blair claimed implicit authorization for the invasion from the United Nations Security Council. Three weeks after the invasion began, U.S. forces formally occupied Baghdad and declared an end to Saddam Hussein's rule. (Hussein was captured that December.) On May 1, 2003, President Bush landed on the aircraft carrier *USS Abraham Lincoln* and delivered a speech proclaiming the "end of major combat operations" in Iraq, with a banner stating "Mission Accomplished" clearly visible in the background. Five days later Bush appointed L. Paul Bremer III to oversee the reconstruction of Iraq as head of the Coalition Provisional Authority (CPA), which would function as Iraq's temporary government until a democratically elected civilian government could be established. On June 28, 2004, the CPA transferred power to the newly appointed Iraqi interim government and disbanded, marking a formal end to the United States' occupation of Iraq. Elections were held, and transitional and permanent governments were formed. But despite these political developments, insurgency and mounting sectarian violence continued in Iraq, and more than 100,000 U.S. troops remained on the ground there. By June 2005, President Bush was calling Iraq "a central front in the war on terror."[86]

The U.S.-led invasion and occupation of Iraq gave rise to a massive U.S.-run detention system in that country. By 2008, the United States was detaining more than 21,000 individuals in Iraq, nominally under the authority of the Multi-National Force–Iraq (MNF–I), the U.S.-dominated international coalition in postinvasion Iraq.[87] U.S. detention operations, which initially sprawled over five facilities, were ultimately concentrated in two prisons: Camp Bucca in southern Iraq, and Camp Cropper, located near the Baghdad International Airport. In addition to U.S. prisoners, by 2008, more than

23,000 people were being held by the Iraqi government in jails throughout the country.[88]

The legal basis for the MNF–I and for U.S. detention operations in Iraq stemmed primarily from several UN Security Council resolutions. On May 22, 2003, the Security Council passed Resolution 1483, stating that the United States and United Kingdom were occupying powers acting under a unified command and would administer Iraq to restore security and stability in accordance with the UN Charter and relevant international law.[89] Less than five months later, the Security Council passed Resolution 1511, recognizing the MNF–I and authorizing it to take "all necessary measures to contribute to the maintenance of security and stability in Iraq."[90] Together, Resolutions 1483 and 1511 legitimized the occupation of Iraq under this U.S.-led military force.[91] The subsequent return of formal sovereignty to Iraq in 2004 did not alter the situation, and UN Security Council Resolution 1546 extended the MNF–I's mandate to continue combat and detention operations in Iraq. In particular, that resolution authorized the MNF–I, acting under the "unified command" of U.S. military officers, to "take all necessary measures" to contribute to the maintenance of security and stability in Iraq,[92] including detaining individuals where "necessary for imperative reasons of security."[93] The MNF–I's mandate was subsequently extended through December 2008, after which point Iraq was expected to take over all detention operations in the country.[94] Although the number of prisoners in U.S. custody declined, the United States continued detaining more than five thousand prisoners into 2010.[95]

The United States did not initially claim that it could detain prisoners in Iraq outside any legal framework, as it did at Guantánamo, Bagram, and the CIA "black sites." In April 2003, the Defense Department announced that it was holding detainees captured in Iraq in accordance with the Geneva Conventions.[96] Before long, however, U.S. detention operations in Iraq started to resemble U.S. detention operations at those other prisons: prolonged security-related imprisonments based on vague suspicions and unverified intelligence rather than reliable evidence, excessive secrecy, torture and other abuse, and a complete denial of judicial review.

Faced with an increasingly aggressive insurgency and a need for better intelligence to combat it, U.S. commanders in Iraq began turning to the same tactics used in the "war on terror." In May 2003, they introduced a new legal category that did not exist under the Geneva Conventions but was already familiar at Guantánamo: "unlawful combatant." U.S. commanders subsequently adopted another category that did not exist under the Geneva Conventions: "security detainees." Within a year, the number of security detainees in Iraq grew to more than 6,300, more than 3,000 of whom were being held at Abu Ghraib, the dusty and decrepit compound outside Baghdad that quickly became the United States' main detention center in the country. High-level U.S. officials responsible for implementing harsh interrogation measures at Guantánamo and Bagram were brought to Iraq to implement those tactics there.

To denote their "significant intelligence or political value," a small number of security detainees were labeled "high-value detainees" and held in secret.[97] Meanwhile, the number of detainees held as prisoners of war continued to dwindle.[98] "They are not EPWs [enemy prisoners of war]," remarked one senior military commander about prisoners in U.S. custody in Iraq. "They are terrorists and will be treated as such."[99] Such statements sowed confusion and sent a message through the ranks that aggressive treatment, even abuse, was permissible. "The gloves are coming off regarding these detainees," a U.S. intelligence officer said in a widely distributed email message from August 2003.[100] By September 2003, Lieutenant General Ricardo S. Sanchez, the commander of coalition forces in Iraq, had a new policy modeled on Guantánamo that sanctioned interrogation methods such as stress positions, the use of military dogs, sleep and sensory deprivation, and exposure to extreme temperatures.[101] Because detainees in Iraq were "unlawful combatants," Pentagon officials reasoned, SERE techniques could be reverse-engineered and used against them, just as they were used against detainees at Guantánamo and Bagram.[102]

U.S. officials continued to assert publicly that detentions in Iraq were conducted "in the spirit" of the Geneva Conventions, which require that an occupying power establish a "regular procedure" for the periodic review of the internment of civilians (or nonprisoners of war).[103] But the reviews conducted by the MNF–I failed to meet these requirements and lacked important safeguards.[104] Prisoners were routinely denied any meaningful opportunity to see or confront the evidence against them.[105] They also were refused the chance to be present at their review hearings.[106] The Fourth Geneva Convention permits the detention of civilians only where it is "necessary for imperative reasons of security" or for penal prosecution.[107] But Iraqi civilians picked up in random military sweeps of entire neighborhoods and at highway checkpoints were held for months, or even years, without prosecution and without evidence that their confinement was, in fact, "necessary for imperative reasons of security."[108] As a United Nations report explained, the MNF–I held detainees "for prolonged periods without judicial review of their cases," and based on administrative review procedures that "do not fulfill the requirement to grant detainees due process in accordance with internationally recognized norms."[109]

The United States also failed to institute an effective system for identifying and tracking detainees. Some prisoners simply got lost in the confusion.[110] Others were deliberately taken off the regular rolls or registered under false names.[111] This practice, known as "ghosting," violated the Geneva Conventions and human rights law. It allowed the CIA and military intelligence officers to hold prisoners incommunicado and hide them from the ICRC, which regularly inspects prisons to monitor compliance with the Geneva Conventions.[112] Ghosting was also intended to facilitate the CIA's transfer of detainees from Iraq to other countries for interrogation—a grave breach of the Geneva Conventions subject to prosecution as a war crime.[113] One U.S. Army general speculated that there may have been as many as one hundred "ghost detainees" in Iraq.[114]

U.S. officials argued that the normal rules did not apply to the war against terrorism. Due process, they insisted, "is a human rights concept generally associated with criminal arrests and trials" and does not apply to security-related detentions in Iraq.[115] This argument was not only wrong but had devastating consequences.

On April 28, 2004, *60 Minutes II* broadcast pictures from Abu Ghraib prison showing the torture and gross mistreatment of detainees by U.S. forces. The pictures quickly spread across the globe through print media and the Internet.[116] They showed U.S. troops subjecting detainees to mock executions, sexual humiliation, beatings, and other mistreatment. One photograph depicted a hooded man standing on a box with electrical wires attached to his hands. Another showed the bloodied body of a prisoner, wrapped in cellophane and packed in ice. Other pictures displayed American soldiers using dogs to terrify prisoners, force prisoners into painful positions, and sexually humiliate them.[117] A U.S. army investigation into the abuses at Abu Ghraib headed by Major General Antonio M. Taguba found numerous instances of "sadistic, blatant, and wanton criminal abuses," including breaking chemical lights and pouring the phosphoric liquids on detainees, pouring cold water on naked detainees, and beating detainees with a broom handle and a chair.[118] These abuses, Taguba's report concluded, stemmed from routine violations of U.S. Army regulations and the Geneva Conventions.[119]

The impact of the Abu Ghraib photographs cannot be overstated. Although written descriptions of prisoner mistreatment already existed, there was no widespread public outcry until these images of American soldiers tormenting Iraqi prisoners were published.[120] As Susan Sontag explained, images of atrocities can incite the public in ways that words alone cannot.[121] The Abu Ghraib photographs did precisely that. They exposed the Bush administration's lie that the United States was treating prisoners humanely and showed why courts and legislators could not blindly trust the president in matters of national security. The photographs also illustrated how the administration's effort to circumvent legal rules and court review could lead to horrific abuse, damaging America's reputation and undermining human rights protections throughout the world.[122]

The abuses were not limited to Abu Ghraib but occurred at other prisons in Iraq, including the infamous Camp Nama. Located just off a dusty road near the Baghdad International Airport, Camp Nama had previously served as a torture chamber for Saddam Hussein's regime. When the Iraqi insurgency intensified in 2004, a U.S. Special Operations unit remade it into an interrogation center. Camp Nama quickly became a black hole for prisoners who were denied access to lawyers, courts, relatives, and the world outside. Prisoners were interrogated in a windowless cell known as the Black Room, where the eighteen-inch hooks hanging from the ceiling served as a reminder of the torture inflicted under Saddam Hussein. Members of a military unit known as Task Force 6-26—a unit closely related to the task force that had so grossly mistreated prisoners at Abu Ghraib—were assigned responsibility for extracting information about Iraq's most-wanted terrorist, Abu Musab al-Zarqawi. But the task force ended up using the brutal techniques intended for "the worst of the worst" on ordinary Iraqi civilians.[123] Soldiers, for example, beat prisoners with rifle butts and yelled and spit in their faces. "The reality is, there were no rules," commented one Pentagon official.[124] When some interrogators at Camp Nama raised questions, military lawyers arrived at the base within hours to give a PowerPoint presentation defending the treatment and techniques on the ground that the detainees were not prisoners of war but "security detainees" or "enemy combatants."[125] Abuses continued even after warnings from an army investigator and American law enforcement officials. More than thirty-four members of Task Force 6-26 were ultimately disciplined in some way for abusing detainees and three members were convicted of physical assault. In the end, Camp Nama yielded little information to help capture insurgents or save American lives. Instead, it succeeded only in alienating ordinary Iraqis and undermining the United States' mission in that country and its counterterrorism efforts generally.[126]

These abuses may be attributed partly to the tremendous stress placed on American soldiers battling an insurgency that continued to grow in strength.

But they also flowed directly from the Bush administration's decision to circumvent legal rules and embrace torture and detention without due process. "Shit started to go bad right away," remarked one infantry team leader, looking back at detainee operations during the United States' first crucial months in Iraq.[127] The decision to operate outside the Geneva Conventions facilitated the migration of aggressive interrogation techniques from Guantánamo and Afghanistan to Iraq. Major General Geoffrey D. Miller, in particular, sought to "Gitmoize" interrogations in Iraq, where he supervised all U.S.-run prisons, by adopting strategies and techniques honed while previously serving as Guantánamo's commander.[128] Meanwhile, Department of Justice lawyer John Yoo's March 2003 memo legitimizing brutal interrogation methods in the name of national security helped provide legal cover for Miller and others to make detention operations in Iraq "an enabler for interrogation" and helped pave the way for many of the human rights violations that followed.[129]

America's failure to implement adequate screening procedures and its evasion of the Geneva Conventions' prohibition against mistreating prisoners fed off each other. Detainees who presented no threat and who had little or no intelligence value swelled the population of Abu Ghraib and other prisons in Iraq.[130] Detainees were often held for long periods of time based on superficial examinations and screening statements that encouraged the use of abusive interrogation methods.[131] In many cases, the United States failed to notify family members that their loved ones had been seized and imprisoned. Individuals were removed from their homes in the middle of the night with bags over their heads and without explanation. When families asked where their loved ones were being taken, they were told to shut up.[132] Sometimes U.S. troops arrested all adult males present in a house, including elderly, handicapped, and sick people. Iraqi men were pushed around, insulted, and kicked and struck with rifles.[133] All told, approximately thirty thousand to forty thousand Iraqis passed through U.S. detention facilities in the first eighteen months of the occupation.[134]

The United States also resisted releasing even those prisoners who were clearly innocent. As a military intelligence officer explained:

People were afraid to take personal responsibility [for] recommending release of detainees, even when obviously innocent, and often this would lead to condemning statements such as "the detainee told the same story seven times but is lying because he should know such and such information and was therefore uncooperative. Recommend detainee be held in U.S. custody for the duration of hostilities."[135]

Major General Taguba's report noted that more than 60 percent of the civilian inmates at Abu Ghraib had been deemed not to present any threat. Yet many continued to languish in jail.[136] As one army intelligence official later told investigators, the prevailing attitude of U.S. commanders was, "We wouldn't have detained them if we wanted them released."[137] Holding people without charge, without access to a court, or without any other meaningful process helped lead to the prolonged confinement of innocent people, the glutting of jails, and the growing reliance on aggressive interrogation measures, particularly as the insurgency gained strength.[138] It also undermined the United States' operations in Iraq by fueling the same insurgency the United States was trying to quell.

The case of American citizen Donald Vance highlights the United States' "haphazard system of detention and prosecution" in Iraq.[139] A navy veteran from Chicago, Vance went to Iraq in 2004 to work as a security contractor. When he discovered that the company he was working for had a growing cache of weapons that it was selling to suspicious customers with ties to violent militias and death squads, Vance informed the FBI and the U.S. embassy in Baghdad. In return, Vance was arrested and imprisoned by the U.S. military in Camp Cropper as a security detainee for having associated with the very people he had tried to expose. Vance was confined to a tiny cell, where he and other prisoners slept on concrete slabs and where the temperature was only 50 degrees Fahrenheit. During interrogations, officials shackled Vance's hands and feet, covered his eyes, placed towels over his head, and put him in a wheelchair.[140] Vance kept track of the days by making hash marks on the wall of his cell. Vance was denied the assistance of a lawyer at his military review hearings and was prevented from seeing the evidence against him. The only reason Vance was even allowed to be present at those hearings was because he was an American citizen—an opportunity denied to Iraqis and detainees from other countries. Vance was finally released, but only after three months of illegal imprisonment. Of the ten letters that Vance had sent to his fiancée in the United States pleading for help while he was imprisoned, only one arrived, and that letter did not arrive until after Vance had already returned home.[141]

Despite these problems, and despite the fact that more than one hundred people reportedly died in U.S. custody in Iraq and Afghanistan, U.S. detentions in Iraq received relatively little attention aside from scandals like Abu Ghraib. Far more is known about the several hundred detainees at Guantánamo than about the tens of thousands of prisoners in Iraq. The sheer number of detainees in Iraq, the proximity to ongoing combat operations, and the fact that the United States paid lip service to the Geneva Conventions all contributed to a tendency to view Iraq separately from the larger post-9/11 detention system. Yet, Iraq presents an important aspect of that system. It illustrates how the theories and impulses behind the "war on terrorism" could lead U.S. officials to circumvent established rules and spawn a massive detention dragnet without adequate checks against arbitrary imprisonment and abuse. It also shows how fears of terrorism could prompt overreaction and a disregard for legal rules, leading to widespread human rights violations and undercutting the United States' ability to counter insurgency. Iraq, in short, shows how a military operation that was originally supposed to comply with the Geneva Conventions and U.S. law could become "in effect, another Guantánamo."[142] Like Guantánamo, Bagram, and CIA "black sites," Iraq highlights the dangers of extrajudicial detention and the importance of habeas corpus.

4

Crossing a Constitutional Rubicon

The Domestic "Enemy Combatant" Cases

After 9/11, the United States imprisoned hundreds of individuals as "enemy combatants" overseas and only three people as "enemy combatants" inside the United States. But those three cases involved the most aggressive and expansive assertions of executive detention power in the "war on terrorism." In two of them, the Bush administration sought nothing less than the crossing of a constitutional Rubicon, threatening to erase the guarantees of the Bill of Rights and institute a new norm of indefinite military imprisonment. In essence, it claimed the power to seize American citizens and legal residents off the streets of the United States and imprison them in military custody, without charge or trial, based solely on the president's assertion that they presented a danger to the nation's security.

Before 9/11, the United States had prosecuted suspected terrorists in federal court under the country's criminal laws. In the case of foreign nationals, the government had the additional option of seeking the person's removal from the country under its immigration power. Either way, the government's authority to detain depended on promptly bringing formal charges within the civilian justice system.

The Bush administration manipulated and circumvented that system after 9/11. Attorney General John Ashcroft explained that the Justice Department must "think outside the box" and adopt a "prevent first, and prosecute second" strategy to fight terrorism.[1] The problem with this approach was not prevention per se, but the illegal methods the administration used to achieve this end. In the United States, the administration's strategy had two components. The first was exploiting the civilian justice system—in particular, laws governing immigration and material witnesses—to hold people for weeks or even months without charging them with a crime. The second—"enemy combatant" designations—abandoned that system altogether by enabling the president to dispense with a criminal trial in favor of a new and unprecedented regime of indefinite military detention.[2]

One way that the Bush administration exploited the civilian justice system was by misusing immigration law as a tool for preventive detention without evidence of wrongdoing. After 9/11, federal authorities detained more than 750 foreign nationals on immigration violations as part of its investigation into the World Trade Center and Pentagon bombings (code-named the "PENTTBOM investigation").[3] The FBI arrested foreigners based on leads that a subsequent Justice Department inspector general's report criticized as overly general and vague, such as "a landlord reporting suspicious activity by an Arab tenant" or a tip that "too many" Muslims worked at a convenience store.[4] Typically, people were arrested for visa violations or other garden-variety immigration infractions, which served as a proxy for generalized suspicions about their associations, activities, or Arab or Muslim background. They were labeled "of interest" and detained without any effort to identify whether they were actually connected to terrorism.

Federal law required that the government bring charges within twenty-four hours of an arrest for an immigration violation.[5] The U.S. Supreme Court, moreover, had previously ruled that the Constitution prohibited detention for more than forty-eight hours without a judicial determination of probable cause.[6] But a new regulation issued after 9/11 allowed the Immigration and Naturalization Service (now the Department of Homeland Security) to detain foreign nationals without charge for "an additional reasonable period in time" in case of emergency or other extraordinary circumstance.[7] Under the regulation, immigrants arrested in connection with the PENTTBOM investigation were frequently held without charge for up to several months.

In addition, the government sought to prevent these persons' release on bond (or bail) once charges had finally been brought. Previously, most foreign nationals arrested in the United States could obtain bond pending their deportation proceedings if immigration judges found that they were not a flight risk or danger to the community. But after 9/11, the government sought to deny bond to all immigrants arrested in connection with the PENTTBOM investigation without any individualized assessment of whether they were actually dangerous or posed a flight risk. Instead, the Justice Department adopted a "hold until cleared" policy blocking the release of any detainee labeled "of interest" until the release was approved by a section chief in the FBI's Counterterrorism Division. Only those individuals affirmatively deemed not "of interest" were exempt from this "hold until cleared" policy. Under the policy, individuals charged with routine immigration violations were held for months while the FBI completed its criminal investigation, even if there was no basis to detain them under immigration law and they had voluntarily agreed to leave the country.[8] These immigration detainees were also held under highly restrictive conditions and often grossly mistreated. Many were held incommunicado for weeks at a time, locked down in their cells for twenty-three hours a day, prevented from obtaining legal assistance or contacting their families, and physically and verbally abused.[9]

The government also sought to keep these detentions secret. It claimed that the entire PENTTBOM investigation consisted of a "mosaic" of countless bits and pieces of information that only FBI headquarters had sufficient overall information to assess. Although these bits and pieces of information "might appear innocuous in isolation," the government argued, they could be used by terrorist groups to help form a "bigger picture" of the government's counterterrorism investigations, revealing sources and methods and jeopardizing national security.[10] Disclosure of any information in immigration hearings, the government claimed, would compromise national security, and only executive branch officials could assess the dangers of disclosure. To implement this policy, the nation's chief immigration judge directed that proceedings in all "special interest" immigration cases be conducted in total secrecy. As a result, the detainees' names did not appear on the public docket, and their court hearings were closed to the public, including the press and the detainees' families.[11]

The government used immigration law to expand its domestic detention power in other ways as well. It issued a new regulation allowing an immigration prosecutor to automatically freeze an immigration judge's decision to release a detainee pending the prosecutor's appeal of that decision—a process that typically takes months if not more than a year—without requiring the prosecutor to show why the detention was necessary.[12] It also implemented a program known as the "Absconder Apprehension Initiative" to identify, interview, arrest, and deport foreign nationals who had been ordered removed but who nonetheless remained in the country. Although intended to identify people with a link to terrorism, the program largely targeted Arabs and Muslims with no terrorism connection at all, including individuals with long-established community roots.[13] In addition, the government established the "National Security Entry-Exit Registration System," which imposed special registration requirements on foreign nationals from certain Arab and Muslim countries who entered or resided in the United States, including a requirement that such individuals register periodically with the immigration authorities. Purportedly intended to prevent terrorism, the program was used to facilitate the arrest, detention, and deportation of individuals with no ties to terrorism whatsoever.[14]

In total, several thousand people were arrested in the PENTTBOM dragnet, and thousands more were arrested and detained through the special registration and absconder initiative programs. Yet, no one arrested in connection with these measures was charged criminally with any terrorism offense.[15] Instead, immigration arrests were often used as a pretext to target and detain Arabs and Muslims based on suspicion or innuendo. Rather than protecting the nation against future terrorist attacks, these detentions undermined the government's credibility and goodwill in the very Arab and Muslim communities whose cooperation many law enforcement officials and experts considered indispensable to fighting terrorism effectively.[16]

The Bush administration also subverted the civilian justice system by misusing the material witness statute. This statute's express purpose is to enable prosecutors to secure the testimony of witnesses who might otherwise flee to avoid testifying. To arrest and detain someone as a potential witness, the government must show that the witness's testimony is material to a criminal proceeding and that it is impracticable for the government to secure the witness's presence at a trial through a subpoena.[17] A person arrested as a material witness is entitled to a prompt judicial hearing to decide whether there is a basis for detention. In making this determination, a court considers whether the witness poses a flight risk and what conditions of release would ensure his or her appearance to give testimony.[18] Detention remains a last resort, as the government must also demonstrate that the witness's testimony cannot adequately be secured by a deposition or other alternative means.[19]

After 9/11, the Justice Department misused this limited detention authority to secure witness testimony by transforming it into a broad power to arrest and detain people based on suspicion about their activities. According to one report, the number of material witnesses arrested by the federal government increased 80 percent between 2000 and 2002. Yet of the seventy material witnesses detained in connection with the PENTTBOM investigation, approximately half never testified, and many had no relevant information concerning any criminal activity.[20] Like the mass arrest of foreign nationals on routine immigration violations, the arrest of material witnesses served as a pretext for preventively detaining people whom the government suspected of criminal activity but lacked evidence to charge or whom the government simply wanted to interrogate without triggering the legal protections guaranteed to criminal defendants. Michael Chertoff, then an assistant attorney general, described material witness arrests as "an important investigative tool in the war on terrorism" that provided "all kinds of evidence . . . from a witness" besides his testimony, including fingerprints and hair samples. Mary Jo White, the former U.S. attorney for the Southern District of New York, similarly defended the government's use of the material witness statute to arrest and detain people to obtain information and not, as the statute specifically contemplated, because it was necessary to secure their testimony.

Many of those arrested on material witness warrants after 9/11 spent weeks or months in jail.[21] They also were routinely denied the right to a prompt judicial hearing.[22] Moreover, when those hearings were held, they were shrouded in secrecy, which was invoked sweepingly, as it was in the "enemy combatant" context, to hide bad practices and avoid accountability rather than to protect legitimate national security concerns. In some cases, individuals were not even told why they were being held or provided access to the government's evidence. One witness described the Kafkaesque nature of the proceedings: "I kept asking with what am I being charged. They would respond you're not being charged with anything. I asked why I am here. They said I was a witness. I said a witness to what? They said they couldn't tell me."[23]

Material witnesses were held under maximum security conditions. Many were kept in solitary confinement for up to twenty-four hours a day in windowless cells, sometimes in units holding the prison's most dangerous inmates. They were prevented from making legal or family phone calls. Material witnesses were also physically and verbally abused.[24] As in immigration detentions, such harsh treatment was used to help facilitate interrogations.

The Justice Department's misuse of the material witness law inevitably led to the imprisonment of innocent people.[25] Brandon Mayfield's case is a notable example. In May 2004, the FBI arrested Mayfield as a material witness in connection with its investigation of the train bombings in Madrid, Spain, two months earlier that killed almost two hundred people. Before arresting Mayfield, the FBI had secretly searched his home and office. It had collected Mayfield's DNA and listened to his conversations without a warrant. The FBI believed that Mayfield, a U.S. citizen, an army veteran, and a Muslim, had carried out the bombing because his fingerprints matched those on a bag of detonators found near the bombing site. Since the United States did not believe that it had enough evidence to indict Mayfield, it arrested him as a material witness. During his interrogations, Mayfield was threatened with capital charges and held in solitary confinement. When Spanish authorities first informed the FBI that they were concerned that it had mismatched Mayfield's prints, the FBI neglected to tell his attorneys. Instead, it continued to detain Mayfield, holding him for several weeks before a district judge dismissed the material witness warrant. Only then did the government finally acknowledge that it had made a mistake.[26]

In another case, American citizen Abdullah al-Kidd was arrested by the FBI at Washington Dulles International Airport as he prepared to fly to Saudi Arabia for graduate work in Islamic studies. Al-Kidd was held as a material witness, during which time he was strip-searched on multiple occasions and confined in high-security units. Al-Kidd was never called as a witness in the case in which he was detained, and he was never charged with a crime. His detention, which lasted more than two weeks, ultimately cost him his marriage and job.[27] An appeals court in the civil suit that al-Kidd filed after his release described his treatment as "repugnant to the Constitution, and a painful reminder of some of the most ignominious chapters of our national history."[28]

These domestic immigration and material witness detentions resembled the post-9/11 detention of terrorism suspects overseas in several respects. Individuals were held on vague suspicion, without charge and without evidence, just as they were at Guantánamo, Bagram, and CIA "black sites." Their cases were shrouded in secrecy. They also were often grossly mistreated. Nonetheless, the immigration and material witness detentions remained within an existing legal framework—even though that framework was manipulated and subverted—and thus remained subject to some limitations and judicial scrutiny. Immigration and material witness detainees still had access to attorneys and to the courts, even if that access was significantly curtailed. Although these detainees were held for much longer than the law allowed, they were not subjected to the same type of prolonged and open-ended confinement as "enemy combatant" detainees who were held year after year in a never-ending "war on terrorism." Nor were they subjected to the same level of abuse as some "enemy combatants," who were tortured as part of U.S. policy. These distinctions, however, disappeared when the Bush administration sought to supplant the civilian justice system altogether by treating domestic terrorism suspects as "enemy combatants" in the global "war on terrorism."

Jose Padilla was the first person arrested in the United States and subjected to military detention as an "enemy combatant"; the second, and last to date, was Ali Saleh Kahlah al-Marri.[29] Although al-Marri was not a U.S. citizen, in some ways his case represented a more extraordinary power grab and assault on the Constitution, for he was pending trial in federal court when the president terminated the proceedings and condemned him to the legal abyss of "enemy combatant" detention.

A citizen of Qatar, al-Marri arrived in the United States on September 10, 2001, with his wife and five children. His stated purpose was to obtain a master's degree at Bradley University in Peoria, Illinois, where he had previously obtained his bachelor's degree. That December, FBI agents arrested al-Marri as a material witness in connection with the government's PENTTBOM investigation and detained him in a Manhattan jail. Two months later, the government indicted al-Marri for credit card fraud. A subsequent indictment added other charges, including making false statements to the FBI and lying on a bank application. Al-Marri pleaded not guilty and sought to contest the charges at trial. For the next sixteen months, his case proceeded through the criminal justice system.[30] On Friday, June 20, 2003, with the trial less than a month away, the district judge scheduled a hearing to resolve various pretrial motions, including al-Marri's motion to suppress evidence seized without a warrant in violation of the Fourth Amendment. But the hearing and trial never took place. Instead, on the following Monday morning, prosecutors presented the district judge with a one-page redacted order signed by the president. The order, identical in substance to the presidential order issued in Padilla's case, declared al-Marri an "enemy combatant" and directed the secretary of defense to take him into military custody.[31] According to the government, al-Marri was an al Qaeda "sleeper agent" who came to the United States at the request of senior al Qaeda officials to explore possibilities for hacking into computer systems to "wreak havoc" on U.S. banking records and to facilitate other possible terrorist activities.[32] The judge granted the government's request to dismiss the indictment, ending the criminal case against him. That same day al-Marri was taken from a jail in Peoria, Illinois, and flown to the Navy brig near Charleston, South Carolina. Although the government claimed that al-Marri "must be detained to prevent him from aiding al Qaeda," it never explained why indefinite imprisonment as an "enemy combatant," as opposed to criminal prosecution, was necessary to achieve that goal, particularly when al-Marri himself was already incarcerated and awaiting trial.[33]

What made the Padilla and al-Marri cases so important was the nature of the power claimed by the executive. By the mere stroke of a pen, the president had eliminated core safeguards of the Bill of Rights: the right of a defendant to be charged promptly, to be tried by jury, to confront and cross-examine his accusers, and to compel the production of witnesses in his favor. Gone, too, was the presumption of innocence and the burden on the government to justify imprisonment in court. In its place, the president was erecting a new and unprecedented system of detention by executive fiat, according to which a person living in the United States could be seized by the military and held indefinitely without charge and without a hearing. No lawyer could speak to the detainee, and no judge could examine the evidence against him. In short, executive say-so would replace the adversary process of a criminal trial as the method of imprisoning terrorist suspects.

But Padilla's and al-Marri's designation as "enemy combatants" was intended to accomplish more than detention without trial. It also was designed to facilitate the use of torture and other coercive interrogation methods by freeing the government from the constraints of the criminal justice system that acted as a check against those abuses through various rules and safeguards, such as access to counsel and to the courts. The presidential orders declaring Padilla and al-Marri "enemy combatants" hinted at this ulterior motive, noting that both men "possesse[d] intelligence . . . that, if communicated to the U.S., would aid U.S. efforts to prevent attacks by al Qaeda." Secretary of Defense Donald Rumsfeld suggested a similar purpose, explaining that the United States wanted "to try to find out everything" Padilla knew to prevent a future terrorist attack.[34] Attorney General John Ashcroft was even blunter: al-Marri, Ashcroft said, was declared an "enemy combatant" because he "insisted on becoming a hard case" and "rejected numerous offers to improve his lot by cooperating with FBI investigators and providing information."[35] In other words, suspects who did not cooperate and plead guilty could be thrown in a military stockade rather than tried in a court of law—a threat that was made against other criminal defendants during this period.[36]

The United Sates held Padilla and al-Marri incommunicado for well over a year, cutting off access to their families, their attorneys, and anyone else in the outside world. The reason, according to Admiral Lowell E. Jacoby, director of the Defense Intelligence Agency (DIA), was that giving an "enemy combatant" detainee access to a lawyer would jeopardize the government's effort to obtain "vital" intelligence in the detainee's possession and thereby impede the United States' ability to prevent future terrorist attacks. Lawyers, Jacoby observed, undermined the necessary "relationship of trust and dependency" between a subject and an interrogator. Creating that relationship could take "months, or, even years," during which time a detainee had to be held incommunicado. "Even seemingly minor interruptions," Jacoby asserted, "can have profound psychological impacts on the delicate subject-interrogator relationship."[37]

Jacoby did not describe any particular interrogation techniques, refer-ring only obliquely to the administration's "robust program" for interrogat-ing detainees in the "war on terrorism." But he did not need to. Many of those techniques were spelled out in the Joint Task Force 170 memorandum and April 2003 working group report for interrogations at Guantánamo; they included prolonged isolation, exposure to cold temperatures, extreme sensory deprivation, and threats of violence and death, all of which were employed against Padilla and al-Marri by interrogators at the Charleston navy brig.[38]

The DIA manipulated virtually every aspect of Padilla's and al-Marri's confinement to create a sense of hopelessness and despair. Both men were imprisoned in six-by-nine-foot cells containing only a sink, toilet, and hard-ened metal bed affixed to the wall.[39] The only window in their respective cells was painted over, preventing any natural light from entering or the prisoner from seeing anything outside his concrete cell.[40] (Padilla and al-Marri also had no contact with each other the entire time they were at the brig.) For more than two years, al-Marri often had no mattress or blanket.[41] Both men were denied a calendar or a clock, preventing them from knowing the time of day or day of the week.[42] They were also denied books, newspapers, and magazines, heightening their disorientation and sense of total isolation.[43] None of these techniques produced any useful intelligence.

Padilla's and al-Marri's designation as "enemy combatants" marked the zenith of the Bush administration's new and radical vision of executive deten-tion power. Through their cases, the Bush administration effectively claimed the power to suspend the Bill of Rights in America, including the prohibition against imprisonment without a prompt judicial determination of probable cause, the right to a speedy trial by a jury, and basic procedural safeguards such as the right to confront and cross-examine the government's witnesses. The administration sought to erase the long-established line between civil-ian and military jurisdiction and to make the arrest of a criminal suspect at his home in the middle of America the legal equivalent of the capture of an enemy soldier in a foreign war zone. Once designated an "enemy combatant," even an American citizen or legal U.S. resident would be stripped of the most fundamental protection in the Constitution: the right not be detained with-out being charged with a crime and tried in a court of law. The importance of these cases thus transcended the two prisoners. If the president's breathtak-ing claim of detention power were upheld in Padilla's and al-Marri's cases, it would open the door to similar detentions of people arrested inside the country in the future. It would also necessarily bolster the president's claim that he could militarily detain terrorism suspects at Guantánamo and other overseas prisons: if the president had this power in the United States, where constitutional protections were strongest, he could assert it anywhere.

The third person held in the United States as an "enemy combatant" was Yaser Hamdi. After traveling to Afghanistan in the summer of 2001, Hamdi was captured by members of the Northern Alliance and handed over to the U.S. military. The United States initially interrogated Hamdi in Afghanistan before transferring him to Guantánamo in January 2002. Three months later, the United States learned that Hamdi, who had lived most of his life in Saudi Arabia, was an American citizen. Fearful of the potential fallout from imprisoning an American citizen at Guantánamo, the Bush administration quickly transferred Hamdi to the United States, first to a navy brig in Norfolk, Virginia, and then to the navy brig in Charleston, South Carolina, where Padilla and al-Marri were being held.[44]

The government classified Hamdi as an "enemy combatant" and claimed it could continue to hold him without charge. Like Padilla and al-Marri, Hamdi was detained incommunicado and denied access to his lawyers.[45] The government also claimed, as it did with Padilla and al-Marri, that Hamdi had no right to challenge the government's accusations in court. Instead, it argued that the untested hearsay allegations of a Pentagon official—based on second- and third-hand statements and unexamined summaries of raw intelligence reports—were sufficient to imprison Hamdi indefinitely.[46]

Hamdi's case, however, differed from Padilla's and al-Marri's in important respects. Hamdi was not arrested in the United States, nor was he seized in a civilian setting elsewhere. Instead, according to the government, Hamdi was captured on a battlefield in Afghanistan, where he had affiliated with a Taliban military unit, received weapons training, and carried a Kalashnikov assault rifle, which he surrendered to Northern Alliance forces upon his capture. Hamdi thus bore some resemblance to soldiers from earlier wars, and his detention was tied to the war against the Taliban in Afghanistan, as opposed to an amorphous global "war" against a terrorist organization. As a result, subjecting Hamdi to military detention as a wartime prisoner, rather than trying him as a criminal in the regular federal courts, did not itself signal the same dramatic departure from legal precedent and historical practice as the military detention of Padilla and al-Marri.

But the government did not treat Hamdi like the "classic wartime" prisoner it claimed he was.[47] Instead, it denied him the protections of the Geneva Conventions and U.S. military regulations, just as it denied those protections to other prisoners captured in and around Afghanistan, who were being held at Guantánamo and Bagram. Hamdi had not been given the required military status hearing under Army Regulation 190-8 to prevent mistaken detention, nor had he been afforded the binding legal safeguards that shield all enemy prisoners from abusive interrogations and other mistreatment. The government also denied Hamdi any rights under the U.S. Constitution, including the right to due process, even though he was an American citizen and was being imprisoned on American soil. In short, Hamdi had no meaningful opportunity to challenge the accusations against him: to show that he was not a Taliban fighter, as the government alleged, but instead an innocent civilian captured while fleeing the war in Afghanistan and sold by the Northern Alliance to the United States for bounty.[48]

Thus, despite their differences, Hamdi's, Padilla's, and al-Marri's cases all highlighted key features of the post-9/11 global detention system. They showed how the Bush administration conveniently bent and manipulated the "enemy combatant" label to fit a wide array of circumstances, from the domestic arrest of civilians in the United States to the capture of armed soldiers in a foreign combat zone. They also demonstrated the administration's modus operandi of invoking the laws of war to claim sweeping executive detention power while disregarding the limits that the laws of war impose on that power. In all three cases, furthermore, the administration sought to avoid meaningful judicial review and render access to the courts through habeas corpus an empty exercise in which judges had to accept the executive's allegations about the prisoner at face value.

In 2004, Hamdi's case reached the U.S. Supreme Court, along with a challenge by Jose Padilla and a joint challenge by several Guantánamo detainees. These three "enemy combatant" cases gave the Supreme Court its first opportunity to address the Bush administration's sweeping claims of executive power. But before examining these challenges, we shall go back in time in chapters 5 and 6 to look at the means by which those challenges were brought—the writ of habeas corpus—and related principles governing judicial review of executive action at home and abroad.

Part 2

5

Habeas Corpus and the Right to Challenge Unlawful Imprisonment

The writ of habeas corpus first emerged in England around the early thirteenth century as a mechanism to ensure a person's presence in court.[1] Of the several forms of the writ that developed, one, *habeas corpus ad subjiciendum*, enabled a court to examine whether there was a lawful basis for a prisoner's confinement by ordering the jailer to produce both the prisoner and the cause for his commitment. *Habeas corpus ad subjiciendum* was initially used by the king's common law courts to limit the jurisdiction of local and rival central courts, such as the specialized courts that decided ecclesiastical and admiralty matters.[2] Habeas was thus not originally understood, as it is now, as a guarantee of civil or human rights but, rather, as a means for the king to ensure just cause for the imprisonment of any of his subjects.

By the 1600s, habeas corpus started to become viewed "as a safeguard against the arbitrary power of the Crown itself."[3] An important shift occurred with the *Five Knights* case (also known as Darnel's case). King Charles I had imprisoned a number of men for refusing to contribute to a loan to raise money for a war with France and Spain. No charges were filed, and five of the men sought writs of habeas corpus challenging their imprisonment and demanding release on bail. Without formal charges, they argued, "imprisonment shall not continue for a time, but for ever; and the subjects of this kingdom may be restrained of their liberties perpetually" in violation of the Magna Carta's guarantee of due process of law.[4] Attorney General Robert Heath responded on behalf of the Crown that it was the king's prerogative to imprison by his "special command" for "a matter of state . . . not ripe nor timely" for the ordinary process of formal accusation and trial. Heath insisted that the judges defer to the king's judgment about what means were necessary to protect "a conspiracy-threatened commonwealth" from danger and not "inquire further" into matters of state.[5]

Although the king won this particular battle, he lost the larger struggle over the Crown's prerogative. After the court denied relief to the prisoners, Parliament responded with the Petition of Right, proclaiming it illegal for the Crown to imprison based on royal command and without formal charges. Responsible government, the Petition of Right stated, could not coexist with such sweeping claims to emergency powers of arrest and detention.[6] When the king continued to imprison individuals without charge or trial, Parliament enacted the Habeas Corpus Act of 1641, requiring the courts to issue writs of habeas corpus on behalf of prisoners "without delay" and abolishing the Star Chamber, which had become associated with arbitrary exercises of power and other abuses.[7] In 1679, Parliament enacted another habeas corpus act to remedy the perceived loopholes in existing law and to ensure that prisoners would not languish in jail without a prompt judicial examination into the cause of their commitment.[8] William Blackstone praised the 1679 act as a "second magna carta and stable bulwark of our liberties."[9] Yet it was the development of the judicial exercise of common law habeas powers (as opposed to statutory intervention by Parliament) that was most crucial to the writ's emergence as a guarantee of individual liberty.[10] Judges increasingly became willing to uphold challenges to detention by Crown officials through the exercise of their habeas corpus jurisdiction. Amid the political turmoil of the late 1600s, for example, the King's Bench adjudicated numerous habeas petitions involving accusations of treason, treasonous practices, and sedition, often finding that there was no basis to hold the prisoner.[11] The writ had become, and would thereafter remain, "the great and efficacious writ, in all manner of illegal confinement."[12]

Even so, there remained one lawful means to deprive prisoners of the Great Writ's protections: suspension of habeas corpus by Parliament. Through suspension acts, Parliament deprived courts of their authority to adjudicate accusations by Crown officials and asserted its control over detention in matters affecting the security of the state.[13] In 1688, Parliament passed the first suspension act amid armed conflict abroad and fears that King James II would try to regain the throne after his ouster earlier that year in the Glorious Revolution.[14] Other suspension acts followed, authorizing the detention of suspected enemies of state without judicial inquiry.[15] The acts did not suspend habeas corpus itself, however, but the right secured by the writ to test the government's allegations in court.[16] Suspension acts generally contained an expiration date, which was usually a year or less from the time of their passage.[17] Prisoners also could still seek judicial review of whether they fell within the parameters of the given suspension legislation.[18] So, while suspending habeas corpus gave "extreme powers . . . to the executive," those powers were specifically bound by the emergency that necessitated them and remained "distinctly limited by law."[19]

Unless suspended, habeas corpus has traditionally been available to all prisoners in the custody of the Crown, and its protections have been invoked by common thieves and alleged enemies of state alike. Access to habeas corpus did not turn on where a prisoner had been born or his nationality.[20] Indeed, one of the most celebrated habeas cases of the eighteenth century involved a slave who had been purchased in Virginia and detained briefly in England while awaiting voyage to Jamaica. The court granted the writ and ordered the slave released because slavery was not legal in England.[21] In another case involving two men held as "alien enemies and spies," the court not only rejected the government's argument that the prisoners' status as foreigners disqualified them from the benefits of habeas corpus but also ordered them discharged.[22] The question in a habeas corpus proceeding was whether the individual was properly within the Crown's detention authority, not whether he was a subject in the modern sense of citizenship.[23] Or put another way, the focus was less on the rights of the prisoner than on the wrongs committed by the jailer.[24]

Once presented with a habeas corpus petition, a judge was supposed to exercise independent judgment about the sufficiency of the facts and the law asserted in the jailer's response, known as the *return*. The judge's factual inquiry could include scrutinizing opposing allegations and resolving disputed contentions, by either examining affidavits or holding a hearing.[25] Judges were not bound by a jailer's statements in the return but instead could probe the evidence and arguments submitted by prisoners in response, known as the *traverse*.[26] Judges also had to determine whether the detention had a basis in statute or the common law.[27] Their duty was to render decisions independently, grounding their judgment on their "own inferences and understandings" and not on the conclusions of the government officials responsible for the detention.[28] Judges also were obliged to afford "full and speedy justice."[29] This meant both promptly examining a prisoner's habeas corpus petition and ordering his release if there was no lawful basis to hold him.[30]

The nature and scope of habeas review varied with the circumstances. In cases of criminal confinement, for example, the review was narrower because the prisoners either had been or soon would be tried by a jury in accordance with common law due process. Judges thus did not wish to usurp the jury's role by conducting trials in habeas corpus proceedings.[31] But for prisoners held for noncriminal matters, habeas review was more searching. And in cases of executive detention without trial, habeas's protections were strongest, for it was here that the danger of the arbitrary exercise of state power was greatest.[32]

Habeas corpus review continued even in time of war. Although prisoners properly held as enemy aliens or prisoners of war had no right to release from custody, they still could avail themselves of habeas corpus to show that they did not fall within those categories and thus were not properly detained.[33] For example, a court considered a petition by a Swedish sailor filed during the Seven Years War (between Great Britain and France and their respective allies between 1756 and 1763), in which the sailor claimed that he could not lawfully be detained because he was a national of a neutral nation and thus not a prisoner of war. The court ultimately disagreed, but not before first considering the sailor's legal arguments and factual submissions.[34] Courts conducted similar inquiries in other cases, providing wartime captives with at least a limited opportunity to show there was no basis to hold them.[35]

Habeas corpus also had a broad territorial reach. This reach, as Professors Paul D. Halliday and G. Edward White have explained, was rooted in habeas's origins as a prerogative writ by which the Crown, through common law judges of the King's Bench at Westminster, could inquire into the legality of a detention by any Crown official or by another court or tribunal.[36] Judges thus issued writs to jailers throughout the realm of the British Crown, including to so-called exempt jurisdictions that maintained their own local courts and were otherwise exempt from oversight by the central English courts because of ancient privileges predating their acquisition by the Crown.[37] Judges also issued habeas writs to dominions beyond the realm to ensure that there was a lawful basis for a prisoner's confinement.[38] As Blackstone noted, habeas corpus must "run into all parts of the king's dominions; for the king is at all times entitled to have an account, why the liberty of any of his subjects is restrained, *wherever* that restraint may be inflicted."[39] With the expansion of the British Empire, habeas corpus also became available in newly formed local courts in Crown-controlled territory.[40] As long as Crown officials were detaining an individual, and thus exercising power in the king's name, a habeas court could inquire into the legality of the detention, regardless of where that detention took place.[41]

The famed jurist Lord Mansfield cited authority and control, and not formal constructs like political sovereignty, as the main principles governing the writ's reach. There was "no doubt," he said, of the court's power to issue writs of habeas corpus to every one of the king's dominions "where the place is under the subjection of the Crown," even if the territory were outside the realm.[42] Although England may have exercised sovereignty over the various Crown-controlled territories in which habeas corpus was available, sovereignty did not determine whether a court could or would exercise habeas review. Instead, habeas review turned on an assessment of "the exact extent and nature of the jurisdiction or dominion exercised in fact by the Crown."[43] As a practical matter, the availability of habeas corpus thus often depended on whether a court could "judge of the cause" and "give relief upon it."[44]

The development of habeas corpus in India illustrates these principles. In the late 1600s, the British East India Company and other merchant companies established a string of "factories" or trading posts along the coast of India under grants of authority from the English Crown.[45] By the mid-1700s, the East India Company had become a substantial military power, exercising control over large swaths of land.[46] In 1773, English law was introduced in the company's territories, and a supreme court was established in Calcutta, the first of several courts in English-controlled territories in India. Although the English Crown delayed assertions of formal sovereignty over the East India Company's territories for more than four decades,[47] these local English courts issued writs of habeas corpus on behalf of both British subjects and native Indians to remedy arbitrary imprisonment and other abuses of power by company officials.[48] The judges in these cases viewed the exercise of habeas review as part of their common law authority to ensure that there was just cause for a prisoner's confinement, regardless of the formal status of the territory in which the prisoner was held or the nationality of the prisoner himself.[49] Judges continued to exercise that review even after Parliament enacted legislation attempting to curb their power to issue habeas writs.[50]

Given the robust protections that habeas corpus provided against unlawful imprisonment, there were repeated efforts by government officials to evade its reach. This practice proved highly controversial. As early as 1591, England's common law judges protested when Crown officials transported detainees to secret and distant prisons to circumvent their review.[51] In 1667, the Earl of Clarendon was impeached and charged with attempting to undermine the judicial exercise of habeas corpus by sending individuals "to be imprisoned against the law in remote islands, garrisons, and other places . . . to prevent them from the benefit of law."[52] The Habeas Corpus Act of 1679 made it a separate offense to remove prisoners to "Scotland, Ireland, Jersey, Guernsey, Tangier, or into Parts, Garrisons, Islands or Places beyond the Seas, which are or at any time hereafter shall be within or without the Dominions of his Majesty."[53]

The importance of habeas corpus was not lost on the colonists who came to America.[54] Influenced by the writings of famed jurists Sir Edward Coke and William Blackstone, colonial leaders saw habeas corpus as the preeminent safeguard of physical liberty, a natural and inalienable right of mankind.[55] Alexander Hamilton, for example, deemed the writ the most important protection against arbitrary government power.[56] By 1776, habeas corpus was available in all thirteen American colonies.[57]

The framers of the U.S. Constitution naturally sought to secure the writ's protections in their own republic to ensure an adequate check against executive imprisonment. King George III's abuse of royal detention power was expressly cited as one of the grievances in the Declaration of Independence.[58] And the colonists remembered well the acts by Parliament suspending habeas corpus during the American rebellion—acts that underscored not only habeas's significance but also its broad reach (for if habeas had not been available overseas, there would have been no need to suspend it).[59] The desire to restrict the new national government's power to suspend habeas was never controversial.[60] The first proposal to mention habeas corpus at the Constitutional Convention of 1787 stipulated that the writ's protections could be suspended only "upon the most urgent and pressing occasions" and only for a limited period of time. Even this proposal, however, prompted opposition from those who believed that suspension should not be allowed under any circumstances.[61] The compromise version that finally emerged allowed for suspension but limited it to truly exceptional circumstances: "cases of rebellion or invasion," when "the public safety may require it."[62]

This provision—known as the "Suspension Clause"—has been called "the most important human right in the Constitution."[63] It requires that those detained by the government have access to the courts and, in the process, makes possible "the full realization" of other constitutional guarantees.[64] If, for example, a person imprisoned on account of his political opinions had no way to seek review before a judge, the guarantees of freedom of speech and of the press secured by the First Amendment could be rendered meaningless. The Suspension Clause also serves an important structural function under the Constitution's separation of powers by giving the judiciary a powerful check against executive overreaching.

The U.S. Supreme Court first interpreted the Suspension Clause against the backdrop of the upheaval in American politics that followed the presidential election of 1800 and the rift between President Thomas Jefferson and his former vice president, Aaron Burr. Burr was suspected of plotting to sever recently acquired territories in the West from their allegiance to the

United States. In December 1806, the U.S. Army commander in New Orleans seized two of Burr's co-conspirators, Erick Bollman and Samuel Swartwout, and took them on a warship to Baltimore by way of Charleston, South Carolina. In the process, the commander ignored writs of habeas corpus that had been issued on the prisoners' behalf by federal judges in New Orleans and Charleston. President Jefferson recognized that the only legal way to deny the prisoners access to the courts was to suspend habeas corpus. So his supporters introduced legislation in Congress to suspend habeas for three months. But the bill failed in the House, prompting the U.S. attorney general to file formal charges of treason against the men. Bollman and Swartwout then sought relief in the circuit court. After the circuit court denied their habeas petition and remanded them for trial, the prisoners sought a writ of habeas corpus from the Supreme Court.[65]

In his decision for the Court, Chief Justice John Marshall explained that the power to suspend habeas corpus belonged solely to Congress, a view that reflected both historical practice and the Suspension Clause's placement with other legislative powers in Article I of the Constitution.[66] Marshall also discussed the interplay between the Suspension Clause and the Judiciary Act of 1789. That statute had not only created the federal trial and circuit courts but had also specified that judges could issue writs of habeas corpus on behalf of prisoners "in custody, under or by colour of the authority of the United States."[67] The Supreme Court thus appeared to have the authority to issue writs of habeas corpus under the terms of this statute. But Marshall had written four years earlier in *Marbury v. Madison* that Congress could not add to or subtract from the Supreme Court's original jurisdiction under Article III of the Constitution, which specifies the types of cases that the Supreme Court can hear in the first instance as original, as opposed to appellate, matters.[68] To resolve this tension, Marshall determined that the Court had the power to hear the prisoners' petition because habeas review was "appellate" in nature, since the Court was reviewing an "appeal" of the lower court's prior decision remanding the prisoners to custody.[69] After carefully considering the evidence on both sides, the Court discharged Bollman and Swartwout, finding that there was insufficient proof to hold them for the crime of treason.[70]

Another question, however, lingered beneath the surface: What if Congress had not specifically authorized courts and judges to issue writs of habeas corpus in the Judiciary Act? Did the Suspension Clause itself guarantee habeas corpus, or did it merely prohibit its suspension absent rebellion or invasion once Congress had first statutorily authorized courts to issue habeas writs? Chief Justice Marshall's opinion was not entirely clear on the subject.

On the one hand, *Bollman* might be read to suggest that jurisdiction to issue habeas writs must be provided by positive legislation. This left open the possibility that the Suspension Clause could be rendered a dead letter by congressional inaction, making habeas corpus equivalent to government benefits like Social Security that require positive legislation. But Marshall also explained that the Suspension Clause imposed an "obligation" on Congress to make the writ available, indicating that federal habeas jurisdiction was compelled by the Constitution.[71] Although scholars have debated Marshall's intentions, the conclusion that federal habeas jurisdiction is constitutionally mandated is closer to framers' understanding of the writ[72] and is more in line with the writ's purpose as well as later Supreme Court decisions.[73]

Some commentators have also suggested that the Constitution's Suspension Clause was originally intended to limit Congress's ability to suspend the guarantee of habeas corpus secured by individual states.[74] In other words, this theory posits that the Suspension Clause was designed to protect individuals against unlawful detention by federal officers through judicial action by state courts. Whether historically accurate, this theory confronts a problem created by later Supreme Court decisions. During controversy over the Fugitive Slave Act of 1850, the Court ruled that state courts lacked the power to order the release of prisoners held in federal custody, a ruling it reaffirmed after the Civil War.[75] Thus, reading the Suspension Clause as protecting only a state court remedy would create a legal void, denying habeas corpus to prisoners in federal custody and leaving executive detention by the U.S. government unchecked.[76]

For more than two centuries, these debates remained largely academic because habeas corpus was available to federal prisoners under the 1789 Judiciary Act.[77] In fact, the federal habeas statute had expanded over time to cover new categories of prisoners. In 1833, Congress, prompted by Southern resistance to federal revenue policies, amended the statute to allow federal officers confined by state officials to seek relief in lower federal courts.[78] In 1842, Congress again changed the statute to provide for federal jurisdiction over the habeas petitions of foreign nationals held in state custody when the foreign nationals claimed to act under the authority of a foreign state.[79] Most significantly, in 1867, Congress authorized federal courts to issue writs of habeas corpus to any state prisoner held in violation of the Constitution or federal law, thereby paving the way for what became the writ's most common and best-known use: as a remedy for prisoners seeking to challenge their criminal convictions and sentences.[80] In recent decades, Congress and the courts have cut back significantly on federal habeas corpus as a postconviction remedy through the imposition of filing deadlines, heightened evidentiary burdens, bars on successive petitions, and other procedural hurdles.[81] But before 9/11, Congress had never sought to eliminate altogether the statutory guarantee of habeas corpus for individuals detained by the federal government without prior judicial process.

Moreover, the limited authority provided under the Constitution to temporarily suspend habeas corpus was exercised only rarely.[82] The first suspension occurred during the Civil War. On April 27, 1861, following the fall of Fort Sumter, President Abraham Lincoln authorized army generals to suspend habeas corpus when necessary "for the public safety." Initially suspended along the military line between Philadelphia and Washington, the suspension was later extended to places as far north as Maine.[83] Following the outbreak of war, Lincoln feared that the advancing Confederate army would destroy the railways and bridges connecting Maryland to Washington and ultimately overrun the capital.[84] The suspension was challenged by John Merryman, an ardent secessionist who had been arrested at his home in Baltimore on suspicion of aiding the Confederacy and then imprisoned at Fort McHenry. When Merryman filed a habeas petition, Supreme Court Chief Justice Roger B. Taney, sitting as a circuit judge in Baltimore, ordered Merryman's military jailers to produce him in court. The president, Taney said, had no authority to suspend habeas corpus on his own.[85] But Lincoln ignored the instruction. As he later explained, Congress was not in session when he suspended habeas corpus. Since the Suspension Clause "was plainly made for a dangerous emergency," Lincoln argued, the president should not have to wait for the danger to "run its course" to obtain congressional approval. To delay under these circumstances, Lincoln famously said in defense of emergency executive action, would allow "all the laws, but one, to go unexecuted, and the government itself go to pieces, lest that one be violated."[86] In March 1863, Congress enacted legislation ratifying Lincoln's prior suspension, long after the fact.[87] As a result of Lincoln's suspension of habeas corpus, more than thirteen thousand individuals were imprisoned without charge or trial in military jails during the Civil War, including newspaper editors and others considered sympathetic to the Confederate cause.[88]

Habeas corpus was suspended only three other times in U.S. history. Each time, the suspension was authorized by Congress, limited to a specific area, and restricted in duration to the emergency that necessitated it. In 1871, Congress authorized President Ulysses S. Grant to suspend habeas corpus in southern States where post–Civil War violence by the Ku Klux Klan had made it impossible to dispense justice. Grant subsequently invoked that authority in nine counties in South Carolina, leading to the mass arrest of suspects without ordinary criminal process.[89] In 1902, Congress enacted legislation authorizing the governor of the Philippines Territory to suspend habeas corpus where necessary to combat rebellion, insurrection, or invasion.[90] Acting under this authority, the governor suspended habeas corpus in two provinces for approximately nine months to suppress armed violence by organized gangs that had created "a state of insecurity and terrorism among the people."[91] The final suspension occurred in Hawaii during World War II. Congress had previously authorized Hawaii's governor to suspend habeas corpus in the Hawaiian Territory to confront a threat of rebellion or invasion.[92] After Japan attacked Pearl Harbor on December, 7, 1941, the governor invoked this emergency suspension power. Hawaii thus remained under military government until 1944, when habeas corpus was restored and martial law ended.[93]

As in England, habeas corpus in the United States has always been available to individuals regardless of citizenship,[94] and since the nation's founding, foreign nationals have invoked habeas to challenge their detention.[95] In 1797, for example, a circuit court granted the habeas petition of a Spanish prisoner, finding that he could not be prosecuted for treason for acts committed abroad, since he had never been properly naturalized.[96] In another case, Supreme Court Justice Joseph Story, sitting on circuit, found that the arrest of a group of Portuguese sailors for desertion was not authorized by any law or treaty.[97] Even the broader executive powers granted under the Alien Enemies Act of 1798, which authorized the president to detain, relocate, and deport aliens of a nation with which the United States was at war, remained subject to habeas review.[98] In 1813, for example, Chief Justice Marshall, sitting on circuit, ordered the release of an enemy alien on habeas because he had been detained without an opportunity to relocate, as required by the controlling regulations.[99] Modern precedents have followed this practice.[100] Thus, although the Supreme Court has upheld the president's power to detain enemy aliens during a declared war against an enemy nation to remove them from the country, it also has made clear that those held as enemy aliens can challenge the validity of their detention through habeas corpus.[101]

The history of immigration law similarly demonstrates that access to habeas corpus is not limited to American citizens. As a federal judge wrote in 1885 amid efforts to exclude Chinese immigrants from the United States,

If the denial . . . to the petitioner of the right to land, thus converting the ship into his prison-house, to be followed by his deportation across the sea to a foreign country, be not a restraint of his liberty within the meaning of the habeas corpus act, it is not easy to conceive any case that would fall within its provisions.[102]

Courts thus consistently reviewed the decisions of executive branch officials to remove or exclude foreign nationals from the United States under immigration statutes.[103] And while the courts often upheld those administrative decisions on the merits, they did sometimes reject the executive's broad interpretation of a ground for an alien's deportation or exclusion.[104] Courts also helped enforce rudimentary due process requirements, ordering that immigrants be provided notice and an opportunity to be heard before a government official could order their deportation.[105] So while Congress and the executive retain wide latitude to establish immigration policy under what has become known as the "plenary power" doctrine, and thus to determine the grounds for admission to and removal from the United States, courts have still reviewed the exercise of that power in individual cases through their habeas corpus jurisdiction.[106]

In 1996, Congress enacted two statutes purporting to eliminate all federal court review of deportation orders for aliens who had been convicted of certain crimes. Following years of litigation, the Supreme Court ruled in *INS v. St. Cyr* in June 2001 that eliminating this review would raise "serious constitutional questions" and might violate the Suspension Clause.[107] Under the jurisprudential doctrine of "constitutional avoidance" (i.e., of not reaching constitutional questions unnecessarily), the Court read the 1996 laws narrowly and concluded that they did not eliminate the federal courts' statutory habeas jurisdiction.[108] Although the Court thus resolved the issue on statutory, as opposed to constitutional grounds, its decision underscored the enduring commitment to habeas corpus as a check against illegal executive action affecting the liberty of the individual.[109]

Habeas has also historically played a checking role by policing the proper boundaries of military authority. In a case from the War of 1812, for example, a New York state court considered the habeas petition of Samuel Stacy, who had been detained as a spy and traitor at Sackets Harbor on Lake Ontario, an area that both sides viewed as critical to the war effort. Stacy had been captured shortly after British troops had landed in the area and nearly taken control of Sackets Harbor. American military commanders blamed Stacy for the near loss of this critical military post. In response, Stacy claimed he was exempt from military jurisdiction based on his U.S. citizenship, and the court issued a writ of habeas corpus commanding the military to produce him. When the officer refused, New York's chief justice, Chancellor James Kent, sought enforcement, explaining that "a military commander" was "assuming criminal jurisdiction over a private citizen . . . holding him in the closest confinement, and contemning the civil authority of the state."[110] Stacy was subsequently released by the secretary of war, who recognized that the military lacked any power over him.[111]

Habeas corpus petitions frequently challenged the legality of a person's enlistment in the military. Courts, for example, examined whether an individual knowingly joined the armed forces and whether his enlistment was voluntary.[112] Habeas also provided for review of decisions by military courts-martial. To be sure, the scope of this review was relatively narrow. Courts would not use habeas corpus petitions to reexamine questions of innocence or guilt but instead generally deferred to the courts-martial's factual findings.[113] This deference reflected the idea that the armed forces was a separate community whose need for obedience and discipline justified granting it autonomy over the application of military law to service members.[114] Nonetheless, habeas corpus still remained available to ensure that the military remained within its "special and limited jurisdiction." Courts thus reviewed whether a defendant was properly subject to military authority, enforced compliance with prescribed statutory procedures, and determined whether a given sentence was authorized by law.[115]

By the middle of the twentieth century, the Supreme Court suggested a possible expansion of habeas review of courts-martial decisions.[116] But the impetus and need for such review lessened with the development of an elaborate, rights-protective adversary process for courts-martial under the Uniform Code of Military Justice (UCMJ), which was enacted in 1950 and has grown more rigorous over time. Today, the more hands-off stance toward courts-martial may be explained partly by the fact that the UCMJ now contains safeguards for defendants that are similar to—and, in some respects, more robust than—those provided in federal court. The UCMJ also provides for appellate review by civilian judges, a role previously served by habeas corpus.[117]

In addition, habeas corpus has provided a mechanism for reviewing decisions by military commissions, the ad hoc tribunals periodically used in American history to try enemy soldiers for war crimes. In one of the most celebrated cases of American history, the Supreme Court considered the habeas challenge of a prisoner in military custody in the immediate aftermath of the Civil War. Lambdin P. Milligan was a high-ranking member of the Sons of Liberty, a secret paramilitary organization of Southern sympathizers in the border state of Indiana. Milligan was accused of plotting to overthrow the Union government, communicating with the enemy, conspiring to seize munitions, liberate prisoners of war, and commit other violent acts in an area under constant threat of invasion.[118] The military arrested Milligan and detained him without charge under the 1863 act suspending habeas corpus. President Lincoln then issued an order subjecting Milligan to trial by military commission for violating the laws of war. After he was convicted and sentenced to death, Milligan sought habeas review. When the circuit court denied the petition, Milligan appealed to the Supreme Court. The government argued that the president must have the power to deal militarily with dangerous men like Milligan. The Court acknowledged that Milligan stood accused of committing "an *enormous* crime" in "a period of war" at a place "within . . . the theater of military operations" and under threat of invasion by the enemy.[119] But it ruled that Milligan nonetheless remained a civilian, not a combatant, and that the Constitution therefore required that he be tried in the regular courts as long as those courts were open and functioning. The president, the Court explained, could not simply opt out of the criminal justice system because an alleged offender posed a grave danger, even at a time when the nation's survival was at stake.[120] As Justice David Davis declared for the Court's majority, "The Constitution of the United States is a law for rulers and people, equally in war and in peace, and covers with the shield of its protection all classes of men, at all times, and under all circumstances."[121] The Court ordered that Milligan be released, since he had been detained without criminal charge beyond the allowable time limit under the 1863 suspension act. Four other justices agreed with the majority's result, but not its reasoning. As explained in a concurring opinion by Chief Justice Salmon Chase, those justices found that Congress could have authorized Milligan's military trial without violating the Constitution but had not done so.[122]

The Supreme Court's decision in *Ex parte Milligan* demonstrates the importance of habeas corpus in helping maintain the proper boundary of military authority. It also highlights the crucial link between habeas review and the vindication of a defendant's right to a jury trial and other constitutional safeguards against wrongful imprisonment. Hailed as "one of the great landmarks in th[e] Court's history,"[123] *Milligan* illustrates how habeas can prevent the government from supplanting the guarantees of the civilian justice system with military detention or trial.

Milligan, however, did not end military commissions, which remained in use during the military occupation of the South in the Reconstruction period. Military commissions also were revived during World War II. The legal challenges to these later commissions prompted several important Supreme Court decisions addressing the reach of habeas corpus and the role of the courts.

In the summer of 1942, eight Nazi saboteurs, including at least one American citizen, landed on beaches in Long Island and Florida after traveling there aboard German U-boats. Acting under the direction of the German government, the men changed from their military uniforms into civilian clothes. Armed with crates of explosives, they planned to destroy various military targets in the United States. But one of the saboteurs tipped off the FBI, and all eight were apprehended.[124] President Franklin D. Roosevelt chose not to charge the men in the regular civilian courts. No criminal statute on the books at the time authorized the death penalty in these circumstances, and Roosevelt wanted the saboteurs tried and executed quickly.[125] So, on July 2, Roosevelt issued an order establishing a military commission to try the defendants for violations of the laws of war and offenses under the Articles of War (the predecessor of the UCMJ). The order made Roosevelt the final reviewing authority and denied the defendants access to the civilian courts.[126] Privately, Roosevelt told Attorney General Francis Biddle that he would not "hand [the defendants] over to any United States marshal armed with a writ of habeas corpus."[127]

Three weeks into the trial, the saboteurs' military defense counsel filed habeas corpus petitions in federal district court, claiming that the commission lacked legal authority to try the defendants and contravened *Ex parte Milligan* as well as other precedents. After the district court denied relief, the Supreme Court agreed to consider the case on an expedited schedule. Oral arguments took place over two days and lasted nine hours.[128] On July 31, the Court issued a short order upholding the president's authority to try the men by military commission and indicating that a decision explaining its reasoning would follow.[129] The trial resumed and concluded three days later with convictions for all the defendants and a recommendation that Roosevelt impose death by electrocution. By the time the Supreme Court issued its full decision in *Ex parte Quirin* on October 29, six of the saboteurs had already been executed. Roosevelt commuted the sentences of the two remaining defendants to life imprisonment.[130]

Another United States military commission case from World War II involved the trial of Japanese general Tomoyuki Yamashita. At the conclusion of the war, Yamashita was put before a military commission in the Philippines for atrocities committed by troops under his command, including the Manila massacre, which resulted in the deaths of more than 100,000 Filipino civilians. Yamashita was convicted. After the Supreme Court of the Philippines affirmed the conviction, Yamashita sought habeas corpus review in the U.S. Supreme Court. He claimed that the tribunal was not legally authorized, that the charges did not allege violations of the laws of war, and that the trial's procedures failed to meet the standards required under the Articles of War, the Geneva Conventions, and the U.S. Constitution. The Supreme Court granted Yamashita's request for review but rejected his claims on the merits, finding that the tribunal was properly authorized and operated within legal limits.[131] On February 23, 1946, Yamashita was hanged at a prison camp thirty miles south of Manila.

Both *Quirin* and *Yamashita* have been sharply criticized. During deliberations in *Quirin*, Justice Felix Frankfurter warned his colleagues against getting bogged down in legal niceties during the middle of a war. But years later, Frankfurter expressed regrets, explaining that *Quirin* was not "a happy precedent."[132] Chief Justice Harlan Fiske Stone, described writing the *Quirin* opinion—issued after the Court's sentence had already been carried out—as "a mortification of the flesh" and acknowledged that there was only meager authority to support the commission's constitutionality.[133] *Yamashita* also was marred by flaws. None of the five American generals hastily sent from Washington, D.C., to preside over Yamashita's trial had any legal or combat experience.[134] The army officers appointed to defend Yamashita had only three weeks to prepare for trial, and 59 of the 123 charges against Yamashita were filed the same day the trial began. Even so, the defense's request for a continuance to prepare was denied.[135] Much of the evidence against Yamashita consisted of hearsay. Nonetheless, Yamashita himself was prevented from putting on evidence that the troops who committed the atrocities were not under his command, a key issue in the case.[136] As Supreme Court Justice Frank Murphy said in his dissenting opinion, Yamashita was "rushed to trial under an improper charge" and "given insufficient time to prepare an adequate defense."[137] In his separate dissenting opinion, Justice Wiley Blount Rutledge denounced the commission as lacking "any semblance of trial as we know that institution."[138]

But despite their flaws, both *Quirin* and *Yamashita* reaffirmed the resilience of habeas corpus as a mechanism of securing judicial review even in time of war. In *Quirin*, President Roosevelt had sought to exclude the federal courts altogether. But the Supreme Court not only reviewed the legality of Roosevelt's order establishing a military commission but also convened a special session to do so because of the "public importance of the questions raised" and "the duty which rests on the courts, in time of war as well as in time of peace, to preserve unimpaired the constitutional safeguards of civil liberty."[139] *Yamashita* similarly demonstrated the constitutional underpinnings of habeas review. Unless Congress properly suspended the writ, the Court said, the executive could not "withdraw from the courts the power and duty" to inquire into the legal authority of the military tribunal and determine whether a prisoner fell within its jurisdiction.[140] Thus, even as these decisions upheld the president's claimed power to employ military tribunals (thus siding with the executive on the merits), they nonetheless demonstrated that habeas corpus could provide judicial review to those detained and facing trial by the military during wartime, regardless of their citizenship.

Quirin and *Yamashita* did not, however, address the availability of habeas corpus for prisoners detained and tried outside the sovereign territory of the United States. The German saboteurs in *Quirin* were arrested, held, and prosecuted by a military commission inside the country; General Yamashita was tried by an American tribunal in the Philippines when the Philippines was still U.S. territory. The Supreme Court did address whether foreign nationals arrested and detained outside the United States had habeas corpus rights in two other World War II–era military commission cases: *Johnson v. Eisentrager* and *Hirota v. MacArthur*.

In *Eisentrager*, twenty-one German soldiers captured in Nanjing, China, had been tried for war crimes by an American military commission.[141] Following their convictions, the prisoners were transferred from Nanjing to a U.S. military base in Allied-occupied Landsberg, Germany, to serve out their sentences. The prisoners challenged their convictions by filing habeas corpus petitions in federal district court in Washington, D.C. They claimed that their imprisonment was illegal because they did not violate the laws of war and because the military commission lacked jurisdiction to try them.

The district court dismissed the petitions, relying on the Supreme Court's decision in *Ahrens v. Clark*, handed down just months earlier.[142] *Ahrens* was a habeas corpus challenge by more than one hundred foreign nationals detained at Ellis Island, New York, pending their deportation to Germany under the Alien Enemies Act. The petitioners in *Ahrens* brought their action in federal district court in Washington, D.C. The Supreme Court ruled that the district court lacked jurisdiction because the federal habeas corpus statute granting courts the power to issue writs "within their respective jurisdictions" required the prisoner's physical presence within the district court's territorial jurisdiction.[143] That meant that the *Ahrens* petitioners had to sue for relief in federal district court in New York, where they were being physically held, not Washington, even though officials there had the authority to order the petitioners' release. The Court reserved decision on whether judges could exercise review under the habeas statute where the prisoner was held by the United States outside the territorial jurisdiction of any district court, as might be the case when a prisoner was detained abroad.[144] If they could not, as Justice Rutledge warned in his dissenting opinion in *Ahrens*, there might be no remedy at all for illegal detentions overseas.[145]

The court of appeals in *Eisentrager* reversed. Recognizing that *Ahrens* meant that prisoners in Landsberg, Germany, had no right to judicial review under the federal habeas corpus statute (because they were held outside the "jurisdiction" of any U.S. district court), the court looked to the Constitution. The right to habeas corpus, it said, "stem[s] directly from fundamentals."[146] If the government was correct, the appeals court explained, then even U.S. citizens could be denied habeas corpus if held abroad. The "only escape from that conclusion" would be to draw a line between citizens and foreign nationals with only the former receiving the Constitution's protections. That distinction, however, was impermissible, since "constitutional prohibitions apply directly to acts of Government, or Government officials, and are not conditioned upon persons or territory."[147] The Supreme Court agreed to hear the case and thus to address whether foreign nationals tried by military commissions could seek habeas relief in a federal court if their arrest, detention, and trial all took place outside the United States.

Justice Robert Jackson wrote the opinion for a closely divided Supreme Court. Jackson, who had previously served as the chief U.S. prosecutor at the Nuremberg Trials, began by describing a descending scale of entitlement to legal rights, with citizens at the top and foreign nationals, or aliens, below them. "Citizenship as a head of jurisdiction and a ground of protection was old when Paul invoked it in his appeal to Caesar," Jackson wrote, suggesting that an American citizen was entitled to habeas corpus when detained by his own government no matter where that detention occurred.[148] Aliens, Jackson acknowledged, also enjoyed the Constitution's protections, but only as long as they were present in or had a sufficient connection to the United States. Enemy aliens captured and detained outside the United States, he continued, did not necessarily enjoy those protections. Surveying past cases, Jackson noted that "in extending constitutional protections beyond the citizenry, the [Supreme] Court has been at pains to point out that it was the alien's presence within its territorial jurisdiction that gave the Judiciary power to act."[149] Thus, he said, alien enemies whose offense, capture, and trial occur outside the United States do not have a right of access to U.S. courts.

Jackson also expressed separation of powers concerns about courts interfering with the executive's war-making role. Affording habeas corpus review to individuals detained in connection with overseas military operations like the German soldiers in *Eisentrager*, he said, would require the military to "produce the body" and transfer prisoners and witnesses halfway across the world for hearings in federal courts. Injecting courts and judges into military operations in a theater of war, Jackson believed, would improperly encumber field commanders and divert "attention from the military offensive abroad to the legal defensive at home."[150] Jackson thus appeared to accept limits on habeas corpus and other constitutional protections during wartime based on a prisoner's citizenship and the location of his capture and detention.

Justice Hugo Black charted a different course in his dissenting opinion, expressing a view that would seem prescient after 9/11. Black refused to place strict territorial limits on habeas corpus and other constitutional rights. The Constitution, Black insisted, should not be confined to American citizens or to aliens within the United States. Instead, Black articulated what has since been described as a responsibility-based, rather than a rights-based, approach to the Constitution. This approach maintains that the exercise of limits on government power toward any person in U.S. custody must be constrained by law, regardless of that person's citizenship status or physical location.[151] If one purpose of the Constitution is to prevent arbitrary and unlawful exercises of executive power, it is just as impermissible to deny an individual habeas corpus relief because he was arrested or detained abroad, rather than inside the country, or because he is a foreign national rather than an American citizen. To deny habeas corpus and other constitutional protections based on such distinctions would adopt a "broad and dangerous principle," Black explained.[152] Instead, Black urged that habeas corpus should be available "whenever any United States official illegally imprisons any person in any land we govern."[153] Black thus articulated a different vision of the writ than Jackson did, one that saw habeas corpus reaching beyond America's shores and its citizenry, possibly to wherever the United States claimed the power to imprison. It was a vision that more closely embodied the idea of habeas corpus as a guarantee of individual liberty and a limitation on executive power. If, as Chief Justice Marshall had put it, the question in a habeas action is "what authority has the jailor to detain [the prisoner]," where that prisoner happens to be held does not itself provide the answer.[154]

A different but potentially significant limit on habeas corpus surfaced in another military commission case, *Hirota v. MacArthur*, decided the year before *Eisentrager*. Baron Kōki Hirota had served as Japan's prime minister and foreign minister during the first stages of World War II in Asia. After the war, Hirota and other Japanese citizens were tried by the Tokyo war crimes tribunal, formally known as the International Military Tribunal for the Far East (IMTFE).[155] The tribunal had been established by General Douglas MacArthur, the Supreme Commander of the Allied Powers in the Far East. Hirota was convicted and sentenced to death for his role in waging "wars of aggression" in violation of international law and for disregarding his duty to take adequate steps to prevent atrocities, including the so-called rape of Nanjing, a six-week-long massacre that left dead more than 200,000 civilians and prisoners of war.[156]

Following his conviction, Hirota filed a petition for a writ of habeas corpus directly in the U.S. Supreme Court.[157] Hirota's was one of hundreds of "original" habeas petitions filed in the Supreme Court by Axis prisoners convicted of war crimes by American or Allied military tribunals—all of whom would have been barred from seeking habeas review directly in the lower courts under *Ahrens*, since they were not confined within the territorial jurisdiction of any district court.[158] The Supreme Court had previously denied every other "original" habeas petition during this period without argument or an opinion, typically by a four-to-four vote, with Justice Jackson recusing himself because of his prior service at the Nuremberg Trials.[159]

This time, however, Jackson agreed that the Court should consider the appeal, although he then recused himself from participating in any further proceedings.[160] Three days after hearing oral argument, the Supreme Court issued a short unsigned opinion denying the applications for relief. The opinion explained that because the tribunal that had convicted and sentenced Hirota and the other prisoners was "not a tribunal of the United States," a U.S. court had "no power or authority to review, to affirm, set aside or annul the judgments and sentences [it had] imposed." In establishing the tribunal that had sentenced the prisoners, the Court added, MacArthur had acted as "the agent of the Allied Powers."[161] Thus, a U.S. court did not have jurisdiction to hear the prisoners' challenge and could not address such basic questions as whether the IMTFE had legal authority over the prisoners and their offenses or whether the tribunal itself was lawfully constituted.[162] Hirota was hanged at Tokyo's Sugamo Prison three days after the Supreme Court's decision. The Court did not decide any other challenges to the IMTFE, and the following year it refused to hear habeas petitions challenging convictions handed down by war crimes trials at Nuremberg.[163]

• • •

The Bush administration would rely heavily on these World War II–era cases after 9/11. *Quirin* and *Yamashita*, the administration argued, justified detaining alleged terrorists indefinitely as "enemy combatants" or trying them in military commissions rather than the regular federal courts. In different ways, *Eisentrager* and *Hirota* both served as the basis for denying alleged "enemy combatants" access to the courts altogether. *Eisentrager*, the administration argued, meant that foreign nationals arrested and detained outside the United States had no right to habeas corpus; *Hirota* meant that a prisoner had no access to habeas corpus if his detention was based on an international "source of authority," such as a UN Security Council resolution, even if the prisoner was under the United States' power and control.

Whether federal courts could exercise habeas corpus review in cases such as *Eisentrager* and *Hirota* reflected a larger debate over the application of constitutional rights outside the United States. In other words, did basic constitutional guarantees, such as habeas corpus, due process, and equal protection under law, constrain U.S. action abroad? Or were those guarantees limited to the United States, at least insofar as foreign nationals were concerned? *Eisentrager* and *Hirota* addressed only part of this larger debate—a debate that would be pivotal in resolving legal challenges to the treatment of prisoners in the "war on terrorism" and to the role of habeas corpus in confronting the post-9/11 global detention system.

6

The Seeds of a Global Constitution

At the time the United States was founded, little thought was given to whether the Constitution applied outside its territory. Instead, the Constitution's framers focused inward on developing and securing a republican form of government.[1] Although they contemplated the possibility of military action overseas, they did not envision the extent to which America's military power, let alone its political, commercial, and cultural influence, would be projected beyond the country's shores over the next two centuries. Nor could they foresee how law enforcement would one day have to undertake international operations in areas from narcotics trafficking to global terrorism.

History, however, also provides support for a more expansive vision of the Constitution. The Constitution's framers were driven by the ideal of protecting individual liberty from arbitrary and lawless government action. Consequently, they established the Bill of Rights to embody what Professor Louis Henkin has called a "universal human rights ideology," even though that ideology was far from its full realization in 1789 when women, slaves, and non-property-owning males did not share equally in political power or civil society.[2] James Madison, for example, insisted that his proposed Bill of Rights "expressly declare the great rights of mankind," thus implicitly rejecting an "us" versus "them" dichotomy.[3] Madison and others also were deeply suspicious of executive power. Having just thrown off the yoke of a king, they wanted to protect against the exercise of monarchical authority in the new system of government that they were creating. Their desire to ensure both individual liberty and checks on government power helped motivate the inclusion of a habeas corpus guarantee in the Constitution as well as limitations on its suspension. They similarly inspired the inclusion of the Bill of Rights, which helped secure such basic protections as the right not to be deprived of life, liberty, or property without due process of law and the right to a speedy trial by jury for alleged crimes.[4] None of these protections turned on a person's citizenship status or location.[5]

The first skirmish between competing visions of the constitutional rights of noncitizens (or "aliens") took place during the 1790s. The French Revolution and ensuing war in Europe had split America along partisan lines, and the divisions were growing increasingly bitter. The Federalists feared the importation of radical Jacobin ideas and a possible invasion by France. In response to these fears, Congress enacted several measures during John Adams's administration giving the president broad powers over noncitizens in the United States. The Alien Enemies Act authorized the president to detain and expel aliens who were citizens, subjects, or residents of an enemy nation with which the United States was at war. The so-called Alien Friends Act swept more broadly, authorizing the president to detain or expel any alien he deemed "dangerous to the peace and safety of the United States."[6] A third statute, the Sedition Act, made it a crime to publish "false, scandalous, and malicious writing" against the government or its officials.[7]

The Alien Friends and Sedition acts provoked heated debate. Leading Federalists who supported the Alien Friends Act argued that members of the social compact (citizens) could define and limit the rights of nonmembers (aliens) who did not enjoy the compact's protections or benefits. The only protections that aliens could claim, they maintained, were those that the international law of nations afforded.[8] On the other side, Jeffersonian Republicans vigorously opposed the acts, condemning them in the Virginia and Kentucky resolutions as unconstitutional.[9] As the prominent American jurist and statesman Edward Livingston wrote, "Alien friends . . . residing among us, are entitled to the protection of our laws, and . . . during their residence they owe a temporary allegiance to our Government." If alien friends are accused of violating this allegiance, Livingston added, "the same laws which interpose in the case of a citizen must determine the truth of the accusation, and if found guilty [aliens] are liable to the same punishment."[10] James Madison incorporated these ideas of equal treatment in his 1800 report for the Virginia legislature defending the resolutions. He emphasized the link between an alien's allegiance to the United States, on the one hand, and his entitlement to the protection of its laws, on the other. That aliens might not be parties to the Constitution as citizens were, Madison said, did not exclude them from its coverage.[11] "If aliens had no rights under the Constitution, they might not only be banished," he wrote, "but even capitally punished, without a jury or the other incidents to a fair trial."[12]

The Alien Friends Act expired in 1800, along with the Sedition Act; neither was ever renewed. By contrast, Madison's belief that constitutional rights protecting individuals from arbitrary and unlawful government action do not necessarily depend on an individual's citizenship or membership in the political community gathered support over time and was later endorsed by the Supreme Court to varying degrees. In the late nineteenth century, in response to an anti-immigrant backlash, the Supreme Court ruled that noncitizens were entitled to equal protection of the law[13] and, if accused of a crime, to a jury trial under the Fifth and Sixth Amendments to the Constitution.[14] Over time, the Court has also made clear that aliens in the United States are entitled to other constitutional protections as well.[15]

The separate question of whether the Constitution applied beyond America's borders first arose in the nineteenth century during the period of westward expansion. The debate centered on the structure of government for newly acquired territories, procedural components of civil and criminal justice, and the hotly contested issue of slavery.[16] Those who advocated an approach based on membership in the polity argued that the Constitution was created by the people of the states for the states and therefore did not extend beyond the states.[17] But those who espoused a more nationalist vision disagreed. John Marshall, for example, maintained that the Constitution applied throughout the "American empire," extending to any territory over which the United States exercised sovereign power.[18] In a series of decisions before the Civil War, the Supreme Court recognized the Constitution's applicability to newly acquired western territories,[19] as well as to the District of Columbia, where the Constitution had granted Congress full legislative power without conferring statehood.[20] Ironically, the most important decision in this regard was the ignominious *Scott v. Sandford* (the "Dred Scott case"), in which the Court ruled that the Constitution's Due Process Clause protected a slave owner's right to his property in the territories.[21]

When America began to acquire an overseas empire in the late nineteenth century, the courts had to address whether the Constitution applied to U.S. action abroad. In general, courts acknowledged territorial limitations on constitutional rights even when U.S. citizens were in foreign countries but affirmed the application of certain fundamental constitutional rights in the United States' overseas colonial possessions.

In 1891, for example, the Supreme Court considered the appeal of an American seaman who had been tried and convicted by an American consul in Japan for a murder committed aboard an American ship in a Japanese harbor. The seaman, John M. Ross, filed a habeas corpus petition challenging the conviction following his return to the United States, where he had been brought to serve out his sentence. Ross argued that the trial violated his constitutional rights by denying him a grand jury indictment and a jury trial.

The Supreme Court rejected his claim. Writing for a unanimous Court in *In re Ross*, Justice Stephen Johnson Field stated that the Constitution was limited to the United States and "can have no operation in another country." As a result, he said, the Constitution's protections extended "only to citizens and others within the United States, or who are brought there for trial for alleged offenses committed elsewhere, and not to residents or temporary sojourners abroad."[22] Ten years later, the Court upheld the extradition of an American citizen to Cuba to face trial for embezzlement during America's temporary military occupation of Cuba after the Spanish-American War, even though Cuban law did not guarantee him the same protections as the U.S. Constitution. The Court explained that America's constitutional guarantees have "no relation to crimes committed without the jurisdiction of the United States against the laws of a foreign country."[23]

Cases like *Ross* and *Neely* were the product of America's growing empire and expanded military presence in foreign countries. But America also began acquiring new possessions for itself during this period. In 1893, American troops helped overthrow the Hawaiian government and establish a new U.S.-controlled provisional government that paved the way for Hawaii's annexation five years later.[24] In addition, the United States acquired significant parts of Spain's colonial empire, including Puerto Rico, the Philippines, and Guam following the conclusion of the Spanish-American War. The United States also obtained control over Guantánamo Bay during this period, in exchange for terminating its occupation of Cuba.[25] As the United States became an imperial power, questions soon arose over whether and how the United States' Constitution would apply to its newly acquired territories.

The Supreme Court addressed this question in a series of decisions collectively known as the "Insular Cases." The first and most important was the Court's 1901 decision in *Downes v. Bidwell*.[26] *Downes* involved a duty imposed on oranges imported from Puerto Rico by a merchant in New York, requiring the Court to address whether Congress was free from the constitutional requirement of uniform taxation in Puerto Rico. In assessing the legality of the tax, members of the Court staked out three broadly defined positions. The controlling opinion by Justice Henry Billings Brown, which attracted a plurality but not a majority of the Court, held that Congress was not bound by the Constitution in taxing Puerto Rico. Embracing the logic of the membership approach from the debate over the Alien Friends Act a century earlier, Brown explained that the Constitution was "created by the people of the United States, as a union of States, to be governed solely by representatives of the states."[27] Puerto Rico, he said, was a territory "appurtenant and belonging to the United States, but not a part of the United States."[28] While Brown held out the possibility that by legislative action, Congress could extend the benefits of membership to newly acquired territories, the Constitution had no force in those territories until Congress did so.

The elder Justice John Marshall Harlan took the opposite position. He maintained that whenever the United States acquired sovereignty over a territory, the Constitution followed, regardless of that territory's status. Harlan believed that as "the supreme law of the land," the Constitution applied "to all peoples, whether of States or territories, who are subject to the authority of the United States."[29] If the United States governed a territory and exercised jurisdiction over it, the Constitution accordingly applied to all the people there, regardless of whether there had been a determination by the political branches to accord statehood to that territory. This view was encapsulated by the popular credo "The Constitution follows the flag."

The third position, staked out by Justice Edward Douglass White, reflected a compromise. White divided territories into different categories: those that Congress had made part of the United States by either admitting them as states or incorporating them as U.S. territories, and those that Congress had not incorporated. The Constitution's full protections, he said, applied to admitted or incorporated territories, while "unincorporated territories" held a different status. Although the Constitution applied to all U.S. territories (including unincorporated territories like Puerto Rico), not all of the Constitution's provisions applied everywhere and at all times. Instead, White explained, the application of a particular constitutional provision to an unincorporated territory required an inquiry "into the situation of the territory and its relation to the United States."[30] White also pointed out that certain constitutional restrictions were of "so fundamental a nature that they cannot be transgressed."[31] White's view ultimately captured the majority of the Court and served as the basis for a series of decisions in the coming decades that addressed the application of particular constitutional provisions to unincorporated territories.[32]

The Insular Cases have been criticized for sanctioning racist attitudes toward "native islanders" whom United States considered unable to appreciate American values and institutions.[33] The Supreme Court, for example, cited Puerto Rico's different origins, culture, and language in refusing to extend the constitutional right to a jury trial to the island's inhabitants.[34] But the Insular Cases also embodied the idea that America's projection of power abroad must be constrained by certain basic constitutional principles. The Insular Cases thus did not hinge the Constitution's extraterritorial application on formal constructs such as citizenship. Instead, they focused on the actual relationship between the United States and the territory in question to determine which constitutional provisions applied under the circumstances.

While the Insular Cases endorsed the extension of constitutional rights beyond America's shores, they addressed only those territories that the United States possessed and governed. The Supreme Court's earlier statement in *Ross*—that the Constitution had no force in foreign territory—still remained on the books. But by the end of World War II, *Ross's* strict territoriality rule seemed increasingly archaic. America had become a superpower, with military forces, corporations, and other institutions spread across the world. The type of colonial arrangements that prevailed during the imperialist era of the late nineteenth and early twentieth centuries had given way to other, more subtle forms of control and influence. America's expanding and enduring global presence, including its growing number of overseas military bases and service members, had created new reasons to extend constitutional protections abroad.[35]

In 1957, the Supreme Court revisited the question of the Constitution's application in foreign territory. In *Reid v. Covert*, two widows of U.S. servicemen challenged the legality of their convictions by courts-martial for murdering their husbands in England and Japan.[36] Six justices refused to find that they were bound by *In re Ross* but divided in their reasoning. Writing for a plurality of four, Justice Hugo Black said that as U.S. citizens and civilians, the defendants could not be subject to court-martial but instead had to be tried by a jury of their peers, as the Fifth and Sixth Amendments to the Constitution required. Black rejected the notion that the Constitution was limited strictly to U.S. territory. "The United States is entirely a creature of the Constitution," he explained. "Its power and authority have no other source. It can only act in accordance with all the limitations imposed by the Constitution."[37] Black also rejected the suggestion made in the Insular Cases that judges could limit the Constitution's applicability to provisions they deemed "fundamental."[38] "When the Government reaches out to punish a citizen who is abroad," Black said, "the shield which the Bill of Rights and other parts of the Constitution provide to protect his life and liberty should not be stripped away just because he happens to be in another land."[39] Building on concepts first articulated by Madison and other framers of the Constitution from the early years of the republic, Black believed that the United States could not subject defendants to its criminal laws while denying them the constitutional protections that accompany enforcement of those laws, simply because they were located in a foreign land.[40]

Justice Felix Frankfurter and the second Justice John Marshall Harlan (the grandson of the elder Justice Harlan from the Insular Cases) each filed concurring opinions. Both agreed that the Constitution was not limited to U.S. territory. But, they said, that does not mean all constitutional protections necessarily apply when the United States acts abroad. Instead, Frankfurter and Harlan advanced a more contextual approach. The question, Harlan explained, was not whether the Constitution applied abroad (for it applied everywhere) but whether the application of a particular constitutional right was "impracticable" or "anomalous" under the circumstances.[41] As Harvard Law School professor Gerald Neuman has observed, this approach "held out the possibility of more widespread constitutional protection than had previously been afforded but at the cost of diluting its content."[42] It undercut the idea that citizenship necessarily determined the Constitution's application abroad, since in many instances it would be no more impracticable or anomalous to apply a particular constitutional protection to an alien than to an American citizen. On the other hand, it suggested that even an American citizen might not always be able to claim the full protections of the Bill of Rights when outside the United States, since the application of particular constitutional provisions would depend on the circumstances.

In subsequent decisions, the Supreme Court extended the Constitution's jury trial guarantee to civilian dependents of military members overseas prosecuted for noncapital crimes and to civilian employees of the armed forces overseas, again rejecting the idea of strict territorial limitations on constitutional rights.[43] Lower courts, in turn, recognized that other constitutional safeguards applied abroad.[44] But because these cases involved American citizens, they did not address whether, and to what extent, the Constitution extended to foreign nationals outside the United States—the issue presented in World War II era cases like *Eisentrager* and *Hirota*.

The opportunity to address that question instead arose in two types of cases: those involving territories where the United States exercised actual control and jurisdiction but not formal sovereignty; and those involving U.S. law enforcement actions in foreign countries and on the high seas. Although the decisions in these cases did not provide a definitive resolution, they offered further support for the proposition that, at minimum, fundamental constitutional rights applied outside the United States to citizens and noncitizens alike.

After World War II, the United States continued to exercise control over several territories without political sovereignty. In resolving various disputes, federal courts built on the logic of the Insular Cases to find that fundamental constitutional rights applied to noncitizens as well as to citizens, even though these territories were not formally part of the United States.

The Panama Canal Zone provides an instructive example. The United States acquired control of the ten-mile-wide Canal Zone in 1903. A treaty between the United States and the new republic of Panama gave the United States permanent, exclusive, and total control but reserved the host state's ultimate sovereignty over the territory.[45] The treaty provided the United States with "all the rights, power and authority within the zone . . . which the United States would possess and exercise, if it were the sovereign of the territory [of the Canal Zone] . . . to the entire exclusion of the exercise by the Republic of Panama of any such sovereign rights, power or authority."[46] The treaty created a U.S. enclave to serve a strategic national interest: constructing and maintaining a canal across the Isthmus of Panama. The United States exercised jurisdiction over the Canal Zone until 1979, when the Canal Zone was returned to Panama.[47]

Early on, Congress created a district court in the Canal Zone to hear civil and criminal cases, with review to a federal appeals court.[48] Congress later provided for a bill of rights that was modeled on, although not identical to, the Bill of Rights in the U.S. Constitution.[49] By the 1940s, both the district court and the appeals court were subjecting U.S. actions and laws in the Canal Zone to scrutiny under the Constitution.[50] Emphasizing the United States' territorial control over the Canal Zone rather than the personal status of the affected individual, judges consistently acknowledged that fundamental constitutional protections, including due process and equal protection under law, applied to both American citizens and foreign nationals.[51] As the U.S. Court of Appeals for the Fifth Circuit, the appellate court with jurisdiction over the Canal Zone, explained, "It is the territorial nature of the Canal Zone and not the citizenship of the defendant that is dispositive."[52]

Judicial decisions arising from the United States' governance of the Trust Territory of the Pacific Islands in Micronesia reflected the same principle: that fundamental constitutional guarantees accompanied U.S. territorial control, regardless of the nature of the political arrangement under which that control was exercised. After liberating the islands from Japanese control during World War II, the United States sought to retain strategic control over Micronesia. Here, the operative agreement took the form of a special trusteeship granting the United States "full powers of administration, legislation, and jurisdiction over the Territory" without ceding formal sovereignty: a degree of control similar to the Canal Zone and Guantánamo Bay.[53] The U.S. Department of the Interior, which assumed control over Micronesia from the U.S. Navy in 1951, exercised executive and legislative authority and also appointed judges for the trust territory, with review in the federal court of appeals in Washington, D.C.[54] In 1986, the trusteeship formally ended: the Northern Mariana Islands became a U.S. commonwealth, and three other islands chose to become independent while remaining in free association with the United States.[55]

Before the trusteeship ended, courts consistently ruled that fundamental constitutional rights applied both to U.S. citizens and to noncitizens in the Trust Territory, even though the territory was a foreign country under U.S. administration. In one case, for example, the U.S. Court of Appeals for the District of Columbia Circuit in Washington, D.C., which had jurisdiction over cases from the Trust Territory, considered a challenge brought by an inhabitant to a valuation of his property made to compensate him for its destruction. The appeals court ruled that the locally based Micronesian Claims Commission, established to adjudicate such claims, was bound by the constitutional requirements of due process.[56] Applying the reasoning of the Insular Cases, the court found that fundamental constitutional rights applied equally to foreign nationals in the Trust Territory because they were no less subject to U.S. governing power than the American citizens there. "It is settled," the court said, that "there cannot exist under the American flag any governmental authority untrammeled by the requirements of due process of law."[57] Other courts reached the same conclusion in adjudicating legal challenges, finding, for example, that inhabitants of the Marshall Islands dispossessed by nuclear weapons testing at Bikini Atoll and Enewetak Atoll were covered by the Constitution's takings clause, which prohibits the taking of private property for public use without just compensation.[58]

The question of the Constitution's application to noncitizens in nonsovereign U.S. territory also arose at the U.S. Naval Base at Guantánamo Bay during the early 1990s when the United States began using Guantánamo to detain asylum seekers from Haiti intercepted on the high seas. Those whom the United States did not summarily return to Haiti, from where they were fleeing persecution, were brought to Guantánamo and held in newly created "tent cities" encircled by rolls of razor-barbed wire. The asylum seekers—men, women, and children—were denied attorneys and access to U.S. courts. Later, when thousands were intercepted fleeing Cuba in the mid-1990s, the United States took them to Guantánamo and confined them behind barbed wire in "safe-haven" camps. The United States also began erecting similar camps elsewhere in the region, including in the Panama Canal Zone.[59]

Lawsuits challenging America's interdiction policy were filed in Florida and New York. Since the asylum seekers were foreign nationals seized and held outside the United States, the government argued, they had no rights enforceable in any court. The U.S. Court of Appeals for the Eleventh Circuit agreed and rejected the Florida-based challenges, finding that the refugees could not challenge their interdiction or the government's asylum screening procedures.[60] Adopting a line of reasoning that would become familiar after 9/11, the appeals court said that because aliens detained at Guantánamo were foreign nationals outside the United States, they "are without legal rights that are cognizable in the courts of the United States" and must instead depend solely on "the American tradition of humanitarian concern and conduct" for their protection and safety.[61] The New York–based challenges fared better. The U.S. Court of Appeals for the Second Circuit, which had jurisdiction over those challenges, affirmed a lower court's ruling that the refugees be provided access to counsel before being repatriated. In rejecting the government's contention that the refugees had no judicially enforceable legal protections, the court emphasized America's "exclusive control" over Guantánamo, finding that it would be neither "impracticable" nor "anomalous" to accord them fundamental constitutional rights.[62]

The Supreme Court ultimately upheld the United States' interdiction and direct return policy, finding that the 1951 UN Convention Relating to the Status of Refugees and the Immigration or Nationality Act did not prohibit the United States from summarily returning to Haiti individuals seized on the high seas without first determining whether they were entitled to refugee status.[63] The Supreme Court, however, focused only on the extraterritorial application of statutory and treaty-based protections to those fleeing Haiti and interdicted on the high seas; it did not consider whether individuals held indefinitely by the United States at Guantánamo or other offshore prisons under its control, where they had been brought by the United States for detention and interrogation, could invoke the Constitution's protections.

The United States' decision to intercept those fleeing persecution was motivated partly by concerns about the domestic and political effects of a worsening refugee crisis. The United States responded with extreme measures that denied individuals any legal protections or access to U.S. courts and that led to prolonged detention without a fair process as well as to cruel treatment. It also embraced a legal position without limits. New York district judge Sterling Johnson Jr. underscored the position's implications in ruling that HIV-infected Haitian refugees could not be detained indefinitely at Guantánamo and had to be released: "If the Due Process Clause does not apply to the detainees at

Guantánamo," he said, the government "would have discretion deliberately to starve or beat them, to deprive them of medical attention, to return them without process to their persecutors, or to discriminate among them based on the color of their skin."[64] Johnson's warning would prove prescient: after 9/11, the United States would exercise its "discretion" at Guantánamo and other law-free zones to imprison people in secret, deny them due process and access to the courts, and subject them to torture and other abuse.

The extraterritorial application of the Constitution was also the focus of litigation in connection with expanding U.S. law enforcement operations on the high seas and in foreign countries. By the 1970s and 1980s, federal criminal law had become increasingly global in scope as the United States focused on combating the narcotics trade and other international criminal activity. Increased surveillance, searches, and arrests by U.S. officials beyond America's borders raised the question of whether those officials were constrained by the constitutional limitations that applied domestically. While *Reid v. Covert* and its progeny demonstrated that American citizens were protected by the Constitution when abroad, the Supreme Court had never clearly extended these rulings to foreign nationals, and lower courts had rendered conflicting decisions on the Constitution's extraterritorial application to noncitizens.[65] This issue came before the Supreme Court in 1990 through the prosecution of Mexican drug dealer Rene Martin Verdugo-Urquidez.[66]

Verdugo-Urquidez's case began when Mexican police seized him for violations of U.S. law and transferred him to the custody of U.S. officials at the U.S.-Mexico border. The following day, while Verdugo-Urquidez was detained in San Diego, agents from the Drug Enforcement Agency, along with Mexican police, searched Verdugo-Urquidez's home in Mexico without a warrant and found evidence of marijuana smuggling. The United States brought criminal charges against Verdugo-Urquidez and transported him to California. Verdugo-Urquidez moved to suppress the evidence taken from his home and to prevent its introduction at trial. He claimed that the evidence had been seized in violation of the Fourth Amendment's prohibition against unreasonable searches and seizures.[67]

In *United States v. Verdugo-Urquidez*, however, the Supreme Court ruled that the Fourth Amendment did not apply to the search and rejected Verdugo-Urquidez's claim. Writing for a plurality of four justices (one short of a majority), Chief Justice William H. Rehnquist maintained that foreign nationals did not have any Fourth Amendment rights with respect to U.S. government action abroad.[68] Imposing constitutional restraints on how U.S.

officials treat foreign nationals outside the United States, Rehnquist warned, would have "significant and deleterious consequences for the United States in conducting activities beyond its boundaries."[69] "For better or for worse," he said "we live in a world of nation-states in which our Government must be able to function effectively in the company of sovereign nations."[70] In a passage that foreshadowed the arguments against habeas corpus rights for Guantánamo detainees and other foreign nationals after 9/11, Rehnquist remarked that any constraints on U.S. action against noncitizens abroad must come from the political branches, through diplomatic understanding, treaty, or legislation, and not from the courts through judicial enforcement of constitutional safeguards.[71] Rehnquist's approach looked both backward to membership theories of constitutional rights and forward to expanding law enforcement and military operations beyond the United States' borders, which he believed should be conducted free of constitutional constraints.

Justice William J. Brennan Jr. took the opposite approach in a dissenting opinion joined by Justice Thurgood Marshall. Brennan maintained that when the United States acted to enforce its criminal law abroad, subjecting foreign nationals to its pains and penalties, the protections of the Constitution must accompany that extraterritorial exercise of American power.[72] By seeking to prosecute and punish Verdugo-Urquidez, Brennan said, the United States had "treated him as a member of our community" and made him "quite literally, one of the governed."[73] Brennan viewed the extraterritorial application of constitutional rights as essential not only to the idea of fundamental fairness embodied in the Bill of Rights but also to America's commitment to the rule of law. How, Brennan questioned, could the United States criticize other governments for acting lawlessly when it refused to adhere to the requirements of its own Constitution merely because it was acting outside its borders?[74]

Justice Anthony M. Kennedy cast the pivotal fifth and deciding vote, positioning himself between these two poles in a concurring opinion. Kennedy emphasized that no "rigid and abstract rule" governed the Constitution's operation abroad. He instead drew on Justice Harlan's opinion in *Reid*, explaining that in determining the extraterritorial reach of constitutional rights, a court must ask whether the application of a particular constitutional provision is "impracticable" or "anomalous" under the circumstances. The absence of local judges or magistrates, along with the need to cooperate with foreign officials, made it impracticable to apply the Fourth Amendment to the search of a nonresident alien's property in Mexico.[75] But, Kennedy cautioned, other constitutional protections might apply extraterritorially depending on the circumstances. In this important opinion, Kennedy thus signaled his resistance to bright-line rules and his support for a more flexible, case-by-case approach designed to weigh the feasibility of applying a particular constitutional safeguard to a particular situation.[76]

Whether, and to what extent, the Constitution applied to foreign nationals outside the United States became a critical question after 9/11, with far-reaching ramifications for U.S. detentions at Guantánamo and beyond. Habeas corpus actions challenging the military detention and trial of "enemy combatants" would spark intense legal battles and produce three landmark Supreme Court decisions. Those actions would ask, at bottom, whether the United States could deny individuals the basic protections of its laws and Constitution by holding them beyond its shores. They would also raise questions about the scope of the president's power to detain individuals indefinitely without charge, to use military commissions to try suspected terrorists for war crimes, and to engage in torture and other abuse. We turn to those challenges in part 3.

Part 3 —————

A Modest Judicial Intervention

*The First Supreme Court
"Enemy Combatant" Decisions*

On April 20, 2004, the Supreme Court heard argument in *Rasul v. Bush*, the first Guantánamo detainee case to reach the Court.[1] Just over a week later, on April 28, the Court heard argument in the cases of alleged "enemy combatants" Yaser Hamdi and Jose Padilla.[2] That same evening, *60 Minutes II* broadcast the first pictures from Iraq's Abu Ghraib prison documenting the torture and other mistreatment of prisoners by the United States. The pictures validated the concern that several justices had voiced during Hamdi's argument that morning: that by exempting the president's sweeping claims of executive power from habeas corpus review, the Court would insulate the worst forms of illegal detention and abuse from judicial scrutiny. The U.S. solicitor general, Paul D. Clement, had sought to assuage this concern, explaining that the "judgment of those involved" in the detention and interrogation of prisoners is that "the last thing you want to do is torture somebody or try to do something along those lines."[3] The pictures from Abu Ghraib, however, told a different story and told it graphically. They underscored the potential dangers of blindly trusting the executive and reinforced the importance of habeas corpus as a check on illegal government action.

Rasul consisted of two separate actions that had been consolidated in the lower courts. One, *Al-Odah v. United States*, involved twelve Kuwaiti nationals; the other, *Rasul v. Bush*, involved two British citizens and one Australian citizen.[4] Although of different nationalities, the detainees had important facts in common: all had been imprisoned at Guantánamo since early 2002; all were being held incommunicado; and all had been denied any access to a lawyer and to the courts. Their habeas petitions asserted that they were innocent of any wrongdoing and that the United States was detaining them unlawfully. The Kuwaitis' habeas petitions said that the detainees had gone to Afghanistan and Pakistan as volunteers to provide humanitarian aid and had been seized by local villagers in exchange for bounties and turned over to the United States. The British detainees' petitions explained that the men had traveled to Pakistan to attend a marriage ceremony, visit relatives, and continue their computer education.

The issue before the Supreme Court was not whether the government's allegations against the men were true. It was more basic: did the federal courts have the power to consider their habeas corpus petitions and determine whether there was a legal basis for imprisonment? The Court's answer would control the outcome not only for the detainees in the case before them but also for the more than six hundred other prisoners then being held at Guantánamo without judicial process. It would also affect the future role, if any, of the federal courts in reviewing challenges to U.S. detentions at other offshore prisons.

Both the district and appellate courts had ruled against the detainees, adopting the government's argument that foreign nationals held outside the sovereign territory of the United States had no right to habeas corpus or other constitutional protections. The lower courts did not expressly endorse the government's argument that the detainees had no protections under U.S. law or the Geneva Conventions. But they did conclude that federal judges had no role in reviewing those detentions or enforcing any legal protections that the prisoners might have. Instead, they said that the detention and treatment of prisoners at Guantánamo remained a matter for the political branches, and not the courts, to decide.

The Bush administration relied principally on *Johnson v. Eisentrager*, arguing that it established a categorical rule barring the exercise of habeas corpus review over the detention of any foreign national captured and held abroad.[5] The fact that U.S. control over Guantánamo was so extensive that, as one Supreme Court justice noted, "even . . . the Cuban Iguana[s]" are protected, made no difference because Guantánamo remained outside sovereign U.S. territory and thus foreign nationals there had no right to access U.S. courts.[6]

Eisentrager, however, differed from the Guantánamo detainee cases in important respects. The prisoners in *Eisentrager* fell within the well-established and limited category of "enemy aliens"—that is, citizens or subjects of an enemy nation at war with the United States. There also was "no fiction about their enmity" because they all admitted to actively serving the enemy German government.[7] By contrast, most of the Guantánamo detainees came from allied or neutral nations. Furthermore, the overwhelming majority of the detainees maintained that they were innocent of any wrongdoing and were not hostile to the United States or its allies. In other words, their enmity was the very fact in dispute. In addition, Landsberg Prison, where the *Eisentrager* prisoners were held, differed from Guantánamo Bay. Although operated by the United States, Landsberg was located in occupied Germany; Guantánamo by contrast, was located in territory under the long-term and exclusive jurisdiction and control of the United States. In *Eisentrager*, moreover, the courthouse doors were not entirely closed to the prisoners, since the Supreme Court went on to consider their claim that trying them by military commission was illegal, ultimately rejecting it on the merits.[8]

There was still another important distinction. The *Eisentrager* prisoners had been captured during a conflict between nation-states, in which the enemy was clearly defined, the battlefield recognizable, and the end discernable. *Eisentrager* was thus rooted in a world in which the military acted according to defined parameters in terms of whom it could detain and for how long. By contrast, at Guantánamo, the United States claimed the power to imprison people in a "war" without spatial or temporal limits against a loosely defined enemy. As long as the president asserted that an individual had some connection to al Qaeda, the Taliban, or an "associated" force, however tenuous, that person could be held indefinitely without charge, without trial, and without a hearing. There would be no cessation of hostilities or armistice to mark the end of this new war, as there had been in earlier conflicts. Instead, the "war on terrorism" would end only when the president said it was over, and the president was saying that this war—and hence the detentions it justified—would last for generations.

These differences influenced the Supreme Court's decision in *Rasul* by highlighting the importance of habeas corpus as a check against illegal executive action. Yet the Court ultimately distinguished *Eisentrager* on statutory grounds rather than overruling it or grappling directly with the underlying constitutional questions it raised. *Eisentrager*, the Court explained, rested on the Court's earlier decision in *Ahrens v. Clark* that the federal habeas corpus statute required the prisoner's presence within the district court's territorial jurisdiction.[9] *Ahrens*, however, had since been overruled by *Braden v. 30th Judicial Circuit Court of Kentucky* and other decisions that interpreted the habeas statute to require only the jailer's physical presence within the court's territorial jurisdiction, and not the prisoner's.[10] In *Braden*, the Court held that because the writ of habeas corpus acts on the prisoner's custodian by commanding him to justify the prisoner's detention, and not upon the prisoner himself, a district court acts "within [its] respective jurisdiction" under the habeas statute as long as the custodian has a sufficient connection to the district and can be reached by service of process.[11] *Braden,* to be sure, involved circumstances different from cases in which the prisoner is captured and detained by the military overseas. The prisoner in *Braden* was serving a criminal sentence in Alabama and had sought to challenge in a Kentucky district court the detainer that Kentucky had lodged against him, requiring his handover to Kentucky authorities for prosecution upon completion of his Alabama sentence. But *Braden* also relied on precedents in which federal courts exercised jurisdiction over habeas petitions filed by American service-members confined in Guam and Korea, suggesting the broader applicability of the jurisdictional principles it articulated.[12] Although the Bush administration correctly noted that these precedents involved American citizens, not foreign nationals, the language of the habeas corpus statute drew no such distinctions. Thus, these precedents supported the conclusion that the habeas statute extended to any prisoner in U.S. custody, regardless of where he or she was located, as long as the court could exercise jurisdiction over the prisoner's jailer.

Applying the *Braden* rule, the Court held in *Rasul* that Guantánamo detainees could seek review under the federal habeas statute because the official with the power to order their release—the secretary of defense, based in Washington, D.C.—was subject to the jurisdiction of the district court there.[13] Accordingly, there was no need to resort to constitutional "fundamentals," as in *Eisentrager,* since Guantánamo detainees could rely directly on the habeas statute as the basis for federal court jurisdiction and as a source of rights.[14]

Rasul's implications transcended Guantánamo. While the Court emphasized the nature and extent of U.S. control over the Guantánamo naval base, its analysis suggested the possibility of habeas review of U.S. detentions at other overseas prisons, since a court's jurisdiction turned on its power over the prisoner's ultimate custodian (located in Washington, D.C.), rather than on the location of the prisoner himself. Justice Antonin Scalia viewed this prospect with foreboding, criticizing the Court in his dissenting opinion for "boldly" extending the reach of habeas corpus "to the four corners of the earth" and inviting unprecedented interference with the executive in time of war. Scalia also attacked the Court for "spring[ing] a trap" on the president who had assumed, in light of precedents like *Eisentrager,* that the government could detain foreign nationals without habeas corpus as long as they remained outside the United States.[15] The president, Scalia observed, had intentionally brought prisoners to Guantánamo to avoid judicial review based on an understanding of the existing legal landscape, and it was unfair for the Court to change the rules midstream. While Congress was free to pass a law creating habeas corpus review over detentions at Guantánamo, Scalia said, nothing in the habeas statute or the Constitution provided for that review now.

Justice Anthony Kennedy issued a separate opinion, concurring in the judgment. He agreed that Guantánamo detainees were entitled to habeas corpus, but he declined to adopt the majority's interpretation of the habeas statute. Instead, Kennedy opted for a contextual, case-by-case approach, building on his earlier opinion in *Verdugo-Urquidez*. In Kennedy's view, judges should first examine the particular circumstances to determine whether a habeas challenge fell "within the proper realm of the judicial power" or within "a realm of political authority over military affairs where the judicial power may not enter."[16] In some instances, this calculus could foreclose further judicial involvement, as in *Eisentrager*, in which "the existence of jurisdiction would have had a clear harmful effect on the Nation's military affairs."[17] In others, it might permit, if not invite, judicial supervision. That, Kennedy said, was the situation at Guantánamo, where prisoners were being held indefinitely without charge and without an adequate process to challenge their detention in a place that was "in every practical respect a United States territory."[18]

Rasul left open important questions. What would a habeas corpus proceeding look like, and what other rights could Guantánamo detainees assert once they were before a federal judge? Looking beyond Guantánamo, did habeas corpus extend to prisoners held elsewhere outside the United States, whether at Bagram, at CIA "black sites," or in Iraq? And was the habeas right dependent on federal statute and thus potentially subject to restriction by Congress, or was it instead grounded in the Constitution and therefore immune from legislative interference, at least without a valid suspension of the writ? Notwithstanding these questions, *Rasul* marked a turning point. It struck at a central pillar of the "war on terror": that the president could evade judicial review simply by imprisoning people beyond America's shores. Major legal battles remained. But with the Court's ruling upholding federal habeas corpus jurisdiction, Guantánamo's days as a prison entirely beyond the law were over.

The same day that it issued *Rasul*, the Supreme Court handed down its decision in *Hamdi v. Rumsfeld*.[19] The habeas petition in *Hamdi* had originally been submitted by Hamdi's father as "next friend" because Hamdi was being held incommunicado and thus could not petition the court himself. It alleged that Hamdi, an American citizen, had traveled to Afghanistan in the summer of 2001 to do relief work and became trapped there once fighting broke out. The petition disputed that Hamdi had received military training and demanded that he be provided access to a lawyer and a hearing that met the Constitution's requirements of due process.[20] The government responded with a two-page affidavit signed by Michael Mobbs, a self-identified special adviser to the under secretary of defense for policy. According to Mobbs, Hamdi was affiliated with a Taliban military unit and received weapons training after his arrival in Afghanistan. Mobbs also claimed that Hamdi remained with his Taliban unit after the 9/11 attacks and that his unit engaged in combat against the Northern Alliance. When Hamdi's unit surrendered, Mobbs said, Hamdi was forced to hand over his Kalashnikov assault rifle. Notably, Mobbs did not base any of these allegations on firsthand knowledge but relied solely on his review of unspecified records and reports, including reports of Hamdi's interrogations by his captors, all of which had been compiled in a situation in which the United States had refused to follow the Geneva Conventions or its own military regulations on the treatment of enemy prisoners.[21] The government contended that federal court review of Hamdi's habeas petition started and stopped with the Mobbs affidavit. As long as the affidavit provided a bare-bones minimum of "some evidence" to support the president's determination that Hamdi was an "enemy combatant," the government maintained, a court had to dismiss Hamdi's habeas petition without further inquiry and without ever hearing from Hamdi himself.

Robert G. Doumar, the Virginia district judge to whom Hamdi's case had been assigned, refused to countenance such blind deference to the executive. Doumar criticized the generic and hearsay nature of the Mobb's affidavit, calling it "little more than the government's 'say so.'"[22] He therefore directed the Defense Department to give Hamdi access to his lawyers and ordered the government to turn over, for the court's review, records of Hamdi's interrogations, statements of the Northern Alliance regarding Hamdi's capture, and other documents bearing on the legality of Hamdi's detention. Doumar, in short, exercised his habeas corpus powers to create a meaningful process so that he could determine whether there was a legal and factual basis to hold Hamdi.

Before any hearing could go forward, however, the government appealed, protesting the district court's interference with the executive's wartime powers. The U.S. Court of Appeals for the Fourth Circuit agreed to hear the appeal and reversed. The Fourth Circuit ruled that Hamdi's American citizenship did not immunize him from military detention for taking up arms against his country and its allies in a foreign theater of war.[23] The appeals court also found that Hamdi was not entitled to talk to a lawyer or to a hearing in court, citing the burdens on the military of litigating the circumstances of battlefield captures before a federal judge halfway across the globe.²⁴ The appeals court limited its decision to what it described as the undisputed capture of an American citizen in a combat zone overseas.²⁵ But no matter how much the court stressed that Hamdi's continued military detention fell "neatly within our historical concepts of war,"²⁶ a fundamental problem remained. The circumstances of Hamdi's capture, as Judge Diana Gribbon Motz noted in her dissenting opinion, were not "undisputed," since Hamdi had never been given an opportunity to explain what he was doing in Afghanistan, whether to a judge or to a properly constituted military tribunal.²⁷ The government, in short, had never provided any legitimate process to determine whether Hamdi was, in fact, a combatant who took up arms against the United States and its allies with a Taliban regiment in Afghanistan or instead was an innocent aid worker in the wrong place at the wrong time.

Judge Motz's analysis ultimately prevailed. In its *Hamdi* decision, the Supreme Court narrowly upheld the president's legal authority to detain as an "enemy combatant" a person allegedly captured on a battlefield where he was fighting alongside enemy government forces against the United States and its allies—a person, that is, whose detention the Court said was supported by clearly established and long-standing law-of-war principles. But the Court resoundingly rejected the proposition that Hamdi could be detained indefinitely without due process and therefore mandated that he be given a judicial hearing through his habeas corpus petition to challenge the allegations against him.

Justice Sandra Day O'Connor wrote the controlling opinion for a plurality of four justices. She determined that Congress had authorized the president to detain Hamdi as an "enemy combatant" under its September 2001 Authorization for Use of Military Force (AUMF) *if* the allegations against him were true. O'Connor cited the Supreme Court's World War II decision in *Ex parte Quirin* for the proposition that American citizens were not immune from military capture and detention when they took up arms against their own government on behalf of an enemy nation. (At least one of the Nazi saboteurs in *Quirin* had been an American citizen.) But O'Connor declined the government's invitation to read the AUMF more broadly by endorsing Hamdi's detention as part of a global "war on terrorism." Instead, she based the government's legal authority to detain on Hamdi's alleged participation in the armed conflict in Afghanistan with the Taliban. While O'Connor left open the possibility that the definition of "enemy combatant" might encompass other situations and fact patterns, she limited the definition of that term in *Hamdi* to individuals who were "part of or supporting forces hostile to the

United States or its coalition partners in Afghanistan and who engaged in an armed conflict against the United States there."[28] O'Connor further emphasized that Hamdi could not be detained indefinitely for purposes of interrogation, thus rejecting one of the government's main justifications for holding him.[29]

O'Connor, however, saved her sharpest language for the government's contention that it could imprison Hamdi based solely on the Mobbs affidavit. A "state of war," she said, "is not a blank check for the President when it comes to the rights of the Nation's citizens."[30] Only a suspension of the writ of habeas corpus could vest the executive with such extraordinary power. Unless Congress took that momentous step, O'Connor said, an American citizen could not be detained without due process, which at its irreducible minimum included a meaningful opportunity to rebut the government's allegations before a neutral decision maker. Due process also meant that a prisoner be provided access to his lawyers, something the government had not allowed Hamdi until shortly before the Supreme Court heard argument in his case and only then as a matter of executive grace, which meant that the access could be revoked at any time.[31]

O'Connor also identified some possible limits on these due process guarantees in order to accommodate the potential burdens on the government of having to litigate an overseas battlefield capture in a U.S. district court. Hearsay, she said, might be the most "reliable available evidence" so that military officers would not necessarily have to travel halfway across the world to testify during a war.[32] O'Connor also suggested that a legally authorized and properly constituted military tribunal might satisfy the requirements of due process for battlefield captures like Hamdi's, as long as the tribunal was provided promptly and in the manner required by applicable military regulations and international law.[33] But when the required hearing was not provided in the first instance by such a tribunal, as in Hamdi's case, a federal court must supply an adequate process itself through a habeas corpus hearing in federal court.

Two other opinions staked out broader positions, each rejecting the government's claim that Hamdi could be held by the military as an "enemy combatant," even assuming that the allegations against him were true. In one of those opinions, Justice David Souter, along with Justice Ruth Bader Ginsburg, found that the AUMF lacked the clear statement necessary to sanction the indefinite detention of an American citizen held on U.S. soil.[34] Souter cited the mass internment of Japanese American citizens during World War II and found no reason why Congress would have seen any need to expand executive power to deal with allegedly dangerous citizens in the United States, given the array of existing federal criminal laws designed for the prosecution of those suspected of plotting, supporting, or committing terrorism.[35] Souter acknowledged that the AUMF could be interpreted to permit the military detention of soldiers captured on a battlefield during wartime based on customary law of war principles. But he refused to sanction Hamdi's detention as an "enemy combatant" because the administration had flouted those very principles by holding Hamdi incommunicado and denying him the required military hearing, conducted close in time and place to Hamdi's capture, to show that he was entitled to prisoner of war status or to release as an innocent civilian.[36] Souter, in short, criticized the president's reliance on the laws of war to augment his power as commander in chief while deliberately avoiding the constraints that the laws of war imposed on the exercise of that power. Or, put another way, what O'Connor sought to remedy through a habeas hearing in district court, Souter sought to nullify by denying any legal authority for Hamdi's military detention altogether.

The most sweeping rejection of the administration's position, however, came from Justice Scalia, ordinarily one of the Court's most conservative jurists. Scalia's opinion, which was joined by Justice John Paul Stevens, one of the Court's most liberal jurists, concluded that Congress could not authorize the military detention of an American citizen in the United States without suspending habeas corpus. Scalia's conception of habeas corpus differed from O'Connor's in the following respect. Habeas, Scalia said, did not simply guarantee a prisoner a meaningful judicial inquiry into the basis for his detention. Instead, habeas corpus secured the protections of a full criminal trial under the Bill of Rights unless Congress took the momentous step of suspending it.

The Constitution, Scalia said, permitted detention without criminal process in only a few well-recognized instances, such as civil commitment of the mentally ill and the wartime detention of enemy aliens. There was no precedent or basis for dispensing with that constitutional requirement in Hamdi's case, in which the prisoner was being held without trial based on suspicion of dangerousness. To the contrary, Scalia explained, suspected enemies of state had traditionally been subject to criminal prosecution for treason or other criminal offenses.[37] The Bush administration had deviated from that norm after the September 11 attacks by claiming the power to hold individuals indefinitely without trial as long as the president labeled them "enemy combatants." No longer would the government's accusations be tested through the criminal process. Henceforth, suspects could simply be incarcerated under the AUMF rather than charged, tried, and punished for their alleged crimes. Thus, whereas O'Connor sought to balance competing concerns of liberty and national security by giving prisoners habeas corpus hearings to challenge their military detention, Scalia drew a line in the sand, rejecting the possibility of detention without trial altogether. The habeas corpus Suspension Clause, he said, provided the basis for that line and barred the executive from holding Hamdi without charging him with a crime unless Congress exercised its emergency power of suspending the writ.

Yet Scalia's opinion was also exceedingly narrow. It applied only to American citizens in the United States. It did not apply to American citizens detained overseas, prompting O'Connor to criticize the opinion for creating a "perverse incentive" to keep American citizens abroad instead of bringing them to the United States when captured outside the country.[38] More important, Scalia's opinion did not apply to foreign nationals. It thus offered no solace to the thousands of foreign nationals held by the United States without charge or due process at Guantánamo, Bagram, and other offshore prisons.[39] The right to be free from unlawful detention, under Scalia's reasoning, was not a human right but a right that depended on a person's citizenship and location. This right, therefore, not only was confined to a limited category of people but also remained subject to manipulation by the executive who controlled where a prisoner would be held.

Clarence Thomas was the only justice to endorse the Bush administration's position.[40] He called for a hands-off policy in reviewing detentions during wartime, even when the detainee was an American citizen imprisoned in the United States. In his view, habeas corpus guaranteed review only of whether the president had legal authority to hold the prisoner as an "enemy combatant" and did not afford any review of the president's factual assertions. Thomas thus envisioned only the most minimal judicial involvement. Judges, he said, could not "second-guess determinations made by the President" in the "war on terrorism."[41] Thomas's view, however, garnered no support on the Court. And although *Hamdi*, like *Rasul*, left important questions unaddressed, it repudiated the Bush administration's claim of unreviewable executive detention power and reaffirmed the importance of habeas corpus as a check against arbitrary and illegal government action.

The third "enemy combatant" case before the Supreme Court that term, *Rumsfeld v. Padilla*, involved the boldest assertion of presidential power: the indefinite military detention of an American citizen arrested in the United States. The Court, however, avoided deciding whether Padilla's detention was legal. Instead, it resolved the case on narrow and technical grounds: that Padilla (or, more precisely, Padilla's lawyers, since Padilla was being held incommunicado at the time) had filed the habeas petition against the wrong person and in the wrong court. Writing for a majority of five, Chief Justice Rehnquist said that a prisoner must normally bring a habeas action against his immediate custodian and in the judicial district where he was confined. For Padilla, that meant suing the commander of the navy brig where he was imprisoned (not the secretary of defense or the president) and filing suit in federal district court in South Carolina, where the navy brig was located (not in New York where Padilla was originally detained as an "enemy combatant"). Rehnquist acknowledged an exception to this general rule when neither the prisoner's immediate custodian nor his place of confinement was within the jurisdiction of any district court—the very situation that the Court confronted in *Rasul*, in which both the Guantánamo detainees and their physical jailers were located outside the territorial jurisdiction of any federal court. But Rehnquist refused to relax that rule for alleged "enemy combatants" held inside the United States.[42] As a result, Padilla had to start all over again by filing a new habeas petition in South Carolina. So did Ali al-Marri, whose case was pending review by the Supreme Court at the time. Like Padilla, al-Marri had filed his habeas corpus petition in the district where he had originally been declared an "enemy combatant" (in al-Marri's case, the Central District of Illinois) rather than in the district where he was subsequently confined following his transfer to military custody (the District of South Carolina).[43] The *Padilla* decision thus meant that the government would be able to litigate these two test cases challenging the president's domestic military detention power in the Fourth Circuit, which included South Carolina and which was widely considered the most politically conservative federal circuit in the country. It also meant that definitive resolution of this most extraordinary assertion of executive detention authority—one that habeas corpus was designed to remedy promptly—would be further delayed as the two cases had to work their way through the federal courts once again.

Rehnquist's decision prompted a sharp dissent from Justice Stevens, which three other justices (Souter, Ginsburg, and Stephen Breyer) joined. Stevens criticized the Court for mechanically applying a general rule—that habeas actions should be brought against the jailer in the prisoner's present district of confinement—to a situation that cried out for an exception. The Court had relaxed this rule before, and the facts of Padilla's case demanded it do so again to fulfill the writ's historic purpose of affording relief from unlawful confinement. "At stake," Stevens insisted, "is nothing less than the essence of a free society."[44] Stevens focused his anger on the Bush administration's machinations and circumvention of the legal process. He chastised the administration for secretly whisking Padilla from New York to South Carolina and then using that transfer to delay judicial review of his detention by claiming that Padilla's lawyer had filed the habeas petition in the wrong court. Stevens also rebuked the government for holding Padilla incommunicado to extract information, warning that America "must not wield the tools of tyrants even to resist an assault by the forces of tyranny."[45]

When Padilla refiled his habeas petition in South Carolina, he would be entitled to at least the same judicial process that the Supreme Court had ordered for Hamdi, who had been seized in an overseas war zone, not arrested in the United States. Padilla thus would be granted access to his counsel and some opportunity to present facts in his defense. But the critical, threshold legal question of whether Padilla could be subject to military confinement based on his alleged criminal activity—a question that cut to the core of the president's detention powers in the "war on terror"—remained unresolved.[46]

The Battle for
Habeas Corpus Continues

On October 5, 2004, District Judge Robert G. Doumar issued an ultimatum. Yaser Hamdi's case had just been remanded from the Supreme Court. Under the Court's decision, the government could continue to detain Hamdi as an "enemy combatant" only if it proved that Hamdi was, in fact, a Taliban soldier who had fought against the United States in Afghanistan. The government and Hamdi's lawyers had already notified Judge Doumar that they were negotiating an agreement for Hamdi's return to Saudi Arabia. But Doumar was growing impatient with the delay. So he scheduled a hearing for the following week and, in advance of that hearing, ordered the government to turn over various documents to Hamdi's lawyers, including statements allegedly made by Hamdi during his interrogations so that Hamdi would have a fair chance to rebut the accusations against him.[1]

The day before the hearing was scheduled to take place, a U.S. military aircraft carrying Hamdi landed in Saudi Arabia. Hamdi then took a commercial flight to a city on Saudi Arabia's eastern coast where he was reunited with his family. In exchange for his release, Hamdi agreed to renounce his American citizenship and not to travel outside Saudi Arabia for five years or to the United States for ten years. The agreement did not require or request that Saudi Arabia detain him. To the contrary, the government stated that "considerations of United States national security do not require [Hamdi's] continued detention." After brief questioning by Saudi authorities following his arrival, Hamdi was released.[2]

The resolution of Hamdi's case illustrated the importance of habeas corpus. For nearly three years, the Bush administration had claimed Hamdi posed such a grave danger to the United States that he had to be detained without charge and without access to a lawyer. Indeed, the administration had said Hamdi was so dangerous that a federal judge must approve Hamdi's indefinite detention without even giving Hamdi himself a chance to be heard. Hamdi's release suggests that what the administration feared most was not Hamdi but a hearing before a judge who would scrutinize its evidence and inquire into Hamdi's treatment. The government's decision to release Hamdi to avoid that hearing raised serious doubts not only about the strength of its evidence that Hamdi was a member of the Taliban who fought against the United States in Afghanistan but also its evidence against hundreds of similarly situated prisoners at Guantánamo who were being held based on untested and unexamined hearsay allegations. In addition, it highlighted the government's fear that its abuse of detainees would be examined and exposed. The government responded in the Guantánamo cases by trying to prevent the habeas petitions from going forward and thus avoiding any meaningful judicial inquiry.

On July 7, 2004, just days after the Supreme Court issued *Rasul v. Bush*, Deputy Secretary of Defense Paul Wolfowitz announced the creation of the Combatant Status Review Tribunal (CSRT) for Guantánamo detainees. The CSRT purported to provide detainees a chance to contest their designation as "enemy combatants" before three-member panels of military officers.[3] But the CSRT's real purpose was to create the appearance of a process while rubber-stamping earlier decisions by the executive branch that the detainees were "enemy combatants," decisions that had already been made "through multiple levels of review by officers of the Department of Defense" and that the CSRT presumed were "genuine and accurate."[4]

The CSRT lacked every element of a fair process. Detainees remained shackled hand and foot for the entire hearing. They were denied the opportunity to see most of the allegations against them, which remained classified, or to confront their accusers. They also were denied all legal advice and assistance. Instead, they were provided with "personal representatives," who often proved worse than no representative at all. In most cases, these personal representatives met with a detainee once for no more than ninety minutes a week before the detainee's CSRT hearing. The bulk of the meeting, moreover, was spent discussing the nature of the CSRT process and the representative's role rather than the facts of the case itself. In more than one-third of the CSRT hearings, the personal representative made no substantive comments, and, in more than half the cases in which the representative did make substantive comments, he or she advocated *against* the detainee.[5]

The CSRT hearings amounted to mini–show trials. The government did not produce a single witness at any of the hundreds of CSRT hearings. It also failed to provide any documentary evidence to the detainees before their hearings in 96 percent of the cases. Instead, the government relied almost exclusively on unreliable hearsay, which often consisted of statements made by one detainee against another in order to curry favor with interrogators. The detainees, meanwhile, could not present evidence in their defense unless the tribunal deemed it "reasonably available." Typically, this meant no opportunity to present any evidence at all. The CSRT denied requests by detainees to produce evidence showing their innocence 74 percent of the time, including every request to produce a witness who was not already at Guantánamo. Other requests included contacting a close family member by telephone to verify a detainee's story; locating a detainee's passport to demonstrate his whereabouts; obtaining medical records from a hospital; and getting documents from court proceedings that exonerated the prisoner.[6]

In one case, the prisoner, Haji Bismullah, asked the CSRT to locate his brother, an Afghan government spokesman. Bismullah maintained that his brother would verify that he had fought alongside the United States to defeat the Taliban and had served as a local official in the transitional government in Afghanistan. The CSRT acknowledged that Bismullah's brother's testimony would be relevant but claimed that he could not be located. The CSRT also failed to consider letters and petitions sent to U.S. military and diplomatic officers from Afghan government officials and community elders refuting the government's claim that Bismullah was an enemy combatant.[7]

The CSRT frequently relied on evidence secured through torture and other coercion. Not only is such evidence "offensive to a civilized system of justice,"[8] but it is inherently unreliable because prisoners tend to fabricate or distort the truth to stop their suffering.[9] As the *Army Field Manual* on interrogations explains, the "use of torture and other illegal methods is a poor technique that yields unreliable results, may damage subsequent collection efforts, and can induce the source to say what he thinks the [interrogator] wants to hear."[10] Nonetheless, the CSRT routinely ignored detainees' claims that they had made statements under duress. The CSRT refused even to check or verify available evidence such as medical records that would have confirmed the use of harsh interrogation methods and thus undermined the reliability of the statements on which it was relying.[11] In one case, three British detainees falsely confessed under torture that they were "affiliated with" Osama bin Laden. One technique used against them was known as "short shackling." As the men explained, "We were forced to squat without a chair with our hands chained between our legs and chained to the floor. If we fell over, the chains would cut into our hands." The CSRT, however, did nothing to establish the veracity of the confession—a confession that British intelligence later determined was false.[12]

The CSRT also routinely relied on statements of other prisoners obtained through torture and abuse. Mohammed al-Qahtani, the victim of some of the most abusive interrogation tactics at Guantánamo, reportedly implicated thirty other detainees.[13] None of those detainees, however, ever knew that al-Qahtani had named them or had an opportunity to show that al-Qhatani's accusations were false. The CSRT similarly relied on statements obtained from prisoners tortured at CIA "black sites" without giving detainees a chance to examine or rebut the allegations.[14]

The CSRT's procedural shortcomings and reliance on torture were exacerbated by its embrace of sweeping detention authority. Wolfowitz's order defined "enemy combatant" far more broadly than the Supreme Court had done in *Hamdi* or than the law of war contemplated. *Hamdi* upheld the president's authority to detain a soldier captured on a battlefield in Afghanistan alongside Taliban forces fighting against the United States and its allies—what the government had itself previously described as "classic wartime detention."[15] The CSRT, however, broadly authorized the detention of any individual who was part of or who supported al Qaeda, the Taliban, or "associated forces" anywhere in the world.[16] This support, moreover, did not have to be intentional. Under the CSRT, the president could detain even "a little old lady in Switzerland who writes checks to what she thinks is a charity that helps orphans in Afghanistan but [what] really is a front to finance al-Qaeda activities."

The U.S. government insisted that it needed to detain "enemy combatants" to prevent them from "returning to the battlefield."[17] But its concept of the battlefield often bore little relation to reality. A study of the government's own unclassified data estimated that only a small percentage of Guantánamo detainees had actually fought on a battlefield.[18] The Bush administration also defined "returning to the battlefield" so broadly that it included detainees who had "returned to militant activities" by speaking out publicly against their mistreatment after leaving Guantánamo[19] or publishing an op-ed in the *New York Times* criticizing the United States' detention policy.[20]

The evidence to support the government's claim that a detainee was an "enemy combatant" was often shockingly weak, sometimes consisting only of vague assertions, hearsay statements of other detainees, and summaries of raw, unverified intelligence reports of questionable accuracy. When called on to defend its allegations, the government frequently did no better than to say that the allegations must be true since the government said they were, ultimately prompting one incredulous judge to invoke Lewis Carroll's poem *The Hunting of the Snark*: "I have said it thrice: What I tell you three times is true."[21] The CSRT thus helped institutionalize an open-ended, extrajudicial global detention system that dispensed with any concern for credible evidence or the costs of its own errors.

The Defense Department conducted its first CSRT hearing in August 2004. In most cases, the tribunal reached a decision the same day that the hearing began. Within two months, nearly all the CSRT hearings had been completed.[22] The CSRT found all except thirty-eight of the 558 detainees whose cases it considered to be "enemy combatants."[23] And in those thirty-eight cases, the CSRT concluded that the detainees were "no longer enemy combatants," that is, that they had ceased to be "enemy combatants," not that an error had been made in classifying them as such. Words like *innocent* and *mistake* were not in the CSRT's vocabulary.[24]

The Defense Department also instituted a second internal review procedure: the Administrative Review Board (ARB). But the ARB did nothing to remedy the CSRT's flaws. The ARB provided an annual hearing to determine whether those determined to be "enemy combatants" should remain in custody.[25] The ARB thus did not determine whether a detainee was an "enemy combatant" but, rather, assumed the detainee was an "enemy combatant" and decided only whether release was appropriate at that particular juncture. In practice, the ARB had little, if any, impact on whether a prisoner was released, a decision that typically turned on political factors and the pressures exerted by the detainee's home government rather than on an individualized assessment of the detainee himself. Thus, many detainees cleared to leave Guantánamo after ARB hearings continued to remain in custody. Meanwhile, dozens of detainees who were returned to their home countries or were declared eligible to leave were never cleared through the ARB process. Indeed, many of those detainees purportedly cleared for release by the ARB failed even to show up for their ARB hearings.[26]

In addition to creating bogus procedures like the CSRT and ARB, the Bush administration undermined the Guantánamo detainees' right to habeas corpus by resisting their access to counsel. Talking to a lawyer, the administration said, was a privilege. As such, it existed at "the Government's pleasure and discretion" and was subject to whatever limitations the government saw fit to impose.[27] Those limitations, the administration said, included real-time audio and visual monitoring and review of the contents of detainees' legal mail: flagrant violations of the attorney-client privilege that were intended to impede the development of attorney-client relationships necessary for effective representation.[28] "We were just throwing up these obstacles in the way of implementing the *Rasul* decision," a former navy lawyer remarked of the government's tactics.[29]

Federal district judge Colleen Kollar-Kotelly rejected the government's proposed limits on attorney-client communications, finding them inconsistent with the requirements of habeas corpus. The Supreme Court had ruled that Guantánamo detainees had the right to habeas corpus. If that right meant anything, Kollar-Kotelly asserted, detainees must have meaningful access to a lawyer. She emphasized that lawyers helped fulfill a core function of habeas: enabling prisoners to challenge the basis for their detention, including by providing them a "full opportunity" to present facts to a court.[30]

In September 2004, the first civilian attorney traveled to Guantánamo since the government started bringing prisoners there more than two-and-one-half years earlier.[31] Over time, hundreds of lawyers made the journey from the United States to Guantánamo, and their visits helped transform the detention center by shedding light on practices that had previously been shrouded in secrecy. No longer would the U.S. government be the only source of information about Guantánamo. Lawyers would henceforth help provide an alternative—and dramatically different—account of who was at Guantánamo, why they were being detained, and how they were being treated.[32] Media, human rights advocates, and others, including some law enforcement, military, and intelligence officials, also played an important role in making the pervasive abuses at Guantánamo public. And once released, a number of detainees spoke out about their mistreatment.[33] But lawyers remained the only nongovernment source of information about those still detained at Guantánamo, as the United States continued to refuse the requests of international bodies and organizations to meet with prisoners.[34] Lawyers' accounts, made possible by the habeas corpus process, helped alter public perception, exposing the lie that Guantánamo contained only the "worst of the worst" and that its prisoners were all being treated "humanely."

Lawyers, however, also operated under significant restrictions, limiting their ability to communicate with and advocate for their clients. These restrictions were codified in a protective order entered by federal district judges in every Guantánamo detainee habeas corpus case. Although the protective order provided for unmonitored attorney-client communications and established procedures for attorneys to visit detainees, it also stated that anything attorneys learned from their clients was presumptively classified and had to be submitted to and reviewed by a government "privilege team" before it could be made public.[35] Consequently, attorneys' notes taken during client meetings had to be submitted for review, and lawyers, who were based all over the United States, had to view any materials not approved for public disclosure at a secure facility near Washington, D.C., creating enormous logistical obstacles to effective representation. The protective order also prohibited lawyers from sharing any classified information with their clients, including the very information the government was relying on to detain them.[36]

These restrictions, however, paled in comparison with the government's other efforts to shut down the habeas corpus litigation. In October 2004, the Bush administration moved to dismiss all the habeas corpus petitions that had been filed in federal court, arguing that the detainees had no rights to enforce and that, in any event, the CSRT satisfied any rights they had. In essence, the government took the position that for Guantánamo detainees, habeas corpus meant nothing more than the right to file a piece of paper in court; once the clerk stamped it "received," the judge had no choice but to dismiss it, without conducting any inquiry into the government's allegations. In January 2005, two district judges in Washington, D.C., issued conflicting rulings on the basic issue of whether the courts had any meaningful role to play.

In one decision, District Judge Richard J. Leon endorsed the government's position. All the Supreme Court had decided in *Rasul*, Leon said, was that Guantánamo detainees could file habeas corpus petitions under the federal habeas statute. The Supreme Court, he reasoned, did not say that Guantánamo detainees had any rights to enforce. Leon then determined that in fact, Guantánamo detainees did not have any rights under the Constitution because they were aliens captured and held outside the United States. Furthermore, he maintained, any rights the detainees might have under international law, including the Geneva Conventions, could be enforced only by the political branches, and not by the courts.[37] Judge Leon also ratified the CSRT's broad definition of "enemy combatant," finding that the president could seize individuals anywhere in the world and detain them indefinitely, based on their alleged involvement in or association with terrorism.[38]

Judge Joyce Hens Green reached the opposite conclusion in an opinion issued just days later.[39] "It is clear," she said, "that Guantánamo Bay must be considered the equivalent of a U.S. territory in which fundamental constitutional rights apply."[40] Drawing on the logic of both the Insular Cases and *Rasul*, Judge Green concluded that "there cannot exist under the American flag any governmental authority untrammeled by the requirements of due process of law."[41] The only question then was whether the CSRT provided the fair hearing that the Constitution required be given to individuals held for years in a U.S. enclave like Guantánamo. And her answer was an emphatic no: the CSRT relied primarily on classified evidence that a detainee could not see or challenge, denied detainees the assistance of a lawyer, and freely considered evidence gained by torture and other coercion. In addition, Judge Green found that the CSRT's definition of "enemy combatant" swept too broadly, sanctioning detention based on mere association without any proof of direct involvement in hostilities or individual guilt.[42]

Judge Green pointed to the hearing transcript of Mustafa Ait Idr to illustrate the CSRT's Kafkaesque nature. The United States had accused Idr of "associat[ing] with a known Al Qaida operative" while living in Bosnia. How, Idr protested, could he possibly refute that accusation if the tribunal refused to tell him the operative's name? As Idr explained:

> Maybe I knew this person as a friend. Maybe it was a person that worked with me. Maybe it was a person that was on my team. But I do not know if this person is Bosnian, Indian or whatever. If you tell me the name, then I can respond and defend myself against the accusation.[43]

But the government gave Idr no information that would enable him to defend himself, relying instead on secret evidence that Idr had no chance to see or rebut.

The plight of another detainee, Murat Kurnaz, is similarly instructive. The United States said that Kurnaz was an "enemy combatant" because he attended a mosque in Bremen, Germany, which housed a branch of Jama'at-al-Tabliq, a missionary organization that allegedly supported terrorist organizations. It also claimed that Kurnaz had been friends with a suicide bomber and had traveled to Pakistan to attend a Jama'at-al-Tabliq school. But the United States never alleged that Kurnaz himself planned to be a suicide bomber or that he directly supported, let alone engaged in, terrorist activity. The government nevertheless sought to detain Kurnaz based on classified documents that he never had an opportunity to see or rebut. Judge Green not only found this one-sided proceeding unfair but, after examining the classified material herself, stated that the secret evidence "call[ed] into serious question the nature and thoroughness" of the government's determination that Kurnaz was an "enemy combatant."[44]

Portions of those classified documents were later made public in response to a Freedom of Information Act lawsuit. The disclosed portions revealed that in 2002 German and American intelligence officers had found no link between Kurnaz and terrorist cells or enemy fighters and had recommended his release. They also revealed that as early as 2003, the commanding general of the Pentagon's Criminal Investigation Task Force found no evidence of terrorist activity by Kurnaz. Nonetheless, Kurnaz remained behind bars at Guantánamo for three more years based on a CSRT determination that relied on the flimsiest of evidence. By way of example, that evidence included a U.S. brigadier general's statement that Kurnaz had once prayed while the U.S. national anthem was sung in the prison and had "asked how tall the basketball rim was" in the prison yard, which the general said suggested a desire to escape.[45]

Reliance on secret evidence, Judge Green found, was not the CSRT's only flaw. The tribunal also accepted evidence procured by torture and other coercion. In one case, an Egyptian-born Australian citizen named Mamdouh Habib claimed that a false confession had been wrung from him in Egypt, where he had been rendered following his seizure in Pakistan. Habib described being beaten routinely to the point of unconsciousness, locked in a room and forced to stand for hours while the room was gradually filled with water to a level just below his head, and suspended from a wall with his feet resting on the side of a large electrified cylindrical drum, forcing him to choose between the pain caused by hanging from his arms and electric shocks to his feet.[46] Even so, the CSRT simply relied on Habib's confession without conducting any further inquiry. The CSRT's refusal to examine Habib's allegations of torture was particularly shocking, since the U.S. State Department had repeatedly criticized Egypt for engaging in the practice.[47] Finally, after Habib filed a habeas corpus petition, and when it seemed that a federal judge might actually examine Habib's claims of mistreatment, the United States quickly sent Habib back to Australia to avoid scrutiny.[48]

Judge Green's ruling offered the promise of fair hearings. But those hearings did not take place. Instead, a few days later Judge Green granted the government's application to stay the proceedings pending appeal.[49] Judges in other habeas cases followed suit, issuing stays in their cases until the higher courts had an opportunity to address the government's latest effort to render habeas corpus a dead letter.[50] In the meantime, the detention of hundreds of prisoners went unexamined. By February 2005, the Guantánamo habeas corpus litigation had come to a virtual standstill and remained that way for almost three-and-one-half years while the executive branch, soon joined by Congress, fought tooth-and-nail to deny detainees meaningful access to the courts.

Although most Guantánamo detainees continued to languish without charge or trial, President Bush sought to prosecute a handful of Guantánamo prisoners in the military commissions he had created in his November 2001 executive order. One of those prisoners was Salim Ahmed Hamdan. A Yemeni citizen with a fifth-grade education, Hamdan had traveled to Afghanistan in 1996. Attracted by the idea of jihad, he had gravitated toward al Qaeda and Osama bin Laden. According to his lawyers, Hamdan was a simple-minded man from an impoverished background who was thankful for the money that al Qaeda paid him for working as a driver and mechanic but who generally remained in the dark about the organization's terrorist activities.[51] After 9/11, Hamdan fled and was seized by Afghan warlords near the Afghanistan-Pakistan border. They tied Hamdan with electrical wire and, a few days later, handed him over to the Americans for a $5,000 bounty. For the next six months, the United States held Hamdan at Bagram and Kandahar, where he was grossly mistreated, before transferring him to Guantánamo in May 2002.[52]

In July 2003, Bush announced his intention to try Hamdan and five other Guantánamo detainees for violations of the laws of war.[53] That December, Lieutenant Commander Charles D. Swift, a navy defense lawyer, was appointed to represent Hamdan.[54] Swift's instructions from superior officers were to negotiate a deal, not to advocate zealously for his client, as JAG lawyers were bound and trained to do. The Bush administration had deliberately chosen for prosecution detainees who, it believed, would plead guilty and thereby give some legitimacy to the military commission process and the Guantanamo detention system generally. But Swift fought back, demanding that Hamdan be afforded the right to a speedy trial under the Uniform Code of Military Justice (UCMJ). When the legal adviser to the convening authority for the commissions refused, Hamdan's lawyers turned to the federal courts. In April 2004, they filed a petition for habeas corpus challenging the legality of the military commission process itself.[55]

The government moved to dismiss Hamdan's petition, claiming that the courts lacked jurisdiction to hear it. The Supreme Court's decision in *Rasul* two months later made clear that federal courts had jurisdiction over the petition under the habeas statute. So the administration changed tactics, trying to move forward with Hamdan's military trial quickly before his habeas challenge could be resolved. In July 2004, the president formally charged Hamdan, claiming that he had conspired with al Qaeda to attack civilians, commit murder, and engage in terrorism. The indictment further alleged that Hamdan had acted as Osama bin Laden's "bodyguard and personal driver," had transported weapons on al Qaeda's behalf, and had received weapons training at an al Qaeda sponsored camp.[56] It did not accuse Hamdan of having any command responsibilities, playing a leadership role, or planning any terrorist acts. Instead, the indictment charged only the offense of conspiracy, an offense historically prosecuted in civilian courts under federal criminal law, not in military tribunals under the laws of war.

Hamdan's habeas petition did not argue questions of guilt or innocence but something more basic: that the military commission established by presidential edict did not comply with federal statutes or international treaties and thus lacked the power to try him. District Judge James Robertson, himself a former naval officer, agreed.[57] In November 2004, Robertson enjoined military commission proceedings in Hamdan's case. He ruled that the commission was invalid because there had been no determination by a competent tribunal that Hamdan was subject to trial by military commission—a determination required under the Third Geneva Convention. Without such a determination, Robertson insisted, Hamdan must be treated like all other prisoners of war and therefore could be tried only by court-martial, the system the United States used to try its own service members.[58] Robertson further concluded that even if a competent tribunal were to find Hamdan eligible for trial by a military commission, Bush's commission still could not try him because it lacked important safeguards, including a defendant's right to be present at his own trial.[59]

In July 2005, a three-judge panel of the U.S. Court of Appeals for the District of Columbia Circuit reversed Judge Robertson's ruling. The appeals court adopted a far more deferential view of the president's creation of military commissions and his interpretation of the Geneva Conventions. Two judges ruled that the Geneva Conventions did not apply to al Qaeda or the "war on terrorism," endorsing President Bush's earlier determination that he was free to treat suspected terrorists as "enemy combatants" while simultaneously denying them any protections under the treaties and customs that make up the laws of war.[60] The third judge, Stephen Williams, joined the ruling but disagreed in one notable respect. Williams found that Common Article 3 of the Geneva Conventions applied to the armed conflict with al Qaeda even if other provisions of the Geneva Conventions did not and that this provision explicitly prohibited trials except by "a regularly constituted court affording all the judicial guarantees which are recognized as indispensable by a civilized people." Yet Williams also concluded that enforcement of Common Article 3 must be left to the political branches, not to the courts, and thus joined the panel's decision to dismiss Hamdan's habeas challenge.[61]

Hamdan petitioned the Supreme Court for review, and in November 2005, the Court agreed to hear his case.[62] The administration and its allies in Congress sprang into action. The following month Congress enacted legislation threatening to deprive the Court of its power to hear Hamdan's appeal. The new law, entitled the Detainee Treatment Act (DTA), amended the federal habeas statute to eliminate habeas corpus rights for detainees at Guantánamo.[63]

Only once before had Congress tried to take away the Supreme Court's power to hear a habeas corpus appeal. In that case, the Court upheld Congress's withdrawal of its appellate jurisdiction under an 1867 statute to consider a habeas challenge brought by a newspaper publisher and former Confederate soldier who had been jailed by the military in the Reconstruction South. The Court, however, left open the possibility of Supreme Court review by another means: an "original" habeas petition filed under the 1789 Judiciary Act.[64] This time, however, there was no alternative avenue for seeking habeas relief. Instead, Congress instituted a more limited form of judicial review under the DTA that excluded, for example, consideration of any factual determinations by the military commission and the commission's compliance with international law. Moreover, the DTA said that this limited review could take place only after the military commission trial had taken place.[65] The DTA would thus prevent precisely the type of challenge that Hamdan sought to bring and that habeas corpus had long secured: a challenge to the power of a military commission to try a person in the first instance.[66] Also, since only those detainees sentenced to a term of imprisonment of ten years or more had the right to invoke the DTA's limited review mechanism, those sentenced to lesser terms could be denied all court review.[67]

The DTA also threatened to terminate the habeas corpus petitions of the hundreds of other prisoners at Guantánamo who were being held without charge. By recognizing Guantánamo detainees' habeas corpus rights, *Rasul* had sought to ensure a meaningful judicial process. The DTA purported to eliminate that process and replace it with an inferior one: narrow review by an appeals court of the sham CSRT hearings. As written, the DTA allowed the D.C. Circuit Court of Appeals to consider only whether the CSRT had followed its own standards and procedures and whether those standards and procedures were constitutional. The appeals court therefore could never do what a district court could do on habeas corpus: hold a hearing, consider evidence presented by both sides, and rule on disputed facts. Indeed, it was unclear whether the appeals court even had the power to order a prisoner's release from unlawful detention, traditionally a *sine qua non* of habeas corpus. In addition, under the DTA, no prisoner could challenge his mistreatment or conditions of confinement. Nor could he seek review of his transfer from Guantánamo to another country, even if he faced a substantial risk of torture in that country.

In short, the DTA sought to prevent federal courts from playing a meaningful role in reviewing the detention, treatment, trial, or transfer of prisoners at Guantánamo. And while the DTA's court-stripping provision applied only to Guantánamo, it implicitly bolstered the administration's contention that foreign nationals held elsewhere outside the United States—and in territory over which the United States' control was less permanent or complete than at Guantánamo—had no habeas rights.

The debate over the DTA helped expose the falsehoods and distortions at the heart of the "war on terror." Leading supporters of the DTA's habeas-stripping amendment, such as U.S. Senators Lindsey Graham (R-SC) and Jon Kyle (R-AZ), alternatively characterized the Guantánamo detainees as classic military combatants, on the one hand, and hardened terrorists, on the other. The detainees, Graham and other lawmakers said, were just like enemy soldiers from past wars. If the tens of thousands of German and Japanese prisoners of war in the United States did not have access to the federal courts during World War II, they reasoned, why should today's "enemy combatants" enjoy such access? "Never in the history of the law of armed conflict has an enemy combatant, irregular component, or POW been given access to civilian court systems to question military authority and control, except here," Graham remarked, referring to the Supreme Court's decision in *Rasul*.[68] At the same time, Graham and other supporters of the DTA observed, all the Guantánamo detainees were terrorists who had to be punished for their misdeeds, thus likening them not to soldiers but to alleged criminals ordinarily charged and tried in the regular civilian courts.

But wartime prisoners had not always been barred from U.S. courts, as cases like *Quirin* and *Milligan* showed.[69] The United States, moreover, had previously limited the military detention of combatants to those affiliated with nation-states. Thus, not only was the effort to detain suspected terrorists as "combatants" entirely new, but the definition of the "enemy combatant" category was incredibly broad and elastic. Furthermore, the past conflicts to which Graham and others referred typically did not involve the same type of factual disputes over who could be detained. Battlefields were geographically defined, and soldiers wore uniforms and carried arms openly to signify their military status. In more recent conflicts in which it became more difficult to tell friend from foe, such as the Vietnam War, the United States implemented additional safeguards to help prevent errors. In addition, wars previously had a clear ending point: the cessation of hostilities or the signing of a peace treaty between governments. By contrast, the very nature of terrorism—the difficulty of determining the enemy, the absence of defined battlefields, and the potentially permanent nature of the conflict—increased both the likelihood and the costs of mistaken detention. Terrorism, in short, demanded greater process, not less, and a more robust judicial role.

In addition, characterizing Guantánamo detainees as terrorists suggested that they all had been found guilty of a crime. In fact, only a handful of detainees had ever been charged with an offense, and those detainees all had been charged in the inferior military commissions, not the regular civilian courts or military courts-martial. So the government alternatively claimed that the detainees were combatants held for the nonpunitive purpose of preventing their "return to battlefield." Supporters of the DTA thus manipulated words like *combatant* and *terrorist* to justify eliminating habeas corpus and dispensing with the protections of both the criminal justice system and the laws of war.

Assuming that all the Guantánamo detainees were terrorists also begged a critical question presented by the habeas cases: whether the detainees were, in fact, who the government said they were. Graham and Kyl's suggestion that the Guantánamo detainees' habeas petitions raised frivolous claims about conditions of confinement was simply false.[70] Those prisoners who were challenging their treatment were not complaining about Internet access and mail delivery but were challenging their torture, prolonged isolation, and other gross mistreatment. And all the prisoners who sought habeas relief were contesting the right of the government to detain them in the first place.

On November 10, 2005, Graham's amendment to eliminate federal court jurisdiction over Guantánamo detainee habeas corpus petitions passed the Senate and was added to the Defense Authorization Act.[71] When several lawmakers voiced concerns about the amendment's impact on pending habeas cases, Senators Graham, Kyl, and Carl Levin (D-MI) sponsored another amendment altering the provision's effective date.[72] On December 30, 2005, President Bush signed the Detainee Treatment Act into law, including the habeas-stripping Graham-Kyl-Levin amendment.

Ironically, an original impetus behind the DTA had been to strengthen protections against detainee abuse. Revelations about mistreatment at Abu Ghraib, Bagram, secret CIA prisons, and Guantánamo had prompted concerns among lawmakers, including Senator John McCain (R-AZ), a former torture victim, that the Bush administration was exploiting what it viewed as a lacuna in the law. The administration had argued that while U.S. criminal law prohibited torture (which it defined narrowly to exclude "enhanced interrogation techniques" like waterboarding), no law barred the lesser forms of abuse known as cruel, inhuman, or degrading treatment (CID) if committed against foreign nationals held abroad. The administration asserted that existing prohibitions against CID in human rights treaties, such as the Convention against Torture and the International Covenant on Civil and Political Rights, did not apply to Guantánamo or to any other territory outside the United States. At the same time, the administration claimed that because the Guantánamo detainees were "unlawful combatants," they also had no protections under the Geneva Conventions, including Common Article 3, which prohibited even a broader range of mistreatment than the Convention against Torture. To remedy this perceived gap, the DTA prohibited the "cruel, inhuman, or degrading treatment or punishment" of any prisoner in U.S. custody or control, "regardless of nationality or physical location."[73]

But the DTA's prohibition on CID came at a high a price: the elimination of habeas corpus and the ability of courts to remedy illegal detention and abuse. Moreover, the DTA's ban on CID was weakened in several ways. The DTA, for example, failed to bar the use of evidence gained through torture and other mistreatment. It said that in future Guantánamo cases, the CSRT must determine whether statements derived from a detainee were "obtained as a result of coercion" and must assess the "probative value (if any)" of those statements. Those future tribunals, however, would inquire whether evidence had been gained through coercion only "to the extent practicable" and could still rely on such coerced evidence if they chose to.[74] This minimal requirement also did not apply to the CSRT hearings that had previously been conducted for the hundreds of prisoners at Guantánamo. The post-9/11 system of detention based on evidence gained through torture and other coercion thus remained firmly in place.

In addition, the Bush administration took steps to nullify the DTA's ban on CID. The DTA defined CID by incorporating the test under the Due Process Clause of the Fifth Amendment to the Constitution, which asked whether the particular conduct in question "shocks the conscience."[75] The administration continued to maintain that an interrogation tactic would not "shock the conscience" unless undertaken for the specific purpose of inflicting pain, as opposed to gathering information to prevent a terrorist attack. Under this theory, officials could continue to justify almost any tactic, no matter how brutal. This was precisely the view embraced by two secret memos drafted in May 2005 by the Office of Legal Counsel, before the DTA was enacted, to create a permanent loophole around any effort by Congress to restrict the president's latitude to interrogate prisoners in the "war on terrorism" and to preclude liability for past abuse.[76] If this were not enough, Bush also issued a statement when he signed the DTA into law that said he would interpret the

DTA's ban on CID in light of his "constitutional authority . . . to supervise the unitary executive branch and as Commander in Chief and consistent with the constitutional limitations on judicial power."[77] This signing statement—one of many that Bush issued—reflected his view that the president could override federal laws if he believed it necessary for national security.[78]

The detention and treatment of prisoners at Guantánamo cried out for meaningful judicial review. Yet the DTA threatened to emasculate that review by eliminating habeas corpus. The DTA's ban on CID, meanwhile, remained vulnerable to continued manipulation by an administration determined to circumvent it. Congress had taken one step forward and two steps back.

If court-stripping legislation was one way to avoid meaningful judicial scrutiny, eleventh-hour action by executive branch officials was another. In Yaser Hamdi's case, this meant abruptly releasing the prisoner to avoid a habeas corpus hearing. In Jose Padilla's case, it meant bringing criminal charges after three and one-half years of military imprisonment to avoid Supreme Court review of the president's claim of sweeping domestic detention power.

Previously, the Supreme Court had declined to address the merits of Padilla's challenge because it ruled that he had mistakenly sought relief from a federal court in New York rather than in South Carolina where he was confined as an "enemy combatant." Padilla promptly refiled his habeas petition in South Carolina and argued once again that the president could not detain him without criminal charge and trial.[79] This time, the district judge agreed with Padilla.[80] The U.S. Court of Appeals for the Fourth Circuit reversed that decision, upholding the president's power to imprison Padilla in military custody as an "enemy combatant."

Judge Michael Luttig's opinion for the Fourth Circuit began by emphasizing the "exceedingly important question" presented by the case: the indefinite military detention of an American citizen arrested in the United States.[81] Judge Luttig explained that the president had authority to hold Padilla as an "enemy combatant" because, before coming to the United States to engage in terrorism, Padilla had fought in Afghanistan alongside the Taliban and al Qaeda. (This was a newly minted allegation that the government added after the first go-round in the Supreme Court to bolster its case by making Padilla seem more like a traditional soldier and his military detention less radical.) Consequently, Luttig said, Padilla could be detained for the duration of hostilities "to prevent his return to the battlefield."[82] The fact that Padilla had been arrested at Chicago's O'Hare International Airport, rather than captured on a battlefield in Afghanistan, did not alter the president's power to hold him as an "enemy combatant." Instead, Judge Luttig asserted, Padilla was just like the German saboteurs from *Quirin*, who had been arrested in Florida and New York and tried by a military commission rather than a civilian court. The fact that Padilla was being detained in connection with a global armed conflict against al Qaeda and other terrorist organizations rather than a war against another nation, as in *Quirin*, made no difference.

Padilla sought Supreme Court review. But two days before its response to Padilla's certiorari petition was due, the government announced that it was indicting Padilla on terrorism-related charges in federal court in Miami. Those charges did not contain any of the accusations on which the president had relied in detaining Padilla as an "enemy combatant." [83] Instead, the indictment placed Padilla at the fringe of a nebulous conspiracy during the 1990s to provide support for Muslim struggles in Bosnia, Kosovo, and Chechnya.[84]

In announcing the indictment, Attorney General Alberto Gonzales referred only obliquely to Padilla's prior military detention, noting that the case began as a "classic intelligence investigation" and that the criminal justice system represented "one of the tools" that the president had at his disposal to combat terrorism. Gonzales never explained why the administration decided to employ that "tool" only when the Supreme Court was on the verge of considering the legality of its other "tool": indefinite military detention. But Gonzales did not need to say anything. The administration clearly feared that the Court would reject its position and thus undercut a main pillar of its post-9/11 detention regime: the authority to seize individuals anywhere in the world and hold them indefinitely without charge or trial as part of the global "war on terror."

Gonzales also failed to mention why the United States did not include the most serious accusations against Padilla in the indictment. Other administration officials, however, acknowledged that those accusations had been derived from statements by al Qaeda suspects Abu Zubaydah and Khalid Sheikh Mohammed, both of whom had been tortured at secret CIA prisons. Unlike in a CSRT or military commission, the government could not simply launder coerced evidence in a federal criminal prosecution.[85] If the indictment's timing showed the lengths to which the administration would go to avoid judicial review of its "enemy combatant" detentions, its content highlighted how thoroughly these detentions were permeated by torture and other abuse.

The administration's gamesmanship did not please the Fourth Circuit. After charging Padilla, the government asked the appeals court to approve Padilla's transfer from military to civilian custody to clear the way for his prosecution. The Fourth Circuit refused. In a sharply worded opinion, Judge Luttig criticized the government for creating the impression that it was deliberately circumventing Supreme Court review.[86] That Padilla's case was imbued with such tremendous public importance, Luttig said, made the government's actions all the more troubling. How could the government claim that it was "imperative" to America's security to hold Padilla as an "enemy combatant" for three and one-half years, only to bring criminal charges when the nation's highest court was finally poised to rule on the matter?[87] Even those who agreed with the government's underlying position, as Luttig did, recognized that the government's conduct tarnished the integrity of the judicial process.

Although the Supreme Court quickly approved Padilla's transfer to civilian custody, the Court took more than four months to decide whether to grant review of the legality of his military detention. Ordinarily, such a change in circumstances would have provided a strong reason to deny review, since Padilla had effectively received the relief he had sought in his habeas petition: the right not to be detained without criminal charge. But Padilla maintained that the Supreme Court should still hear his challenge because the president insisted that he could redesignate Padilla an "enemy combatant" if he were acquitted at trial and that he could continue to detain others like Padilla as "enemy combatants" in the future. The Supreme Court ultimately declined to hear Padilla's case. Three justices (Roberts, Stevens, and Kennedy) did, however, take the unusual step of issuing an opinion expressing concerns about the changes in Padilla's custody status, while three other justices (Breyer, Ginsburg, and Souter) said that the Court should have heard the case (Four votes are required for a grant of certiorari.).[88] Thus, while habeas corpus had helped end Padilla's military imprisonment, it had not produced a definitive answer to the underlying question about the scope of the president's detention power.

The federal criminal prosecution of Padilla went forward in Miami. In August 2007, the jury returned a verdict convicting Padilla and his codefendants of all counts, including conspiring to commit illegal violent acts outside the United States and providing material support to terrorists. District Judge Marcia G. Cooke sentenced Padilla to seventeen years and four months in prison. Cooke, however, rejected the government's argument that Padilla should be given a life sentence, noting that that there was no evidence linking Padilla and the other defendants to specific acts of terrorism. Cooke also gave Padilla credit for the time he had spent in military detention, over the government's objection.[89]

The Bush administration touted Padilla's conviction as a victory for its detention policy. But the conviction highlighted the policy's flaws. It demonstrated, once again, that federal courts could successfully prosecute, convict, and punish those who planned or committed terrorist acts and could do so without sacrificing the rights central to America's Constitution and values. The criminal justice system, though not perfect, still proved highly effective, capable of handling even the most challenging cases. The claimed need for a "new paradigm" of indefinite military detention to fight terrorism, by contrast, seemed increasingly like smoke and mirrors.

While the Bush administration succeeded in avoiding Supreme Court review in Padilla's case, it failed to do so in Hamdan's. In June 2006, the Court issued its five-to-three ruling in *Hamdan v. Rumsfeld*, invaliding the military commissions established under Bush's November 2001 order.[90] If *Rasul* had affirmed right of Guantánamo detainees to habeas corpus, *Hamdan* helped show why that right mattered.

In an opinion by Justice Stevens, the Court rejected the government's contention that the DTA had stripped it of its power to hear Hamdan's appeal. It concluded that Congress had repealed jurisdiction only over future habeas corpus cases, not habeas cases pending at the time of the DTA's passage, such as Hamdan's. This determination was based on a close reading of the compromise Graham-Kyl-Levin amendment, which had altered the act's effective date. It also reflected the more general principle that courts must avoid interpreting statutes to repeal habeas corpus jurisdiction as long as another reading is fairly possible. While the Court did not say that Congress lacked the power to eliminate habeas corpus review for Guantánamo detainees, it indicated that Congress would have to speak in the clearest terms to accomplish that momentous end. As Justice Souter remarked during oral argument, the Court would not assume Congress "inadvertently" took the grave step of suspending habeas corpus in enacting the DTA, which would be "just about the most stupendously significant act that the Congress of the United States can take."[91]

Turning to the merits of Hamdan's appeal, the Court found that the president's military commissions suffered from two fatal flaws. First, the commissions deviated impermissibly from courts-martial procedures, including by denying defendants the right to be present at their own trial[92] and by allowing the use of unreliable hearsay statements, including statements obtained through coercion.[93] There was neither any principled basis nor any need, the Court said, for creating a separate ad hoc trial system for terrorism suspects that lacked the established safeguards of military courts-martial. Second, the commissions violated Common Article 3 of the Geneva Conventions, which requires that all trials be conducted by a "regularly constituted court affording all the judicial guarantees which are recognized as indispensable by civilized peoples."[94] Because the United States' "regularly constituted" military courts are courts-martial, and because the military commissions fell far short of courts-martial standards, the Court said, the commissions violated Common Article 3.[95] Four justices found an additional problem: conspiracy, the offense with which Hamdan had been charged, did not violate the law of war and thus could not be prosecuted by a military commission, even if the commission's procedures had been fair.[96]

Hamdan was an important decision on several levels. It rejected the asymmetrical use of the law of war to assert sweeping military jurisdiction over terrorism cases while avoiding the restrictions that the law of war places on the trial and treatment of detainees. *Hamdan* also bolstered the broader constitutional system of checks and balances, cautioning that even during wartime the president cannot "disregard limitations that Congress has, in proper exercise of its own war powers, placed on [the president's] powers."[97] Here, Congress in the UCMJ had required that any military commission conform largely to courts-martial procedures. Just as important, *Hamdan* vindicated the judiciary's role in that system, showing how courts could serve as a bulwark against illegal executive action by exercising their habeas corpus review. As Justice Stevens wrote in striking down the president's military tribunals, "the Executive is bound to comply with the Rule of Law that prevails in this jurisdiction."[98]

By finding that all detainees were protected by Common Article 3, the Court also dealt an important blow to the United States' post-9/11 global detention system. That system had assumed that individuals held as "enemy combatants" in the "war on terrorism" had no rights and, consequently, that their treatment remained a matter of executive discretion. This, in turn, opened the door to the torture and other abuse that spread like a virus through lawless enclaves from Guantánamo to secret CIA "black sites." *Hamdan* helped halt that virus's spread by reaffirming that no person in U.S. custody was beyond the law. At a minimum, the Court said, Common Article 3 applied to all prisoners in U.S. custody during wartime. It prohibited not only unfair trials by military commissions but also "outrages upon personal dignity," including "humiliating and degrading treatment."[99] Without actually saying so, the Supreme Court had made clear that harsh interrogation methods—including those that did not rise to the level of torture—were illegal and that any official who engaged in them exposed himself to criminal prosecution under the War Crimes Act.[100]

Hamdan, however, had several limitations, all of which soon became apparent. It had invalidated Bush's power to try terrorist suspects through his military commissions, but not his power to detain them indefinitely without charge. Since only a handful of Guantánamo prisoners had actually been charged before a military commission and since there was no requirement that any prisoner be charged or tried at any point, the government could circumvent *Hamdan* simply by continuing to hold prisoners without charge. As Guantánamo's commander explained, as long as the military could continue to detain people as "enemy combatants," *Hamdan's* practical impact would be "negligible."[101]

Hamdan also rested on the president's failure to seek appropriate authorization from Congress. It therefore did not bar Congress from creating new military commissions in the future. Similarly, although the Court ruled that the DTA had not eliminated habeas corpus review over Guantánamo detainee cases, the Court did not say that Congress lacked the power to eliminate this review through new legislation. In resting its ruling on statutory rather than constitutional grounds, the Court thus set the stage for another legislative battle. Once again, the Bush administration would seek congressional approval for broad powers to detain and try terrorist suspects without habeas corpus. This time, however, the powers it claimed would be even more far-reaching.

Tackling Prisons beyond the Law

Guantánamo Revisited

On September 6, 2006, President Bush delivered a nationally televised speech describing the current state of U.S. detention policy. He began by recalling the tragic events that had occurred almost five years to the date and reiterating his promise to do everything within his power—and "within America's laws"—to prevent another terrorist attack. The president then publicly acknowledged for the first time that the CIA operated a "separate program" of secret imprisonment, although the program's existence had been widely reported for years. The president said that the program targeted so-called high-value detainees like Abu Zubaydah, Khalid Sheikh Mohammed (KSM), and Ramzi bin al-Shibh. He also said that information wrested from these men through the CIA's secret detention program had helped prevent terrorist attacks and saved American lives. Now that the questioning had been completed, Bush explained, the program's remaining fourteen prisoners could be moved "into the open." They would be transferred to Guantánamo and brought "to justice." The president acknowledged that aggressive interrogation methods had been used. But, he assured the American public, "the United States does not torture. It's against our laws, and it's against our values."[1]

The president then told the country that the Supreme Court's decision in *Hamdan v. Rumsfeld* had imposed constraints on the United States' ability to confront terrorism and put the nation at risk. So Bush announced that he was sending new legislation to Congress to "clarify the rules for our personnel fighting the war on terror." This legislation not only would establish new military commissions but also would reinterpret the United States' obligations under the Geneva Conventions to allow the government to resume the secret CIA detention program without fear of exposing officials to criminal liability. And the legislation would seek—once again—to eliminate habeas corpus rights for those the administration designated as "enemy combatants."[2]

As political propaganda, the president's speech was a success. In one stroke, he put opponents on the defensive, seizing the high ground in the fight against terrorism and telling the American public that he was protecting both its values and its safety. Secret detention and harsh interrogation methods, he suggested, not only were vital to the nation's security; they also were legal. The United States did not engage in torture but merely in aggressive tactics that were necessary to produce valuable information and that remained within the letter, if not the spirit, of the law. Also, by transferring to Guantánamo the handful of detainees allegedly responsible for the 9/11 attacks, such as KSM, Bush breathed new life into the myth that most prisoners at Guantánamo were dangerous terrorists.

But Bush's speech was inaccurate and misleading. Guantánamo did not "bring prisoners to justice." Of the nearly eight hundred men imprisoned there since 2002, only a handful had ever been charged with any crime, and most would never be brought to trial in any court, let alone in a legitimate forum. Also, even based on the government's own untested allegations, most prisoners were not dangerous terrorists, and many were wholly innocent.

The speech also misled the American people about torture. Bush suggested that the government needed to keep "specific [interrogation] methods secret"; otherwise, terrorists would "learn how to resist questioning." But the United States' use of waterboarding, cold cell, and other forms of torture was already widely known. The real reason for the secrecy was to cover up conduct that was not only embarrassing but potentially criminal.

In addition, the speech created the false impression that the Bush administration had terminated the secret CIA detention program. But just days before Bush's speech, the Justice Department had issued secret legal opinions concluding that the conditions of confinement in CIA prisons complied with both federal law and Common Article 3 of the Geneva Conventions.[3] And the president reserved the right to continue the program, which he continued to defend as "small, carefully run, lawful, and highly productive," and to use "enhanced interrogation techniques" in the future.[4]

The Bush administration, in short, transformed its defeat in *Hamdan* into an opportunity to justify to the American public extrajudicial detention, military commissions, and torture and to institutionalize those practices through new legislation. Following Bush's speech, the focus shifted to Capitol Hill, as lawmakers began to debate the administration's proposals to restrict habeas corpus, establish new military commissions, rewrite America's obligations under the Geneva Conventions, and insulate government officials from liability for past abuses. On September 29, Congress passed the Military Commissions Act (MCA), and the next month the president signed the bill into law.[5]

The MCA resurrected military commissions to try foreign nationals in the "war on terror," providing the congressional sanction that the Supreme Court in *Hamdan* had said was lacking. The new commissions were authorized to try a wide range of offenses that traditionally had been treated as criminal offenses and not war crimes, such as conspiracy and "material support" for terrorism.[6] The MCA did improve on the previous commissions, for example, by giving a defendant a partial right to be present at his trial and by affording him a greater opportunity to examine and respond to the government's evidence.[7] But the commissions continued to suffer from flaws that undermined their fairness and integrity. For example, the commissions still limited a defendant's access to exculpatory information.[8] They also allowed for the admission of coerced evidence, including evidence gained by cruel, inhuman, or degrading treatment, as long as the evidence was obtained before the passage of the Detainee Treatment Act of 2005—precisely the period during which the worst abuses had occurred.[9] Furthermore, even though the commissions now formally prohibited evidence gained by torture, the Bush administration continued to define torture so narrowly as to render that prohibition all but meaningless. Statements wrung from other detainees by means of physical and mental abuse also could be laundered through lax evidentiary rules or could escape scrutiny altogether if classified as intelligence "sources" or "methods."[10]

The MCA, however, did more than revive military commissions; it sought to legitimize and institutionalize other key features of the post-9/11 global detention system. While the MCA paid lip service to the United States' Geneva Convention obligations, it gave the president unilateral authority to interpret the conventions while hindering their enforcement in the courts by prohibiting individuals from invoking them in habeas corpus or other judicial proceedings.[11] The MCA also sought to foreclose criminal prosecution for past breaches of the Geneva Conventions and to limit the risk of prosecutions in the future by confining liability under the War Crimes Act to a specific list of "grave breaches" of Common Article 3 set forth in the legislation. Even though that list included cruel and inhuman treatment as well as torture, the MCA limited the definition of such treatment to conduct that caused substantial risk of death, physical disfigurement, and organ loss or impairment. It also excluded degrading and humiliating treatment entirely.[12] The Bush administration, meanwhile, continued to maintain that interrogation methods such as stress positions, religious and sexual humiliation, and sleep deprivation did not violate Common Article 3.[13] The MCA thus helped prepare the groundwork for a subsequent presidential order that both reinitiated the CIA's secret detention program and sanctioned the continued use of highly coercive interrogation methods.[14] Once again, the Justice Department supplied legal cover, concluding that the CIA's use of various "enhanced interrogation techniques," including prolonged sleep deprivation (of up to ninety-six hours), dietary manipulation, and physical force, did not violate Common Article 3 or the War Crimes Act.[15]

The MCA also sought to eliminate habeas corpus, which had proved to be the single most effective check against arbitrary detention and abuse. Unlike the DTA, however, the MCA did not limit the habeas repeal to Guantánamo. Instead, it purported to eliminate habeas corpus for any foreign national the president designated an "enemy combatant."[16] The Bush administration subsequently interpreted the repeal in the broadest manner possible, arguing that its bar on habeas jurisdiction extended not only to foreign nationals at Guantánamo and other prisons outside the United States but also to those arrested and detained inside the country. In the administration's view, a legal immigrant could be seized by the military at home, at school, or his or her place of work and be imprisoned without access to a lawyer or a court if the president determined that he or she was an "enemy combatant." In addition, the MCA barred "any other action" by an alleged "enemy combatant," thus preventing detainees from receiving any compensation for illegal detention or torture they had suffered in the past.[17]

Lawmakers once again justified the restrictions on habeas corpus by distorting the truth. They portrayed the Guantánamo prisoners as soldiers "captured on the battlefield," even though many had not been captured on or near a battlefield.[18] The familiar rhetoric about legal proceedings wasting government resources and interfering with the "day-to-day operation" of the military attempted to mask a much darker theme: that courts and lawyers had no place in "war on terrorism" and that the president must have unfettered power to detain and interrogate in the name of national security.[19] Or as one senator candidly explained, the purpose of the MCA was "to get the lawyers out of Guantánamo Bay."[20]

Opponents denounced the MCA as a violation of cherished principles. Senator Russ Feingold (D-WI) lamented that America would look back on the MCA as "a stain on our nation's history."[21] The *New York Times* called it "our generation's version of the Alien and Sedition Acts."[22] After the MCA's passage, several bills were introduced in Congress to repeal the provisions of the act eliminating habeas corpus. But none gained sufficient support to overcome an expected filibuster or a presidential veto, and the focus shifted again to the courts.[23]

The first four years after the 9/11 attacks had largely pitted the executive branch against the judiciary in the battle over habeas corpus, other constitutional safeguards, and America's compliance with international law. The Detainee Treatment and Military Commissions Acts altered that dynamic. By 2006, majorities in Congress had twice approved key aspects of the post-9/11 detention regime. Some supporters of that regime even argued that it was the Supreme Court, and not the executive, that had engaged in a "stunning power grab," which Congress rectified in the MCA by restoring the president's command over the conduct of the "war on terrorism."[24] If previous Supreme Court decisions like *Rasul* and *Hamdan* had emphasized the president's unilateral action in defiance of Congress, post-MCA legal challenges would have to take on Congress and the executive by showing that both branches had exceeded the limits that the Constitution placed on their respective powers.

As lawyers for the government and the detainees prepared for another legal showdown, the situation at Guantánamo continued to worsen. Prisoners increasingly turned to hunger strikes to protest the denial of due process, inhumane living conditions, isolation, religious degradation, and other mistreatment. One strike in mid-2005 involved more than two hundred detainees, approximately fifty of whom were given intravenous treatment for dehydration. The government responded with heavy-handed measures, including strapping detainees into restraint chairs to facilitate force-feeding through nasal tube insertions, placing them in uncomfortably cold air-conditioned isolation cells, and withholding "comfort items" like blankets and books.[25]

In June 2006, Guantánamo experienced its first reported prisoner suicide: the Bush administration announced that three detainees had hanged themselves from the mesh walls of their cells with nooses made of bed sheets. The three detainees had been on hunger strikes and had been force-fed. An article later published in *Harper's* questioned the truth of the government's account, describing how the men had been moved after their deaths from a secret prison within Guantánamo called "Camp No" (as in "No," it doesn't exist) and explaining how the government's investigation into the deaths had been a cover-up.[26] Another detainee reportedly committed suicide the following year. By 2007, twenty-five different prisoners had made more than forty suicide attempts.[27]

The Bush administration denied any responsibility for the deteriorating situation at Guantánamo. Instead, it said a detainee who attempted to take his own life was committing an act of "asymmetrical warfare." Suicides were relabeled "PR stunts" intended to create support for the plight of the detainees,[28] and attempted suicides were dismissed as "manipulative, self-injurious behavior."[29] The administration completely ignored its role in creating a detention system in which individuals were held for years without due process, subjected to torture and other abuse, and isolated from the rest of the world, including from their own families.

Public criticism of Guantánamo, meanwhile, continued to mount.[30] The president of the ICRC took the unprecedented step of condemning the United States for imprisoning individuals for years without charge or an adequate process.[31] Amnesty International labeled Guantánamo "the gulag of our time."[32] Calls to close Guantánamo also came from America's closest allies. Lord Steyn, a justice on Britain's highest court, castigated Guantánamo as a "monstrous failure of justice."[33] By 2007, some high-level officials within the Bush administration, including Defense Secretary Robert M. Gates, were pressing for the prison's closure. Guantánamo, Senator John McCain declared, was "an image throughout the world which has hurt [America's] reputation."[34] The Bush administration's flagship prison in the "war on terrorism" had become a political and public relations liability that outweighed any benefits it provided.[35]

Simply closing Guantánamo and moving the prisoners to the United States, however, would not address the underlying problem of detention without trial or the use of second-class tribunals like military commissions. Instead, it would only replicate Guantánamo within the United States. It also would do nothing to address the continued potential for lawless detentions beyond America's shores, whether at other military prisons like Bagram or secret CIA "black sites." Indeed, simply closing Guantánamo without confronting the larger detention system Guantánamo embodied could increase the government's incentive to bring prisoners to other U.S.-run offshore jails or to render them to foreign governments to avoid scrutiny and accountability.

Guantánamo's future thus remained linked to the United States' broader detention policy. At the same time, if the battle for habeas corpus and other fundamental constitutional safeguards could not be won at Guantánamo, where the United States had long exercised complete, exclusive, and permanent control, it could not be won at prisons farther from America's shores and over which U.S. control might be less clear or complete.

The legal challenge to the latest court-stripping measure thus headed to the Supreme Court laden with significance. Ironically, though, the Supreme Court almost never heard it.

In February 2007, a federal appeals court in Washington, D.C., upheld the MCA's elimination of habeas corpus. In a two-to-one decision, the court determined that the Guantánamo detainees were not protected by the Suspension Clause or any other provision of the Constitution because they were foreign nationals held outside the United States.[36] Writing for the majority, Judge A. Raymond Randolph contended that habeas corpus had never been available to enemy aliens detained abroad and that when the Constitution was written, it would "not have been available to aliens held at an overseas military base leased from a foreign government" such as Guantánamo.[37] Furthermore, Randolph said, the Supreme Court's decision in *Johnson v. Eisentrager* foreclosed any claim of a constitutional entitlement to habeas corpus by prisoners at Guantánamo because it established a bright-line rule prohibiting the Suspension Clause's reach to noncitizens held outside the United States. The Court's more recent decision in *Rasul*, he said, addressed only the Guantánamo detainees' statutory right to habeas corpus—a right Congress was free to revoke, as it had done twice since *Rasul*, first through the DTA and then through the MCA.[38] Randolph also distinguished the Insular Cases, arguing that these decisions involved territory over which the United States exercised political sovereignty—a *sine qua non* for extending the Constitution's protections to noncitizens abroad, no matter how extensive or complete the United States' control over the territory or prisoner in question.[39] Randolph's opinion did not merely affirm the denial of habeas corpus for Guantánamo detainees. It also endorsed a central premise of the post-9/11 global detention system: that at least with respect to noncitizens, the president was not constrained by the Constitution as long as he acted outside the borders of the United States.

The habeas petitioners who had brought the appeal—a group of approximately thirty Guantánamo detainees—sought Supreme Court review. But the Court declined to hear the case, as the petitioners fell one vote shy of the four votes necessary to grant certiorari. In an unusual step, Justices John Paul Stevens and Anthony M. Kennedy issued an opinion explaining their vote to deny certiorari. "Despite the obvious importance of the issues raised," they said, the Court should adhere to its usual practice of avoiding unnecessary adjudication of constitutional questions and of requiring the "exhaustion of available remedies as a precondition to accepting jurisdiction over applications for the writ of habeas corpus."[40] That meant the Guantánamo detainees first had to seek review of their respective Combatant Status Review Tribunal (CSRT) findings in the D.C. Circuit Court of Appeals—the same court that had just ruled that they had no constitutional rights— through the procedure Congress created in the DTA to replace habeas corpus, despite that procedure's manifest shortcomings.[41] The Guantánamo detainees would thus remain imprisoned without a meaningful hearing while they exhausted this seemingly futile review process, even though many were already well into their sixth year of confinement.

The detainees asked the Supreme Court to reconsider its decision. Such rehearing petitions are invariably denied; the Court had not granted one in approximately forty years. But this time, the Supreme Court reversed course and agreed to hear the case.[42] Although the Court gave no explanation, many suspected that Justice Kennedy—the critical swing vote—had been moved by a new and devastating critique of Guantánamo's CSRT process from within the military itself.

In a sworn declaration provided to the Supreme Court with the rehearing petition, Lieutenant Colonel Stephen Abraham, a twenty-six-year veteran of military intelligence, offered an inside account of how the CSRT actually functioned.[43] Abraham had previously served in the Office for Administrative Review of the Detention of Enemy Combatants (OARDEC), the division of the Defense Department responsible for implementing the CSRT-ARB process. Abraham's description shattered any remaining pretense this process had to legitimacy. The OARDEC, Abraham explained, had no intelligence-gathering capabilities. Instead, its efforts were confined to making arbitrary and incomplete requests to outside agencies for information about particular detainees. In turn, those agencies could, and often did, withhold exculpatory evidence about the detainees in question. Moreover, the OARDEC's staff lacked training and experience in collecting and using intelligence information and was under tremendous time pressure to complete hundreds of CSRTs within four months. Another military official who sat on forty-nine CSRT panels provided additional details about the CSRT's inadequacy. The tribunal's officers, for example, did not understand the difference between conclusory statements, which constituted the bulk of the material presented, and actual evidence.[44]

As Abraham explained, detention decisions were instead based on summaries of interrogations and boilerplate intelligence information. Rather than carefully assessing the evidence (or lack thereof), the OARDEC's members would "cast broad nets for any information, no matter how marginal, no matter how tenuous, no matter how dated, no matter how generic, no matter how dubious the source, so long as it could be connected to the detainee."[45]

That information would be "cut and pasted" into documents given to CSRT panels, without any critical assessment of its accuracy or reliability.[46] When no information about a detainee was available, as was often the case, the search would shift to broad-brushed categories, such as the region from which the detainee came, his ethnic group or country of origin, or the organization with which the detainee was alleged to have been associated.[47] The CSRT would then label the detainees "enemy combatants" based on this haphazard and incomplete collection of generic information that "lacked even the most fundamental earmarks of objectively credible evidence."[48]

Command influence exacerbated these problems. On the few occasions that a CSRT panel determined a detainee should not be classified as an "enemy combatant," Abraham said, the OARDEC's director and deputy director questioned the validity of the finding. They ordered that a new CSRT hearing be conducted to allow for the presentation of new evidence. The only "new" information presented at these do-over hearings, however, was "a different conclusory intelligence finding, which was not justified by the underlying evidence."[49] If the panel failed to alter its conclusion, the OARDEC would conduct an inquiry into "what went wrong."[50] Insider accounts like Abraham's made the point more powerfully than any legal brief could: Guantánamo detainees had been imprisoned for years based on a process that was rotten to the core, and they should not have to wait any longer for the Supreme Court to decide whether they were entitled to habeas review under the Constitution.

In December 2007, the Supreme Court heard argument in the Guantánamo detainees' challenge to the MCA. The following June, the Court issued its decision in *Boumediene v. Bush*, ruling that Guantánamo detainees had a constitutional right to habeas corpus.[51] This meant that neither the president nor Congress could deprive Guantánamo detainees of habeas corpus without a valid invocation of the limited emergency powers provided under the Suspension Clause. The Court also determined that the mechanism the Bush administration and Congress had created to replace habeas corpus—limited appellate review of CSRT decisions via the DTA—failed to provide a constitutionally adequate substitute. As result, the Court invalidated the MCA's elimination of habeas corpus and directed district judges to conduct prompt hearings into the legality of the prisoners' confinement.

The Court's ruling in *Boumediene* transcended Guantánamo and the fate of the approximately 265 detainees who remained there at the time of the decision. Above all, the Court rejected the proposition—urged by the government—that formal constructs like political sovereignty determined whether the habeas corpus Suspension Clause and other constitutional protections extended to foreign nationals held beyond America's borders. In place of any bright-line rule, the Court adopted a functional test that examined not only the prisoner's citizenship but also the nature of the detention, the surrounding circumstances, and the adequacy of the process the prisoner had received in determining whether a given constitutional provision applied abroad. While this test did not guarantee habeas corpus wherever the United States detained a prisoner, it nonetheless rejected the idea that the president could avoid judicial review simply by choosing to hold that prisoner outside the country.

Justice Kennedy's opinion for the Court emphasized the critical role of habeas corpus in America's Constitution and system of government. "The Framers," Kennedy explained, "viewed freedom from unlawful restraint as a fundamental precept of liberty, and they understood the writ of habeas corpus as a vital instrument to secure that freedom."[52] Habeas corpus, he pointed out, not only protects individuals from the arbitrary and unlawful exercise of state power; it also serves as "an essential mechanism in the [Constitution's] separation-of-powers."[53]

Kennedy looked to English history to determine whether under English common law precedents, detainees held in circumstances similar to Guantánamo would have had access to habeas corpus. Although history provided no direct analogies, Kennedy said, it also did not support the government's argument that habeas corpus was available only in territory over which the executive exercised political sovereignty. Thus, from a historical perspective, the fact that Cuba retained formal ownership over the U.S. naval base at Guantánamo offered "scant support" for the government's contention that this territory was necessarily beyond the reach of the Constitution's Suspension Clause.[54]

Kennedy next examined the Court's own precedents addressing the Constitution's extraterritorial application. During the first century of the nation's history, he noted, there was no need to address this issue, since the United States extended its laws and Constitution to new territory acquired during its westward expansion. The question of whether the Constitution also followed the flag to territories that were not incorporated into the United States first arose after the United States began acquiring overseas possessions in the late nineteenth century. In the Insular Cases, discussed in chapter 6, the Supreme Court ruled that the Constitution had independent force in these so-called unincorporated territories even if Congress had not made the political decision to extend its protections there. But, Kennedy observed, the Insular Cases also recognized some potential obstacles to applying the Constitution in its entirety and displacing the existing legal systems in these territories. The question, therefore, was not *whether* the Constitution applied but "*which* of its provisions were applicable by way of limitation upon the exercise of executive and legislative power in dealing with new conditions and requirements."[55] And the answer turned not on formal constructs like "political sovereignty" but on other, more pragmatic considerations.[56]

The Supreme Court, Kennedy said, had employed a similar approach a half century later in *Reid v. Covert*.[57] While Justice Hugo Black's plurality opinion in *Reid* focused on U.S. citizenship in concluding that the Constitution's jury trial guarantee applied to American civilians tried by an American military court in a foreign country, Justices John Marshall Harlan's and Felix Frankfurter's concurring opinions emphasized other, more practical, considerations related to the place of the prisoners' confinement and trial. Kennedy's reading of *Reid* aligned the Court more closely with the Harlan-Frankfurter position. Citizenship, Kennedy said, was merely one factor considered in *Reid* in determining whether the right to a jury trial extended extraterritorially. If this diminished the importance of citizenship, it also strengthened the idea that the Constitution could extend more widely to foreign nationals in U.S. custody, regardless of location. It thus moved the Court closer to the idea that freedom from arbitrary and unlawful detention was a human right and not just a right of American citizens.

Justice Kennedy also distinguished *Johnson v. Eisentrager*, the World War II–era decision that had been the linchpin in the government's effort to resist habeas corpus review for Guantánamo detainees. As Kennedy explained, *Eisentrager* did not in fact establish "a formalistic, sovereignty-based test for determining the reach of the Suspension Clause."[58] *Eisentrager* instead turned on its unique factors, including the absence of plenary U.S. control over Landsberg Prison in Germany, which Kennedy contrasted with the total, exclusive, and permanent U.S. control over Guantánamo. *Eisentrager* thus did not mean what the Bush administration had been arguing since the first Guantánamo habeas petitions were filed: that the United States could deny prisoners access to its courts by detaining them beyond its borders.

Boumediene thus turned the government's separation of powers argument on its head. In recognizing that Guantánamo detainees had a constitutional right to habeas corpus protected by the Suspension Clause, the judiciary was not interfering with executive prerogative but was preventing executive manipulation of the judiciary and the Constitution itself. Accepting the government's political sovereignty test meant that the United States could act at will and without constraint whenever it exercised power outside the country.

And if the United States could do this at a place like Guantánamo, a territory under its permanent, total, and exclusive control, it could do so anywhere beyond its shores. *Boumediene* rejected this argument in no uncertain terms. The actions of the United States, the Court maintained, are always subject to constitutional constraints, even when those actions concern foreign nationals and occur abroad. The political branches did not have the power to "switch the Constitution on or off at will" by altering the locus of detention.[59] "The test for determining the scope of [the Suspension Clause]," the Court said, "must not be subject to manipulation by those whose power it is designed to restrain."[60]

In place of formal constructs like political sovereignty, *Boumediene* set forth a multifactored test to determine whether the habeas corpus Suspension Clause applied abroad. In addition to the citizenship of the detainee, the test also factored in the adequacy of any previous process the detainee had received, the nature of the sites where his apprehension and detention took place, and the practical obstacles inherent in resolving his entitlement to the writ.[61] Applying this test, the conclusion that the Suspension Clause reached Guantánamo was a virtual slam dunk. Although they were not American citizens, the Guantánamo detainees had been detained for years based on a determination by the woefully inadequate CSRT process. The prison where they were held was under the total and exclusive control of the United States. And the government had presented "no credible arguments that the military mission at Guantánamo would be compromised if habeas corpus courts had jurisdiction to hear the detainees' claims."[62]

The question remained, however, whether appellate review under the DTA could cure the problem by providing an adequate substitute for habeas corpus. If so, there would be no constitutional violation, since the detainees would effectively be receiving what habeas guaranteed them, only under a different name. The Supreme Court, however, found that the DTA was no substitute for habeas. Instead, in enacting the DTA, Congress had deliberately sought to create an inferior remedy for individuals who it believed had no right to habeas in the first place.[63] Congress's elimination of habeas corpus for Guantánamo detainees thus differed significantly from earlier amendments to the federal habeas corpus statute, which were intended to create a similar remedy in a different forum, for example, by requiring federal prisoners to challenge their criminal convictions in the district court that sentenced them rather than in the jurisdiction where they were imprisoned after sentencing.[64] More important, the Court concluded that Congress had in fact created an inferior remedy. It highlighted three points about habeas corpus: first, that the court's role is most important in cases of executive detention without prior judicial review; second, that habeas review is more searching where the underlying process lacks rigorous safeguards; and third, that habeas is itself a flexible remedy that can be adapted to the circumstances and tailored to achieve its underlying purpose: relief from unlawful imprisonment.

Measured in light of these standards, DTA review of CSRT hearings fell short. The CSRT was patently deficient as a remedy for executive imprisonment: it denied detainees access to a lawyer, relied largely on secret evidence, limited detainees' ability to present evidence in their favor and to confront the evidence against them, and contained virtually no restrictions on the use of hearsay. Such a "closed and accusatorial" proceeding, the Court said, carries "considerable risk of error"—a "risk too significant to ignore" given the potential length of the prisoners' confinement, which the Court recognized could last a generation or more.[65] And appellate review under the DTA could not compensate for these deficiencies. As the Supreme Court explained, one flaw of the DTA could not be overcome no matter how creatively the statute was read: the absence of any meaningful opportunity for a detainee to rebut the allegations against him. The DTA, for example, barred courts from considering new evidence or conducting a hearing to resolve the factual disputes around which so many cases turned. A *sine qua non* of habeas corpus, the Court said, was the authority it gave a judge to "conduct a meaningful review of both the cause for detention and the Executive's power to detain."[66] The DTA substantially curtailed that authority and undermined a judge's power to correct errors, a power that was even more critical given the CSRT's manifest flaws. In brief, no substitute for habeas corpus could allow a prisoner to be locked away—potentially for life— unless it provided him a meaningful opportunity to test the legal and factual basis for his detention before a neutral decision maker.

But even though the victory was momentous, the margin was narrow, resting on a five-to-four vote. Chief Justice John Roberts and Justice Antonin Scalia each filed dissenting opinions, which Justices Clarence Thomas and Samuel Alito joined. "The Court," Roberts said, "strikes down as inadequate the most generous set of procedural protections ever afforded aliens detained by this country as enemy combatants."[67] Its decision, Roberts continued, also contradicts previous statements in *Hamdi* that a military status tribunal, coupled with judicial review, could satisfy even an American citizen's right to due process—precisely what the Bush administration and Congress had created via the DTA-CSRT review scheme. Roberts thus chastised the Court for failing to defer to this alternative process and undercutting the considered judgment of the political branches.[68]

But Roberts ignored both the larger context of the Guantánamo detentions and the specific flaws of the DTA-CSRT review scheme. Unlike prisoners of war from past conflicts, Guantánamo detainees were being held in connection with a loosely defined armed conflict of perpetual duration and under a definition of "enemy combatant" that vastly exceeded all recognized military detention authority in its breadth and scope. To be sure, the Court in *Hamdi* had referred to a legally sanctioned military status tribunal acting pursuant to Army Regulation 190-8 and the Geneva Conventions in describing the process Hamdi had failed to receive. But it did so only for individuals seized on a battlefield where they were fighting alongside enemy armed forces (in Hamdi's case, the Taliban). *Hamdi* never considered whether such tribunals could be used to justify the prolonged detention of individuals— many of whom were seized outside any battlefield or hostilities—based solely on their suspected affiliation with, or activity on behalf of, a terrorist organization. *Hamdi* also assumed that habeas corpus would be available to correct errors when the regular military process had not been provided in the first instance. Moreover, Roberts looked only at the CSRT process on paper, not how it functioned in practice, and ignored the unrefuted evidence of the CSRT's excessive reliance on secret evidence, its pervasive command influence, and its kangaroo-court style "hearings." CSRT determinations sanctioned potentially lifelong detention; yet, they provided fewer protections than a person in the United States ordinarily receives in contesting a speeding ticket.

Whereas Roberts focused on the DTA-CSRT scheme as a substitute for habeas review, Scalia denied that any substitute was necessary, since the Guantánamo detainees had no constitutional right to habeas in the first place. Building on his dissent in *Rasul*, Scalia sought to limit the Suspension Clause to its original meaning, which, he maintained, excluded from its protections foreign nationals seized and detained outside the United States. The Suspension Clause's unprecedented extension to Guantánamo detainees, Scalia insisted, not only contradicted the intent of the Constitution's framers but also undermined the separation of powers by ceding too much authority to judges.[69] What the Court's majority saw as executive manipulation in bringing prisoners to Guantánamo to avoid habeas corpus, Scalia viewed as unwarranted judicial interference with the president's wartime prerogative to detain alien prisoners seized abroad without court review. "'Manipulation' of the territorial reach of the writ by the Judiciary," Scalia charged, "poses just as much a threat to the proper separation of powers as 'manipulation' by the Executive."[70]

Scalia, however, misunderstood the tradition and precedents he cited. Power and control over the jailer and a judge's ability to enforce the writ's command, not formal notions of sovereignty, had traditionally guided determinations about the writ's territorial reach. The availability of habeas corpus also had never turned on a prisoner's citizenship status—a limitation that contradicted the writ's role as a safeguard against arbitrary and unlawful executive action. Elevating citizenship or territorial sovereignty to a bright-line rule or "litmus test" was a modern invention. Such a rule, moreover, ultimately could not be reconciled with a system of government predicated on the idea of checks and balances and commitment to the rule of law. Guantánamo itself demonstrated how tethering the Constitution's reach to formal constructs like political sovereignty opened the door to the creation of lawless enclaves, arbitrary detention, and torture.

Boumediene thus rejected one of the animating ideas behind the post-9/11 global detention system: that prisoners could necessarily be denied habeas corpus review as long as they were held beyond America's shores. The right to habeas corpus secured by the Suspension Clause, the Court said, was not limited to American citizens or the mainland United States. Instead, it could apply to any U.S. detention anywhere in the world, from Guantánamo (where the Court found it applied) to Bagram in Afghanistan and CIA "black sites" (where the Court might one day reach the same conclusion).

Yet *Boumediene* also contained several important qualifications. The Supreme Court did not rule that the Suspension Clause necessarily reached all prisoners held by the United States abroad. *Boumediene's* functional test implicitly recognized that some prisoners would not have a right to habeas corpus and left open exactly where the writ might extend beyond Guantánamo. The Court acknowledged that in "cases involving foreign citizens detained abroad by the Executive, it likely would be both an impractical and unprecedented extension of judicial power to assume that habeas corpus would be available at the moment the prisoner is taken into custody."[71] This reinforced the idea that there remained some undefined realm of extraterritorial detention—temporally, if not spatially—that habeas corpus would not reach. Furthermore, the Court cautioned that in assessing where the habeas right applied, "proper deference can be accorded to reasonable procedures for screening and initial detention under lawful and proper conditions of confinement and treatment for a reasonable period of time."[72] Thus, an adequate military process might delay or foreclose habeas review altogether. The Court's functional test also meant that where and when habeas was available depended partly on an individual judge's assessment of what was appropriate and practicable—an assessment that was, by its nature, subjective and malleable. How long was too long? How much process was enough? How much control over the detention site or the prisoner was necessary? The prolonged detention of several hundred individuals at a U.S. enclave like Guantánamo based solely on a determination by a tribunal as deeply flawed as the CSRT provided a relatively easy answer. But other overseas detentions—when U.S. control over the territory was less complete, when the detentions were shorter and the military process more robust, and when the prison was in or nearer to a theater of armed conflict—might present a closer call. *Boumediene* thus not only created future uncertainty but also implied that the political branches could still act in some places without legal constraint, a result in tension with the decision's stated purpose.

A sign of *Boumediene*'s potential reach as well as its potential limitations first came in litigation challenging U.S. detentions at Bagram. In April 2009, a district judge handed down a decision in *al-Maqaleh v. Gates*, the first jurisdictional ruling in a Bagram habeas corpus case.[73] The challenge involved four prisoners, at least three of whom had been seized outside Afghanistan, including in places as distant as Thailand and Dubai. All four had been imprisoned at Bagram as "enemy combatants" for more than six years.

The district judge, John D. Bates, rejected the government's effort to limit *Boumediene* to Guantánamo, finding that the Supreme Court had definitively rejected any bright-line test for determining the reach of habeas corpus and other constitutional protections. Applying *Boumediene*'s functional test, Bates instead looked at the nature and degree of U.S. control over Bagram, the adequacy of the process afforded the detainees there, and the practical obstacles, if any, to habeas review. He acknowledged that the United States' control over Bagram was not as complete as its control over Guantánamo and that Bagram was located in an active theater of war. But he also found that the degree of U.S. control at Bagram was not appreciably different from that at Guantánamo and was "practically absolute." It also was significantly greater than U.S. control over Landsberg Prison during post–World War II Germany, when the Supreme Court decided *Eisentrager*.[74] In addition, Bates found that ongoing military operations in Afghanistan did not present a significant obstacle to habeas review and that any practical barriers to such review were "largely of the Executive's choosing" where the prisoners had been apprehended elsewhere and brought to Bagram.[75] He also found that the process used to determine the status of Bagram detainees fell "well short" of the process that the Supreme Court had declared unconstitutional at Guantánamo and failed to provide meaningful access to the government's evidence, an opportunity to be heard, or a neutral decision maker.[76]

Judge Bates therefore ruled that three of the petitioners before him had a constitutional entitlement to habeas review. However, he rejected habeas rights for the fourth prisoner on the ground that he was an Afghan national. Bates explained that for Afghan nationals, as well as for detainees apprehended in Afghanistan, the balance of factors cut against habeas review. He focused on the possible friction with the Afghan government, since according to the United States, a significant percentage of Afghan detainees at Bagram were expected to be transferred to Afghan custody. Tensions could arise, he said, if a U.S. court were to entertain an Afghan detainee's habeas petition and reach a different result than an Afghan court did, for example, by ordering the detainee's release.[77] Bates also suggested that for detainees apprehended inside Afghanistan, there might be greater practical obstacles to habeas review because of the ongoing military hostilities there.

On the one hand, *al-Maqaleh* showed how the Supreme Court's rejection of categorical limits on habeas jurisdiction could help prevent the creation of "new Guantánamos" in other parts of the world, with the executive free to transport prisoners across geographic lines to avoid court review. On the other hand, *al-Maqaleh* highlighted *Boumediene*'s potential limits as the district court's application of the Supreme Court's malleable, multifactored test afforded habeas rights to only some Bagram detainees. Under Judge Bates's ruling, prisoners brought to Bagram from other countries could contest their detention in U.S. courts (at least if they were not Afghans), but those seized inside Afghanistan—the overwhelming majority of detainees at Bagram— could not, even though their detention might be based on the same flimsy evidence, the same inadequate military hearing, and the same overbroad definition of "enemy combatant." Furthermore, nothing required that the United States transfer any prisoner to Afghan custody, and until such transfer, which could take years to be carried out (if ever carried out at all), that prisoner had no access to Afghan or U.S. courts.

Boumediene's potential limitations became more apparent in the government's appeal of Judge Bates's decision granting some Bagram detainees habeas rights. The three-judge panel—which included liberal judges David S. Tatel and Harry T. Edwards—ruled that none of the petitioners should have access to habeas corpus and ordered that their cases be dismissed.[78] The D.C. Circuit panel acknowledged that the Supreme Court had rejected any bright-line test for determining the application of the Suspension Clause and other constitutional rights outside the United States and had refused to limit its decision in *Boumediene* to territories over which the United States exercised de facto sovereignty, such as Guantánamo. In applying *Boumediene*'s multi-factored test, the panel also agreed with Judge Bates that the military process that the Bagram detainees had received was even more flawed than the process used for Guantánamo detainees.[79] But the panel nevertheless held that Bagram's location in an active theater of war and the practical obstacles to habeas review over detentions there trumped the factors favoring jurisdiction.[80] Notably, the Court said it was only "speculation" that the United States had brought prisoners from other countries to Bagram to avoid habeas corpus review, even though it appeared that, at least from the time of the Supreme Court's decision in *Rasul*, the United States had been confining prisoners at Bagram rather than bringing them to Guantánamo for precisely this reason.[81] The panel also pointed to a risk that habeas review might cause friction with Afghanistan, even though U.S. detentions at Bagram violated Afghan law, which does not authorize indefinite detention without charge and which prohibits detention without due process.[82]

The D.C. Circuit's decision in *al-Maqaleh* made clear that the malleability of the *Boumediene* test was both a strength and a weakness: while it created the possibility that extraterritorial detentions by the United States would be subject to habeas review, it by no means ensured that review. To the contrary, it gave judges wide discretion to balance various factors and decline to exercise jurisdiction based on what they perceived as practical concerns. Without a reversal of *al-Maqaleh*, no Bagram detainee would have access to habeas corpus, no matter how long he had been held or how inadequate the process he had received, at least without additional evidence that he had been brought to Bagram deliberately to avoid habeas review.

The same day that it issued *Boumediene*, the Supreme Court handed down *Munaf v. Geren*, which involved habeas corpus challenges filed on behalf of two American citizens detained in Iraq.[83] Both men—Mohammad Munaf and Shawqi Omar—had been seized by U.S. forces in Iraq and held at U.S.-run facilities there for more than two years. *Munaf*, like the Bagram litigation, thus grappled with the lurking issue of U.S. overseas detentions beyond Guantánamo. It also raised the question of whether habeas corpus reached U.S. detentions conducted as a part of an international force—in this case, as part of the Multi-National Force-Iraq (MNF–I)—but answerable to U.S. authority. While the Supreme Court ruled that the federal courts had jurisdiction to review the two petitions, it placed potentially significant limits on the scope and intensity of that review.

In upholding habeas jurisdiction, the Court distinguished *Hirota v. Mac-Arthur*, the World War II–era case involving war criminals convicted and sentenced by the International Military Tribunal for the Far East. There, the Supreme Court had ruled that the tribunal was "not a tribunal of the United States" and that "the courts of the United States ha[d] no power or authority to review, to affirm, set aside or annul [its] judgments and sentences."[84] The government invoked *Hirota* in *Munaf* just as it had invoked *Eisentrager* in the Guantánamo detainee litigation: as a categorical bar to habeas jurisdiction. It argued that the international character of the MNF–I, like the multinational character of the tribunal in *Hirota*, meant that the MNF–I was "not a United States entity subject to habeas."[85] But *Hirota*, the Supreme Court said, differed from *Munaf*. It involved enemy aliens, not U.S. citizens. More important, the tribunal that convicted and sentenced the petitioners in *Hirota* was not clearly subject to U.S. authority. *Munaf* thus confirmed that habeas corpus could reach U.S. detentions overseas and that the executive could not evade judicial scrutiny simply by acting as part of a multinational force or pursuant to an international source of authority, such as a UN Security Council Resolution.

The Supreme Court nevertheless also concluded in *Munaf* that the habeas petitions should be dismissed because a U.S. judge could provide no relief.[86] As framed by the Court, *Munaf* concerned the exercise of habeas jurisdiction over individuals detained by the United States in another country for criminal prosecution under the laws of that country. The Court therefore evaluated the actual exercise of habeas review against the long-standing rule that "the jurisdiction of [a] nation within its own territory is necessarily exclusive and absolute."[87] A host country may cede that jurisdiction in certain instances, the Court reasoned, through measures like status-of-forces agreements that give a foreign government primary jurisdiction over offenses committed by its troops stationed in the host country. But without such provisions allocating jurisdiction to the foreign government, the host nation retains an absolute right to enforce its criminal law within its territory. In light of these principles, the Court concluded that "prudential concerns," such as comity and the orderly administration of criminal justice, require a habeas court to forgo its usual inquiry when the United States is detaining a prisoner for prosecution by the host state.[88]

The Supreme Court also rejected the petitioners' alternative claim, that their threatened transfer to Iraqi jailers lacked the requisite legal authorization and impermissibly exposed them to a risk of torture. The Court acknowledged that habeas corpus jurisdiction can provide for review of a prisoner's transfer from U.S. custody to another government. In extradition cases, for example, such transfers require legal authorization, such as a treaty, and habeas courts routinely review the prisoner's transfer to ensure compliance with the treaty's terms and with applicable statutory requirements.[89] But when the transfer occurs solely within the territory of a host government for purposes of criminal prosecution, the Court stated, no specific authorization is necessary. To the contrary, without a law, treaty, or agreement restricting the transfer, the executive is free to hand the prisoner over to the host government for prosecution under the host government's laws.[90]

The Court thus approved Munaf's and Omar's transfer to Iraqi custody without a hearing, even though both men had presented evidence that they faced possible torture there. The Court pointed to a U.S. policy against transferring American citizens in Iraq to likely torture. "The Judiciary," it said, "is not suited to second-guess such determinations—determinations that would require federal courts to pass judgment on foreign justice systems and undermine the Government's ability to speak with one voice in this area."[91] The Court's decision, however, did not foreclose all review of transfer-to-torture claims. It left open the possibility that in implementing the Convention against Torture through the Foreign Affairs Reform and Restructuring Act, Congress had authorized the courts to consider such claims.[92] Justice David Souter suggested another important qualification in a concurring opinion. He insisted that a judge could prohibit a prisoner's transfer when "the probability of torture is well documented, even if the Executive fails to acknowledge it."[93]

Munaf, together with *Boumediene*, demonstrates the broad ambit of habeas corpus and its ability to reach U.S. detentions overseas. Just as the absence of American citizenship and political sovereignty did not foreclose habeas jurisdiction in *Boumediene*, U.S. participation in a multinational operation did not preclude habeas review in *Munaf*. And the reason that this review was so circumscribed in *Munaf*, the Court explained, was that the prisoners were subject to criminal prosecution for violating the laws of the foreign nation (Iraq) where they had been seized and were being detained. If the prisoners were instead being held for other purposes, such as for continued detention by the United States for its own security interests rather than for prosecution by the host nation, habeas review would not be subject to this limitation.

But *Munaf* also suggested that there might be other, more signifcant restrictions on habeas corpus. The Court ordered that the habeas petitions be dismissed without any factual inquiry into the basis for the prisoners' detention or the risk of torture following transfer to Iraqi authorities. The United States avoided this scrutiny in *Munaf* by successfully characterizing the prisoners' cases as U.S. detentions for the purpose of prosecution by the host government whose criminal laws the United States was helping enforce, and not continued U.S. detention without charge in an extraterritorial U.S. enclave. Yet this rationale was in tension with the record in the case and underscored the risk that the United States could simply circumvent habeas review by invoking the specter of another nation's criminal process to shield its own detentions from review. In Munaf's and Omar's cases, Iraqi criminal proceedings were initiated only after habeas relief had been sought from a U.S. court. Furthermore, at least in Omar's case, the United States suggested that it could still detain the petitioner even if he were acquitted by Iraqi courts, based on the theory that he was not only a security detainee subject to criminal prosecution by Iraq but was also an "enemy combatant" in America's global "war on terrorism." This U.S.-based detention interest was shielded, however, from habeas review by the specter of Iraqi proceedings.

Munaf's impact was soon felt in other habeas cases challenging prisoner transfers. Relying on *Munaf*, a divided three-judge panel of the D.C. Circuit Court of Appeals subsequently ruled that Guantánamo detainees had no right to contest their transfer to another country.[94] As long as the executive could point to a policy forbidding transfers to likely torture, the appeals court said, a judge could not second-guess the executive's decision to transfer a particular prisoner. Nor, the appeals court said, could a judge examine a prisoner's claim that he was being transferred for the purpose of further detention in the receiving country. If the prisoner was held pursuant to another sovereign's laws, a U.S. court could not question the decision or inquire whether the continued detention was at the United States' behest. As the dissent correctly noted, the panel's decision undermined habeas corpus because it allowed transfers intended to remove a prisoner from the court's reach by handing the prisoner over to another sovereign.[95] The Supreme Court, however, declined to hear the prisoners' appeal of the panel decision, leaving that decision in place.[96]

Boumediene and *Munaf* were the Supreme Court's last two "war on terrorism" decisions during Bush's presidency. Both decisions rejected the Bush administration's effort to avoid habeas review by invoking formalistic or bright-line tests: political sovereignty and citizenship status in *Boumediene* and U.S. participation in a multinational force in *Munaf*. *Boumediene* further demonstrated that habeas corpus remained an important means of cutting through sham proceedings like the CSRT and providing a meaningful examination of the basis for a prisoner's confinement.

The decisions, however, also pointed to some potential limitations on habeas corpus: *Boumediene* employed a malleable and functional test that left open the possibility that at least some overseas U.S. detentions would remain beyond judicial review; *Munaf*, in contrast, served as a reminder that habeas review itself could be exceedingly narrow, especially if the United States successfully tied the prisoner's detention to possible criminal prosecution by another state. Moreover, habeas corpus review did not itself determine the permissible scope of the president's detention authority. The availability of habeas thus did not resolve the circumstances under which the United States could imprison an individual indefinitely without charge or prosecute that person in a military commission rather than in the regular federal courts. Nor did it determine what other constitutional or legal rights a detainee might claim in challenging his confinement. Habeas did provide a vehicle for courts to address these questions through the exercise of their jurisdiction over individual cases. But as recent history has shown, habeas review of important legal questions, such as the scope of the president's military detention power, could be avoided by eleventh-hour machinations by the executive through the transfer or release of the prisoner, thereby leaving those questions unresolved and the government free to engage in the same unlawful conduct again in the future.

The availability of habeas corpus also did not answer the question of what remedy a court could order if it found the prisoner's detention unlawful but the prisoner could not be safely returned to his home country and could not be repatriated to a third country. Could, for example, a habeas court in Washington, D.C., order the prisoner's release into the United States? If not, what could the court do to remedy illegal detention? Part 4 addresses these and other issues.

Part 4

Toward a Better Understanding
of Habeas Corpus

*Individual Rights and the Role of
the Judiciary during Wartime*

Centuries ago, the king declared people enemies of the state and locked them away in the Tower of London. After the attacks on September 11, 2001, the president called them "enemy combatants" and imprisoned them at Guantánamo and other offshore prisons. In both instances, habeas corpus emerged as a critical check against executive detention without judicial review.

Some people have claimed that habeas corpus undermines the fight against terrorism and jeopardizes America's security. The most extreme critics have even accused the detainees' attorneys of waging "lawfare," as though defending a person deprived of his liberty in court was a form of combat against the United States.[1] Those who oppose extending habeas rights to detainees held in connection with the "war on terror" argue that judges, legislators, and the public should instead defer to the president's decisions about whom to imprison and for how long. They also contend that the treatment of prisoners, including the methods of their interrogation, is a matter solely for the executive to decide. But it is the very nature of terrorism and the pressures it can exert on even well-intentioned public officials to exceed legal limits in the name of security that make habeas corpus so important. As Supreme Court Justice Louis Brandeis cautioned long ago, "The greatest dangers to liberty lurk in insidious encroachment by men of zeal, well-meaning but without understanding."[2]

By rejecting bright-line categories such as a detainee's citizenship or territorial sovereignty as the basis for habeas rights, the Supreme Court sought to limit the possibility of detentions outside the law. Its decision in *Boumediene v. Bush*, as Professor Gerald Neuman has explained, serves as an important

protection to "security detainees who have been the innocent victims of . . .
extraterritorial arrests."[3] It also alters "conceptions of sovereignty, territoriality, and rights in the globalized world," as Professor David Cole has noted.[4]
At a minimum, *Boumediene* ensures that future overseas detentions will take
place in the shadow of potential federal court intervention. The mere possibility of habeas review envisioned by *Boumediene* will likely have a disciplining effect on the executive by causing it to act in ways that give greater
consideration to the dangers of arbitrary detention in order to avoid more
direct judicial intervention.[5]

But *Boumediene* does not go far enough to protect against unlawful
detention and secure adherence to the rule of law. As we have seen, the very
malleability of *Boumediene*'s jurisdictional test, which focuses on whether
the extension of a particular right is "impracticable" or "anomalous" under
the circumstances, allows courts to avoid assuming jurisdiction over future
detention challenges that they deem too complicated or politically sensitive.
It also implicitly contemplates the possibility of detentions beyond the law.
The Supreme Court instead should have made clear that habeas corpus is
available to all individuals detained by the United States, regardless of where
they are held, without a valid suspension of the writ by Congress. The sole
prerequisite for habeas jurisdiction should be detention by, or at the direction of, the United States. Where a prisoner is held and the circumstances
under which he is captured and detained may affect the scope of a court's
inquiry, the substantive law that guides its analysis, and the result it ultimately reaches. But it should not determine the court's power to consider
whether the detention is legal.

Extending habeas corpus to all U.S. detentions, regardless of location, inevitably raises difficult questions, especially during wartime. What is the legal
basis for this assertion of jurisdiction, and how does it square with previous
understandings of the writ's application? How would habeas review work in
practice when a prisoner is captured and held in a theater of military operations halfway across the world—a concern raised in prior wartime habeas
decisions like *Johnson v. Eisentrager*?[6] Would it cause courts to improperly
second-guess military decisions and micromanage wartime operations from
the bench? Would the courts themselves be inundated by petitions filed by or
on behalf of prisoners in military custody?

Previously, foreign nationals captured and detained outside the United
States were thought to be excluded from the writ's reach. In *Boumediene*,
however, the Supreme Court rejected the proposition that a prisoner's citizenship and location necessarily determined the availability of habeas cor-

pus. Instead, the Court stated that citizenship and location were among the factors to consider in determining whether the Constitution's Suspension Clause guaranteed habeas review over a particular detention abroad. The Court's ruling accorded with habeas's history and purpose insofar as it rejected any bright-line or categorical limits on its availability.

Historically, habeas corpus was available to individuals regardless of their citizenship. It also had a broad territorial ambit under common law, capable of reaching any jailer under the Crown's command. When the king's jailers occasionally sought to transport prisoners overseas to avoid habeas review, reforms were enacted to curb the practice. In the United States, habeas corpus was similarly understood as a vital check against arbitrary and unlawful executive confinement. Since 1789, federal law had authorized judges to grant writs of habeas corpus to any person "in custody under or by color of the authority of the United States" without regard to citizenship status or location—a provision that remained in effect until Congress amended it in the Detainee Treatment Act of 2005 and the Military Commissions Act of 2006.[7] Even more important, the Constitution expressly prohibits the suspension of habeas corpus except in narrowly defined circumstances, without reference to a prisoner's citizenship or location.[8]

Territorial and citizenship-based limitations similarly are at odds with the writ's purpose. Habeas corpus does not just protect individuals against illegal confinement; it also helps ensure that the power of the state is exercised lawfully. Restricting habeas corpus based on citizenship not only violates the principle of equal protection under law but also creates a perception that U.S. detentions are arbitrary and lawless. Citizenship, to be sure, can be relevant to determining the government's authority to detain in a particular situation. Immigration law, for example, may authorize the detention of certain foreign nationals pursuant to their removal from the United States. So may the Alien Enemies Act of 1798, with respect to citizens or subjects of an enemy government in time of war.[9] But citizenship itself does not resolve whether a person's detention is lawful, nor does it determine the power of a court to address that question. Thus, even when a person's noncitizenship is an essential element of a given detention, as in the immigration and alien enemy contexts, habeas review remains available to ensure the detention comports with law.[10]

Conditioning habeas corpus on a prisoner's location also increases the risk of the type of arbitrary and lawless executive action that took place after 9/11. Terrorism today is global, and an effective counterterrorism policy depends on transnational action by law enforcement, intelligence agencies, and the military, sometimes in combination. Counterterrorism thus potentially involves the seizure of terrorist suspects abroad and the projection of U.S. power overseas in ways not contemplated either at the nation's founding or in prior military conflicts. An effective counterterrorism policy also requires gathering information to prevent future attacks. As long as access to habeas corpus depends on where a prisoner is detained, there will be an incentive for the government to find new locations where it can imprison and interrogate without a judicial check—precisely the dynamic that helped prompt the Bush administration to create a network of overseas prisons after 9/11. For habeas corpus to fulfill its checking function in an age of transnational law enforcement and military operations, it must be even more broadly conceived than in the past. The global reach of U.S. detention power to fight terrorism, in short, begets a broader conception of habeas rights to help ensure that this power is exercised lawfully—a conception that aligns with habeas's historic purpose as a bulwark against wrongful imprisonment.

War poses a more difficult challenge to the idea of global habeas corpus. Relatively few precedents involve combatants detained during wartime who challenged their detention or military trial by habeas corpus, whether successfully or unsuccessfully. The United States has never fought a war with judges on the sidelines conducting hearings in federal court on behalf of every person whom American forces capture during combat. Habeas review during wartime risks injecting judges and lawyers into matters beyond their expertise and competence and interfering with military operations. But that does not mean courts have no role to play, and the further the United States drifts from clear and well-defined legal boundaries, the more aggressive the judicial role must be.

Take the supposed problem of numbers. Guantánamo, the principal battleground over habeas rights after 9/11, held fewer than eight hundred prisoners in total. Given the tens of thousands of postconviction habeas petitions decided by the courts every year, many brought by individuals imprisoned for murder and other violent crimes, the number of Guantánamo detainee habeas actions has always been relatively small and posed little risk of overwhelming the courts. The question that always loomed in the background during this litigation was where else habeas rights might apply once they were recognized at Guantánamo. Would, for example, the writ also reach the hundreds of U.S. detainees in Afghanistan, the thousands of prisoners the United States held in Iraq, and all the others whom the United States might capture and detain abroad in future armed conflicts? Or looking back, would habeas rights have extended to the more than one million German,

Italian, and Japanese soldiers the United States captured during World War II, including the 400,000 prisoners of war held inside America's borders?[11] Where and how should the courts draw the line? If a prisoner's location and citizenship do not justify restricting access to habeas corpus, then perhaps the realities of war do.

A closely related concern is the impact that so many habeas petitions could have on the military. The government repeatedly argued during the Guantánamo litigation that affording habeas rights to "enemy combatants" would jeopardize military operations and decision making in the "war on terror."[12] In *Boumediene*, the Supreme Court noted the interference that habeas petitions from enemy prisoners could have caused in post–World War II Germany, where the United States became responsible for maintaining order in an occupation zone encompassing more than 57,000 square miles with a population of 18 million. The D.C. Circuit raised similar concerns about interfering with military operations in *al-Maqaleh* when ordering the dismissal of habeas petitions filed on behalf of prisoners at Bagram in Afghanistan on the ground that Bagram was located in an active theater of war.

In addition to these practical considerations, wartime habeas review also raises questions about maintaining the proper separation of powers among the branches of government. The Constitution envisions the war power as shared between Congress and the executive. It grants to Congress, for example, the power to declare war, to raise and support armed forces, and to make rules concerning military captures.[13] The Constitution also stipulates that the president shall be the commander in chief of the armed forces.[14] The meaning and scope of the Constitution's commander-in-chief clause was at the center of many of the debates over the Bush administration's post-9/11 detention policies, from declaring prisoners "enemy combatants" to trying them in military commissions. The Bush administration invoked the commander-in-chief clause to support far-reaching claims of presidential authority, including the power to ignore laws that the president said encroached on his discretion to define and to wage war as he saw fit. Even laws prohibiting torture, administration lawyers argued, must yield before the president's assertions of military necessity and national security. Yet merely because one commander in chief exceeded his constitutionally delegated power neither resolves the proper scope of that power for future presidents nor settles the question of the judiciary's appropriate role in reviewing military detentions during wartime. Indeed, it is possible that courts could overcompensate for the abuses and excesses of one administration by inserting themselves into matters beyond their proper sphere and competence.

These concerns, although understandable, are rooted in misconceptions about the nature of habeas corpus review and the importance of that review in modern transnational counterterrorism operations. Properly understood, habeas corpus does not interfere with legitimate military operations or executive functions. Instead, habeas helps ensure that to the extent the U.S. government detains prisoners, those detentions adhere to applicable legal requirements. While this more expansive conception of habeas rights will inevitably lead to greater judicial review of military detentions than in the past, that is a consequence of the military's increased role in combating terrorism, the different legal framework governing armed conflicts outside the traditional state-versus-state context, and the heightened risk of error posed by national security detentions without criminal process.

The potential volume of wartime habeas petitions does not necessarily mean that courts would be overwhelmed. The mere fact that thousands of prisoners *could* seek habeas relief does not mean that they *would* do so, especially once it became clear that there was no prospect of relief. But even if the courts were somehow flooded with lawsuits filed by or on behalf of prisoners seized during wartime military operations, judges could still handle the volume because of the nature and flexibility of habeas review, which can vary significantly depending, for example, on the nature of the conflict, the breadth of the government's claimed detention power, and the procedures and protections provided to the prisoner. Thus that review might be extremely limited, even *pro forma*, in some circumstances. In others, however, it might be appropriately robust, with a court conducting a searching inquiry into legal and factual basis for a prisoner's detention.

In an armed conflict between two or more nations—known as an "international armed conflict"—habeas review is narrow as long as the government demonstrates that it is adhering strictly to the Geneva Conventions and other applicable legal requirements.[15] If it does, a court can promptly dismiss a habeas petition. If the government fails to adhere to those well-established legal requirements, however, a court can remedy the failure, such as by ordering that the process used to determine a prisoner's status comply with the Geneva Conventions. Thus, although international armed conflicts, such as World War II, have traditionally involved the greatest number of prisoners, it is precisely in this context that habeas review is most circumscribed.

The limited but important function of habeas in international armed conflicts is to demand that the government show that its detentions are being conducted under the proper legal framework, that it is providing prisoners with the required hearings and other protections to prevent error, and that it is complying with the rules mandating humane treatment and prohibiting torture and other forms of abuse. To make this showing, the government would not have to present live testimony but could submit a sworn statement by a high-level official describing how it was treating prisoners seized in the conflict and confirming that the same standards and procedures were being applied to the particular prisoner in question.

Some habeas petitioners might claim that military officials made a mistake in their particular case. For example, a petitioner might claim that he was improperly denied prisoner-of-war status under Article 4 of the Third Geneva Convention. Another might argue that she never provided support to the enemy army and was improperly interned as a civilian under the Fourth Geneva Convention. But for individuals captured in an international armed conflict and held in accordance with the Geneva Conventions, a court need not conduct an individualized inquiry into each detainee's allegations. Instead, a court could defer to the findings of a properly constituted military tribunal that assessed the detainee's status as long as that status was legally authorized (i.e., that the category of persons who could be detained was correctly defined as prisoner of war or civilian) and the tribunal reached its determination through the required process to minimize the risk of error (i.e., a hearing conducted in accordance with Article 5 of the Third Geneva Convention and applicable military regulations). Commanders and soldiers in the field would neither have to testify at habeas hearings in federal court nor rebut the specific allegations made by every prisoner in U.S. custody who filed a petition challenging his or her detention. Although a court would always retain the power to probe further on habeas, particularly if confronted with egregious or widespread evidence of illegal detention and abuse, the ordinary rule would be summary dismissal of wartime petitions in international armed conflicts.

There are sound reasons for cabining habeas review under these circumstances. The military detention of combatants during armed conflicts with enemy nations is firmly rooted in both international law and the Constitution, which grants Congress the power to declare war and to make rules governing the capture of prisoners[16] and which gives the president the power to prosecute the war as commander in chief.[17] As an original matter, the Constitution's framers understood war as existing only between sovereign states.[18] War might vary in its magnitude and intensity—hence, the difference between "perfect" and "imperfect" wars—but war, in the legal sense, existed only between two or more governments.[19] This view persisted long after the country's founding. During the Civil War, for example, when President Abraham Lincoln commissioned the first codification of the laws and usages of war, he defined public war as a "state of armed hostility between sovereign nations or governments."[20] Similarly, the cases on which the Bush administration leaned most heavily after 9/11 to defend its indefinite military detention of suspected terrorists as "enemy combatants"—*Eisentrager* and *Quirin*—understood war as existing between nation-states. Thus, while the Constitution recognizes broad executive power during wartime—including the extraordinary power to detain without criminal charge and trial—it also contemplates that power as operating within fixed and well-defined parameters.

In an international armed conflict, it also is generally clear who may be detained, both legally and factually. Not only are the legal categories clear (i.e., prisoner of war or civilian), but the fact-finding process—a military status hearing conducted close to capture in both time and place—provides a meaningful safeguard against mistakes. Put simply, in international armed conflicts, in which combatant status is based on membership in the enemy government's armed forces and that status is ordinarily easy to discern (e.g., because soldiers wear uniforms and carry weapons openly), the Geneva Conventions' more streamlined process of Article 5 hearings is generally sufficient to prevent error. At the same time, given the finite and discernable temporal limits of such conflicts (i.e., when hostilities between nations cease), the costs of mistaken detention are less severe. Military detention in these circumstances is thus best understood as a limited exception to, rather than a permanent abrogation of, ordinary due process requirements. In this context, military procedures, implemented in accordance with the Geneva Conventions and U.S. military regulations, can also be viewed as providing an adequate substitute for habeas corpus.

By contrast, military detention outside international armed conflict lacks a constitutional foundation or pedigree. To be sure, American history contains a number of examples in which military force was used against nonstate actors, such as pirates and slave traders. But those captured in military operations against nonstate actors were generally prosecuted under civilian law, not held as prisoners of war or otherwise treated as "combatants" exempt from the ordinary requirement of criminal charge and trial.[21] The main exception—a civil war—is more a variation than a departure, as the party in opposition claims and exercises the functions of a sovereign state (e.g., a governmental structure, organized army), as the Confederacy did during the American Civil War.[22] Thus, the very notion of indefinite military detention outside the strictures of an international armed conflict or a conflict against a de facto state in a civil war raises serious constitutional questions. If the United States can effectively treat the members or supporters of al Qaeda and other terrorist organizations anywhere in the world as combatants in a perpetual war, what are the limits? Can the same power to detain indefinitely without trial be employed against an inner-city gang or drug cartel that the government views, rightly or wrongly, as endangering the public safety? Military detention in these circumstances not only threatens individual liberties but also raises concerns about military intrusion into the civilian sphere of criminal law enforcement.

Armed conflicts that are not between nation-states are referred to as noninternational armed conflicts. Since World War II, international law has developed to address conflicts that do not involve two or more opposing states. The rational behind these developments is not to maximize the detaining state's power or to avoid legal constraints, as the Bush administration did after 9/11 by selectively invoking and manipulating the law of war. Rather, it is to ensure that all individuals seized during armed conflict have some protection against arbitrary detention and mistreatment. In noninternational armed conflicts, however, there is a presumption that the domestic law of the state in which the detention occurs will continue to govern and that those detained will be prosecuted under that state's laws. This presumption reflects the fact that civilians who engage in hostilities (also called *unprivileged belligerents*) have no status in international law, since there is no conflict between two or more sovereigns, and seeks to avoid interference with a state's right to treat insurrection, insurgency, or terrorism within its borders as a crime under its laws.[23] In noninternational armed conflicts, international law also requires adherence to the due process guarantees of human rights law, including meaningful access to a court, whereas in international armed conflicts, many of these guarantees are addressed by the Geneva Conventions.[24]

In addition, the risk of mistaken detention is generally much greater in noninternational armed conflicts than in international armed conflicts. It is precisely because insurgents, guerrillas, and other nonstate forces do not always wear uniforms, bear arms openly, or otherwise seek to distinguish themselves from the civilian population that it is more difficult to identify those subject to detention in a noninternational armed conflict. Accordingly, whereas in international armed conflict, there is generally little factual uncertainty about the enemy, in noninternational armed conflict, there is often some, if not a great deal, of factual uncertainty. This uncertainty is multiplied when, as the United States did after 9/11, a country seeks to detain, as part of a global "war on terrorism," people who were never present on or near a battlefield, who never engaged in hostilities, and who, in some instances, had no connection to armed conflict at all.

At the same time, the cost of error is greater, given the uncertain and potentially extended duration of a noninternational armed conflict against insurgents, terrorists, or other nonstate groups. The United States, for example, maintains that it is engaged in an armed conflict against al Qaeda and "associated" terrorist organizations that is not only global in scope but also generational in duration. Both the risks and the costs of erroneous detention in such a conflict are thus far greater than in an armed conflict between nations, in which under the Geneva Conventions prisoners must be promptly released and repatriated at the end of hostilities.[25]

For these reasons, detention in noninternational armed conflict warrants broader habeas review. A court must do more than simply confirm that the government is complying with the Geneva Conventions and holding combatants as prisoners of war, as it would do in an international armed conflict. In a noninternational armed conflict, in which international law does not supply a basis for detention, a court must address who may properly be subject to detention without charge: that is, the category of persons—if any—subject to military confinement or administrative detention rather than prosecution in the regular criminal courts. A court must also determine whether the individual prisoner is himself detainable. In other words, even if the government is properly authorized to detain a limited category of persons militarily (such as members of an organized military force of a nonstate actor engaging in hostilities against U.S. or allied forces in a theater of war), a court must determine that a prisoner actually falls into that category as a factual matter—whether by conducting that fact-finding inquiry itself or ensuring that there is an adequate alternative process to make that determination. Any such process must contain the safeguards required by human rights and customary international law, including access to an independent and impartial body and to a legal representative.[26]

Habeas review is especially critical in two circumstances: when the government fails to follow the laws of war and other applicable rules in its treatment of prisoners seized during armed conflict and when wartime detention power is extended beyond the bounds of armed conflict itself. Both circumstances occurred after 9/11 in the United States' detention of "enemy combatants."

These detentions, to be sure, traded on familiar concepts: incapacitating the enemy's soldiers to prevent their "return to the battlefield" and refusing to afford prisoner-of-war status to those who fight outside regular military units and do not adhere to the laws of war.[27] The notion that individuals could engage in hostile acts without the protected status afforded to regular members of an enemy armed force has a long history. Francis Lieber, who wrote one of the first codifications of the laws of land warfare during the American Civil War and helped lay the groundwork for the 1899 and 1907 Hague Conventions defining rights and duties during armed conflict, cited the differing levels of protection that might apply to irregular bands of armed men who did not obey the rules and customs of warfare.[28] Likewise, the 1949 Geneva Conventions distinguish between privileged and unprivileged belligerents by giving combatant immunity only to prisoners of war and singling out for special treatment spies, saboteurs, and others whose activities jeopardize the security of an occupying power and who can be prosecuted under domestic law for taking up arms.[29]

Modern developments have increased the challenges of unprivileged belligerency, with the traditional model of uniformed armies squaring off against one another in rank-and-file formation giving way to amorphous and wide-ranging methods of warfare in which individuals can act as guerrillas, partisans, spies, or saboteurs.[30] Terrorism presents additional challenges. Terrorists do not wear uniforms or openly acknowledge their identities but instead try to blend in with the ordinary population. They also indiscriminately target civilians.[31]

The Bush administration, however, exploited these challenges to maximize executive power and avoid all legal constraints. It maintained that terrorists were just like the spies, saboteurs, and others before them who engaged in warlike acts without adhering to the laws of war. This, the administration stated, made them "unlawful combatants," and meant that any level of involvement—even the mere provision of support to al Qaeda or an "associated group"—could justify a person's indefinite military detention or trial for war crimes before a military commission that failed to meet the standards of the regular civilian courts or military courts-martial. The Bush administration thus claimed the power to fight an armed conflict of global scope and infinite duration against an enemy whose members and affiliates could be treated as combatants in order to exempt them from regular due process requirements but who had no privilege of belligerency, rendering even otherwise lawful acts of war a war crime, and no legal protections against arbitrary detention and abuse.

This approach was deeply flawed. First, combatant status developed in the context of international armed conflict and has long been tied to a person's connection to an enemy nation's armed forces. The prevailing view, including that of the ICRC, which monitors compliance with the 1949 Geneva Conventions, was that no wartime prisoner in international armed conflict fell outside the category of combatants under the Third Geneva Convention or civilians under the Fourth Geneva Convention. To be a combatant under the Geneva Conventions was to be a prisoner of war; all others were civilians who, if they took a direct part in hostilities, were "unprivileged belligerents" and could be prosecuted criminally under domestic law.[32] There was, in other words, no separate category of "unlawful combatant."[33] Only a person who was a combatant in the first instance had the privilege of belligerency, which included taking up arms against the enemy's soldiers and attacking its military targets with legal impunity. That person could expose himself to criminal sanctions for violating the laws of war, as did the German soldiers in *Quirin* who committed perfidy by removing their uniforms and surreptitiously entering the United States to attack military targets, thereby rendering their belligerency unlawful. All other persons, however, were noncombatants (i.e., civilians) and did not have the combatant's privileged status to engage in armed conflict.[34]

Civilians who engage in hostilities—including terrorists—are thus more accurately described as "unprivileged belligerents" than as "unlawful combatants." Although unprivileged belligerents may be targeted with military force when they are directly participating in hostilities, they remain civilians for purposes of detention and trial. This does not mean they are immune from punishment. To the contrary, unprivileged belligerents may be prosecuted for murder or related offenses under domestic law. The Bush administration thus deviated from long-standing rules and customary practice by seeking to treat those who allegedly were connected to or supported al Qaeda and associated organizations as combatants subject to indefinite military detention or military prosecution as war criminals rather than as civilians subject to criminal prosecution under domestic law.

The Bush administration also manipulated the "enemy combatant" label to create a category of prisoners without legal protection under any body of law, civilian or military, domestic or international. All individuals taken into custody during armed conflict, even if denied prisoner-of-war status, are still entitled to protections against arbitrary detention and abuse under other provisions of the Geneva Conventions, customary international law, and, in noninternational armed conflicts, international human rights law.[35] Indeed, much of the post–World War II development in international humanitarian law was intended to ensure that no prisoner in armed conflict—even armed conflict outside the traditional state-based framework of the 1949 Geneva Conventions—is beyond the law. Nonetheless, the Bush administration sought to treat the fight against terrorism as a global armed conflict and to deny the prisoners that it captured any legal protections or access to the courts by labeling them "enemy combatants."

The administration thus extended the concept of war beyond the parameters of a conflict against another nation-state and also beyond the confines of any country or theater of operations where U.S. forces were engaged in hostilities. There was no material difference, it argued, between an armed soldier seized during combat against U.S. forces on a battlefield near Kandahar and a student arrested at his home in Peoria by the FBI on suspicion that he was providing support to a terrorist organization or plotting a terrorist crime.

The troubling implications of this argument were highlighted by the *al-Marri* and *Padilla* cases, in which the president claimed he could order the military to seize and detain citizens and legal residents inside the United States as part of the global "war on terrorism." These cases made clear that the United States was not just imprisoning people captured during military operations in Afghanistan and Iraq outside the Geneva Conventions, human rights law, and the Constitution. It also was applying its unbridled military detention power inside the country, threatening fundamental safeguards against detention without charge or trial.[36]

Finally, the Bush administration denied prisoners any meaningful process to challenge their detention. During the international armed conflict in Afghanistan (i.e., from the U.S.-led invasion that began in October 2001 until the fall of the Taliban regime that December and the establishment of a new government in June 2002), the Bush administration failed to provide the required military process—Article 5 hearings under the Geneva Conventions—to determine whether Taliban soldiers and militia under their command were entitled to prisoner-of-war status. These hearings would have given individuals the opportunity to testify, to attend open sessions, and to call witnesses if reasonably available, all before a neutral three-officer adjudicatory panel, while also prohibiting the use of evidence gained by torture or other coercion, whether physical or mental. Although summary in nature, the hearings would have been held close in time and place to the prisoner's capture to maximize accuracy.[37] The United States also failed to follow international law during the subsequent noninternational armed conflict in Afghanistan (i.e., when the United States and allied forces were no longer fighting the Afghan regime but assisting that regime against insurgents in the country), by detaining individuals without charge, due process, or court review. In addition, the administration failed to bring charges against or provide any meaningful process to those seized outside Afghanistan and held in connection with the global "war on terror" at Guantánamo, CIA "black sites," and Bagram, where some prisoners were rendered after having been seized in other countries. Instead, it compounded the problem by engaging in torture and other coercive interrogation tactics and then relying on the fruits of the information it obtained as the basis for the detentions.

In short, the United States tried to wage war without rules and to extend war without limit. The costs of this legal breakdown were profound and far-reaching. Individuals were swept up by mistake or sold for bounty and imprisoned for years without a fair hearing and without any process for correcting errors. Stripped of any legal protections and without any clear recourse to the courts, a system of torture, arbitrary detention, and abuse took hold and festered.

Habeas corpus does not guarantee that U.S. detention standards and procedures will adhere to legal requirements. But it does at least subject those standards and procedures to an independent checking mechanism. The prospect of habeas review also means that the United States is more likely to define the scope of its detention power more carefully and responsibly, to limit military confinement to appropriate circumstances, and to institute an adequate process of error correction up front to minimize the risk of more expansive judicial involvement later.

Federal habeas corpus jurisdiction over all U.S. detentions, regardless of location, would undoubtedly lead to increased judicial review of military action during wartime. But following *Boumediene* and its rejection of bright-line limitations on the Constitution's extraterritorial application, more litigation is inevitable. As long as the United States continues to detain prisoners in counterterrorism operations overseas, courts will be called on to address such basic issues as who may be detained, what rights they must be given, and what procedures the government must employ to protect against wrongful imprisonment. But whereas jurisdictional litigation is a deadweight loss, all sides benefit from clear detention rules. So, for example, it is better for a court to adjudicate whether the standards and procedures used by the United States at Bagram meet applicable legal and constitutional requirements than for a court to say it has no power to make that determination and thus no power to remedy potentially illegal detentions. Jurisdiction, in other words, should not be in dispute: as long as a prisoner is in U.S. custody, a court should have the power to review the lawfulness of his confinement.

Habeas review also does not require an individualized judicial hearing for every person captured by U.S. forces during military operations. In many cases, it may not require any such hearing at all. Most important, it does not ordinarily require such a hearing in an international armed conflict that is conducted in accordance with the Geneva Conventions. Thus, while courts in theory could have exercised habeas jurisdiction over the detention of individuals held as prisoners of war during World War II, those petitions would have been summarily dismissed on the merits because the detentions were clearly lawful.

Under U.S. law, habeas also may not require a judicial hearing for some prisoners seized in a noninternational armed conflict—as long as the legal standard for detention is properly limited and the prisoners are given a hearing before an impartial and independent body that comports with due process and is subject to judicial review. As the Supreme Court explained in *Hamdi*, it is possible that a properly constituted military tribunal can fairly determine a battlefield detainee's status. Similarly, in *Boumediene*, the Court observed that when an adequate military process has been provided to protect against wrongful detention, a habeas judge may be able to defer to its findings, provided that the military is acting within its proper sphere. But the Court also made clear that without a meaningful process to test the government's allegations, habeas corpus must be available to supply such a process directly.

Even when courts supply a fact-finding process, moreover, that does not mean that judges will necessarily conduct live hearings. Habeas practice itself has evolved over the centuries so that the jailer (or custodian, in habeas terms) no longer has to produce the body of the prisoner in court to justify the prisoner's detention. Courts now have at their disposal other tools to receive evidence, from admitting affidavits to taking testimony through audio or video links. When necessary, there also is the possibility of using special masters or magistrates to assist judges in adjudicating cases.

In addition, this type of individualized review by a U.S. court would be unnecessary if the United States provided access to a court in the state in which the detention occurs. Thus at Bagram, for example, if the United States provided prisoners seized in Afghanistan with access to Afghan courts in accordance with international law—as other countries operating there as part of the International Security Assistance Forces normally do by transferring prisoners to Afghan custody within ninety-six hours of their arrest rather than detaining them indefinitely—a U.S. habeas court's review would be circumscribed because the detention would be pursuant to Afghan law.[38]

Viewing increased litigation and national security as opponents in a zero-sum game is a mistake. Guantánamo, Abu Ghraib, and secret CIA "black sites" have undermined, not enhanced, America's safety because they have created a perception of lawlessness. Legal norms have great strategic value, and the United States disregards them at its peril.[39] It is for this reason, for example, that the U.S. *Army–Marine Corps Counterinsurgency Manual* highlights the harmful strategic impact of "illegitimate actions . . . involving the use of power without authority," including "unlawful detention, torture, and punishment without trial."[40] Successful military operations, particularly those waged against insurgents or others who contest the state's legitimacy, depend on a perception that the state—or another state that detains on its behalf—is bound by the rule of law. As the Supreme Court recently explained, "Security subsists, too, in fidelity to freedom's first principles," chief among them being "freedom from arbitrary and unlawful restraint and the personal liberty that is secured by adherence to the separation of powers."[41] Habeas corpus helps promote this fidelity by requiring a jailer to account for the detention and treatment of prisoners in his custody or control.

Finally, greater judicial involvement is the natural result of expanding the military and intelligence agencies into new areas and the novel questions it raises. Detention in a "war on terrorism" not only is prolonged and indefinite. It also is not based on clear indicators of status (e.g., membership in a nation's armed forces) or narrowly circumscribed (e.g., taking up arms on a battlefield or in a theater of operations where U.S. forces are engaged in hostilities). Instead, it turns on an assessment of a person as a "security risk" based on his perceived dangerousness or associations or simply a belief that he might provide information about others. In these circumstances, military detention jeopardizes both the presumption of innocence and the Constitution's prohibition against imprisonment without trial for suspected crimes. Increased litigation is unavoidable as well as appropriate because it enables the judiciary to fulfill its required role under the Constitution by protecting individuals against arbitrary and unlawful executive action.

— 11 —

The Elusive Custodian

Some Potential Limits of Habeas Corpus

The enduring strength of habeas corpus is that it requires the state to justify a prisoner's detention before an independent court that has the power to find the detention illegal and order the prisoner's release. But in that strength lies a weakness: the incentive it creates for the state to structure its detention operations to avoid habeas corpus altogether or to curtail the court's ability to grant an effective remedy, an incentive that can be particularly strong in matters affecting national security.

Actions taken after the September 11 attacks illustrate this paradox, from the Bush administration's decision to transfer prisoners to Guantánamo in early 2002 to Congress's twice enacting legislation seeking to repeal habeas corpus and overturn Supreme Court decisions recognizing the Guantánamo detainees' right to the writ. The desire to avoid habeas corpus also influenced the Bush administration's decision to detain people at other, more remote and secret offshore prisons, from military facilities like Bagram to CIA-operated "black sites."

Even though the Bush administration went to extraordinary lengths to avoid habeas corpus, it was not the first, and it will not be the last, administration to try to escape accountability. The nature of terrorism, with its potential both to inflict death and destruction and to instill fear, can lead public officials to err on the side of security and secrecy rather than liberty and transparency. This is why recognizing that habeas corpus applies to all individuals in U.S. custody, regardless of where they are detained, is essential to preventing the creation of more prisons beyond the law or "new Guantánamos." But habeas corpus will always be vulnerable to those who want to circumvent it. Future administrations will seek to find new ways to avoid judicial review if they believe it is necessary to do so. One way of concealing responsibility is to claim that the prisoner is in the custody and control of another government. Another is to avoid detaining the prisoner altogether and rendering him to another country for further detention and interrogation. Both were done after 9/11 and helped transform overseas detentions into a shell game in which prisoners were moved from one jail to another to escape judicial scrutiny.

For a federal court to exercise habeas corpus jurisdiction, an individual must be in the custody or control of a U.S. official. The text of the habeas corpus statute authorizes courts to issue writs of habeas corpus only when an individual is "in custody under or by color of the authority of the United States" or "in violation of the Constitution or laws or treaties of the United States."[1] Habeas was not meant to address unlawful detentions by another government, and a U.S. judge has no authority to order a foreign official to release a prisoner, not even an American citizen. Habeas, in other words, does not make U.S. courts the world's policemen for human rights violations. Instead, it is directed at imprisonment by, or at the behest of, U.S. officials (or state government officials, as the case may be).

Detentions in the "war on terrorism" have thus posed significant challenges to habeas corpus review, not only because they have largely occurred outside the United States, but also because U.S. officials have often tried to conceal their role. In the CIA's "black sites," for example, the United States detained prisoners in secret. In the related practice of "ghosting," the CIA and military intelligence detained prisoners at known Defense Department facilities, such as Bagram in Afghanistan and Abu Ghraib in Iraq, but hid the detainees' existence, even from the ICRC. Proxy detention is another, more subtle way that the United States has masked its involvement. Here, the United States does not exercise formal or exclusive control over the prisoner but instead exercises varying degrees of control and influence through the intermediary of a foreign state. In some forms of proxy detention, physical custody is shared by the United States and a foreign government; in others, the United States may direct the detention without any physical involvement at all. And in the closely related practice of extraordinary rendition, the United States "outsources" the detention and interrogation to a foreign country, typically one that has both a close relationship with U.S. intelligence agencies and a record of torture.[2]

Secret detention and extraordinary rendition are forms of forced disappearance. They rank among the worst human rights abuses committed by the United States after 9/11 and were central to the Bush administration's program of state-sanctioned torture. Paradoxically, though, secret detention and extraordinary rendition, as well as proxy detention, pose some of the most significant challenges to habeas corpus because they deliberately seek to conceal or minimize the United States' role and thus make it more difficult to establish the necessary prerequisite to the exercise of habeas jurisdiction: a finding that the prisoner is in U.S. custody or control.

A brief discussion of the meaning of the "in custody" requirement makes clearer its implications for habeas review of these forms of detention. This requirement has traditionally been interpreted flexibly to achieve the writ's purpose. At common law, custody was understood to reach "all manner of illegal confinement."[3] The federal habeas corpus statute, which incorporated these common law principles, eschewed narrow and formalistic limitations on the writ's scope.[4] The original 1789 statute referred to any prisoner "in custody, under or by colour of the authority of the United States," and not just those in physical U.S. custody.[5] The 1867 amendments to this statute, which extended federal habeas jurisdiction to prisoners in state custody, was similarly broad, encompassing any prisoner in custody "in violation of the Constitution or laws or treaties of the United States."[6]

Courts, in turn, have liberally interpreted custody to achieve the writ's larger purpose. "The custody requirement," the Supreme Court wrote, "is designed to preserve the writ of habeas corpus as a remedy for severe restraints on individual liberty."[7] Judges have thus found habeas corpus jurisdiction in a variety of situations in which the petitioner was not in the jailer's actual physical custody in order to determine whether the restraint on the petitioner's liberty was lawful.[8] Under a theory of "constructive custody," for example, courts have considered challenges by habeas petitioners imprisoned in one state and subject to a detainer in another state;[9] petitioners in federal or state prisons and subject to a deportation order seeking their removal from the United States under immigration law;[10] those on parole but nonetheless restrained by the conditions imposed on them;[11] and foreign nationals seeking review of a decision denying them entry to the United States, even though they were free to go to another country.[12] In all these cases, the habeas statute's "in custody" requirement was satisfied because a federal or state government official was responsible for significant restraints on the petitioner's freedom, even if those restraints did not take a direct or tangible form.[13]

It is true that none of these situations addressed proxy detention or other forms of confinement in which a prisoner is in the physical custody of a foreign government. But the basic principle is the same. Detention by U.S. officials exercised through or in conjunction with another government should be considered detention by the United States for purposes of habeas jurisdiction. Indeed, proxy detention and related forms of secret imprisonment present a particularly compelling case for habeas review because they are a deliberate and calculated attempt to circumvent the writ. They are the modern version of the age-old attempt to transport prisoners beyond the seas—an abuse that prompted landmark habeas legislation more than four centuries ago.[14] Preventing the government from being able to manipulate jurisdiction by moving prisoners around was, after all, one of the Supreme Court's main justifications for upholding habeas jurisdiction over the Guantánamo detentions. To deny jurisdiction because the custody is constructive rather than actual would frustrate the purpose of habeas corpus and create a loophole for the United States to continue a practice of extrajudicial detention.

A broad view of constructive custody is reinforced by human rights norms that apply even in a noninternational armed conflict against al Qaeda and other terrorist organizations. Human rights treaties and customary international law prohibit detention without due process and transfers to torture—both of which lie at the heart of secret prisons, proxy detention, and extraordinary rendition. The International Covenant on Civil and Political Rights (ICCPR) prohibits arbitrary arrest and detention while mandating prompt judicial review when an individual is deprived of his liberty.[15] The ICCPR also has been interpreted to contain a *non-refoulement* obligation barring transfers when the risk of torture or other cruel, inhuman, and degrading treatment or punishment is significant.[16] Furthermore, the Convention against Torture and Other Cruel, Inhuman or Degrading Treatment or Punishment (CAT) contains an explicit and absolute ban against transfers to torture that applies even in a state of war or a time of public emergency.[17]

Although the ICCPR has been deemed "non-self-executing"—which means that Congress must enact separate implementing legislation for individuals to enforce its protections affirmatively in domestic litigation[18]—some courts have suggested that the treaty's protections can be invoked through the federal habeas corpus statute and that denying its protections to prisoners would raise serious problems under the Constitution's Suspension Clause.[19] The ICCPR also can help inform the interpretation of federal laws to avoid violating individual rights.[20] The CAT has been implemented through legislation and regulations, although there is continuing debate over whether its provisions may be enforced directly by courts outside the limited context of immigration removal proceedings.[21] The CAT also strengthens the *non-refoulement* obligation by requiring judicial review of "diplomatic assurances," the representations made by a receiving country that the transferred prisoner will not be tortured or abused,[22] and by prohibiting reliance on those assurances when the receiving country systematically or repeatedly engages in torture.[23]

Human rights bodies have interpreted these provisions to achieve their underlying purpose, rejecting the suggestion that there is a lacuna in the system for illegal actions taken outside a state's territory. (The United States does, however, take the contrary view that the ICCPR does not apply to U.S. action abroad.) The Human Rights Committee, which monitors and implements the ICCPR, has construed the *non-refoulement* obligation to apply extraterritorially to situations in which one government either retains effective control over the territory of another government or exercises personal control over the prisoner without territorial control.[24] The Committee against Torture, which is responsible for monitoring and implementing the CAT, has similarly applied that treaty's *non-refoulement* obligation to territory under a state's effective control.[25] Notably, the CAT's drafting history indicates that this obligation should apply to "any person who, for *whatever reason*, is in danger of being subjected to torture if handed over to another country . . . [and] cover *all measures* by which a person is physically transferred to another State."[26]

Regional human rights bodies have reached similar conclusions. For instance, the European Court of Human Rights has ruled that state officials can be held responsible for violating the rights of individuals that they seize or detain, even when those officials act abroad.[27] The Inter-American Commission on Human Rights likewise has explained that "individual rights inhere simply by virtue of a person's humanity . . . [and] the inquiry turns not on the presumed victim's nationality or presence within a geographic area, but on whether, under the specific circumstances, the State observed the rights of a person subject to its authority and control."[28]

Thus, an important principle underlying international treaties and customary norms is that a state must respect and guarantee the human rights of all persons in its custody or effective control, including the right not to be detained without due process or to be transferred to likely torture or other abuse. That principle covers an array of extraterritorial actions by the U.S. government in the "war on terrorism," from the operation of secret detention centers, like the CIA "black sites" (effective control over a place), to the abduction of individuals, like the kidnapping of Abu Omar off the streets of Milan (effective control over a person). It also mirrors the traditional understanding of habeas corpus: that a court has authority to enforce the writ against the jailer, regardless of where the custody or control is exercised, in order to ensure that there is a lawful basis for the prisoner's detention.

The case of Ahmed Abu Ali illustrates how the concept of constructive custody can be applied to overseas counterterrorism detentions. Abu Ali was a twenty-four-year-old American citizen who traveled to a university in Saudi Arabia to study after completing high school in Virginia, where he had grown up. Saudi officials arrested Abu Ali in June 2003, when he was taking his final exams at the university, and detained him without charge or access to counsel.[29] Approximately five days after Abu Ali's arrest, and at about the same time that FBI agents raided Abu Ali's home in Virginia, FBI agents visited the Saudi prison where Abu Ali was being held and observed his interrogation.[30] In the following months, FBI agents traveled to Saudi Arabia and interrogated Abu Ali directly while he was being detained by the Mubahith, Saudi Arabia's state security service, widely believed to engage in torture. Abu Ali later told his mother that the FBI agents had threatened to declare Abu Ali an "enemy combatant" and send him to Guantánamo if he did not cooperate.[31] In the meantime, Abu Ali's family began to press U.S. government officials to help him.

In June 2004, more than a year after his arrest, Abu Ali's family, acting as "next friend," filed a habeas corpus petition on his behalf in federal district court in Washington, D.C. The petition claimed that the United States was violating Abu Ali's constitutional rights by detaining him without charge and demanded that he be returned to the United States and charged with a crime, or released.[32] The petition presented evidence that the United States, and not Saudi Arabia, was directing Abu Ali's detention. That evidence included statements from Saudi government officials that they had no intention of charging Abu Ali, that they were instructed to "stay away" because the United States was "behind the case," and that the Saudi officials would release Abu Ali to American authorities if the United States made a formal request.[33] The petition also presented evidence that Abu Ali had been tortured. One witness said Abu Ali was in so much pain that he was not even able to pick up a pen to sign documents, and a federal prosecutor allegedly remarked that Abu Ali "doesn't have to worry about clipping his fingernails anymore."[34] The government did not produce any evidence to the contrary. Instead, it argued that a federal judge was precluded from inquiring into the matter because Abu Ali was in the custody of a foreign government and because the absence of actual custody by a U.S. official precluded habeas corpus review.

The district judge rejected the government's argument. The petition, the District Judge John D. Bates said, alleged a violation of the constitutional right to be free from arbitrary detention by the executive and therefore fell within the heartland of habeas corpus.[35] While Judge Bates did not determine that Abu Ali was in the custody of the United States, he ruled that the petition presented sufficient evidence to warrant further fact-finding. If that fact-finding demonstrated that Abu Ali was in constructive U.S. custody, Bates said that he would exercise jurisdiction to determine whether Abu Ali's detention was unlawful and, if so, order appropriate relief.[36]

In the end, this inquiry—known as "jurisdictional discovery"—never took place. The U.S. government avoided further scrutiny of Abu Ali's proxy detention by bringing criminal charges and returning him to America. The indictment, filed in the Eastern District of Virginia, alleged that Abu Ali had plotted to assassinate President Bush and hijack commercial airliners. Abu Ali was subsequently convicted and sentenced to life in prison.[37] In obtaining the conviction, the government relied on confessions elicited during Abu Ali's interrogations in Saudi Arabia, which the district court allowed into evidence after finding that the confessions were voluntary.[38]

At first glance, Judge Bates's decision to order jurisdictional discovery in Abu Ali's case might seem to have limited relevance, since it was explicitly confined to American citizens. American citizens, Bates observed, can claim the protection of habeas corpus when they are held by their own government, even when that detention occurs overseas. But this ruling predated *Boumediene*, in which the Supreme Court made clear that the same protection can also encompass foreign nationals held outside the United States. Read together, *Boumediene* and *Abu Ali* suggest that habeas corpus can reach proxy detention and other forms of secret imprisonment carried out beyond America's shores and in collusion with other governments, regardless of the prisoner's citizenship.

In this context, the challenge to accessing the courts through habeas corpus is as much practical as legal: discovering the existence of someone detained in secret or by proxy and obtaining the information necessary to pierce the veil of non-U.S. involvement. In many ways, Abu Ali's case was unusual. His family had managed to obtain extensive evidence from American and Saudi officials that the United States was pulling the strings behind his detention. This type of evidence has been—and will continue to be—more difficult to obtain in other cases, however, unless a court is willing to authorize some discovery and probe beneath the surface to examine the true nature of the Unites States' role. In some instances, the location of the prisoner itself may be unknown, as with individuals held in secret CIA jails. In other instances, the location may be known, but the evidence of U.S. involvement may be more circumstantial, as was the case with hundreds of prisoners held in Pakistan after 9/11.[39] A district judge can—and should—conduct the same kind of limited inquiry into the United States' role in an overseas detention whenever there is a good-faith basis to support it. In practice, however, courts may be reluctant to engage even in preliminary fact-finding over executive branch officials' objections that any such inquiry would interfere with the internal affairs of another sovereign nation and encroach on sensitive foreign policy concerns.

The transfer of detainees between governments and countries also can hinder the exercise of habeas jurisdiction. Historically, habeas corpus has provided for review of some international prisoner transfers. But that review has typically taken place when custodial control is officially acknowledged. The best example is extradition cases. There, habeas review is triggered when one country requests the return of a fugitive from another country, thereby commencing a formal legal process that results in a judge from the country where the fugitive is located ordering the fugitive's return to the requesting country. Although habeas review in extradition cases is relatively narrow, it does provide for judicial review of whether there is a legal basis for the transfer. But habeas review of prisoner transfers is compromised whenever the custodial control is fluid, the transfer secret, and the process intentionally extralegal and extrajudicial. Simply put, it is more difficult for courts to examine the lawfulness of a transfer when prisoners are moved around the globe and held in secret. Ultimately, some of those prisoners may resurface, as Binyam Mohamed and others did following their eventual transfer to Guantánamo, making habeas review more feasible. But that review comes only after months, if not years, of illegal detention, and after the worst abuses have likely occurred.

The fact that proxy detention is more difficult to reach through habeas corpus makes it an attractive option when U.S. officials want to avoid accountability, as the following case illustrates. In early 2007, the United States launched two air strikes at suspected al Qaeda targets in Somalia. The strikes were not an isolated occurrence but were part of ongoing U.S. counterterrorism operations in the Horn of Africa since the late 1990s. While the strikes received wide publicity, less is known about the role of American officials in the secret detention, interrogation, and rendition of civilians seized following the renewed violence in Somalia. One prisoner who fled the violence there, only to become ensnared in a U.S.-backed detention dragnet, was a twenty-four-year-old American citizen from New Jersey named Amir Mohamed Meshal.[40]

In late 2006, Meshal had traveled to Somalia for educational and religious purposes, drawn by the effort to create an Islamic state there. At the time, Somalia was enjoying a period of relative tranquillity after years of unrest.

But shortly after Meshal's arrival, fighting again erupted in the country and Ethiopian forces bombed the airport in the capital city of Mogadishu. Fearing for their safety, Meshal and others tried to flee Somalia by land. In late January 2007, Meshal was seized by Kenyan soldiers near the Somalia-Kenya border, stripped of his possessions, and taken to Nairobi, where he was detained without charge. Although nominally in Kenyan custody, Meshal was repeatedly interrogated by American officials, several of whom identified themselves as FBI agents. For several days, the agents came to Meshal's jail and took him to a small hotel in a residential neighborhood where they grilled him for more than six hours at a time. During those interrogations, agents threatened Meshal, warning him that he was in a "lawless country" and that if he did not cooperate and confess to involvement with al Qaeda, they would send him to Israel or to Egypt, where he would disappear. Meanwhile, a Kenyan human rights group was protesting the treatment of those seized fleeing the violence in Somalia and had challenged their detention without charge by filing habeas corpus petitions in Kenyan courts. But before the courts could act, Meshal and other prisoners were secretly rendered to Somalia, where they were detained in makeshift camps. Meshal and a number of other prisoners were then taken to Ethiopia.[41]

In Ethiopia, Meshal was detained in a secret jail near Addis Ababa. The other prisoners at the jail came from more than a dozen countries and included women and children. Like Meshal, many had fled the violence in Somalia. For the next three months, Meshal was interrogated repeatedly by American officials. U.S. officials also interrogated other prisoners at this Ethiopian secret jail. "I was kept in solitary [confinement] for a month, shackled ankle and feet, night and day," said a South African accountant who had traveled to Somalia to do charity work and was imprisoned in Ethiopia for almost five months. "The Ethiopians would come collect me, blindfold me and drive to some apartment in Addis [the capital]. And the Americans would be there waiting behind a desk, asking me over and over about my terrorist connections."[42]

During the months they were held in Ethiopia, Meshal and his fellow prisoners were never brought before a judge or permitted to see a lawyer or the evidence (if any) against them. Instead, they received only a cursory hearing before a secret military tribunal. The tribunal told them that they had no rights because they had been declared "enemy combatants"—prisoners in "Africa's Guantánamo," as it become known locally. The link was not merely metaphorical. At least one of the detainees swept up in Somalia, Mohammed Abdul Malik, was taken by the United States to Guantánamo.[43]

Meshal was eventually released in late May 2007 and returned to the United States in the face of mounting public and political pressure. His case, however, highlights some of the potential obstacles to addressing proxy detentions through habeas corpus unless judges view their authority to conduct jurisdictional discovery broadly. Initially, Meshal's detention was entirely secret. And even when a newspaper later reported that Meshal was being held in Kenya and then in Ethiopia, critical details about his detention and the United States' role in it remained unknown. Was the United States directing or conspiring with Kenyan and Ethiopian officials to detain Meshal? Were U.S. officials hiding behind the fiction of foreign custody so that they could interrogate Meshal without affording him the guarantees they would have had to provide to him if they acknowledged that he was in U.S. custody? Did U.S. officials order or approve Meshal's rendition from Kenya so that he could be further detained and interrogated outside the law, despite the grave risk of harm to him? It is possible that a habeas petition could have prompted a judicial inquiry similar to the inquiry ordered in Abu Ali's case and assessed whether the United States was exercising custody over Meshal. But it also is possible that a court would simply have dismissed the petition for failing to demonstrate U.S. custody (whether actual or constructive), leaving Meshal without a judicial remedy for the United States' role in his illegal detention.

The case of Naji Hamdan exemplifies similar problems posed by secret and proxy detentions, although its outcome suggests that habeas can still affect those detentions even when a court declines to exercise jurisdiction. Hamdan, a U.S. citizen and businessman from California, was living in the United Arab Emirates (UAE) with his wife and children. In August 2008, Hamdan was interrogated at the U.S. embassy in Abu Dhabi by FBI agents who had flown from Los Angeles to question him. A few weeks later, Hamdan was arrested by UAE police at his home and then disappeared into the hands of Emirati security forces, which held him virtually incommunicado and tried to coerce a confession from him. Although nominally in UAE custody, there was evidence that Hamdan was being held at the United States' request, including a statement from an Emirati official stating that the United States was responsible for Hamdan's detention. But when Hamdan's wife filed a habeas corpus petition on his behalf in federal district court in Washington, D.C., Hamdan was transferred by the state security forces to face prosecution in Abu Dhabi.[44] Hamdan's habeas petition was then dismissed on the ground that he had been charged in the UAE for a criminal offense and was no longer in U.S. custody, if he had ever been.[45] Hamdan was later convicted by a UAE court of terrorism charges and sentenced to eighteen months in prison. Even though Hamdan's habeas petition failed, it may have helped end his legal limbo by prompting the filing of criminal charges (albeit leading to his conviction).

Another example of proxy detention is the continued U.S. control and influence over prisoners who have been repatriated to other countries from U.S. detention at Guantánamo and Bagram. Take the case of Afghan prisoners returned to Afghanistan. In 2005, the United States and Afghanistan signed a joint declaration providing for the "gradual transfer of Afghan detainees to the exclusive custody and control of the Afghan Government."[46] As part of the agreement, the United States said it would finance the rebuilding of an Afghan prison block and help equip and train an Afghan guard force.[47] Accordingly, the United States spent more than $30 million constructing the new high-security Afghan National Detention Facility (ANDF) located in the Pul-i-Charki prison on the outskirts of Kabul.[48] The United States also tried to persuade Afghanistan to adopt a Guantánamo-like model that permitted the indefinite detention of "enemy combatants" and military commission trials at "Block D," as the ANDF is known locally.[49] When Afghanistan refused, the two countries agreed that former Guantánamo and Bagram prisoners at the ANDF would be detained and prosecuted under Afghan criminal law.[50] As of April 2008, more than 250 Guantánamo and Bagram detainees had been transferred to Block D,[51] which had the capacity to hold up to 700 prisoners in its 350 cells.[52]

The transfer of prisoners from U.S. detention at Guantánamo and Bagram to Afghan detention at the ANDF, however, did not necessarily end U.S. control or influence. The United States, for example, implemented some forms of "soft" control by requiring that Afghanistan share intelligence information with U.S. officials, conduct surveillance, and restrict the prisoners' travel following their release.[53] The United States also exerted more direct forms of control, such as preventing Afghan defense attorneys from meeting with their clients.[54] As the chairman of the Afghanistan Human Rights Organization commented in 2007 on the continuing U.S. involvement, "Everyone knows who's really in control. They just won't say it."[55]

Habeas corpus is not the only remedy for illegal detention. Civil damages suits also provide an opportunity for redress. Most important, they hold out the possibility of compensation for those who have been unlawfully imprisoned and mistreated. In addition, they can help deter abuses in the future by putting officials on notice that they may be held liable for human and civil rights violations. But damages actions also face hurdles of their own even when the plaintiff has solid evidence to support his claims: for example, the United States has invoked the "state secrets" privilege to bar lawsuits by victims of torture and extraordinary rendition on the ground that any litigation would reveal sensitive national security information;[56] it also has asserted affirmative defenses like qualified immunity that insulate government officials from liability for violating constitutional rights that were not clearly established at the time they were committed.[57] Damages actions, moreover, have an inherent limitation: unlike habeas petitions, they are intended to remedy past wrongs, not to obtain release from continued detention.

Other safeguards can help decrease the risk of extrajudicial detention and renditions. One possibility is legislation outlawing secret detention by the CIA or any other agency and preventing the United States from engaging in proxy detention. Such legislation could, for example, prohibit the United States from entering into a formal or informal agreement with a foreign government to detain a person on behalf of the United States as well as impose restrictions on U.S. interrogations of individuals in foreign custody to ensure compliance with due process requirements and to discourage U.S. officials from outsourcing detention to avoid accountability. Congress could also make explicit that it was implementing the United States' *non-refoulement* obligation in domestic law with respect to any prisoner transfer (including transfers made from outside the United States) and that the Convention against Torture prohibits transfers to countries that have a demonstrated pattern of engaging in torture, regardless of any assurances those countries might provide in an individual case.

In addition, federal agencies could be required to issue formal rules for transferring prisoners from U.S. custody in order to make those agencies accountable and to facilitate habeas review. The State Department has promulgated regulations for extradition cases, and the Department of Homeland Security has issued regulations for immigration removal decisions, helping subject those decisions to review for compliance with the United States' *non-refoulement* obligations under the Convention against Torture and implementing legislation.[58] Extradition and immigration removal, however, involve transfers from the United States to another government. None of the relevant federal agencies has issued formal regulations governing extraterritorial prisoner transfers, the context in which extraordinary rendition typically occurs. The Defense Department has described its policies on prisoner transfers from Guantánamo but has neither issued any formal rules nor made clear what policies govern prisoner transfers outside Guantánamo. Meanwhile, the CIA, the agency principally responsible for extraordinary rendition, has never disclosed what, if any, rules govern its transfer of prisoners to other governments. Requiring agencies to promulgate rules would help provide more concrete and transparent procedures for extraterritorial transfers, assuming those agencies continued to engage in the practice. It would also facilitate pretransfer review through habeas corpus to determine whether the United States is complying with its *non-refoulement* obligations by replacing the secret handover of prisoners with a more formal legal process.

This chapter has focused on some practical obstacles to habeas review when the detention is secret (CIA "black sites"), carried out in collusion with another government (proxy detention), or temporary because of the prisoner's impending transfer to another government (extraordinary rendition). But another potential limitation of habeas review will persist even when courts exercise habeas jurisdiction because that limitation is inherent in habeas itself.

Habeas corpus requires that the jailer justify a prisoner's detention to a court. But the mere availability of habeas corpus does not itself ensure a correct outcome. Habeas does not, for example, determine how a court will analyze various precedents, statutes, and legal doctrines and apply them to the facts of the case before it. Nor does it answer threshold questions concerning the proper scope of the military's detention authority—that is, who may be held as an "enemy combatant" or prosecuted before a military commission for war crimes. Habeas instead provides a mechanism and a forum for the judiciary to supply its answer to those and other questions, as well as a process for the detainee to challenge the government's allegations against him. The availability of habeas also does not dictate the remedy in all situations, for instance, when there is no lawful basis to detain but the prisoner cannot be returned to his home country. As a result, a number of Guantánamo detainees have been held for years even after it was established that they were not "enemy combatants" because the United States could not send them home or repatriate them to another country and because judges did not believe they had the power to order their temporary release into the United States.

The force of habeas corpus can thus be diminished if a reviewing court misapplies the law, if the underlying law itself grants too much power to the executive or licenses arbitrary action, or if the court misconstrues its ability to grant an effective remedy. Indeed, habeas review can even legitimize the very abuses that it is meant to prevent by giving illegal executive action a judicial stamp of approval. We need only recall the Supreme Court's decisions upholding challenges to the internment of 120,000 Japanese Americans during World War II to realize that judicial review does not necessarily ensure justice or vindicate constitutional rights.[59]

In the next chapter, therefore, we return to questions raised earlier that a habeas corpus petition can ask but that the law of habeas itself does not answer—questions that go to the heart of current debates about U.S. detention policy. Central among them is whether suspected terrorists can be subjected to indefinite military detention and/or prosecuted before military commissions or whether they instead should be charged and tried in the regular federal courts.

Terrorism as Crime

Toward a Lawful and Sustainable Detention Policy

As the Bush presidency neared its end, approximately 250 prisoners were still being held at Guantánamo, hundreds more in Bagram, thousands in Iraq, and an undefined number in secret or proxy detention. One person was still being detained as an "enemy combatant" inside the United States. For more than five and a half years, Ali al-Marri had been imprisoned without criminal charge or trial at a navy brig in Charleston, South Carolina. Al-Marri had been detained by the military even though he did not meet any traditional or legal definition of a combatant: he was not a member of the armed forces of an enemy state; he had never taken up arms against U.S. or allied forces; and he was not seized on a battlefield or in connection with any military activity. Instead, al-Marri had been arrested at his home in Peoria, Illinois, by FBI agents and then prosecuted in federal court until the president declared him an "enemy combatant" less than a month before trial and on the eve of a hearing to suppress the evidence against him.

Could the president deprive al-Marri of his constitutional right to a criminal trial based on the allegation that he was plotting terrorist acts in the United States and imprison him indefinitely in military custody? The answer to that basic—but critical—question remained uncertain. In June 2007, a three-judge panel of the U.S. Court of Appeals for the Fourth Circuit, which sits in Richmond, Virginia, had ruled that al-Marri's military detention was illegal.[1] The full appeals court, however, agreed to rehear the case and then reversed the panel's judgment in a narrowly divided and fractured decision. The full court ruled, by a five-to-four vote, that the president had legal authority to detain al-Marri as an "enemy combatant" if, as the government alleged, he had come to the United States to engage in terrorist activities on behalf of al Qaeda. The court's decision rested on the Authorization for Use of Military Force (AUMF), enacted by Congress in the immediate aftermath of the September 11 attacks. The court also ruled, however, by a different five-to-four majority, that al-Marri was entitled to greater protections than the district court had afforded him in challenging those allegations and remanded the case to the district court for further proceedings.[2]

Judge Diana Gribbon Motz wrote both the original panel decision and the opinion for the four judges who voted to invalidate al-Marri's military detention.[3] Judge Motz looked to the laws of war to help determine what domestic military detention power the AUMF granted and the Constitution allowed. According to the Supreme Court's decisions, she explained, the legal definition of a "combatant" had always rested on a person's affiliation with the military arm of an enemy nation.[4] In *Hamdi*, moreover, the Court had expressly cautioned against stretching the AUMF's grant of military detention power beyond long-standing law-of-war principles, such as soldiers who take up arms on a battlefield alongside enemy government forces. No precedent supported treating al-Marri as a combatant in a global military conflict against a terrorist group and thereby imprisoning him without the guarantees of the Bill of Rights. Instead, Motz said, al-Marri was a civilian, and under the Constitution, civilians must be charged and tried for their alleged crimes in the ordinary courts as long as those courts are open and functioning—a principle embodied by Supreme Court decisions such as *Ex parte Milligan*.

Judge Motz also observed that Congress had specifically addressed the detention of domestic terrorism suspects at virtually the same time it enacted the AUMF. In the Patriot Act, Congress increased law enforcement's power to investigate and prosecute suspected terrorists, and it enhanced the attorney general's authority to detain alien terrorist suspects seized in the United States. But Congress also cabined that detention power, stating that suspected alien terrorists had to be charged within seven days of arrest and rejected the Bush administration's request for the power to detain indefinitely.[5] By relabeling al-Marri an "enemy combatant," the administration had therefore thwarted not only the Constitution but Congress as well.

Judge Motz underscored the broader threat that al-Marri's military detention posed to the Constitution. The notion that the president could simply designate allegedly dangerous people as enemies of the state and thereby deny them the right to a criminal trial defied the country's core principles. Today it was an alleged al Qaeda agent, but tomorrow it might be someone who merely associated with a terrorist group or knew a terrorist; one day, it might be someone accused of other crimes such as drug trafficking; and eventually, it might be a politically disfavored group. Once the "enemy combatant" category was stretched beyond established law-of-war principles and severed from membership in the armed forces of an enemy nation or participation in hostilities on a battlefield, there was no principled limit. This unprecedented expansion of military detention authority gave tremendous discretion to executive branch officials, allowing them to circumvent the fair-trial guarantees of the Constitution when they lacked evidence of criminal activity or wanted to engage in coercive interrogations, or both.

"To sanction such presidential authority to order the military to seize and indefinitely detain civilians," Judge Motz warned, "would have disastrous consequences for the Constitution—and the country."[6] Allowing the president to designate suspected criminals—even suspected terrorists—"enemy combatants" was a more radical step than temporarily suspending habeas corpus during an emergency, Motz said, because it represented the permanent evisceration of not one constitutional guarantee but the many guarantees embodied in the Bill of Rights.[7] Al-Marri was accused of serious crimes and, if convicted, should be punished severely. But, Motz added, al-Marri's military detention must cease.

The majority ruled, however, that the executive branch's allegations of suspected terrorist activity on behalf of al Qaeda, an organization with which the United States was at war, was sufficient to strip lawful residents of the United States of their constitutional right to a criminal trial. Yet the majority could not agree on the meaning of "enemy combatant," issuing three separate opinions in an effort to define the term. If nothing else, the fractured ruling itself highlighted the problems with trying to treat the fight against terrorism as a global armed conflict and to equate suspected terrorists seized in civilian settings in the United States with soldiers captured on a battlefield.

Judge J. Harvie Wilkinson III offered the most elaborate defense of presidential power. He recognized that the military detention of a person lawfully in the United States "is a momentous step" that raises serious constitutional concerns. He also acknowledged that this detention power would apply equally to citizens and noncitizens for, as the Hamdi and Padilla cases showed, citizens no less than aliens could be "enemy combatants."[8] Wilkinson maintained, however, that it was necessary for the United States to take this step into uncharted waters. Terrorism posed an unprecedented threat, as "thousands of human beings can be slaughtered by a single action and . . . large swaths of urban landscape . . . leveled in an instant."[9] Congress had responded to this threat in the AUMF by authorizing the president to use "all necessary and appropriate force" against those responsible for the 9/11 attacks. It was therefore incumbent on the courts, Wilkinson argued, to develop an appropriate legal framework for implementing this broadly worded congressional command to protect the nation against future attacks.

In Wilkinson's view, the criminal justice system was not the only way to address terrorism. The president, he maintained, must also have the flexibility to deviate from the normal legal rules by treating terrorism suspects, including those arrested inside the United States, as combatants subject to military detention. Limiting military detention to persons who affiliate with an enemy nation or take up arms on a battlefield, Wilkinson asserted, reflected an outmoded view of war ill suited to today's struggle against al Qaeda and other terrorist groups. In this new war, the struggle was not being waged against armies or on battlefields but was being fought everywhere and at all times. Constitutional protections had to give way. America, he insisted, cannot fight this new and unconventional enemy with its "hands tied with Marquess of Queensberry rules."[10]

One problem with the criminal justice system, in Wilkinson's view, was its inability to prevent disclosure of classified or other sensitive information.[11] By scrupulously protecting defendants' rights, he argued, terrorism trials could jeopardize national security. They also exposed jurors and judges to threats of violence and possible attack.[12] Given the stakes, requiring the government to charge terrorism suspects in federal court was impractical and potentially dangerous. Some cases, Wilkinson said, had to be handled outside the criminal justice system. Indefinite military detention under a war paradigm provided an alternative.

But Wilkinson's opinion was flawed, both legally and empirically. He discounted the criminal system's success in handling terrorism cases, on the one hand, and the problems with detaining prisoners without trial, on the other. He also underestimated the dangers of giving the executive license to circumvent the criminal justice system simply by alleging that a person had supported or engaged in terrorist activity. This danger was particularly grave, since designation as an "enemy combatant" in the "war on terror" could mean a life sentence. Although Wilkinson acknowledged the need for habeas corpus to prevent mistakes, he viewed the habeas process as highly circumscribed, excluding such important protections as the prisoner's right to see the government's evidence and to confront its witnesses.

Al-Marri appealed the Fourth Circuit's ruling to the Supreme Court, arguing that the indefinite military detention of legal residents arrested in the United States exceeded the president's authority and represented a profound departure from more than two centuries of precedent and tradition. Al-Marri's appeal was supported by former top-level Justice Department and military officials as well as a range of nongovernmental organizations and legal experts. The Bush administration opposed it, trying, as it had in Jose Padilla's case, to avoid review by the nation's highest court of its most far-reaching claim of executive detention power—a power that extended both to citizens and non-citizens alike. In December 2008, nearly seven years to the date of al-Marri's initial arrest, the Court announced that it would hear his case. This time, however, the decision whether to defend the indefinite military detention of a person arrested in the United States would fall to a new administration.

The intense controversy over al-Marri's case, whose resolution is discussed in the next chapter, shows that the right to habeas corpus is in some ways the start, not the end, of the conversation about law and national security. Once a court has the power to consider a habeas petition, as it did in al-Marri's case, it must then determine whether the detention is lawful. That inquiry, in turn, encompasses a series of important questions. Who, for example, can be held in military custody? And by what process? Are suspected terrorists to be treated as criminals or combatants? Can they be placed in another category, one that shares attributes of each but necessitates a new set of rules? These and other questions remain central to the continuing debate over U.S. detention policy.

On July 27, 2005, John C. Coughenour, a federal district judge in Seattle, sentenced Ahmed Ressam to twenty-two years in prison for his role in a plot to detonate explosives at Los Angeles International Airport on the eve of the millennium. In handing down the sentence, Judge Coughenour explained why the criminal justice system should remain the legal mechanism for trying suspected terrorists: "Our courts have not abandoned our commitment to the ideals that set our nation apart. We can deal with threats to our national security without denying the accused fundamental constitutional protections." Even though Ressam was a foreign national accused of planning to kill Americans, he "received an effective, vigorous defense, and the opportunity to have his guilt or innocence determined by a jury of 12 ordinary citizens." The accusations against him were tested "in the sunlight of a public trial. There were no secret proceedings, no indefinite detention, no denial of counsel."[13] U.S. Attorney John McKay, whose office prosecuted Ressam, disagreed with the sentence and demanded more jail time. (The court of appeals agreed and subsequently remanded the case for resentencing.) But McKay nonetheless shared Judge Coughenour's assessment that the criminal justice system could handle such cases. In addition, McKay pointed out, Ressam's sentence "sent an important message to would-be terrorists around the world" that "in the United States a fair trial will be given . . . and where it is found that terrorism was committed, a lengthy prison sentence will be imposed."[14]

Terrorism, as Judge Coughenour's comments underscore, is a crime, and terrorists are criminals who should be prosecuted in civilian courts under established laws and procedures. The fact that terrorism is international in scope and has the potential to inflict tremendous damage does not alter its fundamental nature. Moreover, the fact that an organization like al Qaeda may have "declared war" on the United States makes no difference: its members and supporters remain outlaws, not soldiers, and should be treated as such.

Trying terrorists in federal courts is sometimes criticized as giving rights to those who do not deserve them.[15] But those criticisms fail to recognize the utility and importance of treating terrorists as criminals. The criminal justice system has proved time and again that it can effectively incapacitate those who plot or plan to commit terrorist acts in the future, as well as those who have committed such acts in the past. If anything, that system has proved to be a far more capable and sustainable mechanism of incapacitating terrorists than detaining them indefinitely as "enemy combatants" or prosecuting them for "war crimes" in military commissions.

Treating terrorists as combatants also has the perverse effect of dignifying the worst kind of criminality by according terrorists the status of soldiers. Throughout history, terrorists of all stripes have tried to justify their actions by claiming that they are fighting against the forces of injustice, while governments have sought to de-legitimize them as criminals, bandits, and outlaws.[16] Equating terrorists with soldiers—even under the label of "unlawful combatant"—lends credence to their contention that they are engaged in an armed struggle with the United States, a fight between opposing forces, each claiming legitimacy. It plays directly into the hands of terrorists by allowing them to cast themselves in the heroic mold of warriors engaged in a historic struggle against a larger and more powerful opponent and to minimize the murder of innocent civilians as the inevitable casualties of war. To take but one example: treating the fight against al Qaeda through the language and legal framework of armed conflict gave Khalid Sheikh Mohammed, the self-proclaimed mastermind of the 9/11 attacks, a platform to compare himself with George Washington, who, he said, would have been labeled an "enemy combatant" if he had been captured during the American Revolution.[17]

Conversely, treating terrorists as criminals who must be prosecuted in federal court deprives them of the opportunity to invoke the rhetoric of war to justify their actions. Thus when Richard Reid tried to justify attempting to blow up a commercial airliner with explosives hidden in his shoes by announcing he was "at war" with America, Massachusetts District Judge

William Young could credibly reject Reid's diatribe in sentencing him to life in prison:

> You are not an enemy combatant. You are a terrorist. You are not a soldier in any war. You are a terrorist. To give you that reference, to call you a soldier gives you far too much stature. Whether it is the officers of government who do it or your attorney who does it, or that happens to be your view, you are a terrorist.[18]

Labels have strategic consequences. "If we are to defeat terrorists across the globe," explained former NATO Supreme Commander Wesley K. Clark, "we must do everything possible to deny legitimacy to their aims and means, and gain legitimacy for ourselves."[19]

To be sure, America's criminal justice system is not perfect. Like all other systems, it makes errors. It also forces prosecutors to develop evidence that will hold up in the crucible of the adversarial process, which can be a demanding task. The government thus might sometimes find it easier in the short run simply to label a suspect an "enemy combatant" and imprison him without charge, without a lawyer, and without a prompt judicial hearing. But this approach creates tremendous problems in the long run, inevitably leading to the prolonged detention of innocent people, undermining the legitimacy of counterterrorism efforts, and making it harder to bring the guilty to justice.

The United States' use of military commissions after 9/11 exemplifies the problems of trying to devise new, "alternative" systems for dealing with terrorists. The commissions have fallen far short of internationally recognized standards of due process, failed to bring to justice those allegedly responsible for the 9/11 attacks, and tarnished America's reputation. During the Bush administration, military commissions obtained only three convictions. The first person convicted was David Hicks, a naïve kangaroo skinner from Australia who, at worst, had volunteered to serve as a low-level Taliban foot soldier. The second was Salim Hamdan, a Yemeni citizen with a fourth-grade education who had worked as a driver for Osama bin Laden but who had no knowledge of any terrorist attacks and had not engaged in any acts of terrorism. The third, Ali Hamza al-Bahlul, an al Qaeda propagandist, was convicted and sentenced to life in prison after proclaiming his guilt and hatred for America in open court and failing to offer any defense. Summarizing these three cases, former chief military prosecutor Morris Davis lamented that the United States had managed to convict only "a dupe, a driver, and a default."[20]

Even after several attempts at reform, the commissions remained plagued by flaws and engulfed in controversy. While the Military Commissions Act of 2006 (MCA) nominally banned the use of evidence gained by torture, the commissions' top legal adviser, Air Force Brigadier General Thomas W. Hartmann, continued to insist that evidence gained through waterboarding and other "enhanced interrogation techniques" from the CIA's secret detention program was admissible at commission trials. The Defense Department also continued to take advantage of lax rules designed to conceal abusive interrogation methods while allowing the fruits of those methods to be used as evidence. For example, most of the government's evidence against Salim Hamdan was based on statements that he had given to FBI interrogators at Guantánamo after almost two years of incommunicado detention and other gross abuses. In pretrial proceedings against another detainee, Canadian citizen Omar Khadr, who was fifteen years old when he was seized in Afghanistan in 2002, the prosecution tried to hide that its evidence was based on confessions coerced from Khadr while he was severely wounded and detained by the United States at Bagram, before his transfer to Guantánamo.

Secrecy continued to pervade the commissions. Important portions of trials and other legal proceedings were closed to the public, not to protect sensitive information, but to hide the mistreatment of prisoners. Critical exculpatory information was withheld from detainees and their attorneys, including information as basic as an agent's interrogation notes that could help reveal the harsh conditions under which a detainee's statements were obtained.

Political influence still plagued the commissions. On paper, the MCA mandated that prosecutors be free from command influence and able to exercise their professional judgment in selecting cases and moving them forward.[21] But in practice, prosecutors had no such independence, and charging decisions remained highly politicized. For example, high-ranking military officials forced commission prosecutors to bring charges against David Hicks even though he was, at most, a marginal figure. Those officials then negotiated an eleventh-hour plea agreement that resulted in Hicks's return to Australia. The deal not only was negotiated without the prosecutors' knowledge, but was the result of a request to Vice President Cheney from Australia's prime minister John Howard, who was facing increasing demands at home to oppose Hicks's prosecution by a military commission. Hicks's plea highlighted what many had long believed: that a prisoner's release from Guantánamo had less to do with his alleged terrorist or military activities than with the amount of pressure his government was capable of and willing to exert on the United States.

The Convening Authority, the nominally independent body established by the MCA to oversee the commission process, continually forced prosecutors to bring charges for political purposes. Hartmann, for example, demanded that prosecutors bring "sexy" cases to capture the public's imagination and increase support for the tribunals. According to Morris Davis, top Pentagon officials, including Deputy Defense Secretary Gordon England, encouraged him to bring charges against the more notorious detainees before the November 2006 midterm elections for their "strategic political value." The Defense Department's general counsel, William J. Haynes II, told Davis that only guilty verdicts were acceptable. "We can't have acquittals," Haynes reportedly said. "We've been holding these guys for years. How can we explain acquittals? We have to have convictions."[22]

The military commissions also violated Common Article 3's requirement that any trial be conducted by "a regularly constituted court affording all the judicial guarantees which are recognized as indispensable by civilized peoples." The commissions were not "regularly constituted courts" because they were not "established and organized in accordance with the laws and procedures already in force in [the] country." Instead, they were created to punish "war crimes" invented after the fact, and their rules were made up on the fly.[23] The commissions deviated from, rather than mirrored, the regularly constituted courts: federal trials and military courts-martial.[24] Furthermore, by attempting to punish conduct that was not necessarily illegal at the time, the commissions raised serious ex post facto problems.

The commissions generated vigorous resistance from some military judges and prosecutors as well as military defense counsel. In May 2007, during pretrial proceedings in Hamdan's commission case, the military judge, Navy Captain Keith J. Allred, granted a defense motion to bar Hartmann from further participation in the case based on his illegal efforts to influence the prosecution.[25] In another case, the judge, Army Colonel Stephen R. Henley, suppressed evidence against Mohammed Jawad, an illiterate young teenager accused of throwing a hand grenade at a military vehicle in Kabul that injured two U.S. service members and their Afghan interpreter. Henley found that the "confession" the government was relying on to prosecute Jawad was the product of torture, obtained from him after he had been hooded, beaten, and threatened with death.[26] Henley also rejected the government's legal theory that Jawad could be convicted of a war crime based solely on his status as an unlawful combatant (i.e., based solely on Jawad's alleged affiliation with a group "associated" with al Qaeda), without proving that Jawad's conduct itself violated the law of war, as throwing a hand grenade at a military target plainly did not.

In 2007, Morris Davis resigned as chief prosecutor, explaining that unlawful command influence had corrupted the integrity of the commissions and declaring that "full, fair and open trials were not possible under the current system."[27] The following year, Army Lieutenant Colonel Darrel Vandeveld became the fourth prosecutor to resign, citing the Pentagon's mishandling of the Jawad case, in which he had served as lead prosecutor. After reviewing the evidence, Vandeveld believed that Jawad should never have been prosecuted in the first place and tried to negotiate a plea deal that would have allowed Jawad's repatriation to Afghanistan, calculating that this was the quickest way for Jawad to escape the corrupt military commission system and go home. Vandeveld also pointed to Jawad's abuse by U.S. officials, including severe sleep deprivation under the "frequent-flyer program," in which interrogators moved Jawad from cell to cell 112 times during a fourteen-day period to cause disorientation and despair. When Vandeveld's superiors saw that Vandeveld had admitted to Jawad's abuse by Afghan and U.S. officials and argued for more lenient treatment, they reprimanded him and forced him to withdraw the admission. Vandeveld also cited the Pentagon's repeated refusal to disclose exculpatory information to defense counsel, including information that the government had regarding another suspect in U.S. custody who had confessed to the same crime that Jawad was accused of committing. "One would have thought that after six years since the commissions had their fitful start, that a functioning law office would have been set up and procedures and policies not only put in effect, but refined," Vandeveld explained in a sworn statement after his resignation.[28]

The military commissions' failure, however, was not due ultimately to any single flaw but to a larger effort to create an inferior, second-class system of justice. In America, as one journalist protested after observing a military commission proceeding, there are no secret trials and reporters are allowed to see the witnesses and the evidence. "This is not America," a Pentagon spokesperson responded, oblivious to the irony.[29]

Even among those who criticize the Bush administration's detention policies, there remains significant disagreement over the solution. A number of commentators and lawyers, for example, have advocated other methods of detaining and trying terrorist suspects outside the criminal justice system. They sympathize with the Bush administration's effort to create an alternative detention system for suspected terrorists outside the criminal justice system but disagree with the direction that this effort took. They thus seek to preserve important elements of the Bush administration's approach, such as indefinite detention without charge, while strengthening procedural protections and other limits on executive power. In short, they propose to reform Guantánamo, rather than to end it.

Professors Robert Chesney and Jack Goldsmith, for example, argue that neither the criminal nor the military model "in its traditional guise can easily meet the central legal challenge of modern terrorism: the legitimate preventive incapacitation of uniformless terrorists who have the capacity to inflict mass casualties and enormous economic harms and who thus must be stopped before they act."[30] The criminal model, they say, is too focused on preventing error, a commitment embodied in the idea that it is better for some guilty persons to go free than for one innocent person to be convicted. "The problem of modern terrorism demands anticipatory or predictive forms of liability, and may demand a lower rate of erroneous acquittals than the traditional criminal system would tolerate," Chesney and Goldsmith contend.[31] In other words, government officials must be able to incarcerate people before they do something wrong and without having to subject their suspicions and evidence to the same type of adversarial testing that the criminal process requires. The military system, by contrast, provides too much detention power. Its focus reflects the exigencies of combat and contemplates the short-term detention of combatants and civilians on a mass scale. It allows for detention based solely on association (typically, membership in the enemy's armed force), on the one hand, and provides relatively few procedural protections, on the other (such as the streamlined status hearings under Article 5 of the Geneva Conventions). If the criminal model is overly concerned with preventing error, Chesney and Goldsmith argue, the traditional military model goes too far in the other direction. Their solution is a hybrid that combines elements of both: allowing for prolonged detention based on some form of membership in or association with a terrorist organization while offering procedural safeguards more rigorous than traditional military status tribunals but considerably less demanding than a criminal trial.

One hybrid proposal that has gained traction in academic and policymaking circles is that of a separate national security court. Specialized courts are not unknown to the federal system. Some courts, for example, hear only tax or patent cases, and specialized administrative agencies decide cases affecting federal benefits, the environment, and various government programs. But national security courts differ from most other specialized tribunals in that they are not driven by a judge's expertise in a particular subject area but by a desire to evade more rigorous rules and due process protections. National security courts, at bottom, seek to institutionalize a new system for the long-term, preventive detention of terrorist suspects without the constitutional safeguards of a criminal trial.

Proposals for national security courts vary. One championed by Goldsmith and former Georgetown Law School professor and later deputy solicitor general Neal Katyal would have federal judges review preventive detention in specialized proceedings. Detainees would be represented by counsel, drawn from a permanent staff of top-quality defense lawyers with special security clearances to handle classified information. In addition to judicial review of the initial decision to detain, Goldsmith and Katyal's proposal calls for further appellate review of whether there is "a continuing rationale" to hold people "years after" that decision was made.[32] It thus explicitly contemplates long-term incarceration without trial, essentially reforming the model of indefinite detention that developed at Guantánamo under the paradigm of the "war on terror" and incorporating it into the U.S. legal system.[33]

Others recommend using national security courts both to detain and to try terrorist suspects. Former federal prosecutor Andrew McCarthy, for example, has called for prosecutions in separate domestic terror courts.[34] McCarthy contends that federal criminal trials are ineffective and also jeopardize national security by giving terrorists the chance to transmit classified or other sensitive information to the public. Former Attorney General Michael B. Mukasey has voiced similar concerns about creating a national security court. "Current institutions and statutes," he argues, "are not well suited to even the limited task of supplementing what became, after September 11, 2001, principally a military effort to combat Islamic terrorism."[35] These new courts would dispense with key safeguards. Defendants would no longer have the right to see and confront the evidence and witnesses against them. Instead, judges would make determinations about the admission and use of evidence in secret, with the input of the prosecutor but without the defendant or his lawyer present.[36] The courts, moreover, would be permanent, creating a new "forum for fairly detaining and trying terrorists no matter how long the war on terror ensues."[37]

Benjamin Wittes of the Brookings Institution has staked out a similar position.[38] The political branches, he says, have failed to create a mature and sustainable legal architecture for the detention and trial of terrorism suspects. Wittes asserts that some form of long-term incarceration of terrorist suspects—outside the criminal justice system—is both desirable and inevitable. The challenge is for Congress to articulate clear legal rules with sufficient safeguards and guidelines to hold the executive accountable and to make the system legitimate. Although the courts would have a meaningful role in this new system, Wittes argues, that role should be limited to deciding cases under legislatively established standards, not devising policy through ad hoc judicial decision making.[39] Wittes envisions a hybrid model—a new law of terrorism—that would provide greater procedural protections than the Bush administration afforded detainees while continuing the practice of long-term detention based on less rigorous standards and rules than in criminal trials. Wittes recognizes that crime, not war, is the more appropriate lens through which to view terrorism, but he argues that the criminal justice system is not up to the task.[40] This hybrid system of preventive detention, he believes, would create a more secure legal architecture while helping detainees through the establishment of clear, legislatively approved rules and procedures.[41]

Despite their technocratic tone, most proposals for national security courts embrace the value judgment that noncitizens deserve less protection than citizens do.[42] "Experience shows," McCarthy argues, "that once alien combatants are permitted access to our courts, . . . judges, under the rubric of due process, will effectively treat them as if they are as vested as citizens with substantive and procedural protections."[43] Even the more nuanced and less openly discriminatory proposals reinforce policy-based arguments with the suggestion that America simply "owes" less to foreign terrorist suspects.[44] These citizenship-based arguments, however, are logically and legally problematic, as well as morally suspect. A person's citizenship does not tell you whether he poses a danger or is responsible for committing a particular terrorist act. Citizens are just as capable of committing grave crimes as foreign nationals are, as the violent acts of homegrown terrorists like Timothy McVeigh demonstrate. Moreover, creating a permanent, second-class detention system for foreign nationals violates the principle of equal protection under law. If past is prologue, the overwhelming majority of people subjected to this new system will be of Arab descent or Muslim background. This discriminatory impact, even if not intentional, will further undermine the United States' reputation in the Arab and Muslim world and encourage the recruitment of terrorists.[45]

Proposals for national security courts are also astonishingly underdeveloped. While they call for more relaxed rules than criminal trials, they typically fail to spell out what those rules would be, leaving unanswered an array of important procedural questions such as the burden of proof, the ability to call and confront witnesses, and the standards governing the admission of evidence. In addition, national security court proposals provide relatively little guidance on perhaps the most important question of all: the category of people they would cover. Most proposals recommend some combination of membership in or association with al Qaeda and other terrorist groups, coupled with some proof of future dangerousness. But how does one determine membership in an amorphous, hydra-headed terrorist organization? What level of association with al Qaeda or other organizations would suffice? And how does one determine "dangerousness" separate from conviction for a crime? The proposals often fail to grapple with these basic questions.

National security court proposals, moreover, ignore the incentive they create for the government to detain individuals without charge and to forgo prosecution altogether. The experience with military commissions at Guantánamo is instructive. In eight years, the Bush administration charged only a handful of Guantánamo prisoners with any crime. One reason is that it was easier to detain them without trial. It would be naïve to expect other administrations to act differently. When given discretion, government officials inevitably gravitate toward a detention option in which the procedures are more flexible and the evidentiary standards lower. Paradoxically, the pressure on government officials to utilize a preventive detention regime with watered-down procedures, rather than developing their cases for trial, will be strongest in those cases in which the government's allegations are more tenuous and its evidence weaker. Yet it is precisely in those situations that the criminal justice system is most vital to protecting individuals against wrongful imprisonment.

In addition, national security court proposals often turn a blind eye to the problem of coercive interrogation. They criticize the criminal justice system's ability to incapacitate terrorist suspects while overlooking the extent to which the desire to interrogate, rather than incapacitate, drove U.S. detention policy after 9/11. "Enemy combatant" detentions in the "war on terrorism" had less to do with any perceived inability to hold prisoners through traditional law enforcement methods than it did with the desire to create a class of prisoners outside the law in order to engage in torture and other abusive interrogation methods to gain information. Proposals for national security courts thus tend to see a problem—lack of detention power—where no problem exists. They also largely ignore that diluting the protections of the criminal justice system will inevitably facilitate the use of harsh interrogation methods, whether by denying suspects access to counsel or allowing for the use of evidence gained through torture and other coercion.

Some, such as Georgetown Law School professor David Cole, have advocated continuing the military detention of a more limited group of suspected terrorists under a law-of-war framework rather than creating new national security courts.[46] Cole argues that the United States should be able to detain al Qaeda and Taliban "fighters" indefinitely and dispense with the constitutional safeguards of a criminal trial, even if the detainees did not directly participate in hostilities and have no connection to a battlefield, as long as it is established that they belong to groups that have asserted that they are at war with the United States. Cole recognizes that imprisonment without trial raises serous concerns, including the potential for error and the targeting of disfavored groups. But he believes that military detention is justified by the shortcomings of the criminal process and the nature of the armed conflict with al Qaeda, which he compares with the struggle against the Axis powers during World War II. Cole also argues that these concerns can be mitigated by improving procedures and by requiring a stronger connection to al Qaeda or involvement in actual hostilities on al Qaeda's behalf to limit this new detention power.[47]

But Cole cannot avoid the problem that detentions in an armed conflict against al Qaeda and other terrorist organizations are not simply indeterminate but generational and, indeed, potentially permanent. His proposed narrowing also is problematic on its own terms. It is difficult to determine what level of participation or association is sufficient to trigger military detention. Moreover, that determination will initially be made by the executive branch, which can unilaterally strip individuals of the safeguards of the criminal process based on the allegations it chooses to make against them, thereby funneling them into a shadow criminal justice system that affords fewer rights and protections, is less accountable, and allows for greater secrecy. Habeas corpus may ultimately help check the exercise of this preventive detention power. But that checking function can take years to produce results, as the Padilla, al-Marri, Hamdi, and Guantánamo detainee cases show. Moreover, it remains unclear as a practical matter when or how individuals seized and placed in military detention would first obtain access to a court. Once the government is freed from the criminal law requirement of promptly bringing a prisoner before a judge for a hearing, the prisoner could simply languish in military custody—potentially in secret—until a family member or friend realizes he is being held, files a habeas petition on his behalf, and persuades a judge to order access to counsel and a hearing.

Furthermore, Cole invokes the rationale of prisoner-of-war military detention to justify imprisoning terrorism suspects without trial, noting that the criminal law model is inappropriate because the laws of war forbid the state from prosecuting enemy soldiers (prisoners of war) for fighting and because those soldiers may be obligated to fight (e.g., by the enemy nation's conscription laws).[48] But neither is true in the case of alleged "al Qaeda fighters": they may be prosecuted criminally consistent with the laws of war (as, indeed, the United States has done and continues to do in federal terrorim cases); and those who join al Qaeda are under no legal obligation to do so and thus can be held accountable for their actions, consistent with the principles of criminal law.

Terrorist organizations, moreover, are often loosely defined and continually evolving. Thus, once terrorism becomes an acceptable basis for detention without criminal process, the rationale for limiting the scope of that detention power to a single group, such as al Qaeda, diminishes. After all, al Qaeda itself has mutated into other groups and formations. (Hence the U.S. government's expansive view of the president's power to detain members of "associated" groups under the AUMF.) The government will inevitably try to extend its detention power to individuals whom it thinks might be dangerous, whether or not they are affiliated with al Qaeda, as it has already done at Guantánamo.

In the end, proponents of a "third way"—whether detentions based on national security courts or the laws of war—believe that the answer lies in sanding down the rougher edges of Guantánamo and the post-9/11 model rather than scrapping it altogether. They acknowledge, to varying degrees, that the Bush administration went too far by circumventing judicial review, engaging in torture and other gross mistreatment, and rejecting any constraints on presidential power. But they nonetheless agree that terrorism cannot be handled effectively through the criminal justice system (or at least not in many cases) and that the United States must develop an alternative legal framework for incapacitating and interrogating terrorism suspects. This premise is fundamentally flawed, however, and fails to recognize the utility and value of treating terrorism as principally a law enforcement problem and prosecuting suspected terrorists through the regular courts.

A common criticism of the criminal justice system is that it punishes past wrongdoing rather than preventing future harm. That backward-looking focus, critics argue, makes criminal law ill equipped to fight terrorism, given terrorism's potential to inflict massive human and economic destruction.[49] But this underestimates the criminal justice system's capacity to prevent terrorism as well as to punish it.

Over time, Congress has cast an increasingly broad net over those who perpetrate terrorism as well as over those who support it or plan future terrorist acts.[50] In enforcing those laws, the government has focused increasingly on prevention. After 9/11, federal prosecutors sought to use every available criminal statute to pursue suspected terrorists before any terrorist act could be committed. The primary goal became detecting, disrupting, and deterring terrorist plots before they could be carried out.[51]

In implementing this preventive approach, prosecutors have an array of powerful tools at their disposal. Among the most important are federal laws that prohibit providing material support or resources to terrorists or terrorist organizations.[52] The first material support law was enacted after the bombing of the World Trade Center in 1993.[53] It defines "material support" broadly to encompass providing property, services, money, lodging, training, weapons, expert advice, or personnel, including one's own person, to facilitate terrorist activity.[54] Another law passed after the 1995 Oklahoma City bombing bans individuals from giving material support to any organization formally designated a foreign terrorist organization by the secretary of state, even if that person did not actually intend to incite or facilitate terrorist activity.[55] All that is necessary is for the person to know that the organization has been so designated or has engaged in terrorist activity.[56] Congress subsequently enacted additional provisions targeting more specific aspects of terrorist financing and attendance at terrorist training camps.[57] It has also extended the reach of the material support provisions so that they apply extraterritorially.[58]

Material support laws have become an increasingly important law enforcement tool to stop terrorism before it occurs.[59] To make a material support case, a prosecutor does not have to prove that any underlying terrorist act took place or even that there was an agreement to carry out such an act. Instead, prosecutors can convict individuals merely for raising money for terrorist organizations, attempting to facilitate arms deals, assisting would-be terrorists to obtain travel documents, and attending terrorist training camps.[60] Not surprisingly, these laws have been used to target low-level players—a terrorist organization's "foot soldiers and sympathizers"—since prosecutors do not have to prove that the defendant intended to facilitate any specific act of terrorism.[61] In one highly publicized case, the federal government indicted six men from Lackawanna, New York, after discovering that they had traveled to Afghanistan to train with al Qaeda. Prosecutors used material support laws to obtain guilty pleas and significant prison sentences.[62] While material support laws have been appropriately criticized for their overbreadth—in particular, how they can be used against individuals without showing any connection between the support provided and terrorism or any intent to further terrorist activity—they underscore the government's capacity to employ criminal statutes to prosecute those who support terrorism without committing any specific terrorist acts.

Conspiracy laws provide another means of disrupting terrorist plots before they materialize. The seditious conspiracy statute, for example, outlaws any agreement to conspire to overthrow or put down the U.S. government, levy war against it, or interfere with the execution of any U.S. law.[63] The statute was enacted in 1861—long before the rise of modern terrorism—to provide "a vehicle for the government to make arrests before a conspiracy ripens into a violent situation."[64] More recently, it was used to prosecute Sheikh Omar Abdel Rahman and his codefendants for plotting to bomb New York City tunnels and landmarks and for planning to assassinate Egyptian president Hosni Mubarak.[65] Under principles of conspiracy liability (or "Pinkerton liability"), as long as one member of the conspiracy takes a step toward carrying out the agreement, other members of the conspiracy can be held accountable for crimes committed in furtherance of that conspiracy, from the lowest to the highest member.

Prosecutors have also used generally applicable criminal statutes to counter terrorism, much as prosecutors previously used the tax laws to convict gangsters like Al Capone. Prosecutors have, for example, convicted terrorists under laws prohibiting fraud, money laundering, racketeering, arms dealing, and the destruction of property.[66] In addition, they have increasingly used statutes involving more "minor" offenses, such as financial or credit-card fraud, making false statements to federal officials, or obtaining false documents. These statues allow for immediate incapacitation through the denial of bail, cast a wide net over possible prohibited conduct, and do not require prosecutors to reveal their suspicions that wider terrorist activity is afoot. Most important, they allow for the detention of individuals when terrorist activity is suspected but there is not sufficient evidence to support terrorism charges.[67] As the Department of Justice has explained, the prosecution of terrorism targets on alternative grounds "is often an effective method—and sometimes the only available method—of deterring and disrupting potential terrorist planning and support activities without compromising national security information."[68] And even though the punishment for such offenses is ordinarily less severe than for terrorism or other violent crimes, substantial jail terms still can be imposed.

The government, moreover, need not wait until it obtains a conviction to detain someone it believes presents a threat to the public. Federal law provides ample authority to detain criminal suspects once they have been charged with a crime. While the Bail Reform Act of 1984 generally requires the release of defendants under the "least restrictive" conditions possible, it allows for their continued detention pending trial if a judge determines that the defendant poses a flight risk or that his pretrial confinement is necessary to ensure the safety of the community. In terrorism cases, the act specifically creates a presumption in favor of detention.[69] The government also may detain non-citizens pending immigration removal proceedings in certain circumstances, and such detention can be mandatory in cases involving terrorism.[70]

Critics of the criminal justice model further contend that terrorism prosecutions risk disclosure of classified information, impose overly onerous requirements that prevent the admission of relevant hearsay evidence, and employ rules that hamstring prosecutors and other law enforcement officers. While national security investigations can present challenges, these criticisms are misguided.

One of the main arguments for indefinitely detaining suspected terrorists as "enemy combatants" instead of trying them in federal court has been the need to protect classified information. But the Classified Information Procedures Act (CIPA) already addresses this concern.[71] Congress enacted CIPA in 1980 to facilitate the prosecution of cold war spies without exposing intelligence assets and information. It has since become a crucial tool in federal prosecutions of suspected terrorists. Under CIPA, the government has been able to use information gained from foreign law enforcement and intelligence sources without compromising the sources' integrity. CIPA has also enabled the government to prosecute terrorism cases without revealing the details of sensitive military and intelligence operations.[72]

CIPA does not change the government's discovery obligations or alter the rules of evidence but instead regulates a defendant's access to and use of classified material. It authorizes a judge to review classified information in a closed hearing to determine whether it is relevant to the case before a defendant can obtain that information during pretrial discovery or use the information at trial. If a judge finds the information relevant, CIPA affords the government a chance to create an unclassified substitute, which may be a redacted version of the classified document (with the sensitive portions blacked out), an unclassified summary, or a statement of the facts that the sensitive material would prove.[73] Regardless of the form it takes, the substitute must "provide the defendant with substantially the same ability to make his defense" as would disclosure of the classified information itself.[74] If the government does not or cannot provide a fair substitute, it can still choose to withhold the information. But there is a cost in doing so. CIPA requires that the court impose an appropriate sanction in such circumstances, not to punish the government, but to ensure the integrity of the trial and judicial process. Sanctions can include barring the government from calling a witness if the defendant is deprived of evidence necessary to effectively cross-examine the witness or dismissing the prosecution altogether if the government refuses to disclose information important to the defense.[75]

CIPA, to be sure, is not perfect, and it can adversely affect a defendant's ability to obtain relevant information and challenge the government's evidence at trial. Under the act, judges must determine what evidence among potentially thousands of pages of law enforcement and intelligence documents is relevant and helpful to the defense and must therefore be disclosed during the pretrial discovery process. To help facilitate this review, courts have ordered disclosure only to members of the defense team with a security clearance and barred the defendant himself from seeing the information. This "cleared counsel" solution, however, presents a problem from a defense perspective. It prevents a defendant from helping his lawyer assess the relevance of materials, thus impairing a defendant's constitutional right to the effective assistance of counsel. It also can jeopardize a defendant's constitutional right to self-representation, since defendants typically lack the security clearance necessary to review classified information themselves.[76] Furthermore, judges can evaluate the relevance of materials requested in discovery *ex parte*, considering arguments by the government but excluding the defendant and his counsel from participating.[77] But its shortcomings aside, CIPA has helped enable terrorism cases to be prosecuted in federal court without jeopardizing the disclosure of sensitive national security information. As Patrick Fitzgerald, the U.S. attorney who helped prosecute the 1998 U.S. embassy bombings case, noted, "When you see how much classified information was involved in that case, and when you see that there weren't any leaks, you get pretty darn confident that the federal courts are capable of handling these prosecutions."[78]

Two examples are commonly cited to show that criminal prosecutions cause the disclosure of sensitive information. Neither has merit. The first involved an alleged breach during the trial of Sheikh Omar Abdel Rahman, when the government handed over to the defense a list of names of individuals alleged to be unindicted co-conspirators, including Osama bin Laden. The list supposedly reached bin Laden in Khartoum, alerting him that his connection to the case had been uncovered.[79] The problem was that the government had neglected to invoke CIPA or any other court-management tool, such as a protective order, to prevent disclosure of the information. Had the government done so, as it has done in other cases, the sensitive information would not have been disseminated.[80] The second example involved the introduction of bin Laden's satellite phone records and other evidence regarding a satellite phone battery pack during the 1998 U.S. embassy bombings trial that supposedly tipped off bin Laden and caused him to stop using the phone.[81] Bin Laden, however, had ceased using the phone long before the material was presented at trial or disclosed to the defense in discovery. The federal prosecution thus was not the source of the problem.[82]

Another criticism of terrorism prosecutions is that the rules are too restrictive and hinder prosecutors from presenting evidence to a jury. "Federal rules of evidence often prevent the introduction of valid factual evidence for public policy reasons that have no application in a trial of a foreign terrorist," former defense secretary Donald Rumsfeld and former deputy defense secretary Paul Wolfowitz told Congress in December 2001.[83] Or as other skeptics of the criminal justice system put it, "It would provoke laughter to suggest that soldiers in Desert Storm should have obtained search or arrest warrants before capturing Iraqi soldiers and their equipment."[84] These broad-brushed attacks ignore the way that the rules of criminal procedure work in practice. They also create a straw man of "battlefield captures" that has little connection to terrorism prosecutions.

One example is the authentication of evidence. Judges understandably need to ensure that a document or recording is what one side represents it to be. The Federal Rules of Evidence implement this commonsense requirement. The rules establish categories of "self-authenticating" documents (such as certified public records) that require no additional proof that they are what they appear to be.[85] They also give a judge wide latitude to allow the admission of other material, requiring only that the party provide "evidence sufficient to support a finding that the matter in question is what its proponent claims."[86] The government generally has not had problems authenticating evidence in terrorism prosecutions, even when some of the evidence came from a theater of military operations. At Jose Padilla's criminal trial, for example, the government successfully introduced an al Qaeda training camp application with Padilla's fingerprints on it that had been uncovered in Afghanistan. The government established the authenticity of the document, despite vigorous objection by the defense, through a confidential witness who described how he came into possession of the document in Kandahar before it was sent to a federal agent in Pakistan to allay concerns about the chain of custody and the document's reliability.[87]

Courts have also applied evidentiary rules flexibly to ensure that a witness with relevant testimony can present it to the jury even in the unusual case when the witness cannot testify in person. Judges, for example, have allowed testimony of witnesses through videotaped depositions or two-way video-conferencing as long as a defendant has an adequate opportunity to cross-examine the witness and a jury can observe the witnesses' demeanor.[88] The same is true for the rule against hearsay, which contains a number of exceptions allowing out-of-court statements to be considered.[89] Judges presiding over terrorism cases have typically applied the rules in a pragmatic fashion so that relevant evidence may be considered without undermining the fairness and integrity of the process.

At the same time, this flexibility is not boundless: the Constitution establishes certain baseline guarantees that cannot be transgressed. A defendant, for example, has the right to a prompt judicial hearing following his arrest and to the assistance of counsel, including for counsel to be appointed at the government's expense if necessary. A defendant must have the opportunity to see and confront the evidence and witnesses against him as well as the ability to compel the production of witnesses in his favor. The government must also disclose to the defendant any material evidence in its possession supporting the defendant's innocence, including any evidence that could be used to impeach a government witness. In addition, the government must establish a defendant's guilt by proof beyond a reasonable doubt. Courts, prosecutors, and defense lawyers, however, all have managed to operate within these fixed parameters in terrorism prosecutions, no matter the size or the complexity of the case.

The Zacarias Moussaoui trial is sometimes cited to show the problems of proscuting terrorism cases in federal court.[90] But this trial shows the opposite, highlighting the ability of federal courts to function under even the most trying circumstances. The district judge in the case confronted a difficult and mentally unstable defendant who fought continually with the court and with his attorneys, refused to enter a plea, and sought to use the courtroom for ideological rants against the United States. Moussaoui also wanted to exercise his constitutional right to represent himself. Self-representation posed challenging legal questions because the case involved classified information that Moussaoui could not see. The judge nevertheless fashioned solutions as new issues arose. For example, she provided standby counsel with access to the classified information that Moussaoui was not permitted to see.[91] This solution was not ideal, and burdened Moussaoui's right to self-represenation.[92] But the same issue has come up in military commission prosecutions, which shows that creating an alternative system does not make tough questions go away but only channels them into a system with less experience, less credibility, and less institutional capacity to address them.[93]

Perhaps the most controversial issue in Moussaoui's trial concerned his effort to question several individuals held at secret CIA "black sites" whose testimony, Moussaoui's attorneys believed, would undermine the government's case for a death sentence by showing his lack of involvement in the 9/11 attacks. The court of appeals eventually rejected the district court's solution of witness depositions in favor of a process in which the jury would receive summaries of the witnesses' testimony.[94] The appeals court's solution, which was modeled on CIPA, has rightly been criticized as limiting a defendant's Sixth Amendment right to compel and examine witnesses in his favor, an important reminder of how constitutional protections can be compromised even when the criminal justice system is used. But those criticisms should not obscure these two points: first, that the court devised a solution that sought to balance the respective interests of the parties, and second, that there would never have been any problem in gaining access to the detainee-witnesses in the first place had those individuals been in lawful criminal custody rather than illegally imprisoned and tortured in a secret CIA jail.

Another frequent criticism of criminal prosecutions is that they impose constitutional requirements like *Miranda* warnings that impede the interrogation of terrorism suspects. Under the Supreme Court's 1966 decision in *Miranda v. Arizona*, law enforcement agents must inform a suspect in custody, before questioning him, that he has the right to remain silent, that anything he says can be used against him, and that he has the right to the presence of an attorney even if he cannot afford one.[95] The purpose of the warnings is to preserve an individual's constitutional right against self-incrimination amid the inherently coercive pressures of custodial interrogations. *Miranda* warnings also seek to prevent false confessions, which can both result in wrongful convictions and lead law enforcement authorities astray. Statements obtained in violation of *Miranda* may be suppressed and cannot be used against a defendant at trial. Once highly controversial, *Miranda* rights have "become embedded in routine police practice to the point where the warnings have become part of our national culture."[96]

Criticisms of applying *Miranda* to terrorism cases rest on several misconceptions. First, *Miranda* applies only to the questioning of individuals who are in custody; it does not limit the government's ability to question those who are not. Officials, moreover, can still question individuals in custody without providing *Miranda* warnings in order to gather information. That is, what *Miranda* restricts is the government's ability to use evidence it obtains from custodial interrogations against the defendant at trial. Thus, as long as the government has other evidence untainted by those interrogations, *Miranda* poses no impediment to prosecution. Furthermore, contrary to popular belief, many terrorism suspects do not stop but continue talking after *Miranda* warnings are provided.

Another criticism of *Miranda* in the national security context is that the warnings would be extended to military operations. Military officials, the argument goes, should not have to administer *Miranda* warnings to soldiers captured on the battlefield. The problem with this argument lies not with *Miranda* but with the failure to limit armed conflict to its proper sphere and with a conception of the battlefield that is so elastic that it is effectively limitless. In practice, *Miranda* has not been an obstacle in counterterrorism investigations, including those conducted overseas, and courts have applied *Miranda* pragmatically in this context.[97] Nor would *Miranda* necessarily impede criminal prosecution in the unusual case in which a terrorism suspect was captured and interrogated in a real battlefield setting. In that situation, a court might find that *Miranda* did not apply, given the nature and exigencies of the situation, thereby making a statement admissible as long as it was made voluntarily.[98] A court might also find that *Miranda*'s "public safety" exception applied to questioning that was urgently needed to secure time-sensitive intelligence.[99] But that is very different from the radical argument made by John Yoo and others: that *Miranda* requirements do not apply to interrogations conducted in the global "war on terror."

An example of the criminal justice system's ability to handle complex terrorism cases is the prosecution of the 1998 U.S. embassy bombings in East Africa that killed more than two hundred people and wounded thousands. The defendants were convicted and sentenced to life in prison for their role in the plot. Three of the four defendants appealed. One defendant, who was an American citizen, claimed that the government had violated his Fourth Amendment right to be free of unlawful searches and seizures when FBI agents raided his home in Kenya and conducted surveillance of his telephone conversations without a warrant. Two other defendants argued that their statements to U.S. and non-U.S. officials after their arrest in Kenya should be suppressed because they were not provided valid *Miranda* warnings and because their statements were not voluntary, given the coercive conditions under which they were held. The appeals court rejected these challenges and affirmed the convictions.[100] The court recognized that the defendants had the same constitutional protections as other criminal defendants, even though they were foreign nationals arrested outside the United States. It then sought to apply those protections to accommodate the demands of overseas terrorism investigations without sacrificing fundamental trial rights. The appeals court concluded, for example, that while *Miranda* warnings must still be administered when the United States actively participates in the interrogation of a suspect in foreign custody, the warnings could be administered in a way that takes into account local conditions, including the fact that outside the United States, a suspect in custody might not be entitled to an attorney right away or at the detaining government's expense. The court also found that while the Fourth Amendment applies to American citizens overseas, its application could vary based on the circumstances. While the United States would still need to demonstrate that the search or surveillance was reasonable to introduce evidence at trial, it would not be required to obtain a warrant to search a person's home or listen to his telephone calls in a foreign country, as it would inside the United States.

Questions can—and should—be asked about whether the court reached the right result on all the issues and whether it erred too much on the side of security. But from the perspective of the extraordinary measures taken by the Bush administration in the "war on terrorism," these debates are at the margins. The prisoners were not detained indefinitely as "enemy combatants," nor were they put before substandard tribunals like the Guantánamo military commissions, as were other individuals accused of involvement in the same terrorist attack. Instead, they were prosecuted in a legitimate, time-tested system and given the same trial rights as other defendants, even if those rights were interpreted in light of the particular circumstances of overseas counterterrorism operations.

Critics of using the criminal justice system to fight terrorism also underestimate its strengths in gaining valuable intelligence. One of prosecutors' most important information-gathering tools is their ability to offer suspects more lenient treatment in exchange for their cooperation.[101] Individuals charged with crimes often provide useful and incriminating information about other suspects in order to avoid going to jail or to lessen their own exposure through the prospect of a reduced jail term. Indeed, the federal sentencing guidelines are structured to obtain this cooperation by reducing sentences for defendants who accept responsibility in pleading guilty[102] and who provide substantial assistance in the investigation of another criminal suspect.[103] At the same time, the government can threaten to seek even longer jail terms against those who do not cooperate.[104] Defense lawyers typically help, not hinder, this process by underscoring the advantages of cooperating and the risks of not cooperating, and by facilitating negotiations with the government when appropriate.

Prosecutors have long used the promise of more lenient treatment in taking down large and complex criminal enterprises like organized crime and drug cartels. More recently, they have used this tactic to infiltrate and build cases against terrorist suspects.[105] By leveraging criminal charges and long prison sentences to induce cooperation from defendants, the Justice Department has obtained "critical intelligence about al-Qaida and other terrorist groups, safe houses, training camps, recruitment, and tactics in the United States, as well as the operation of those terrorists who mean to do Americans harm."[106] In the "Lackawanna Six" case, for example, prosecutors agreed to a reduced sentence for one of the defendants, Yahya Goba, in exchange for Goba's assistance. Goba, in turn, not only provided information that helped lead to the conviction of his codefendants, but also provided important testimony for the government in other terrorism cases.[107]

By their nature, criminal investigations also lead to both more information and greater understanding of the information that has been accumulated.[108] Each investigation offers the chance that new defendants and informants will cooperate and provide valuable information. Those investigations yield search warrants, post-arrest statements, and assistance from foreign governments, all of which contribute to a growing storehouse of knowledge. What may at first seem small and isolated pieces of information can ultimately enable law enforcement to infiltrate terrorist activities and bring prosecutions in court.[109] Those cases produce what national security experts have called a "treasure trove" of new information about terrorism.[110]

The criminal justice system also helps foster reliable intelligence gathering. Prosecutors must anticipate that any information the government receives from an informant or a cooperating witness in a criminal investigation will later be challenged by defense counsel and scrutinized by a judge and jury if introduced in court. Prosecutors therefore have an incentive to ensure that the information is accurate by probing, analyzing, and verifying it. This examination and corroboration process helps ensure the integrity of judicial proceedings and yields more dependable information. As one former prosecutor explained, "When you have to demonstrate probable cause to a judge to get a wiretap, or proof beyond a reasonable doubt to a jury, information must be reliable and corroborated."[111] By contrast, with sham proceedings like the Combatant Status Review Tribunals used to justify detentions at Guantánamo, the government had no incentive to ensure the accuracy of the information, since it believed that the information would never be reviewed by a judge or presented in court. In short, inferior adjudicatory systems encourage shoddy intelligence gathering.

Criminal prosecutions, moreover, will always have the legitimacy that military commissions, national security courts, and other second-class models lack. Often, the most important leads in uncovering terrorist plots come from voluntary statements by members of the community and the general public. Sometimes those tips come from relatives of the perpetrators themselves, as in the case of the attempted bombing attacks of London's transportation system on July 21, 2005.[112] But the people with the most valuable information—the members of the same religious, ethnic, or geographic community as the would-be terrorists—are less likely to offer their assistance if they perceive their group has been singled out for inferior treatment.

Of course, not every terrorist suspect who has information is willing to cooperate. But there is no evidence that terrorist suspects cooperate less frequently than do defendants accused of other serious crimes.[113] It also is possible in some cases that the government may lack sufficient evidence to charge a suspect or that the government has come into possession of information that it cannot use at trial, for example, because it would compromise a source or risk disclosure of sensitive intelligence. But such cases are rare and the problem is not novel; it commonly arises in large drug-trafficking and organized-crime cases. In general, criminal prosecutions have proved effective not only at incapacitating suspected terrorists before they engage in attacks but also at gaining information useful to prevent future terrorist acts. By contrast, creating alternatives to criminal prosecutions to enable the government to interrogate suspects with fewer restrictions and then to use the fruits of those interrogations as a basis for imprisonment, imposes tremendous costs that far outweigh any benefits.

Most intelligence and counterterrorism experts agree that torture and other abusive interrogation practices do not produce accurate information and are counterproductive in the long run. Torture, according to one expert, "overwhelms investigators with misleading information."[114] Robert S. Mueller III, director of the FBI since 2001, has stated that no attacks have been disrupted because of intelligence gained through torture or other mistreatment.[115] The "only thing torture guarantees you," insists a veteran FBI interrogator, "is pain."[116] An extensive report from a group of experts advising U.S. intelligence agencies describes the use of harsh interrogation methods as outmoded, amateurish, and unreliable.[117] General David H. Petraeus, commander of the U.S. Central Command and formerly the top general in Iraq, has stated that torture and other "expedient methods" used to gain information are not only wrong but useless and unnecessary.[118]

Bush administration officials nevertheless claimed repeatedly that harsh interrogation methods saved lives and prevented future attacks by providing valuable information. They often cited the CIA's interrogation of Abu

Zubaydah at a secret prison in Thailand following his capture in 2002—the catalyst for the initial Justice Department torture memos. Under the pressure of its "enhanced interrogation techniques," the CIA claimed, Zubaydah provided leads about a number of terrorism suspects, including Jose Padilla, who was arrested soon after Zubaydah's interrogation. In addition to waterboarding, which the CIA inflicted on Zubaydah eighty-three times in a single month, CIA operatives stripped Zubaydah naked, exposing his injuries (previously suffered during a firefight in Pakistan); raised the air conditioning so much that he "seemed to turn blue"; blasted rock music at him; and made him stand for hours at a time in a frigid cell.[119] (The CIA later subjected Khaled Sheikh Mohammed to waterboarding 183 times in a single month.)[120] The former military psychologist, James Mitchell, led the CIA's interrogation team, announcing that Zubaydah had to be treated "like a dog in a cage" and his power to resist broken.[121] There is no evidence, however, that those techniques produced useful intelligence. Indeed, the interrogators on the ground suggested that the brutal treatment was "unnecessary," but they were overruled by the CIA officials in headquarters who were monitoring the interrogation.[122] By contrast, the FBI agents who initially questioned Zubaydah through standard interview techniques had far greater success.[123] Their progress, however, came to a halt when the CIA team arrived, froze the FBI out of the interrogation process, and turned to torture.[124] In addition to misrepresenting the efficacy of its interrogation methods, the CIA also profoundly overstated Zubaydah's importance: the CIA and top Bush administration officials had sought to justify Zubaydah's treatment on the ground that he was a senior member of al Qaeda and a close associate of Osama bin Laden. Interrogators later realized that Zubaydah was merely a low-level personnel clerk who helped facilitate travel to training camps in Afghanistan.[125] In order to justify Zubadyah's brutal treatment, government officials nevertheless continued to perpetuate the lie for years afterward that Zubaydah was a high-ranking al Qaeda member until eventually abandoning the claim that Zubaydah was even a member of or formally identified with al Qaeda.[126] In the end, not a single plot was thwarted as a result of statements wrung from Zubaydah through torture. As one former intelligence official said, "We spent millions of dollars chasing false alarms."[127]

The most successful U.S. interrogations since 9/11 instead have come through traditional law enforcement methods. In the weeks after the attacks, Ali Soufan of the FBI and Robert McFadden of the Navy Criminal Investigative Service interrogated Abu Jandal, Osama bin Laden's former bodyguard, at a Yemeni prison where Jandal had been held for nearly a year. Jandal refused to cooperate and insisted that the attacks had been orchestrated by Israel's Mossad. Rather than resorting to torture, Soufan got Jandal to open up through a combination of guile and craft, starting the process by giving the diabetic Jandal sugar-free cookies as a sign of friendship and respect. Jandal later provided reams of valuable information about al Qaeda without waterboarding, sleep deprivation, or other harsh interrogation methods, and notwithstanding the fact that he was advised of his constitutional rights.[128] Matthew Alexander, a former military interrogator in Iraq whose efforts helped track down al Qaeda leader Abu Mousab al-Zarqawi, has pointed out that coaxing, cajoling, and tricking terrorist suspects, and not torturing them, is the right way to obtain valuable intelligence.[129] Another professional interrogator, Eric Maddox, credits similar tactics in yielding the information that led to the capture of Saddam Hussein. Maddox got Mohammed Ibrahim, a mid-ranking Baath Party leader with close ties to Hussein, to provide directions to Hussein's whereabouts by creating a false sense of urgency: Maddox told Ibrahim that unless he volunteered the information immediately, Hussein might move, and he could no longer help Ibrahim from going to prison.[130] Substantial intelligence has been gleaned in various other ways—from materials found on detainees after they were captured (known as "pocket litter"), from playing detainees against one another, and from detainees freely volunteering information that they believed their questioners already knew.[131]

Torture is not only ineffective; it also can produce misinformation with devastating consequences, as the case of Ibn al-Shaykh al-Libi illustrates. In late 2001, the United States captured al-Libi in Afghanistan. He initially was interrogated—without torture—by FBI counterterrorism expert Jack Cloonan, who says that he advised FBI agents in Afghanistan to "handle this like it was being done right here, in my office in New York."[132] During interrogations, agents were able to dangle the possibility of favorable treatment for al-Libi's wife. Al-Libi cooperated, and provided detailed information about al Qaeda staff and training camps in Afghanistan and about a plot to blow up a U.S. military base, thus helping avert a potentially deadly attack.[133] Al-Libi also denied any connection between al Qaeda and Saddam Hussein's regime in Iraq, even though FBI agents repeatedly pressed him on this point.[134] The CIA, however, resisted the FBI's effort to treat al-Libi like a potential prosecution witness and wanted to use more aggressive tactics. So, several days into the FBI's interrogation, a CIA agent burst into the cell where the FBI was questioning al-Libi and started shouting at the prisoner, "You're going to Egypt! And while you're there, I'm going to find your mother and fuck her!"[135] Shortly thereafter, al-Libi was strapped to a stretcher, bound and gagged with duct tape, and rendered to Egypt—with the White House's approval.[136]

In Egypt, al-Libi's interrogators pressed him to admit knowing about ties between al Qaeda and Saddam Hussein in Iraq. When al-Libi denied any such connection, he was locked in a tiny cage for eighty hours. After he was finally let out of the box, al-Libi was beaten before being given another chance to "tell the truth." So al-Libi made up a story, accusing three al Qaeda figures he knew of going to Iraq to learn about nuclear weapons.[137] When Egyptian interrogators beat al-Libi again to find out more, al-Libi embellished his tale about Iraq's helping al Qaeda obtain weapons of mass destruction. The information was relayed to the United States, without a description of how it was obtained. Secretary of State Colin Powell later relied on al-Libi's coerced confession in his February 5, 2003, presentation to the United Nations justifying the United States' military intervention in Iraq.[138] "I can trace the story of a senior terrorist operative telling how Iraq provided training in these [chemical and biological] weapons to al Qaeda," Powell said. "Fortunately, this operative is now detained, and he has told his story."[139] Unfortunately, that story—which al-Libi later recanted and the CIA eventually repudiated—was false, and the United States' decision to invade Iraq rested in part on a false confession gained by burying a prisoner alive. Under torture, al-Libi had told his interrogators what they had wanted to hear. Al-Libi was later transferred to a secret jail in Afghanistan and eventually sent to a prison in Libya where he reportedly committed suicide.[140]

Torture also can help fuel terrorism by inculcating the desire for vengeance.[141] Al Qaeda leaders such as Ayman al-Zawahiri have cited their torture and abuse in Egyptian prisons as sparking the desire to take revenge through violence.[142] In addition, torture can alienate moderates from Arab and Muslim communities, undermining the United States' ability to gain support from those whom it needs in fighting terrorism.[143] America's image and standing in the world have been seriously undermined by the brutal and dehumanizing actions committed by U.S. officials at Abu Ghraib, Guantánamo, and secret CIA jails.[144] While some may gravitate toward terrorist groups regardless of how the United States treats prisoners, torture harms America's ability to win the hearts and minds of those who have not yet committed to that path.

Torture, like indefinite detention and sham military trials, also emboldens repressive regimes like Egypt, Sudan, and Syria, which now point to the United States to justify their own human rights violations. As the Parliamentary Assembly of the Council of Europe, an international government organization of forty-six nations, warned:

The commission of unlawful acts—abductions, the exporting of torture to other countries even though they are regarded as "rogue states," the setting up of detention centers beyond judicial supervision—has severely affected the moral authority of the United States. Worse still, the world's greatest power is becoming a negative role model for other countries, which feel that they may legitimately follow the same path and flout human rights.[145]

At the same time, torture makes the United States less willing to share information with other countries, a point of contention with key allies and a source of frustration among counterterrorism officials in Europe.[146] One German court, for example, had to dismiss the charges against a suspected accomplice of the 9/11 hijackers when U.S. officials refused to produce a key witness to testify at trial because that witness was being held and interrogated in secret CIA custody.[147] "The trial and the legal investigation is at the center of our answer to terrorism," explains Armado Spataro, a senior Italian counterterrorism prosecutor who saw a broad terrorism investigation he was conducting disrupted by the rendition and torture of Abu Omar. "In the U.S. situation, the trial is not important."[148]

The 9/11 Commission warned early on about the United States' failure to live up to its legal and moral obligations. "Allegations that the United States abused prisoners in its custody make it harder to build the diplomatic, political, and military alliances the government will need [to fight terrorism]."[149] Members of the commission later reiterated those downsides, citing the United States' mistreatment of "suspected terrorists in military prisons and secret detention centers abroad."[150] The U.S. Senate Intelligence Committee similarly highlighted "the complications" secret detention and extraordinary rendition pose to terrorism prosecutions and to America's image.[151]

Defenders of torture still cling to the myth of the "ticking time bomb"— that torture may be necessary in an emergency when authorities believe a prisoner has information that could prevent an imminent attack. But it is impossible to know in advance whether a person actually has information that would prevent some future attack. As a result, the goal of saving lives— however remote or tenuous the threat—can always be invoked to justify torture because it is always possible in theory that torture will yield valuable information. So while torture might be intended for only the most extreme situations, it will inevitably be used more widely once the door is opened. Another problem is that torture does not occur in a vacuum but infects a country's entire legal and political system, which must continually find ways to hide or excuse it.

Those who defend torture will always claim there are situations in which torture yielded useful information. But one can never know if that same information could have been obtained without it. There is no evidence, for example, that the United States gained any information after 9/11 through torture that could not have been obtained through lawful means. Conversely, much of the evidence gained through torture was false. Legal and moral considerations aside, torture remains a much less effective method of gaining information than the more sophisticated and calibrated tools of criminal law enforcement. Torture also carries tremendous costs beyond the physical and mental harms inflicted on its victims. When a democratic country seeks to sanction or legalize torture, it undermines its own legitimacy, creates a backlash among affected communities, and weakens the rule of law at home and abroad.

The criminal justice system contains other safeguards that help to deter torture, such as the privilege against self-incrimination, the right of access to counsel and a prompt judicial hearing following arrest, and the right to confront one's accusers at trial. But as long as the U.S. government continues to detain terrorist suspects militarily and as long as national security courts and other forms of preventive detention are considered possible alternatives to criminal prosecution, habeas corpus will remain important to preventing torture and other abuse because it provides access to a court and thus helps prevent the type of secret, extrajudicial detention that is torture's breeding ground. It is not simply enough to "trust" the executive (no matter who is occupying the White House): the check of an independent judiciary is essential—and its availability is more, and not less, important in an age of international terrorism given the inevitable tendency of government officials to push against legal boundaries and to engage in coercive interrogation practices.

By the end of the Bush administration, the post-9/11 detention regime was still largely intact, even if some of its worst excesses had been curbed. The United States continued to detain hundreds of individuals indefinitely without charge. It also maintained the prerogative to operate secret prisons and engage in torture and other abuse in the name of national security. Detainees at Guantánamo had finally won the right to habeas corpus. But more than two hundred men were still imprisoned there in legal limbo, and the United States continued to resist access to habeas corpus for prisoners held at Bagram in Afghanistan.

The Bush administration had not only altered and corroded America's laws and institutions; it had also changed public consciousness and perception. Despite the widespread criticism of Guantánamo, many of its key features had gained traction, particularly indefinite detention without charge, military commissions, and the broader concept of a global "war on terror." The Bush administration had also done what before was virtually unthinkable: it had made torture a matter of public debate. Important victories had been won in the courts, abuses uncovered, and habeas corpus defended against executive and legislative assault. But much had changed, and the next administration would have to govern in a legal, political, and cultural climate that was different from any before it.

Continuity and Change

The Detention Policy of a New Administration

On his inauguration as the forty-fourth president of the United States on January 20, 2009, Barack Obama suggested a new direction for America's national security policy: "As for our common defense, we reject as false the choice between our safety and our ideals."[1] Two days later, in one of his first official acts as president, Obama issued a directive mandating the closure of the detention facility at Guantánamo Bay within one year. He also issued three executive orders that day. One banned harsh interrogation methods by confining the CIA to techniques contained in the *U.S. Army Field Manual* and mandating compliance with Common Article 3 of the Geneva Conventions while also directing the closure of any remaining secret CIA prisons.[2] The second created a cabinet-level task force to review existing individual Guantánamo detainee cases.[3] The third called for a comprehensive review of U.S. detention and interrogation policy.[4]

However, important questions remained. Under the president's directive, some Guantánamo detainees would presumably be returned home or repatriated to third countries. But others would not, and Obama did not address how they would be treated. Would they simply be moved to the United States and continue to be held indefinitely as "enemy combatants"? Would some detainees still be tried by military commissions? And what about prisoners at other U.S.-run facilities like Bagram in Afghanistan? A new and larger prison—the Parwan Detention Facility—had been built on the outskirts of the Bagram Air Base. But even though conditions were improving, the underlying question remained: would the United States continue to hold prisoners there without charge and without access to any court? In short, even if the Obama administration closed Guantánamo, would it—or a future administration—maintain key features of the larger detention system that Guantánamo embodied?

The first major test of the new administration's intentions came in the case of Ali al-Marri, which the Supreme Court had decided to hear the month before President Obama took office. The Obama administration consequently was forced to decide almost immediately whether to defend this extraordinary exercise of presidential detention power: the military seizure and imprisonment without trial of a person lawfully residing in the United States based on allegations of terrorism. In February 2009, after al-Marri's opening brief had been filed, and just weeks before the administration's response was due, the Justice Department unsealed a two-count indictment against al-Marri for providing material support to terrorism and sought his transfer from military to civilian custody.[5] The solicitor general simultaneously asked the Supreme Court to dismiss al-Marri's case as moot on the ground that al-Marri had obtained the relief he sought in his habeas petition: the right not to be imprisoned without trial. Faced with a choice, Obama thus elected not to defend the sweeping—and dubious—assertion of executive power made by his predecessor. The Court granted the government's motion and dismissed the petition.[6] Although the Court also vacated the Fourth Circuit's divided ruling upholding al-Marri's possible military detention, thereby erasing that precedent and preventing its use against others in the future, it left unanswered the exceedingly important question about the president's domestic military detention power presented by al-Marri's case. Al-Marri, meanwhile, subsequently pleaded guilty to one count of conspiring to provide material support to al Qaeda and was sentenced to eight years and four months in prison, showing the ability of the criminal justice system to handle even the most challenging cases.[7]

In ongoing litigation elsewhere, however, the Obama administration tacked closely to the prior administration's legal positions. In the Guantánamo habeas cases, which had finally started to go forward with hearings in district court following the Supreme Court's June 2008 decision in *Boumediene v. Bush*, the administration claimed broad power to seize and detain terrorism suspects without charge or trial. While it said a detainee's support for terrorism must be "substantial" and swapped the label "enemy combatant" for that of "unprivileged belligerent," these changes were largely cosmetic. The Obama administration maintained that the government could detain individuals indefinitely without charge as part of the United States' global armed conflict against al Qaeda, the Taliban, and associated groups, even if those individuals were not seized on or near a battlefield and never took up arms against the United States.[8] Moves that had at first appeared to signal a new direction, such as the Obama administration's decision to indict al-Marri rather than defend his military imprisonment, increasingly seemed like efforts to sidestep difficult cases and avoid adverse rulings that might limit its options in the future.

On May 21, 2009, Obama delivered an important speech from the National Archives in Washington.[9] Flanked by the Constitution and the Declaration of Independence, Obama reiterated his vision for the country's national security policy. "My single most important responsibility as President," he said, "is to keep the American people safe." But, he cautioned, "in the long run we also cannot keep this country safe unless we enlist the power of our most fundamental values."[10]

Obama had sharp words for his predecessor. After the attacks of September 11, the United States entered a new era, forced to confront an enemy that presented grave dangers and did not abide by legal rules. Faced with this uncertain threat, he said, the U.S. government "made a series of hasty decisions. . . . Instead of strategically applying our power and our principles, too often we set those principles aside as luxuries that we could no longer afford." To restore those principles, Obama reiterated his commitment to ending torture. Referring to his earlier decision to ban "enhanced interrogation techniques," Obama did not mince his words, denouncing those methods and rejecting the notion that torture was necessary to keep America safe. Obama also defended his decision to close Guantánamo, charging that the prison had tarnished America's reputation and undermined its security by serving as a recruiting tool for terrorists. In addition, he rejected claims of unilateral executive power, asserting instead that an effective national security policy depended on action by all three branches of government. In its rhetoric and sensibility, the speech marked a sharp contrast with President Bush's September 2006 speech defending secret detention and torture.

But Obama's speech also showed that key components of the United States' post-9/11 detention policy were becoming institutionalized. Although Obama stressed the importance of the criminal justice system and the ability of the federal courts to handle terrorism cases, he also stated that federal prosecutions were just one of several tools the U.S. should employ in closing Guantánamo and fighting terrorism. Another tool, he said, was military commissions. While Obama said he would reform the commissions, he never provided a coherent explanation of why commissions should still be used and ignored the harmful consequences of maintaining this tarnished second-class justice system. In addition, Obama indicated that he would continue to hold some Guantánamo detainees indefinitely, thus perpetuating the existence of a category of individuals who could be held, potentially for life, without ever being charged with a crime.[11]

Obama followed a similar approach on other national security issues, embracing the language of change without deviating significantly from the policies of his predecessor. For example, he proclaimed the importance of transparency in government when he released redacted versions of four memos from the Bush administration's Office of Legal Counsel that sought to legalize torture and other detainee mistreatment, including the second, previously classified August 1, 2002, torture memo. But Obama also refused to release photographs depicting the abuse of prisoners by U.S. personnel, arguing that the photographs would endanger American service members. Instead, Obama sought (and subsequently obtained) reversal of an appeals court decision mandating the release of the photos under the Freedom of Information Act.[12]

Obama also said that he intended to reform the "state secrets" privilege that the United States had previously used to shut down litigation by victims seeking damages for torture and illegal detention. And the administration did announce changes designed to curb abuse of the state secrets privilege, including imposing a higher standard to invoke the privilege and strengthening internal Justice Department review.[13] But Obama also refused to modify the government's position in seeking to dismiss lawsuits challenging the CIA's extraordinary rendition program and gross mistreatment of detainees.

In November 2009, Attorney General Eric H. Holder Jr. announced that the United States would bring criminal charges against Khaled Sheikh Mohammed (KSM) and four other Guantánamo detainees for their role in the 9/11 attacks.[14] The decision to prosecute the suspected 9/11 plotters in federal court rather than in military commissions marked a sharp break with previous policy. After years of torture and illegal detention, the prisoners would finally be tried in accordance with the Constitution. Moreover, Holder said the trial would take place at the federal courthouse in New York City, close to where the 9/11 attacks on the World Trade Center occurred, increasing the trial's symbolic importance. The prosecution would send the message that even the most dangerous criminals could be brought to justice in the regular courts.

Holder, however, also stated that some Guantánamo detainees would still be tried in military commissions. Congress had recently enacted legislation improving the commissions, strengthening evidentiary standards, promising more resources to defense counsel, and restricting the use of evidence gained through mistreatment.[15] Notwithstanding these latest reforms, the commissions still failed to meet the standards of either the federal courts or military courts-martial. The commissions, for example, contained fewer protections against the use of hearsay, which could be used to launder evidence gained through coercion, and were more prone to secrecy. The commissions also had larger problems. They continued the error of treating as war crimes such criminal offenses as material support for terrorism and conspiracy. They also lacked the legitimacy of the federal courts, as well as their expertise and track record of trying complex terrorism cases. Furthermore, the commissions still applied only to foreign nationals, violating principles of equal protection under law and reinforcing the perception that the United States discriminated against noncitizens.

In addition, the Obama administration indicated that it would continue to hold some detainees without trial by endorsing the same claim of sweeping military detention power that treated the world as a battlefield in a war against al Qaeda and those associated with it. The administration also did not explain why one detainee might receive a full criminal trial and another no trial at all. Instead, the administration's Detention Policy Task Force created by Obama's executive order listed a number of factors that went into the calculation, including "protection of intelligence sources and methods" and possible "legal or evidentiary problems."[16] This raised the concern that decisions were based on expediency rather than principle. As a practical matter, it meant that when the government believed it could easily convict, it brought charges in federal court; when the government had some doubts about its evidence, it resorted to the more relaxed rules of military commissions; and when the government's case was weakest, it dispensed with a trial altogether and simply held the prisoners indefinitely under a theory previously unknown to American law: that the prisoners were too difficult to try but too dangerous to release. In short, while the Obama administration adopted a preference for trying suspected terrorists in federal court, it remained only that—a preference, not a requirement. The twin system of military commissions and indefinite detention without charge that had developed at Guantánamo remained available whenever the United States did not want to afford a person in its custody the full protection of its laws.

One thing, however, had changed: those detained at Guantánamo were at least no longer deprived of habeas corpus. Nor could Congress pass a statute taking away the right to habeas corpus, as it had tried to do twice before, because the Supreme Court ruled in *Boumediene* that this right was protected by the Constitution. Following the Court's decision in *Boumediene*, district judges in Washington, D.C., were now obligated to conduct prompt habeas corpus hearings in individual Guantánamo detainee cases and to examine whether the detentions were lawful. By the fall of 2008, these hearings had started to move forward, and dozens were underway by the time Obama took office. The results underscored why the government had resisted habeas corpus for so long: in most cases, it simply could not defend the detentions in court.

District judges generally accepted the government's argument that at least some individuals at Guantánamo could be held without charge as "enemy combatants" under the 2001 Authorization for Use of Military Force (AUMF) even if they did not take up arms on a battlefield, a broader detention standard than the Supreme Court had upheld in *Hamdi v. Rumsfeld*. The judges did, however, insist on a stronger connection to and degree of involvement with the Taliban, al Qaeda, or "associated forces" than the government said was required. Judge Reggie B. Walton, for example, adopted the government's position that "substantial support" for the Taliban or al Qaeda provided a basis for detention under the AUMF, but he tethered "substantial support" to actions taken within that organization's "command structure."[17] Another judge, John D. Bates, rejected the government's claim that "substantial support" of al Qaeda or an associated terrorist organization alone justified military detention, finding that an individual had to be "part of" that organization or to have committed a belligerent act to be detained under the AUMF.[18] That determination was rejected by the court of appeals in a ruling that said support alone could be a basis for detention under the AUMF. The court of appeals also suggested that courts could not consider international law in interpreting the AUMF, which contradicted both the Supreme Court's decision in *Hamdi* and well-settled rules of statutory interpretation.[19]

But the district judges also found in a staggering percentage of cases that the government had failed to provide credible or reliable evidence to justify imprisonment; that is, that the government had not established the facts required to show that the prisoner fell within the legal category of "enemy combatant," however defined. By the one-year anniversary of *Boumediene* in June 2009, federal judges had ruled in twenty-six of the thirty-one Guantánamo habeas cases they decided that there was no basis to hold the prisoners; by January 2010, that number was thirty-two out of the forty-one cases decided, meaning that the government had failed to justify the prisoner's detention almost 80 percent of the time. The judges, moreover, were often sharply critical of, if not openly hostile to, the government's claim that the evidence supported detention.

The first habeas hearings were held before district judge Richard J. Leon, the same judge who four years earlier had summarily dismissed several petitions on the ground that the Guantánamo detainees had no rights to enforce through habeas corpus. The first case that Leon considered involved the six

Algerian prisoners who had been before the Supreme Court in *Boumediene*. Leon conducted a weeklong hearing behind closed doors, with the detainees permitted to participate by telephone only in those portions of the hearing that did not involve classified information. Some of the evidence was hidden even from the detainees' lawyers. But this extraordinary secrecy notwithstanding, for the first time in more than seven years, the government was forced to present evidence before a judge. Faced with the prospect of an actual hearing, the government's case no longer seemed so strong. Before the hearing had even started, the government dropped its most serious allegation: that the men had been planning a bomb attack on the American embassy in Sarajevo.[20] By the hearing's conclusion, Judge Leon found that the government had failed to present any credible proof of its remaining allegation against five of the six prisoners: that the men had planned to travel to Afghanistan to fight against U.S. and allied forces there. The government had relied exclusively on information contained in a classified document from an unnamed source without providing sufficient information to adequately evaluate the credibility and reliability of the information.

"To allow enemy combatancy to rest on so thin a reed," Leon announced in his public ruling, "would be inconsistent with the Court's obligation . . . to protect [the prisoners'] from the risk of erroneous detention."[21] Although he upheld the continued detention of the sixth prisoner for providing support to al Qaeda in Afghanistan (a ruling later reversed on appeal), Leon ordered that the other five detainees be released as soon as possible. In addition, Leon took the unusual step of imploring the government not to appeal his decision, warning that "seven years of waiting for our legal system to give them an answer to a question so important . . . is more than plenty."[22] The government did not appeal, and all five men whose habeas petitions had been granted by Judge Leon were eventually repatriated.

Another habeas decision by a different district judge involved a Yemeni citizen accused of traveling to Afghanistan, training at an al Qaeda or Taliban camp, and engaging in hostilities against the United States—the type of broad-brush allegations routinely leveled at many Guantánamo prisoners.[23] The detainee, Ali Ahmed, admitted that he had gone to Pakistan before the 9/11 attacks to attend a religious school to study the Qur'an and denied that he had attended a terrorist training camp, become a member of a terrorist group, or taken up arms against the U.S. or its allies. While Ali Ahmed acknowledged that he was staying at a guesthouse when he was arrested (one the government said was frequented by al Qaeda and Taliban fighters), he denied any connection to terrorism.

The government relied on its "mosaic" theory. According to this theory, the government said, its allegations must be examined together, not in isolation, to determine whether the evidence as a whole supported the conclusion that the detainee should continue to be held under the AUMF. The mosaic approach required the fact-finder to draw inferences from the government's myriad allegations, connecting the dots without hard evidence. Previously used for analysis in the intelligence community, the mosaic approach was imported wholesale into the detention context after 9/11 and used to justify indefinite imprisonment. The district judge, Gladys Kessler, refused to draw the government's requested inferences and instead demanded that each of its allegations be supported by reliable and credible evidence.

> Even using the Government's theoretical model of a mosaic, it must be acknowledged that the mosaic theory is only as persuasive as the tiles which compose it and the glue which binds them together—just as a brick wall is only as strong as the individual bricks which support it and the cement that keeps the bricks in place.[24]

"Therefore," Judge Kessler emphasized, "if the individual pieces of a mosaic are inherently flawed or do not fit together, then the mosaic will split apart, just as the brick wall will collapse."[25] And collapse it did.

As Judge Kessler explained, the government had failed to prove that Ali Ahmed had fought against the United States or supported terrorism. The government's evidence, derived principally from the hearsay statements of other former or current Guantánamo detainees, was generic and "riddled . . . with equivocation and speculation."[26] The judge further noted that some of the evidence was unreliable because it was obtained from detainees at Bagram and at the Dark Prison in Afghanistan who had been chained to walls, deprived of food and water, kept in total darkness with loud music or other sounds blaring for weeks at a time, and subjected to other torture and abuse.[27] Kessler acknowledged that Ali Ahmed had stayed briefly at a guesthouse where alleged al Qaeda and Taliban members stayed during the same time period. But she rejected the government's theory of guilt-by-association and determined that there was "no solid evidence" that Ali Ahmed engaged in or planned any hostilities against the United States or its allies. Judge Kessler also observed that a young Arab man seeking to flee the violence and chaos of a war-torn country might plausibly seek the company of or stay with individuals who shared a language, religion, and culture, and she refused to make the extraordinary leap that this conduct alone constituted evidence of terrorism or other violent activities.[28]

In another case, Judge Leon ridiculed the government's arguments for continued detention.[29] Abdulrahim Abdul Razak Janko was a Syrian citizen who had been taken into custody by U.S. forces in Kandahar, Afghanistan, in January 2002 and brought to Guantánamo. The government argued that Janko traveled to Afghanistan to participate in jihad on behalf of the Taliban; stayed for several days at a guesthouse used by Taliban and al Qaeda fighters and operatives in early 2000, where he helped to clean some weapons; and then briefly attended an al Qaeda training camp. The government conceded that Janko had been tortured by al Qaeda into falsely confessing that he was a U.S. spy and afterward had been imprisoned by the Taliban for more than eighteen months at the notorious Sarpusa Prison in Kandahar where detainees were routinely abused and often died. Nonetheless, the government maintained that Janko still remained part of the Taliban and al Qaeda when he was taken into custody after U.S. forces learned from a reporter of his presence at the prison, where Janko had been left behind with thousands of other Northern Alliance prisoners.[30] The government's position, Judge Leon said, "defies common sense." "Five days at a guesthouse in Kabul combined with eighteen days at a training camp does not add up to a long-standing bond of brotherhood."[31] Furthermore, any modicum of sympathy for al Qaeda or the Taliban that Janko may once have had, Leon noted, was vitiated by his subsequent torture and abuse by those groups.[32]

The case of Afghan prisoner Mohammed Jawad highlighted the mounting judicial frustration over the government's handling of the Guantánamo detentions. Jawad had been a young teenager when he was taken from Afghanistan by the United States for allegedly throwing a hand grenade at a military vehicle, injuring two U.S. Special Forces soldiers and their Afghan interpreter. The government had tried to prosecute Jawad in a military commission under the flawed theory that he had committed a war crime and failed miserably. Although its case was in shambles even in the military commissions, where the deck was stacked heavily in its favor, the government refused to release Jawad and argued that he could be detained indefinitely as an "enemy combatant" even if it chose to forgo prosecution. With the commission proceedings stalled, Jawad sought relief through habeas corpus in federal court. In seeking dismissal of the petition, the government continued to rely on coerced evidence, including a false "confession" that the military judge had already thrown out as the product of torture. Jawad again moved to suppress his prior statements to interrogators on the ground that they were obtained through torture. Jawad's motion detailed his mistreatment by the United States: following his arrest in Kabul, during his forty-nine days at Bagram where he was beaten and threatened with death, and at Guantánamo where he was subjected to extreme isolation, sleep deprivation, and other cruel treatment that drove him to attempt suicide. The day on which its response to the motion was due, the government abandoned its reliance on Jawad's statements, effectively conceding that Jawad had been grossly mistreated. The Court in turn suppressed the statements as the product of torture. Yet the government still continued to argue for Jawad's detention, prompting a scathing rebuke from the district judge, Ellen S. Huvelle. "Your case has been gutted," Huvelle told the government's attorneys. "I don't need to put too fine a point on it."[33] When the government sought an additional delay, Huvelle refused and scheduled a prompt hearing to decide the case, emphasizing how long Jawad had been imprisoned already. "Seven years and this case is riddled with holes," she said. "This case is an outrage."[34] Just days before the hearing, the government finally conceded that Jawad's detention was illegal. Judge Huvelle granted the habeas petition, and Jawad was subsequently returned home to Afghanistan.[35]

Another judge, Colleen Kollar-Kotelly, issued a similarly blistering indictment of the government's evidence. In that case, the government had relied almost exclusively on "confessions" that the prisoner, Fouad Mamoud al-Rabiah, had provided to U.S. interrogators. The government alleged that al-Rabiah had traveled to Afghanistan from his home in Kuwait in 2001 and had met with Osama bin Laden four times, fought in the Tora Bora mountains (the site of a bin Laden complex), and had personal links to al Qaeda members in Afghanistan.[36] But Kollar-Kotelly not only found those allegations unsubstantiated; she also noted that the Justice Department had sought to defend al-Rabiah's detention based on unreliable confessions that even the government's own interrogators did not accept. "The Court is unwilling to credit confessions," Kollar-Kotelly explained, "that the Government cannot even defend as believable."[37] Those confessions, she noted, were wrung through highly coercive methods, including warnings that al-Rabiah could never return to Kuwait if he did not admit to involvement in terrorism and that "no one leaves Guantánamo innocent."[38]

These and other cases demonstrated the importance of habeas corpus. Prisoners had been imprisoned at Guantánamo for years based on the government's allegations that they were dangerous terrorists: "the worst of the worst." Until *Boumediene*, however, none had received anything approaching a fair hearing, let alone been charged and tried in a court of law. The U.S. government had instead waged a relentless campaign to deny the detainees access to a lawyer and a judge, all the while subjecting them to harsh interrogations, prolonged isolation, and other abuse. Once detainees finally were given hearings, and judges had a chance to take a look at the facts, it became clear that in many cases the government had been imprisoning people without any credible or reliable evidence.

The district court habeas decisions helped expose the falsehoods and misrepresentations on which Guantánamo had been built. But they also suffered from a shortcoming that threatened to deprive them of practical effect. Release from imprisonment has long been the remedy in habeas corpus cases.[39] However, at Guantánamo, decisions finding the detentions illegal typically did not end with an order mandating the prisoner's release. Instead, they concluded with language directing the government "to take all necessary and appropriate diplomatic steps to facilitate the [detainee's] release."[40] This language represented a perceived limitation on the power of federal judges to order the release of a prisoner who was unlawfully detained at Guantánamo but who could not be returned to his home country (often because he faced the risk of torture or other persecution there), and for whom no other country had yet been found where he could be safely resettled.

In 2007, the United States was still detaining eight-two people at Guantánamo who, it conceded, were "no longer enemy combatants" or had been "cleared for release."[41] The continued detention of individuals who should have been released persisted even after the Supreme Court's *Boumediene* decision the following year, as some Guantánamo prisoners whose detention had been invalidated by courts in habeas corpus proceedings remained behind bars because the government had been unable to return them to their home country or repatriate them to a third country. In other words, although the detainees now had a right to a court hearing, it remained uncertain whether the court could provide an effective remedy when it found that their detention was illegal. Lakhdar Boumediene, the lead petitioner in the Court's landmark decision bearing his name, remained at Guantánamo for more than six months after Judge Leon ruled that his detention was unlawful, until he was finally resettled in France.[42] Others remained in limbo much longer. Pressure to end such illegal imprisonments reached a boiling point in the cases of seventeen Uighurs, members of a persecuted Muslim minority from western China who had fled their homes for Afghanistan.

In 2002, the Uighurs were seized by the Northern Alliance and bounty hunters, sold to U.S. forces, and brought to Guantánamo. Although the United States eventually admitted that it had no basis to detain the Uighur prisoners, it was unable to resettle them, partly because no country wanted to anger China by accepting them and partly because the United States had branded them dangerous terrorists. When the Uighur detentions were first challenged in court, the Bush administration clung to the theory that they were "enemy combatants." It claimed that the Uighurs were connected with the East Turkestan Islamic Movement (ETIM), which it said was "associated" with al Qaeda, thus bringing them within the government's elastic interpretation of the AUMF. An appellate court ridiculed the government's lack of proof and suggested that the United States had originally designated the ETIM a terrorist association based on Chinese propaganda posted on the Internet.[43] The court held that there was no lawful basis for the prisoners' detention. Following the Supreme Court's decision in *Boumediene*, the Uighurs sought their release through habeas corpus.

In October 2008, district judge Ricardo M. Urbina granted their request, directing that the men be brought to the United States and freed under terms to be ordered by the court. By then, the Uighurs had been imprisoned for more than six years, and the government still had failed to present any credible or reliable evidence that they posed a threat to the United States or its allies. Indefinite detention of the innocent, Judge Urbina ruled, "is not in keeping with our system of government."[44] The Uighurs' continued imprisonment after a court had found there was no basis to hold them would not only gut habeas corpus and undermine the Supreme Court's decision in *Boumediene*, Urbina said, but would also allow the executive to nullify the judiciary in violation of the Constitution's separation of powers.

The Bush administration blocked the order by filing an emergency appeal, arguing that no court could order the prisoners' release into the United States, no matter how long the resettlement process took. A panel of the D.C. Circuit Court of Appeals reversed the district court's order in a divided, two-to-one decision, finding in *Kiyemba v. Bush* that federal courts were powerless to order the release of Guantánamo prisoners into the United States, even when those prisoners had been found not to be "enemy combatants," presented no danger, and had been deemed eligible for release to another country by the U.S. government.[45] The appeals court relied principally on the federal government's power to control immigration, even though the Uighurs were not seeking admission to the United States or legal status under U.S. immigration law, but were asking only for temporary release from imprisonment until another country could be found for them. Given the circumstances, this was the only effective remedy for their indefinite detention. By taking that remedy off the table, *Kiyemba* threatened to render habeas corpus a dead letter for prisoners at Guantánamo who could not be returned to their home nation and whom the United States was unable or unwilling to repatriate to a third country. Taken to its logical conclusion, the ruling meant that no court could end the unlawful imprisonment of a Guantánamo detainee over the executive's objection or as long as the executive represented that it was engaging in diplomatic efforts to secure the detainee's repatriation, no matter how long that process took. Prisoners at Guantánamo could thus continue to win the battle by proving that their detention was illegal, only to lose the war when the judge said that he or she was powerless to order their freedom.

In April 2009, the Uighurs appealed the D.C. Circuit's decision in *Kiyemba* to the Supreme Court. In its brief opposing Supreme Court review, the Obama administration adhered to the Bush administration's position that the federal courts lacked the power to remedy the Uighurs' illegal detention by ordering their release and defended the lower court's decision. At the same time, the new administration stepped up diplomatic efforts to repatriate the prisoners and to avoid another legal showdown over habeas rights by rendering the Uighurs' challenge moot. Four Uighur prisoners were sent to Bermuda; six went to Palau.[46] But the Obama administration was unable to repatriate all the petitioners in *Kiyemba*, and it refused to support their temporary release in the United States. Congress, meanwhile, goaded by right-wing propaganda about the dangers the temporary release of a few Uighurs could pose to America's security, sought to limit the president's ability to transfer Guantánamo detainees to the United States. It added measures to appropriations legislation that imposed conditions on the transfer of Guantánamo detainees to other countries and prohibited the government from bringing Guantánamo detainees to the United States for any purpose other than trial.[47] Amid the cloud of legal uncertainty over the authority of judges to provide actual habeas relief, the Supreme Court granted review in *Kiyemba* in October 2009. But in March, 2010, one month before oral argument, the Court dismissed the Uighurs' petition after the government provided new evidence that all of the remaining Uighur detainees had received offers of repatriation and that some had refused them. The Court vacated the D.C. Circuit's decision and remanded the case to the appeals court to consider the implications of these new facts.[48] Thus, as in the al-Marri case the year before, the Supreme Court did not rule on the critical issue before it. In *Kiyemba*, that meant the Court left unanswered the question of the power of federal courts to provide meaningful relief in habeas corpus cases over which they had jurisdiction.

In addition to opposing the release of any Guantánamo detainee into the United States, the Obama administration maintained that courts could not review the transfer of Guantánamo detainees to another country, even if a detainee presented evidence that he was likely to face torture in that country. The Obama administration thus adopted the prior administration's position that the transfer of prisoners in the "war on terror" remains a matter solely for the executive. In theory, this means that the government could seek to evade habeas corpus simply by moving Guantánamo detainees to another U.S. prison, such as Bagram, or outsourcing their detention to another country that would continue to hold them at the United States' request. At the same time, an Obama administration task force recommended continued reliance on "diplomatic assurances" by other countries that prisoners transferred there by the United States would not be tortured, despite the repeated failure of those assurances in the past.[49] While the task force advised strengthening the reliability of diplomatic assurances, the administration has resisted any court review of transfer decisions. The D.C. Circuit has upheld the administration's position, ruling that federal courts cannot enjoin the transfer of Guantánamo detainees who claim that they would likely be tortured in the receiving state. The Supreme Court has thus far declined to intervene.[50]

The Obama administration's approach to Bagram has followed a similar course: instituting modest reforms without altering the overall paradigm or abandoning broad claims of executive detention power. Since the Supreme Court's decisions recognizing a habeas corpus right for those held at Guantánamo, Bagram has become the principal U.S. detention center in the "war on terrorism." Indeed, Obama administration officials have acknowledged that Bagram's importance as a prison for terrorism suspects rose after the Obama administration barred the CIA from conducting long-term detentions and ordered the closure of the detention center at Guantánamo.[51] The new administration has improved conditions at Bagram and beefed up the military procedures for challenging detention, promising Bagram prisoners greater access to the government's evidence and more ability to present witnesses during hearings before newly created detainee review boards. But the reforms lack important protections. Instead of affording access to counsel, for example, the reforms provide only a nonlawyer personal representative. The reforms also do not ensure the impartiality of the three-member military boards that make the detention decisions, including by failing to make them independent from the chain of command.[52] In addition, the United States continues to rely heavily on classified information, which the detainees are not permitted to review.[53] Most important, the Obama administration continues to resist habeas corpus rights for prisoners held at Bagram, which means no judicial review of the standards or procedures the U.S. government is using and no judicial examination of the factual basis for detention, even though some prisoners at Bagram have been held for as long as those at Guantánamo. At the same time, the Obama administration still asserts the legal authority to bring detainees to Bagram from other countries, thus adhering to the prior administration's view that the executive may seize suspected terrorists anywhere in the world and hold them indefinitely without charge or access to a court by transporting them to a U.S. enclave outside America's borders.[54]

In addition to shaping future detention policy, the new administration must grapple with the past. The evidence is overwhelming that the United States tortured and mistreated prisoners in its custody after 9/11 and that these abuses emanated from policies and directives approved at the highest levels of the U.S. government. One question is whether all evidence of these abuses will be made public. Another is whether those responsible will be investigated and held accountable.

In August 2009, the Obama administration released a partially declassified 2004 report by the CIA's Office of Inspector General (OIG) into the Bush administration's interrogation practices.[55] The report's release—like the release of other formerly secret documents describing post-9/11 detention and interrogation practices—was forced by a Freedom of Information Act suit by the American Civil Liberties Union and other groups. The OIG report focused on the treatment of detainees held in CIA secret prisons outside the United States during 2002 and 2003. Although heavily redacted, the report provided chilling new details about the Bush administration's torture regime. It called the CIA's interrogation program ad hoc and poorly supervised and found that it had led to the use of "unauthorized, improvised, inhumane, and undocumented" techniques.[56] The report described interrogators' staging mock executions to convince detainees that they could be killed, threatening to punish a detainee's family by killing his children, and squeezing a detainee's neck at his carotid artery until he began to pass out.[57] It also detailed, for example, how interrogators put a handgun to the head of one CIA prisoner, Abd al-Rahim al-Nashiri, and, to terrify him further, revved a power drill while he stood naked and hooded.[58]

The OIG report provided additional evidence that CIA interrogation techniques were not only legally suspect but, in some instances, patently criminal. This fact was not lost on those involved at the time. One official warned that agency officers might one day wind up on a "wanted list" to appear before the World Court for war crimes for methods used in secret

CIA jails.[59] Concern about the legality of these methods drove the CIA to shroud its entire detention operation in secrecy. It also caused the agency to seek approval from Justice Department lawyers for the interrogation tactics to help avoid criminal liability—a step taken in some instances *after* agency officials had already engaged in tactics that exceeded the guidelines in effect at the time.[60]

The day the OIG report was released, Attorney General Eric Holder announced that the Justice Department had opened a preliminary investigation into the treatment of prisoners in U.S. custody abroad.[61] The investigation represented a first step toward accountability and one that went against President Obama's stated desire to look forward, not backward, and to leave this dark chapter of American history in the past. But the investigation was limited, focusing on a very small number of cases.[62] Holder, moreover, signaled that the Justice Department would not prosecute those who had acted in good faith or within the bounds of legal guidance. This raised serious concerns about the investigation's scope, suggesting that it would focus only on interrogators who exceeded Justice Department guidelines and not on the architects of the techniques themselves, including those high-ranking administration officials who had authorized torture and the Justice Department lawyers who had facilitated it. Thus, those most responsible for the United States' torture and mistreatment of prisoners would continue to evade scrutiny. At worst, Holder's investigation could result in a whitewash, targeting a few low-level agents and perpetuating the lie that the abuse of prisoners was the result of a handful of bad apples rather than a widespread government policy created by high-level officials. Such a facade of accountability could be worse than no investigation at all, creating a false sense that the United States had come to grips with its descent into torture.

President Obama, to be sure, had inherited a colossal mess. When a government acts outside the law for eight years, it creates a host of legal complications and practical problems that are difficult to overcome. Obama also had to navigate an increasingly treacherous political terrain, with members of the opposing party continually trying to make him appear weak on national security, often by distorting the facts, and with some members of his own party resisting his efforts to close Guantánamo and bring terrorism suspects to trial in the United States. In addition, Obama faced internal resistance from some senior military and intelligence officials determined to maintain the status quo. These pressures helped limit the extent to which the new administration was willing to risk political capital by breaking from the practices of its predecessor.

By the end of Obama's first year in office, he had not only failed to close Guantánamo. In the face of mounting public pressure, Obama also indicated that he might abandon the plan to try KSM and the other plotters of the 9/11 attacks in federal court and return them to a military commission.[63] Indefinite detention of terrorism suspects remained U.S. policy. And even though Obama had banned torture, the loopholes for abusive interrogation techniques, such as those created by 2006 amendments to the *U.S. Army Field Manual*, had not yet been closed.[64] If the pendulum was starting to swing back, it still had a long way to go.

It would be a mistake, however, to view these developments simply through the lens of individual presidents and their administrations. The United States' continuation of centerpieces of the "war on terror," such as indefinite detention and military commissions, is about more than the "good" or "bad" choices of its leaders. Ultimately, it is about how far-reaching, even radical changes in law and policy can become institutionalized and accepted as mainstream. It is about how political leaders, commentators, and the public inevitably gravitate toward tough-sounding responses to security threats even if the evidence shows that those responses are unnecessary, unlawful, and even harmful to the country's safety. And it is about how terrorism unleashes impulses to find new ways to detain beyond the law, interrogate without restriction, and avoid accountability. Thus, for example, even as President Obama ordered the closure of secret CIA prisons, reports emerged about the continued use of secret jails within existing Defense Department prisons like Bagram: new microspaces for lawless government action.[65]

The response to the Christmas Day 2009 attempted airplane bombing shows just how much public perception and discourse have shifted since 9/11. After Nigerian Umar Farouk Abdulmutallab failed to detonate an explosive hidden in his underwear while aboard a Northwest Airlines flight bound for Detroit, he was arrested and charged with attempted murder and use of a weapon of mass destruction. Politicians and pundits then attacked the Obama administration for prosecuting Abdulmutallab in federal court rather than in a military commission, even though federal prosecutors had obtained four hundred convictions in terrorism-related cases since 9/11 and military commissions had obtained only three, all of which were mired in controversy.[66] Unable to claim that the criminal justice system could not incapacitate the failed bomber (who was behind bars under maximum security conditions and facing almost certain conviction), critics pressed the equally spurious claim that a criminal prosecution would undermine the government's ability to gain useful intelligence because it prevented the use of harsh interrogation methods and required that the defendant be afforded a lawyer. Ironically, no one had considered a military commission for Richard Reid when he was arrested in Boston after attempting to detonate a shoe bomb on an airplane only months after 9/11 or criticized President Bush for prosecuting Reid in federal court. Nor had anyone proposed denying Reid access to a lawyer to interrogate him aggressively. Eight years later, however, military commissions, indefinite detention, and coercive interrogations had become mainstream, while criminal prosecutions in accordance with the Constitution had become merely an option—one, moreover, that carried the political risk of being painted as weak on terrorism.

The failed car bombing in New York City's Times Square the following May similarly illustrates how the creation of a "new normal" for addressing terrorism paves the way for overreaction and for a continuing erosion of constitutional rights and values. The suspect, an American citizen named Faisal Shahzad, was arrested at John F. Kennedy International Airport as he tried to flee the country and was charged with conspiring to use weapons of mass destruction and other crimes. Although Shahzad quickly began to cooperate with law enforcement officials, the Obama administration was criticized for prosecuting him in the civilian justice system and providing him the rights guaranteed by the Constitution to criminal defendants. "I would not have given him *Miranda* warnings after just a couple of hours of questioning. I would have instead declared him an enemy combatant," remarked former New York City mayor and federal prosecutor Rudolph Giuliani. Two senators, Joe Lieberman (I-CT) and Scott Brown (R-MA), introduced a bill, widely denounced as both senseless and unconstitutional, that would empower the government to revoke the citizenship of anyone who supported or joined a foreign terrorist group, without their even having been convicted of a crime.[67] The administration, bowing to political pressure, subsequently announced that it would seek legislation expanding the *Miranda* "public safety" exception to give the government more leeway to interrogate suspects in terrorism cases without informing them of their rights.[68]

The dark cloud cast by U.S. detention policy after 9/11 is not, however, without a silver lining from the standpoint of human rights and constitutional values. The Bush administration's decision to use Guantánamo as a detention center was based on its belief that individuals could be denied habeas corpus and other legal protections as long as they were imprisoned outside the United States. Guantánamo, as we have seen, was not just a prison; it was an idea, the product of a new system of prisons beyond the law. Yet Guantánamo, in turn, gave rise to landmark Supreme Court decisions rejecting the proposition that the executive could avoid the Constitution simply by moving prisoners across a geographic line and render the Geneva Conventions and other legal safeguards a nullity by labeling prisoners "enemy combatants" in a "war on terrorism." Designed to limit the Constitution, Guantánamo triggered the Constitution's reconceptualization and expansion. It did more than galvanize the human rights movement in the United States, create alliances with international actors and institutions, and build bridges with those law enforcement, military, and intelligence officials who understand that upholding the rule of law helps keep America safe as well as free. Guantánamo also breathed new life into the idea of a transnational Constitution, capable of reaching arbitrary detention, torture, and other illegal government action regardless of where it occurs. Premised on the idea that noncitizens lack even basic constitutional rights, Guantánamo affirmed the notion that rights protect individuals, not just American citizens. Designed to exploit international law, Guantánamo helped demonstrate the continued importance of the Geneva Conventions and other international rules that restrict the power of governments in time of war.

Above all, Guantánamo underscored the enduring need for habeas corpus, which proved to be the single most important check against executive overreaching. The most significant resistance to extrajudicial detention, military commissions, and abusive interrogations came from the courts. Congress, after finally awakening from its post-9/11 slumber, repeatedly showed its willingness to ratify, if not expand on, the sweeping claims of executive power asserted by President Bush and to deprive the courts of any meaningful role. Although the press had played an important part in helping expose torture, extraordinary rendition, and other abuses, these exposés had done little to curtail illicit practices. Only the courts, through the exercise of habeas corpus jurisdiction, had imposed real limits on the government's detention and treatment of terrorism suspects. The federal judiciary remained the one branch in which law and facts mattered, even if they did not matter enough, in which the incarceration of human beings was not reduced to sloganeering or partisan gamesmanship, and in which decisions could be rendered with at least some immunity from the fear, hysteria, and irrationality that had so thoroughly infected the public debate over national security.

Habeas corpus, to be sure, remains both a limited and imperfect tool for curtailing illegal executive action. Courts ultimately may not find that habeas rights extend to the overseas detention of foreign nationals except at Guantánamo. And even if they do, habeas by its nature has difficulty reaching more secret forms of confinement: when the prisoner's location is unknown, the U.S. role is hidden behind a foreign proxy, or the prisoner is simply transferred to another country for continued detention and interrogation. Moreover, the mere availability of habeas does not ensure an answer, let alone the correct answer, to the issues presented. Indeed, more than nine years into the "war on terror," the courts have still not definitively answered perhaps the most basic question it raised: who is a civilian and who is a combatant, that is, who is properly subject to military detention and thus exempt from the ordinary requirement of criminal charge and trial under the Constitution. Finally, as the Guantánamo litigation shows, even "winning" a habeas petition does not itself ensure a prisoner's prompt release from custody, particularly given the reluctance of judges to intervene in the area of prisoner resettlement.

But if habeas is not the only component of a rights-respecting national security policy, it is an indispensable one. The vitality of habeas has become clearer since 9/11, both despite and because of the sustained efforts by the executive and Congress to eliminate it. As long as terrorism remains a problem, there will be a risk that the United States will continue to imprison people without charge or prosecute them before second-class military tribunals rather than in the regular federal courts, to deny them due process, and to engage in torture and other illegal methods of interrogation. Supreme Court decisions have helped ensure the possibility of habeas review over any U.S. detention, regardless of a prisoner's citizenship or location. Those decisions thus serve as a check against further abuses and deterrent against the creation of more law-free zones like Guantánamo. At the same time, not only does indefinite military imprisonment outside the laws of war continue, but there are new proposals for national security courts and other forms of preventive detention that threaten to institutionalize violations of basic constitutional and human rights. In the face of intensifying pressures to detain allegedly dangerous people without charge, without a lawyer, and without access to a court, habeas corpus will continue to be the most important bulwark of individual liberty and safeguard against illegal executive action.

The government must protect the public, and terrorism's capacity to inflict massive damage means that the government must be unflagging and hypervigilant in carrying out that duty. But the United States also must not forgo its Constitution and values in the process. Despite its limits and imperfections, habeas remains—as it has been for centuries—critical to preventing arbitrary and unlawful detention and securing the government's adherence to the rule of law.

Notes

INTRODUCTION

1. Rollin C. Hurd, *A Treatise on the Right of Personal Liberty, and on the Writ of Habeas Corpus*, 2d ed. (Albany, NY: W. C. Little & Co., 1876), 266.

CHAPTER 1

1. A literal translation of al Qaeda from Arabic is "the foundation" or "the base." The origin of organization can be traced to the Soviet invasion of Afghanistan in 1979, when foreign Arab mujahideen, with financial backing from bin Laden and other wealthy Muslim contributors, joined the fight against Soviet occupation of the country. By the mid-1990s, al Qaeda had evolved into a militant terrorist organization, and by the late 1990s, the group had carried out several attacks against U.S. targets. See generally Lawrence Wright, *The Looming Tower: Al Qaeda and the Road to 9/11* (New York: Random House, 2006).

2. Louise Richardson, *What Terrorists Want: Understanding the Enemy, Containing the Threat* (New York: Random House, 2006), 144.

3. NBC News, *Meet the Press*, transcript for September 14, 2003. See also Nancy Gibbs, "What a Difference a Year Makes," *Time*, September 9, 2002.

4. Authorization for Use of Military Force, Pub. L. No. 107-40, 115 Stat. 224 (2001).

5. George W. Bush, "Address to a Joint Session of Congress and the American People, September 20, 2001," in *Public Papers of the Presidents of the United States: George W. Bush, 2001* (Washington, DC: U.S. Government Printing Office, 2003), book 2, 1140–44.

6. Jeffrey Rosen, "Conscience of a Conservative," *New York Times*, September 9, 2007; Michael Dorf, "The Justice Department's Change of Heart regarding Torture: A Fair-Minded and Praiseworthy Analysis That Could Have Gone Still Further," *Findlaw*, January 5, 2005.

7. George W. Bush, "Remarks by the President to Employees at the Pentagon and an Exchange with Reporters in Arlington, Virginia, September. 17, 2001," in *Public Papers of the Presidents of the United States: George W. Bush, 2001*, book 2, 1120.

8. John C. Yoo to Timothy Flanigan, Memorandum Opinion for the Deputy Counsel to the President, September 25, 2001, in *The Torture Papers: The Road to Abu Ghraib*, ed. Karen J. Greenberg and Joshua L. Dratel (New York: Cambridge University Press, 2005), 3–24. See also Frederick A. O. Schwarz and Aziz Z. Huq, *Unchecked and Unbalanced: Presidential Power in a Time of Terror* (New York: New Press, 2006), 73–74.

9. Memorandum for Alberto R. Gonzales, Counsel to the President, and William J. Haynes III, General Counsel, Department of Defense, from John C. Yoo, Deputy Assistant Attorney General, and Robert J. Delahunty, Special Counsel, Re: *Authority for Use of Military Force to Combat Terrorist Activities within the United States*, October 23, 2001.

10. 18 U.S.C. § 1385.

11. Uniting and Strengthening America by Providing Appropriate Tools Required to Intercept and Obstruct Terrorism Act of 2001, Pub. L. No. 107-56, 115 Stat. 272 (2001).

12. 18 U.S.C. §§ 3123(a), 3127(3)-(4).

13. 18 U.S.C. § 3103a.

14. 50 U.S.C. § 1861.

15. 18 U.S.C. § 2331.

16. Jane Mayer, *The Dark Side: The Inside Story of How the War on Terror Turned into a War on American Ideals* (New York: Doubleday, 2008), 93–94.

17. Ibid., 95–97.

18. Ibid., 97.

19. See Hague Convention (IV) Respecting the Laws and Customs of War on Land, October 18, 1907, T.S. No. 539. See also Marco Sassòli and Antoine A. Bouvier, *How Does Law Protect in War* (Geneva: International Committee of the Red Cross, 1999), 67.

20. The other two conventions cover the wounded and sick on land (Geneva I) and the wounded, sick, and shipwrecked at sea (Geneva II).

21. Geneva Convention [III] Relative to the Treatment of Prisoners of War, art. 13, August 12, 1949, 6 U.S.T. 3316, 75 U.N.T.S. 135 (Third Geneva Convention). See also ibid., art. 17 (describing protections of prisoners of war against coercive interrogation).

22. Ibid., art. 118.

23. Ibid., art .4.

24. Ibid., art. 5.

25. Oscar Uhler and Henri Coursier, *Commentary on the Geneva Conventions of 12 August 1949*, vol. 4 (Geneva: International Committee of the Red Cross, 1958), 51. See also *Prosecutor v. Delalic et al.*, Case IT-96-21-T, Judgment (Trial Chamber), November 16, 1998, para. 271 (explaining that "there is no gap between the Third and Fourth Geneva Conventions" because one is either a prisoner of war entitled to protection under the Third Geneva Convention or a civilian entitled to protection under the Fourth Geneva Convention).

26. See Joseph Margulies, *Guantánamo and the Abuse of Presidential Power* (New York: Simon & Schuster, 2006), 73–83.

27. U.S. Department of the Army, *Army Field Manual 34-52: Intelligence Interrogation* (May 8, 1987).

28. Military Order, "Detention, Treatment, and Trial of Certain Non-citizens in the War against Terrorism," November 13, 2001, in Greenberg and Dratel, *The Torture Papers*, 25–28.

29. Ibid. § 2(a).

30. Winfield Scott, *Memoirs of Lieut.-General Scott, L.L.D.* (New York: Sheldon & Company, 1864), vol. 2, at 392–93 (also available at http://www.archive.org/details/memlieut-geno2scotrich). Previously, during the American Revolutionary War, British Major John André was hanged for conspiring with Benedict Arnold. André, however, was not tried by a military commission; he was instead referred to a "Board of General Officers," an

advisory panel and not a court, which decided that he should suffer death for spying. See David Glazier, "Precedents Lost: The Neglected History of the Military Commission," 46 *Virginia International Law Review* 5, 18–20 (2005).

31. Louis Fisher, *Military Tribunals and Presidential Power: American Revolution to the War on Terrorism* (Lawrence: University Press of Kansas, 2005).

32. Tim Golden, "After Terror, a Secret Rewriting of Military Law," *New York Times,* October 24, 2004. The group included John Yoo, David Addington, and former deputy White House counsel Timothy E. Flanigan.

33. Ibid. See also *Amicus* Brief of Retired Generals and Admirals and Milt Bearden in Support of Petitioner, *Hamdan v. Rumsfeld,* No. 05-184 (U.S. Sup. Ct. 2006).

34. Golden, "After Terror."

35. Ibid.

36. Ibid.

37. Ibid. (quoting Richard L. Shiffrin, former Pentagon deputy general counsel for intelligence matters).

38. John Yoo and Robert J. Delahunty to William J. Haynes II, Memorandum: "Application of Treaties and Laws to al Qaeda and Taliban Detainees," January 9, 2002, in Greenberg and Dratel, *The Torture Papers,* 38–79.

39. Jay S. Bybee to Alberto R. Gonzales and William J. Haynes II, Memorandum: "Application of Treaties and Laws to al Qaeda and Taliban Detainees," in Greenberg and Dratel, *The Torture Papers,* 81–117.

40. The War Crimes Act of 1996, Pub. L. No. 104-192, 110 Stat. 2104 (1996) (codified at 18 U.S.C. § 2441).

41. Third Geneva Convention, art. 129.

42. The memo was reportedly drafted by David Addington. See Barton Gellman and Jo Becker, "A Different Understanding with the President," *Washington Post,* June 24, 2007.

43. Alberto R. Gonzales to President Bush, Memorandum: "Decision Re Application of the Geneva Conventions on Prisoners of War to the Conflict with al Qaeda and the Taliban," January 25, 2002, in Greenberg and Dratel, *The Torture Papers,* 118–21.

44. Colin L. Powell to Counsel to the President, Memorandum: "Draft Decision Memorandum for the President on the Applicability of the Geneva Convention to the Conflict in Afghanistan," January 26, 2002, in Greenberg and Dratel, *The Torture Papers,* 122–25.

45. William H. Taft IV to Counsel to the President, Memorandum: "Comments on Your Paper on the Geneva Conventions," February 2, 2002, in Greenberg and Dratel, *The Torture Papers,* 129–33.

46. George W. Bush to the Vice President, the Secretary of State, the Secretary of Defense, the Attorney General, Chief of Staff to the President, Director of the CIA, Assistant to the President for National Security Affairs, and Chairman of the Joint Chiefs of Staff, Memorandum: "Humane Treatment of al Qaeda and Taliban Detainees," February 7, 2002, in Greenberg and Dratel, *The Torture Papers,* 134–35.

47. Ibid.

48. Ibid.

49. Memorandum from Jay S. Bybee, Assistant Attorney General, Office of Legal Counsel, to Alberto R. Gonzales, Counsel to the President, August 1, 2002 (unclassified August 1, 2002, memo), in Greenberg and Dratel, *The Torture Papers,* 172–222; Barton Gellman

and Jo Becker, "Pushing the Envelope on Presidential Power," *Washington Post*, June 25, 2007.

50. Foreign Relations Authorization Act, Fiscal Years 1994 and 1995, Pub. L. No. 103-236, 108 Stat. 463 (1994) (codified at 18 U.S.C. §§ 2340-B).

51. Convention against Torture and other Cruel, Inhuman or Degrading Treatment or Punishment, art. 16, December 10, 1984, S. Treaty Doc. No. 100-20, 1465 U.N.T.S. 85.

52. 18 U.S.C. §§ 2340-A.

53. David Luban, "Liberalism, Torture, and the Ticking Bomb," in *The Torture Debate in America*, ed. Karen J. Greenberg (Cambridge: Cambridge University Press, 2006), 35–83.

54. Unclassified August 1, 2002 memo.

55. Memorandum for John Rizzo, Acting General Counsel of the Central Intelligence Agency, "Interrogation of al Qaeda Operative," from Jay S. Bybee, August 1, 2002 (classified August 1, 2002, memo).

56. Douglas Jehl and David Johnston, "White House Fought New Curbs on Interrogations, Officials Say," *New York Times*, January 13, 2005; Ron Suskind, *The One Percent Doctrine: Deep Inside of America's Pursuit of Its Enemies since 9/11* (New York: Simon & Schuster, 2006), 115.

57. Release of Declassified Narrative Describing the Department of Justice Office of Legal Counsel's Opinions on the CIA's Detention and Interrogation Program, Senator John D. Rockefeller IV (April 22, 2009), 3–4.

58. Classified August 1, 2002, memo, 1–4.

59. International Committee of the Red Cross, "ICRC Report on the Treatment of Fourteen 'High Value Detainees' in CIA Custody" (February 2007), 22.

60. Classified August 1, 2002, memo, 3–4.

61. Editorial, "The Torturers' Manifesto," *New York Times*, April 19, 2009.

62. Jack Goldsmith, *The Terror Presidency: Law and Judgment inside the Bush Administration* (New York: W. W. Norton, 2007), 144. See also Mark Danner, "U.S. Torture: Voices from the Black Sites," *New York Review of Books*, April 9, 2009.

63. Dana Priest, "CIA Puts Harsh Tactics on Hold; Memo on Methods of Interrogation Had Wide Review," *Washington Post*, June 27, 2004.

64. Jane Crawford Greenburg et al., "Bush Aware of Advisers' Interrogation Talks," *ABCNews*, April 11, 2008; R. Jeffrey Smith and Peter Finn, "Harsh Methods Approved as Early as Summer 2002; Holder Declassifies Timeline of Actions by Top Bush Administration Officials regarding Interrogation," *Washington Post*, April 23, 2009.

65. Greenburg et al., "Bush Aware of Advisers' Interrogation Talks."

66. Scott Shane and Mark Mazzetti, "In Adopting Harsh Tactics, No Look at Past Use," *New York Times*, April 21, 2009.

67. Memorandum for William J. Haynes, General Counsel of the Department of Defense, Re: "Military Interrogation of Alien Unlawful Combatants Held Outside the United States," March 14, 2003 (March 2003 memo).

68. Dan Eggen and Josh White, "Memo: Laws Didn't Apply to Interrogators: Justice Dep't Official in 2003 Said President's Wartime Authority Trumped Many Statutes," *Washington Post*, April 2, 2008.

69. March 2003 memo, 6–10.

70. Ibid., 11–19.

71. Ibid., 13.

72. Ibid., 74–79.

73. Paul Kramer, "The Water Cure: Debating Torture and Counterinsurgency—A Century Ago," *New Yorker*, February 25, 2008.

74. These abuses were documented by the Wickersham Commission. See U.S. National Commission on Law Observance and Enforcement (1931).

75. Suskind, *The One Percent Doctrine*, 62.

76. Harold H. Koh, "Regarding the Nomination of the Honorable Alberto R. Gonzales as Attorney General of the United States" (Statement to the U.S. Senate Committee on the Judiciary, January 7, 2005).

77. Ruth Wedgwood and R. James Woolsey, "Law and Torture," *Wall Street Journal*, June 28, 2004.

78. Eggen and White, "Memo: Laws Didn't Apply to Interrogators."

79. Goldsmith, *The Terror Presidency*, 148.

80. See Dep't of Justice, Office of Professional Responsibility, "Investigation into the Office of Legal Counsel's Memoranda Concerning Issues Relating to the Central Intelligence Agency's Use of 'Enhanced Interrogation Techniques' on Suspected Terrorists," July 29, 2009. A separate report by the Justice Department, however, concluded that Yoo and Bybee were not guilty of professional misconduct, although it agreed that they used flawed reasoning and exercised poor judgment. See Eric Lichtblau and Scott Shane, "Report Faults 2 Authors of Bush Terror Memos," *New York Times*, February 19, 2010.

81. Levin, "Legal Standards Applicable under 18 U.S.C. §§ 2340-2340A."

82. Memorandum for John A. Rizzo, Senior Deputy General Counsel, Central Intelligence Agency, Re: "Application of 18 U.S.C. §§ 2340-2340A to Techniques That May Be Used in the Interrogation of a High Value al Qaeda Detainee," from Steven G. Bradbury, Principal Deputy Attorney General (May 10, 2005).

83. Memorandum for John A. Rizzo, Senior Deputy General Counsel, Central Intelligence Agency, Re: "Application of 18 U.S.C. §§ 2340-2340A to the Combined Use of Certain Techniques in the Interrogation of High Value al Qaeda Detainees," from Steven G. Bradbury, Principal Deputy Attorney General (May 10, 2005).

84. Memorandum for John A. Rizzo, Senior Deputy General Counsel, Central Intelligence Agency, Re: "Application of United States Obligations under Article 16 of the Convention against Torture to Certain Techniques That May Be Used in the Interrogation of High Value al Qaeda Detainees," from Steven G. Bradbury, Principal Deputy Attorney General (May 30, 2005).

85. Ibid., 32–39.

86. *The Federalist* No. 47 (James Madison), ed. Clinton Rossiter (New York: Penguin, 1961), 301.

87. *The Federalist* No. 69 (Alexander Hamilton), 386.

88. U.S. Const., art. I, § 8.

89. *Youngstown Sheet and Tube Co. v. Sawyer*, 343 U.S. 579, 643–44 (1952) (Jackson, J., concurring).

90. Unclassified August 1, 2002, memo.

91. Schwarz and Huq, *Unchecked and Unbalanced*, 156–60.

92. Goldsmith, *The Terror Presidency*, 85–90; Mayer, "The Hidden Power."

93. Margulies, *Guantánamo and the Abuse of Presidential Power*, 45.

94. Suskind, *The One Percent Doctrine*, 54–55, 75.

95. Katharine Q. Seelye, "A Nation Challenged: The Detention Camp; U.S. to Hold Taliban Detainees in 'the Least Worst Place,'" *New York Times*, December 28, 2001. The administration had considered, but ruled out, bringing the prisoners to Guam, because of security concerns expressed by residents there. The administration also had considered and rejected the idea of detaining prisoners on ships at sea because it would limit the number of detainees that could be held.

96. Agreement between the United States of America and the Republic of Cuba for the Lease to the United States of Lands in Cuba for Coaling and Naval Stations, February 23, 1903, art. 3, U.S.-Cuba, T.S. No. 418.

97. Treaty between the United States of America and Cuba Defining Their Relations, May 29, 1934, T.S. No. 866, 48 Stat. 1682 (1934).

98. Robert E. Harkavy, *Great Power Competition for Overseas Bases: The Geopolitics of Access Diplomacy* (New York: Pergamon Press, 1982), 3, 5, 206–9.

99. Marion E. Murphy, *The History of Guantanamo Bay*, 2d ed. (U.S. Naval Base, District Publications and Printing Office, Tenth Naval District), 7. See also "Caribbean Leased Bases Jurisdiction," *Jag Journal* 161, 166, no. 15 (October/November 1961): (explaining that Cuba retained "at most a 'titular' sovereignty" over Guantánamo).

100. Jeffrey Toobin, "Camp Justice," *New Yorker*, April 14, 2008.

101. See *United States v. Rogers*, 388 F. Supp. 298, 301 (E.D. Va. 1975) (federal criminal trial of U.S. citizen for actions committed during his employment on Guantánamo); *United States v. Lee*, 906 F.2d 117, 117 n.1 (4th Cir. 1990) (federal criminal trial of Jamaican national for actions committed on Guantánamo); *Huerta v. United States*, 548 F.2d 343, 344, 346 (Ct. Claims 1977) (assuming federal court may decide breach of contract and takings clause claims by Cuban national for loss of property located on Guantánamo).

102. Gerald L. Neuman, "Closing the Guantanamo Loophole," 50 *Loyola Law Review* 1, 34, 39 (2004).

103. Patrick F. Philbin and John C. Yoo to William J. Haynes II, Memorandum: "Possible Habeas Jurisdiction over Aliens Held in Guantánamo Bay, Cuba," December 28, 2001, in Greenberg and Dratel, *The Torture Papers*, 29–37.

104. *Shaughnessy v. United States ex rel. Mezei*, 345 U.S. 206, 218–19 (1953) (Jackson, J., dissenting).

105. See Brandt Goldstein, *Storming the Court: How a Band of Yale Law Students Sued the President—And Won* (New York: Scribner, 2005).

CHAPTER 2

1. Julian Borger, "Cargo of 'Worst' al-Qaida Captives Unloads in Cuba," *The Guardian*, January 12, 2002; Ben Fenton, "Prisoners Locked in Seats: U.S. Takes Tough Precautions as Flights to Guantanamo Begin," *The Gazette*, January 11, 2002; James Dao, "A Nation Challenged: Military; U.S. Is Taking War Captives to Cuba Case," *New York Times*, January 11, 2002; Michael Hedges, "America Responds; Detainees Rights Not Violated, U.S. Insists after Plane Lands," *Houston Chronicle*, January 12, 2002; Sue Anne Pressley, "At Guantanamo Bay, a Peaceful Night; Afghan War Detainees Sleep Soundly after 27-Hour, 8,000-Mile Trip," *Washington Post*, January 13, 2002; David Rose, "World Exclusive: Inside Guantanamo: How We Survived Jail Hell," *The Observer*, March 14, 2004; Katharine Q. Seelye, "A Nation Challenged: The Prisoners;

First 'Unlawful Combatants' Seized in Afghanistan Arrive at U.S. Base in Cuba," *New York Times*, January 12, 2002.

2. Carol D. Leonnig and Julie Tate, "Some at Guantanamo Mark 5 Years in Limbo," *Washington Post*, January 16, 2007.

3. Joseph Margulies, *Guantánamo and the Abuse of Presidential Power* (New York: Simon & Schuster, 2006), 63–65; Rose, "World Exclusive: Inside Guantanamo."

4. "The Changing Face of Guantánamo Bay," *Miami Herald*, May 15, 2007; Margulies, *Guantánamo and the Abuse of Presidential Power*.

5. Margulies, *Guantánamo and the Abuse of Presidential Power*, 67; Jeffrey Toobin, "Inside the Wire; Can an Air Force Colonel Help the Detainees at Guantanamo?" *New Yorker*, February 9, 2004; Carol J. Williams, "At Guantanamo: Hard Time and a View of What Could Have Been," *Los Angeles Times*, October 7, 2006.

6. Jeffrey Toobin, "Camp Justice," *New Yorker*, April 14, 2008.

7. Michelle Shephard, "The View from Guantánamo Bay," *Toronto Star*, February 4, 2007.

8. Kathleen T. Rehm, "Detainees Living in Varied Conditions at Guantánamo," *American Forces Press Service*, February 16, 2005; *Miami Herald*, "Web Extra: A Prison Camps Primer," February 6, 2008, *available at* http://www.miamiherald.com/news/more-info/v-fullstory/story/102770.html (last updated April 27, 2010).

9. Shephard, "The View from Guantánamo Bay."

10. Toobin, "Camp Justice."

11. Tim Golden, "The Battle for Guantánamo," *New York Times*, September 17, 2006.

12. Toobin, "Camp Justice"; Jane Mayer, "The Experiment," *New Yorker*, July 11, 2005.

13. U.S. Department of Defense, "DoD News Briefing on Military Commissions," March 21, 2002.

14. Remarks by Alberto R. Gonzales, Counsel to the President, American Bar Association, Committee on Law and National Security, February 24, 2004, at 3.

15. James Taranto, "War inside the Wire," *Wall Street Journal*, September 16, 2006.

16. Gerry J. Gilmore, "Rumsfeld Visits, Thanks U.S. Troops at Camp X-Ray in Cuba," *American Forces Press Services*, January 27, 2002.

17. Neil A. Lewis and Eric Schmitt, "Guantánamo Prisoners Could Be Held for Years, U.S. Officials Say," *New York Times*, February 13, 2004.

18. Maura Reynolds, "No Tax Hike for Bridges," *Los Angeles Times*, August 10, 2007, A12.

19. Mark Denbeaux and Joshua Denbeaux, "Report on Guantánamo Detainees: A Profile of 517 Detainees through Analysis of Department of Defense Data" (Newark, NJ: Seton Hall Law School, 2006). See also Mark Denbeaux et al., "The Empty Battlefield and the Thirteenth Criterion" (Newark, NJ: Seton Hall Law School, 2007).

20. Mark Denbeaux and Joshua Denbeaux, "Second Report on the Guantánamo Detainees: Inter- and Intra-Departmental Disagreements about Who Is Our Enemy" (Newark, NJ: Seton Hall Law School, 2006).

21. Jared A. Goldstein, "Habeas without Rights," *Wisconsin Law Review* 1165, 1170 (2007).

22. Denbeaux et al., "The Empty Battlefield." This report does not consider the fourteen so-called high-value detainees transferred to Guantánamo in September 2006.

23. Petition for a Writ of Certiorari, *Boumediene v. Bush* (No. 06-1195), at 4–5: The men had been arrested in October 2001. After a three-month investigation, Bosnian officials concluded there was insufficient evidence to support prosecution, and on January 17, 2002, the Supreme Court of the Federation of Bosnia Herzegovina ordered the prisoners' release.

24. Ben Russell, "Camp Delta Protests," *Independent*, January 9, 2007.

25. United Nations Development Program, United Nations Office for Coordination of Humanitarian Affairs, "Assistance for Afghanistan Weekly Update," issue no. 429, September 12, 2001.

26. RAND National Defense Research Institute, "Aid during Conflict: Interaction between Military and Civil Assistance Providers in Afghanistan," September 2001–June 2002, at 26–37; prepared for the Office of the Secretary of Defense and the United States Agency for International Development (2004).

27. Denbeaux and Denbeaux, "Report on Guantánamo Detainees," 15.

28. Associated Press, "U.S. Hopes $25 Million Reward Will Lead to bin Laden," November 20, 2001.

29. Declaration of Colonel Lawrence B. Wilkerson (ret.), dated March 24, 2010, para. 9; prepared for submission in *Hamad v. Bush*, 05cv1009 (D.D.C.) (JDB) (Wilkerson Decl.)

30. Pervez Musharraf, *In the Line of Fire: A Memoir* (New York: Free Press, 2006).

31. U.S. Department of the Army, "Enemy Prisoners of War, Retained Personnel, Civilian Internees and Other Detainees," Army Regulation 190-8, § 1-6e (November 1, 1997) (Army Regulation 190-8).

32. Frederick L. Borch, *Judge Advocates in Combat: Army Lawyers in Military Operations from Vietnam to Haiti* (Washington, DC: U.S. Army, Office of the Judge Advocate General and Center of Military History, 2001), 22.

33. Ibid., 104–6.

34. U.S. Department of Defense, *Conduct of the Persian Gulf War: Final Report to Congress*, (Washington, DC: U.S. Government Printing Office, 1992), L-3.

35. Jane Mayer, "The Hidden Power: The Legal Mind behind the White House's War on Terror," *New Yorker*, July 3, 2006.

36. Army Regulation 190-8, § 1-6. See also Judge Advocate General's School, *Operational Law Handbook*, O'Brien ed. (2003), 10.

37. Tim Golden, "Tough Justice: Administration Officials Split over Stalled Military Tribunals," *New York Times*, October 25, 2004.

38. Denbeaux and Denbeaux, "Report on Guantánamo Detainees," 14–16.

39. Wilkerson Decl. para. 9a.

40. Margulies, *Guantánamo and the Abuse of Presidential Power*, 68.

41. Leonnig and Tate, "Some at Guantanamo Mark 5 Years in Limbo."

42. *Parhat v. Gates*, 532 F.3d 834, 838 (D.C. Cir. 2008); Josh White and Julie Tate, "4 Men Cleared of Terrorism Links but Still Detained," *Washington Post*, May 20, 2006, A18.

43. Tim Golden, "Expecting U.S. Help, Sent to Guantánamo," *New York Times*, October 15, 2006, A1.

44. Margulies, *Guantánamo and the Abuse of Presidential Power*, 70; Leonnig and Tate, "Some at Guantanamo Mark 5 Years in Limbo."

45. Margulies, *Guantánamo and the Abuse of Presidential Power*, 65.

46. Mayer, "The Hidden Power."

47. John Mintz, "Most at Guantánamo to Be Freed or Sent Home, Officer Says," *Washington Post*, October 6, 2004, A16.

48. Christopher Cooper, "Detention Plan: In Guantánamo, Prisoners Languish in Sea of Red Tape," *Wall Street Journal*, January 26, 2005, A1.

49. See Leonnig and Tate, "Some at Guantanamo Mark 5 Years in Limbo" (quoting Pierre-Richard Prosper, former U.S. ambassador-at-large for war crimes issues). For an excellent study of the Guantánamo detainees, see Andy Worthington, *The Guantánamo Files: The Stories of the 774 Detainees in America's Illegal Prison* (London: Pluto Press, 2007).

50. Tim Golden, "After Terror, a Secret Rewriting of Military Law," *New York Times*, October 24, 2005, A1.

51. Golden, "Tough Justice: Administration Officials Split over Stalled Military Tribunals."

52. Ibid.

53. Jess Bravin, "U.S. Seeks Death Penalty for Gitmo Six," *Wall Street Journal*, February 11, 2008.

54. See Karen J. Greenberg, *The Least Worse Place: Guantanamo's First 100 Days* (New York: Oxford University Press, 2009).

55. Lieutenant Colonel Jerald Phifer, Memorandum for Commander, Joint Task Force 170, Re: "Request for Approval of Counter-Resistance Strategies," October 11, 2002, in *The Torture Papers: The Road to Abu Ghraib*, ed. Karen J. Greenberg and Joshua L. Dratel (New York: Cambridge University Press, 2005), 227.

56. The statements were memorialized in the Counter Resistance Strategy Meeting Minutes and were released by the Senate Armed Services Committee on June 18, 2008 (Counter Resistance Strategy Meeting Minutes). See also Marty Lederman, "How Did the Department of Defense Decide to Authorize Torture, Cruel Treatment, and Violations of the Uniform Code of Military Justice?" *Balkinization*, June 17, 2005.

57. Counter Resistance Strategy Meeting Minutes.

58. Ibid.

59. U.S. Department of the Army, *Army Field Manual 34–52: Intelligence Interrogation* (1992), 1–8.

60. Memorandum for Commander, Joint Task Force 170, in Greenberg and Dratel, *The Torture Papers*, 227–28.

61. Jane Mayer, *The Dark Side: The Inside Story of How the War on Terror Turned into a War on American Ideals* (New York: Doubleday, 2008), 220.

62. Diane E. Beaver, Legal Brief on Proposed Counter-Resistance Strategies, October 12, 2002, in Greenberg and Dratel, *The Torture Papers*, 229.

63. Ibid., 233–35.

64. Ibid., 233.

65. Marty Lederman, "GTMO: Where Was the Law? Whither the UCMJ," *Balkinization*, June 14, 2005; Mayer, "The Experiment"; Jane Mayer, "The Memo: How an Internal Effort to Ban the Abuse and Torture of Detainees Was Thwarted," *New Yorker*, February 27, 2006.

66. Mayer, "The Experiment."

67. Lederman, "How Did the Department of Defense Decide to Authorize Torture?" *Balkinization*, June 17, 2008; Mark Benjamin, "A Timeline to Bush Government Torture," Salon.com, June 18, 2008.

68. Philippe Sands, *Torture Team: Rumsfeld's Memo and the Betrayal of American Values* (New York: Palgrave Macmillan, 2008), 127–30.

69. Ibid., 109–10.

70. William J. Haynes Jr., Action Memo, "Counter-Resistance Techniques," in Greenberg and Dratel, *The Torture Papers*, 236.

71. Ibid.

72. See Margulies, *Guantánamo and the Abuse of Presidential Power*, 86–88; Adam Zagorin and Michel Duffy, "Inside the Interrogation of Detainee 063," *Time*, July 20, 2005; Bill Dedman, "Can '20th Hijacker' of Sept. 11 Ever Stand Trial? Aggressive Interrogation at Guantanamo May Prevent This Prosecution," *MSNBC*, October 26, 2006. *Time* first published a portion of the secret interrogation logs in July 2005; the complete interrogation logs were published in March 2006.

73. Mayer, *The Dark Side*, 208–9.

74. Bob Woodward, "Detainee Tortured, Says U.S. Official," *Washington Post*, January 14, 2009 (quoting Susan J. Crawford, the convening authority for military commissions).

75. Memorandum for William J. Haynes, General Counsel of the Department of Defense, Re: "Military Interrogation of Alien Unlawful Combatants Held outside the United States," from John Yoo, March 14, 2003.

76. Senator Carl Levin, "Senate Floor Speech on the Amendment to Establish an Independent Commission on Detainee Treatment," November 4, 2005; Marty Lederman, "Silver Linings (or the Strange but True Fate of the *Second* (or Was It the Third?) OLC Torture Memo," *Balkinization*, September 21, 2005.

77. "Working Group Report on Detainee Interrogations in the Global War on Terrorism: Assessment of Legal, Historical, Policy, and Operational Considerations" (April 3, 2003), in Greenberg and Dratel, *The Torture Papers*, 286, 341–42.

78. Mayer, "The Memo."

79. *In re Guantánamo Detainee Cases*, 355 F. Supp. 2d 443, 474 (D.D.C. 2005). See also Center for Constitutional Rights, "Report on Torture and Cruel, Inhuman, and Degrading Treatment of Prisoners at Guantánamo Bay, Cuba" (July 2006), 15–16, 21, 24, 28.

80. Joby Warrick, "Detainees Allege Being Drugged, Questioned," *Washington Post*, April 22, 2008.

81. U.S. Department of Justice, Office of Inspector General, "A Review of the FBI's Involvement in and Observations of Detainee Interrogations in Guantanamo Bay, Afghanistan, and Iraq" (May 2008); Carrie Johnson and Josh White, "Interrogation Tactics Were Challenged at White House," *Washington Post*, May 22, 2008.

82. Mayer, "The Experiment"; Mayer, "The Memo."

83. Neil A. Lewis, "Red Cross Finds Detainee Abuse in Guantánamo," *New York Times*, November 29, 2004.

84. Mayer, "The Memo."

85. Mayer, *The Dark Side*, 160.

86. *KUBARK Counterintelligence Interrogation*—July 1963 (quoted in Mark Danner, "U.S. Torture: Voices from the Black Sites," *New York Review of Books*, April 9, 2009).

87. Inquiry into the Treatment of Detainees in U.S. Custody, Report of the Committee of the Armed Services of the U.S. Senate, 110th Cong., 2d sess. (November 20, 2008) (SASC Report on Interrogation), 14–15; Spencer Ackerman, "Report Details Origins of Bush-Era Interrogation Policies," *Washington Independent*, April 21, 2009.

88. SASC Report on Interrogation, 19–22; Ackerman, "Report Details Origins of Bush-Era Interrogation Policies."

89. Memorandum for John Rizzo, Acting General Counsel of the Central Intelligence Agency: "Interrogation of al Qaeda Operative," from Jay S. Bybee, Assistant Attorney General, August 1, 2002.

90. SASC Report on Interrogation, 38; Sheri Fink, "The Reluctant Enablers of Torture," Salon.com, May 5, 2009.

91. Scott Shane, "China Inspired Interrogations at Guantánamo," *New York Times*, July 2, 2008.

92. SASC Report on Interrogation, 6.

93. Mayer, *The Dark Side*, 190 (quoting Michael Gelles, the chief clinical forensic psychologist for the Navy's Criminal Investigative Service and an outspoken critic of the interrogation techniques used at Guantánamo).

94. SASC Report on Interrogation, 154, 194–95.

95. Ibid., xxiii–xxiv.

96. Mayer, "The Experiment."

97. Andrew Buncombe, "U.S. Torture at Guantánamo 'Increasingly Repressive,'" *The Independent*, December 1, 2004.

98. Memorandum for Secretaries of the Military Department, "Medical Program Principles and Procedures for the Protection and Treatment of Detainees in the Custody of the Armed Forces of the United States," June 3, 2005, at 2; Mayer, "The Experiment."

CHAPTER 3

1. Stephen Grey, *Ghost Plane: The True Story of the CIA Torture Program* (New York: St. Martin's Press, 2006), 48–51.

2. Ron Suskind, *The One Percent Doctrine: Deep Inside America's Pursuit of Its Enemies since 9/11* (New York: Simon & Schuster, 2006), 117.

3. Grey, *Ghost Plane*, 53.

4. Ibid., 59.

5. *Mohamed v. Obama*, Civ. No. 05-1347 (GK), 2009 WL 4884194, at *20 (D.D.C. December 16, 2009).

6. Phil Hirschkorn, "Pentagon IDs Suspected Terror Accomplice," CNN.com, December 10, 2005.

7. Peter Finn, "Key Allegations against Terror Suspect Withdrawn," *Washington Post*, October 15, 2008; Richard Norton Taylor et al., "Binyam Mohamed Returns to Britain after Guantánamo Ordeal," *The Guardian*, February 23, 2009.

8. *Rumsfeld v. Padilla*, 542 U.S. 426 (2004).

9. Order Declaring Jose Padilla an Enemy Combatant, June 9, 2002.

10. Transcript of the Attorney General John Ashcroft regarding the Transfer of Abdullah al Muhajir (Born Jose Padilla) To the Department of Defense as an Enemy Combatant, June 10, 2002.

11. Mark Danner, "U.S. Torture: Voices from the Black Sites," *New York Review of Books*, April 9, 2009.

12. Devlin Barrett, "CIA Destroyed 92 Interrogation Recordings," Associated Press, March 3, 2009.

13. Eliza Griswold, "The Other Guantánamo: Black Hole," *New Republic*, May 7, 2007; Tim Golden and Eric Schmitt, "A Growing Afghan Prison Rivals Bleak Guantánamo," *New York Times*, February 26, 2006.

14. Griswold, "The Other Guantánamo"; Reed Brody, *The Road to Abu Ghraib* (New York: Human Rights Watch, 2004), 21.

15. Golden and Schmitt, "A Growing Afghan Prison Rivals Bleak Guantánamo."

16. Ibid.; Alissa J. Rubin, "Afghans Detail Detention in 'Black Jail' at U.S. Base," *New York Times*, November 28, 2009.

17. Golden and Schmitt, "A Growing Afghan Prison Rivals Bleak Guantánamo."

18. Griswold, "The Other Guantánamo."

19. Tim Golden, "Foiling U.S. Plan, Prison Expands in Afghanistan," *New York Times*, January 8, 2008.

20. Nicholas D. Kristof, "Sami's Shame, and Ours," *New York Times*, October 17, 2006.

21. Tim Golden, "Years after 2 Afghans Died, Abuse Case Falters," *New York Times*, February 13, 2006.

22. Tim Golden, "In U.S. Report, Brutal Details of 2 Afghan Inmates' Deaths," *New York Times*, May 20, 2005; Golden, "Years After 2 Afghans Died, Abuse Case Falters."

23. Tim Golden, "Army Faltered in Investigating Detainee Abuse," *New York Times*, May 22, 2005.

24. Golden, "Foiling U.S. Plan."

25. Declaration of Colonel Rose M. Miller, paras. 10–12, filed in *Ruzatullah v. Rumsfeld*, No. 06-1707 (D.D.C.) (GK) (Miller Declaration).

26. Golden and Schmitt, "A Growing Afghan Prison Rivals Bleak Guantánamo."

27. Ibid.; Golden, "Foiling U.S. Plan."

28. See "Accommodation Consignment Agreement for Lands and Facilities at Bagram Airfield between the Islamic Republic of Afghanistan and the United States of America," Exhibit 1 to Miller Declaration.

29. Golden and Schmitt, "A Growing Afghan Prison Rivals Bleak Guantánamo."

30. Ibid.

31. William Safire, "War Words," *New York Times*, June 20, 2004.

32. Association of the Bar of the City of New York and Center for Human Rights and Global Justice, "Torture by Proxy: International and Domestic Law Applicable to 'Extraordinary Renditions,'" October 29, 2004, at 15.

33. Grey, *Ghost Plane*, 132–34; *United States v. Yunis*, 924 F.2d 1086 (D.C. Cir. 1991).

34. See *United States v. Alvarez-Machain*, 504 U.S. 655 (1992) (refusing to dismiss prosecution of Mexican national forcibly kidnapped and brought to the United States to face charges for the murder of a U.S. Drug Enforcement Administration agent). For earlier decisions setting forth the basic rule, see *Ker v. Illinois*, 119 U.S. 436 (1886) (upholding the conviction of a fraudulent banker who had taken refuge in Peru and was forcibly abducted and transferred to the United States by Pinkerton detectives), and *Frisbie v. Collins*, 342 U.S. 519 (1952) (upholding the conviction of a defendant who had been arrested, beaten, and forcibly transferred from Illinois to Michigan).

35. See D. Cameron Findlay, "Abducting Terrorists Overseas for Trial in the United States: Issues of International and Domestic Law," 37 *Texas International Law Journal* 1, 2–3 (1988).

36. Presidential Decision Directive 39, "U.S. Policy on Counter-Terrorism," June 21, 1995.

37. "Torture by Proxy," 15–16.

38. Jane Mayer, "Outsourcing Torture," *New Yorker*, February 14, 2005.

39. Grey, *Ghost Plane*, 143.

40. National Commission on Terrorist Attacks upon the United States, *The 9/11 Commission Report: Final Report of the National Commission on Terrorist Attacks upon the United States* (New York: Norton, 2004), 176.

41. "Torture by Proxy," 16–17.

42. "Torture by Proxy," 9; Katherine R. Hawkins, Note, "The Promises of Torturers: Diplomatic Assurances and the Legality of 'Rendition,'" 20 *Georgetown Immigration Law Journal* 235, 236–37 (2006); Mayer, "Outsourcing Torture."

43. Mayer, "Outsourcing Torture."

44. The White House, "The Vice President Appears on *Meet the Press* with Tim Russert," September 16, 2001.

45. Mayer, "Outsourcing Torture."

46. Grey, *Ghost Plane*, 25–32; Mayer, "Outsourcing Torture."

47. Grey, *Ghost Plane*, 32–39.

48. This summary of Arar's case is derived from "Torture by Proxy," 11–12; *Arar v. Ashcroft*, 414 F. Supp. 2d 250, 252–55 (E.D.N.Y. 2006); Grey, *Ghost Plane*, 63–78.

49. Commission of Inquiry into the Actions of Canadian Officials in Relation to Maher Arar, *Report of the Events Relating to Maher Arar: Analysis and Recommendations* 59 (2006).

50. Ian Austen, "Canada Will Pay $9.75 Million to Man Sent to Syria and Tortured," *New York Times*, January 27, 2007.

51. Scott Shane, "Justice Dept. Amends Remark on Torture Case," *New York Times*, September 21, 2006.

52. Scott Shane, "Canadian to Remain on U.S. Terrorist Watch List," *New York Times*, January 23, 2007.

53. The account of Abu Omar's rendition is derived from Grey, *Ghost Plane*, 190–213.

54. Tracy Wilkinson and Maria De Cristofaro, "Italy Indicts 33 in Abduction Case; 26 Americans Charged in Alleged CIA Abduction," *Chicago Tribune*, February 17, 2007; "Italy Orders CIA Kidnapping Trial," *BBC News*, February 2, 2006.

55. Rachel Donadio, "Italy Convicts 23 Americans for C.I.A. Renditions," *New York Times*, November 4, 2009; Jamie Smyth, "U.S. Will Not Extradite CIA Agents to Italy," *Irish Times*, March 1, 2007.

56. Grey, *Ghost Plane*, 207, 213.

57. See Margaret L. Satterthwaite, "Rendered Meaningless: Extraordinary Rendition and the Rule of Law," 75 *George Washington Law Review* 1333, 1343 (2007).

58. Ibid.

59. United Nations Convention against Torture and Other Cruel, Inhuman or Degrading Treatment or Punishment, art. 3, December 10, 1984. S. Treaty Doc. No. 100-20, 1465 U.N.T.S. 85 (1988). The Convention against Torture also prohibits the direct commission of torture and cruel, inhuman, or degrading treatment or punishment; mandates that states criminalize, investigate, and prosecute torturers; and prohibits states from relying on evidence gained by torture.

61. International Covenant on Civil and Political Rights, G.A. Res. 2200A (XXI), art. 7, U.N. GAOR, 21st Sess. Supp. No. 16, U.N. Doc. A/6316, 999 U.N.T.S. 171 (December 19, 1966); UN Human Rights Comm., *General Comment* 20, art. 7, U.N. Doc. A/47/40 (1992), reprinted in *Compilation of General Comments and Recommendations Adopted by Human Rights Treaty Bodies*, UN Doc. HRI/GEN/1/Rev.1 at 30 (1994); UN Human Rights Comm.,

General Comment 31, Nature of the General Legal Obligation on State Parties to the Covenant, UN Doc. CCPR/C/21/Rev.1/Add.13 (2004), ¶ 12.

62. UN Doc. No. CAT/C/USA/CO2/ at ¶ 20. See also Satterthwaite, "Rendered Meaningless," 1375; Leila Nadya Sadat, "Ghost Prisoners and Black Sites: Extraordinary Rendition under International Law," 37 *Case Western Reserve Journal of International Law* 309, 319–21 (2006).

63. President Bush, Press Conference of the President, April 28, 2005.

64. Condoleezza Rice, U.S. Secretary of State, Remarks upon Her Departure for Europe (December 5, 2005).

65. United States, "Reply of the Government of the United States of America to the Report of the Five UNCHR Special Rapporteurs on Detainees in Guantánamo Bay, Cuba," March 10, 2006.

66. For an elaboration of these arguments, see John Yoo, "Transferring Terrorists," 79 *Notre Dame L. Rev.* 1183 (2004).

67. Elisabeth Bumiller, David E. Sanger, and Richard W. Stevenson, "Bush Says Iraqis Will Want G.I.s to Stay to Help," *New York Times,* January 28, 2005.

68. President Bush, Press Conference of the President, April 28,2005 (italics added).

69. The United States has specifically employed this defense against charges that it violated the Convention against Torture: "In those exceptional cases where the United States conducts renditions of individuals, the United States does not transport anyone to a country if the United States believes he or she will be tortured. Where appropriate, the United States seeks assurances it considers to be credible that transferred prisoners will not be tortured." United States, "List of Issues to Be Considered during the Examination of the Second Periodic Report of the United States of America: Response of the United States of America," 37.

70. Satterthwaite, "Rendered Meaningless," 1380–81; Julia Hall, "Still at Risk: Diplomatic Assurances No Safeguard against Torture," 17–19 (New York: Human Rights Watch, 2005); "Torture by Proxy," 37–40.

71. Satterthwaite, "Rendered Meaningless," 1390.

72. Grey, *Ghost Plane,* 223.

73. Dana Priest and Barton Gellman, "U.S. Decries Abuse but Defends Interrogations: 'Stress and Duress' Tactics Used on Terrorism Suspects Held in Secret Overseas Facilities," *Washington Post,* December 26, 2002.

74. The United States refused to confirm or to deny that such a directive even existed until it was finally forced to acknowledge its existence in response to a Freedom of Information Act lawsuit brought by the ACLU. See ACLU, "CIA Finally Acknowledges Existence of Presidential Order in Detention Facilities Abroad," November 14, 2006.

75. Dana Priest, "CIA Holds Terror Suspects in Secret Prisons," *Washington Post,* November 2, 2005; Human Rights Watch, "Statement on US Secret Detention Facilities in Europe," November 7, 2005; Council of Europe, Committee on Legal Affairs and Human Rights, "Secret Detentions and Illegal Transfers of Detainees Involving Council of Europe Member States: Second Report" (Explanatory Memorandum), June 7, 2007; "List of 12 Operatives Held in CIA Prisons," *ABC News,* December 5, 2005; Matthew Cole, "Officials: Lithuania Hosted Secret CIA Prison to Get 'Our Ear,'" *ABC News,* August 20, 2009.

76. Jane Mayer, *The Dark Side: The Inside Story of How the War on Terror Turned into a War on American Ideals* (New York: Doubleday, 2008), 147–48.

77. The term "ghost detainees" was first used by the U.S. Army in Iraq and was described in the report of Major General Antonio M. Taguba into alleged abuse of prisoners at Abu Ghraib. See Antonio M. Taguba, Major General, U.S. Department of the Army, Article 15-6 Investigation of the 800th Military Police Brigade, reprinted in *The Torture Papers: The Road to Abu Ghraib*, ed. Karen J. Greenberg and Joshua L. Dratel (New York: Cambridge University Press, 2005), 405 (Taguba Report).

78. "U.S. Bars Access to Terror Suspects," *BBC News*, December 9, 2005.

79. Mayer, "Outsourcing Torture."

80. Mayer, *The Dark Side*, 166–67.

81. Ibid., 284.

82. The account of el-Masri's case is derived from Grey, *Ghost Plane*, 79–102, and *El-Masri v. Tenet*, 479 F.3d 296, 300 (4th Cir. 2007).

83. Jabour's detention is described in Joanne Mariner, "Ghost Prisoner; Two Years in Secret CIA Detention" (New York: Human Rights Watch, 2007).

84. Ibid., 33.

85. Scott Shane, "Rights Groups Call for End to Secret Detentions," *New York Times*, June 7, 2007; Amnesty International et al., "Off the Record: U.S. Responsibility for Enforced Disappearances in the 'War on Terror'" (June 2007); Mark Benjamin, "The CIA's Latest 'Ghost Detainee,'" Salon.com, May, 22, 2005.

86. Office of the Press Secretary, "President Addresses Nation, Discusses Iraq, War on Terror," June 28, 2005.

87. UN Assistance Mission for Iraq (UNAMI), *Human Rights Report*, July 1–December 31, 2007, ¶ 56 & n. 68 (December 2007 UNAMI Report).

88. Ibid.

89. S. C. Res. 1483, U.N. Doc. S/RES/1483 (May 22, 2003).

90. S. C. Res. 1511, ¶ 13, U.N. Doc. S/RES/1511 (October 16, 2003).

91. Andrew Carcano, "End of the Occupation in 2004? The Status of the MultiNational Force in Iraq after the Transfer of Sovereignty to the Interim Iraqi Government," 11 *Journal of Conflict & Security Law* 41 (2006); Gregory H. Fox, "The Occupation of Iraq," 36 *Georgetown Journal of International Law* 195 (2005).

92. S.C. Res. 1546, ¶ 10, U.N. Doc. S/RES/1546 (June 8, 2004).

93. Ibid., Annex, at 11.

94. S.C. Res. 1790, U.N. Doc. S/RES/1790 (December 18, 2007).

95. "U.S. Still Holds 5,000 Prisoners in Iraq," *Radio Free Europe*, January 26, 2010.

96. Senior Military Official (unnamed), "Interrogation Procedures and Detention Facilities in Iraq," Defense Department Background Briefing in Pentagon Briefing Room, Arlington, VA (May 14, 2004).

97. Major General Donald J. Ryder, "Report on Detentions and Corrections in Iraq," November 5, 2003 (Ryder Report/Taguba Annex 19).

98. Human Rights First, "Ending Secret Detentions," 11–12 (June 2004).

99. Thomas E. Ricks, *Fiasco: The American Military Adventure in Iraq* (New York: Penguin, 2006), 283.

100. Ibid., 197.

101. Mayer, *The Dark Side*, 242.

102. Ibid., 247.

103. Geneva Convention (IV) Relative to the Protection of Civilian Persons in Time of War, art. 78, August 12, 1949, 6 U.S.T. 3516, 75 U.N.T.S. 287 (Fourth Geneva Convention).

104. December 2007 UNAMI Report ¶ 69.

105. Alex Barker and Demetri Sevastopulo, "Hands Tied: The U.S. Struggles to Get out of the 'Detention Business' in Iraq," *Financial Times*, July 16, 2007.

106. Ibid.; Michael Moss, "Iraq's Legal System Staggers beneath the Weight of War," *New York Times*, December 17, 2006. Even Iraqi members of the Combined Review and Release Board (CRRB), which conducted the review hearings, received only a "summary of classified information" on each case, prompting Iraq's minister of justice to suspend participation in the CRRB. December 2007 UNAMI Report ¶ 69.

107. Fourth Geneva Convention, art. 78.

108. Seymour M. Hersh, "Torture at Abu Ghraib," *New Yorker*, May 10, 2004.

109. December 2007 UNAMI Report ¶ 66.

110. Eliza Griswold, "American Gulag: Prisoners' Tales from the War on Terror," *Harpers*, September 2006.

111. Josh White, "Army Documents Shed Light on C.I.A. 'Ghosting,'" *Washington Post*, March 24, 2005.

112. Margaret L. Satterthwaite, "Rendered Meaningless," 1397–98; Human Rights First, "Ending Secret Detentions," 13; White, "Army Documents Shed Light on C.I.A. 'Ghosting.'"

113. Douglas Jehl, "U.S. Action Bars Right of Some Captured in Iraq," *New York Times*, October 26, 2004; Dana Priest, "Memo Lets CIA Take Detainees out of Iraq: Practice Is Called Serious Breach of the Geneva Conventions," *Washington Post*, October 24, 2004. The Fourth Geneva Convention prohibited the deportation, transfer, or evacuation of individuals from Iraq unless they were prisoners of war or nationals of the United States or another member nation of the coalition forces. Fourth Geneva Convention, art. 49.

114. Bradley Graham and Josh White, "General Cites Hidden Detainees; Senators Told CIA May Have Avoided Registering Up to 100," *Washington Post*, September 10, 2004; Eric Schmitt and Douglas Jehl, "Army Says C.I.A. Hid More Iraqis Than It Claimed," *New York Times*, September 10, 2004.

115. December 2007 UNAMI Report ¶ 66 and n.84.

116. Seth F. Kreimer, "Rays of Sunlight in a Shadow 'War': FOIA, the Abuses of Anti-Terrorism, and the Strategy of Transparency," 11 *Lewis & Clark Law Review* 1141, 1199–1200 (2007).

117. See Joan Walsh, Michael Scherer, and Mark Benjamin, "The Abu Ghraib Files," Salon.com, March 14, 2006. See also Hersh, "Torture at Abu Ghraib."

118. Taguba Report, 16–17; Scott Wilson and Sewell Chan, "As Insurgency Grew, So Did Prison Abuse," *Washington Post*, May 10, 2004.

119. Taguba Report; Hersh, "Torture and Abuse at Abu Ghraib."

120. M. Angela Buenaventura, "Torture in the Living Room," 6 *Seattle Journal for Social Justice* 103, 114 (fall/winter 2007).

121. Susan Sontag, *Regarding the Pain of Others* (New York: Farrar, Straus & Giroux, 2002).

122. Human Rights First, "Ending Secret Detentions," 27–28.

123. John H. Richardson, "Acts of Conscience," *Esquire*, August 2006.

124. Eric Schmitt and Carolyn Marshall, "In Secret Unit's 'Black Room,' A Grim Portrait of U.S. Abuse," *New York Times*, March 19, 2006.

125. Richardson, "Acts of Conscience."

126. Schmitt and Marshall, "In Secret Unit's 'Black Room.'"

127. Ricks, *Fiasco*, 278.

128. Wilson and Chan, "As Insurgency Grew"; Jane Mayer, "The Memo: How an Internal Effort to Ban the Abuse and Torture of Detainees Was Thwarted," *New Yorker*, February 27, 2006.

129. Taguba Report, 8. See also Marty Lederman, "[Post 2] Full Employment Memo for Bloggers (and Prosecutors?)," *Balkinization*, April 1, 2008.

130. Ricks, *Fiasco*, 261.

131. [Name Redacted], Sworn Statement of CW2, A/519th MI Bn, DoD000867—DoD00871, Obtained from American Civil Liberties Union's Government Documents on Torture Search: http://www.aclu.org/accountability/released.html.

132. Jeffrey Gettleman, "The Struggle for Iraq: The Detainees," *New York Times*, March 9, 2004.

133. Ricks, *Fiasco*, 235.

134. Ibid., 199.

135. [Name Redacted], Sworn Statement of Individual Augmentee, B/470th MI Group, assigned to Detainee Assessment Board, DoD000859-000862, Obtained from American Civil Liberties Union's Government Documents on Torture Search.

136. Taguba Report; Hersh, "Torture at Abu Ghraib"; declaration of Colonel Lawrence B. Wilkerson (Ret.), dated March 24, 2010, para. 12b; prepared for submission in *Hamad v. Bush*, 05cv1009 (D.D.C.) (JDB).

137. Ricks, *Fiasco*, 239.

138. Hersh, "Torture at Abu Ghraib."

139. Michael Moss, "Former U.S. Detainee in Iraq Recalls Torment," *New York Times*, December 18, 2006.

140. Ibid. Vance's fellow prisoners were subjected to the same treatment, including another American citizen named Nathan Ertel who had similarly tried to expose misdeeds by his and Vance's company.

141. Moss, "Former U.S. Detainee in Iraq Recalls Torment."

142. Hersh, "Torture at Abu Ghraib."

CHAPTER 4

1. Attorney General John Ashcroft, Testimony before the House Committee on the Judiciary, September 24, 2001.

2. Alberto R. Gonzales, Counsel to the President, "Statement to the American Bar Association Standing Committee on Law and National Security," Washington, DC, February 24, 2004.

3. Rachel L. Swarns, "Thousands of Arabs and Muslims Could Be Deported, Officials Say," *New York Times*, June 7, 2003.

4. U.S. Department of Justice, Office of the Inspector General, "The September 11 Detainees: A Review of the Treatment of Aliens Held on Immigration Charges in Con-

nection with the Investigation of the September 11 Attacks," April 2003, at 17, 186 (OIG Report).

5. 8 C.F.R. § 287.3(d) (pre-September 11 regulation); 66 Fed. Reg. 48, 334 (September 20, 2001) (amending 8 C.F.R. § 287.3(d)).

6. *County of Riverside v. McLaughlin*, 500 U.S. 44 (1991).

7. 8 C.F.R. § 287.3(d); David Cole, *Enemy Aliens: Double Standards and Constitutional Freedoms in the War on Terrorism* (New York: New Press, 2003), 31. Congress also authorized the detention of suspected alien terrorists for up to seven days without charge in the Patriot Act, although this provision was never invoked. See Uniting and Strengthening America by Providing Appropriate Tools Required to Intercept and Obstruct Terrorism Act of 2001, Pub. L. No. 107-56, § 412(a), 115 Stat. 350 (October 26, 2001) (codified at 8 U.S.C. § 1226a).

8. OIG Report, 37–71.

9. Ibid., 115–17, 157–63.

10. See Declaration of Dale L. Watson, Executive Assistant Director of Counterterrorism and Counterintelligence for the Federal Bureau of Investigation, at 4 (Watson Declaration)

11. *North Jersey Media Group, Inc. v. Ashcroft*, 308 F.3d 198 (3d Cir. 2002).

12. See Review of Custody Determinations, Interim Rule, 66 Fed. Reg. 54,909 (October 31, 2001) (codified at 8 C.F.R. § 1003.19). This process, a former INS commissioner noted, soon became used "routinely and without careful calculation." See David A. Martin, "Preventive Detention: Immigration Law Lessons for the Enemy Combatant Debate," 18 *Georgetown Immigration Law Journal* 305, 312 (2004).

13. Migration Policy Institute, "America's Challenge: Domestic Security, Civil Liberties, and National Unity after September 11," 51 (2003), (citing memorandum from Deputy Attorney General to the Commissioner of the INS, Director of the Federal Bureau of Investigation, Director of the United States Marshals Service, and U.S. Attorneys (January 25, 2002)); Susan Sachs, "Traces of Terror: The Detainees; Cost of Vigilance, This Broken Home," *New York Times*, June 4, 2002.

14. Susan M. Akram and Maritza Karmely, "Immigration and Constitutional Consequences of Post-9/11 Policies Involving Arabs and Muslims in the United States: Is Alienage a Distinction without a Difference," 38 U.C. *Davis Law Review* 609, 630–31 (2005).

15. Ibid.

16. See Neil A. Lewis, "Immigrants Offered Incentives to Give Evidence on Terrorists," *New York Times*, November 29, 2001; William Lyons, "Partnerships, Information and Public Safety," 25 *Policing: An International Journal of Police Strategies and Management* 530 (2002).

17. 18 U.S.C. § 3144.

18. 18 U.S.C. § 3142.

19. 18 U.S.C. § 3144.

20. Anjana Malhotra, "Witness to Abuse: Human Rights Abuses under the Material Witness Law since September 11," (New York: Human Rights Watch, 2005), 2, 16, 81.

21. Ibid., 26.

22. Ibid., 47–48. On the right to a prompt hearing, see, for example, *Barry v. Barchi*, 443 U.S. 55 (1979).

23. Malhotra, "Witness to Abuse," 48–50.

24. Ibid., 41–47.

25. Ibid., 2, 81.

26. "FBI Apologizes to Lawyer Held in Madrid Bombings," MSNBC, May 25, 2004; Steven T. Wax and Christopher J. Schatz, "A Multitude of Errors: The Brandon Mayfield Case," *The Champion* 6 (September/October 2004); Malhotra, "Witness to Abuse," 20–22, 32.

27. *Al-Kidd v. Ashcroft*, 580 F.3d 949, 952-54 (9th Cir. 2009).

28. Ibid., 981.

29. I served as lead counsel to al-Marri in his habeas corpus challenge to his military detention.

30. In May 2003, the indictment in New York was dismissed on venue grounds and promptly refiled in Peoria, Illinois, where most of the alleged events had taken place.

31. Order Declaring Ali Saleh Kahlah al-Marri an Enemy Combatant, June 23, 2003.

32. Declaration of Mr. Jeffrey N. Rapp, Director, Joint Intelligence Task Force for Combating Terrorism, dated September 9, 2004.

33. Ibid.

34. News Briefing, U.S. Department of Defense, June 11, 2002.

35. John Ashcroft, *Never Again: Securing America and Restoring Justice* (New York: Center Street, 2006), 168–69.

36. In another case, the government successfully coerced guilty pleas from several defendants by threatening to declare them "enemy combatants." Eric Lichtblau, "Threats and Responses: Terror; U.S. Cites Al Qaeda in Plot to Destroy Brooklyn Bridge," *New York Times*, June 20, 2003; Dan Herbeck, "2 Defendants Feel Pressure for Plea Deals," *Buffalo News*, April 6, 2003.

37. Declaration of Vice Admiral Lowell E. Jacoby (USN), Director of the Defense Intelligence Agency, dated January 9, 2003, filed in *Padilla ex rel. Newman v. Rumsfeld*, 243 F. Supp. 2d 42 (S.D.N.Y. 2003).

38. Complaint, *Al-Marri v. Rumsfeld.*, ¶¶ 68-73, No. 2:05-2259 (D.S.C.) (HFF); Certification of Andrew J. Savage III, ¶¶ 23–29, No. 2:05-2259 (D.S.C.) (HFF) (Savage Certification); First Amended Complaint, *Padilla v. Rumsfeld*, ¶¶ 33, 38-39, 42, 44–46, No. 2:07-cv-00410 (D.S.C.) (HFF).

39. Complaint, *Al-Marri v. Rumsfeld*, ¶ 35; Savage Certification ¶ 13; First Amended Complaint, *Padilla v. Rumsfeld*, ¶ 36. For a detailed discussion of al-Marri's treatment, see Transcript of Sentencing Hearing, *United States v. Al-Marri*, Crim. No. 09-10030 (C.D. Ill.) (MMM) (Oct. 29, 2009).

40. Complaint, *Al-Marri v. Rumsfeld*, ¶¶ 45–46; Savage Certification ¶ 11; First Amended Complaint, *Padilla v. Rumsfeld*, ¶ 36.

41. Complaint, *Al-Marri v. Rumsfeld*, ¶¶ 39–41.

42. Savage Certification ¶ 21; Complaint, *Al-Marri v. Rumsfeld*, ¶ 76; First Amended Complaint, *Padilla v. Rumsfeld*, ¶ 38.

43. Complaint, *Al-Marri v. Rumsfeld*, ¶¶ 54–56; Savage Certification ¶ 18; First Amended Complaint, *Padilla v. Rumsfeld*, ¶ 59.

44. *Hamdi v. Rumsfeld*, 542 U.S. 507, 509-11 (2004) (plurality opinion).

45. Ibid., 511.

46. Ibid., 512-13.

47. Brief for the Respondents, 20–21, 27, *Hamdi v. Rumsfeld*, 542 U.S. 507 (2004) (No. 03-6696).

48. Joel Brinkley and Eric Lichtblau, "Held 3 Years by U.S., Saudi Goes Home," *International Herald Tribune*, October 13, 2004; Jerry Markon, "'Combatant' Returned to Saudis; U.S. Citizen Had Been Detained Almost 3 Years," *Washington Post*, October 12, 2004.

CHAPTER 5

1. R. J. Sharpe, *The Law of Habeas Corpus*, 2d ed. (New York: Oxford University Press, 1989), 1–2.

2. Ibid., 4–7; Jonathan L. Hafetz, Note: "The Untold Story of Noncriminal Habeas Corpus and the 1996 Immigration Acts," 107 *Yale Law Journal* 2509, 2521–22 (1998).

3. William F. Duker, *A Constitutional History of Habeas Corpus* (Westport, CT: Greenwood Press, 1980), 80. For examples of the writ's early use to challenge the king's authority, see *Searche's Case*, 74 Eng. Rep. 65 (C.P. 1587) (discharging a prisoner detained for arresting a surety indirectly designated by the queen to receive protection from arrest); *Howel's Case*, 74 Eng. Rep. 66 (C.P. 1587) (releasing a prisoner imprisoned by the Privy Council without cause). For a general discussion, see J. H. Baker, *An Introduction to English Legal History*, 2d ed. (Oxford: Oxford University Press, 1979), 126.

4. *Darnel's Case*, 31 Howell's State Trials 1, 8 (K.B. 1627); Magna Carta art. 39 (1215) ("No freeman shall be taken, or imprisoned . . . except by the lawful judgment of his peers or by the law of the land.").

5. *Darnel's Case*, 31 Howell's State Trials at 37, 45 (arguments of Attorney General Robert Heath); Robert Searles Walker, *The Constitutional and Legal Development of the Writ of Habeas Corpus as the Writ of Liberty* (BookSurge Publishing (amazon), 2006), 67.

6. Petition of Right, 3 Car. 1, c.1, §§ 5, 10 (1628); Duker, *A Constitutional History of Habeas Corpus*, 141.

7. 16 Car. 1, c.10, §§ 2-3, 6 (1641).; see also Dallin H. Oaks, "Legal History in the High Court—Habeas Corpus," 64 *Michigan Law Review* 451, 460 (1966).

8. 31 Car. 2, c. 2 (1679); Sharpe, *The Law of Habeas Corpus*, 18–20; *Crosby's Case*, 88 Eng. Rep. 1167, 1168 (K.B. 1694).

9. William Blackstone, *Commentaries on the Laws of England* (1765–69), vol. 1, 137.

10. Paul D. Halliday and G. Edward White, "The Suspension Clause: English Text, Imperial Contexts, and American Implications," 94 *Virginia Law Review* 575, 631–32 (2008). Since the 1679 act applied only to criminal matters, the common law writ remained the principal mechanism for challenging noncriminal forms of detention by government officials and private actors until 1816, when a statute was enacted expressly providing for habeas corpus in noncriminal matters. See William S. Holdsworth, *A History of English Law*, 2d ed. (London: Sweet & Maxwell, 1938), vol. 9, 117–18; Hafetz, "The Untold Story," 2522–23.

11. Halliday and White, "The Suspension Clause," 626.

12. William Blackstone, *Commentaries on the Laws of England* (1765–69), vol. 3, 131 .

13. Halliday and White, "The Suspension Clause," 625–28.

14. 1 Will. and Mary, c. 7 (1688).

15. See, for example, 19 Geo 2, c. 1 (1746) (suspension to secure the peace and security of the kingdom from a threatened rebellion in Scotland); 17 Geo. 2, c. 6 (1744) (suspension to protect against the danger of foreign invasion by those acting "in concert with

disaffected persons in England"). See generally William Forsyth, *Cases and Opinions on Constitutional Law* (London: Stevens & Haynes, 1869), 452.

16. Sharpe, *The Law of Habeas Corpus*, 94.

17. Albert V. Dicey, *Introduction to the Study of the Law of the Constitution* (London: Macmillan, 1908), 226.

18. Duker, *A Constitutional History of Habeas Corpus*, 142 and n. 120; *R. v. Earl of Orrey*, 88 Eng. Rep. 75, 77 (K.B. 1722).

19. Sharpe, *The Law of Habeas Corpus*, 95.

20. See, for example, *Case of the Hottentot Venus*, 104 Eng. Rep. 344 (K.B. 1810); *Case of Three Spanish Sailors*, 96 Eng. Rep. 775 (C.P. 1779); *R. v. Schiever*, 97 Eng. Rep. 551, 96 Eng. Rep. 1249 (K.B. 1759).

21. *Somersett's Case*, 20 Howell's State Trials 1 (K.B. 1772).

22. Brief of Legal Historians as *Amici Curiae* in Support of Petitioners, at 6–7, *Boumediene v. Bush*, Nos. 06-1195, 06-1196 (U.S. Sup. Ct. 2007) (discussing manuscripts underlying *DuCastro's Case*, 92 Eng. Rep. 816 (K.B. 1697)); Halliday and White, "The Suspension Clause," 606–7, n. 76. See also Brief of Legal Historians, *Boumediene v. Bush*, at 6, n. 5 (citing cases involving foreign merchant sailors wrongfully impressed into service on warships).

23. *Sir Matthew Hale's The Prerogative of the King* (London: Selden Society, D.E.C. Yale ed., 1976), 52; Brief of Legal Historians, *Boumediene v. Bush*, at 5, n. 4.

24. Halliday and White, "The Suspension Clause," 595–97.

25. *R. v. Delaval*, 97 Eng. Rep. 913, 915–16 (K.B. 1763) (examining affidavits showing girl's indenture was "plainly and manifestly, for bad purposes"); *R. v. Turlington*, 97 Eng. Rep. 741 (K.B. 1761) (ordering medical inspection and reviewing evidence from inspection to determine whether a woman had been properly committed to a "mad house"); *Barney's Case*, 87 Eng. Rep. 683 (K.B. 1701) (examining affidavits showing prisoner held based on "malicious prosecution").

26. See, for example, *Goldswain's Case*, 96 Eng. Rep. 711 (K.B. 1778) (refusing to accept admiralty's assertion that a bargeman had been properly impressed into service in the face of the petitioner's response that he was protected from impressment by virtue of his service in the Navy Board carrying cargo for the king).

27. Hafetz, "The Untold Story," 2530–34; Sharpe, *The Law of Habeas Corpus*, 39; *R. v. Nathan*, 93 Eng. Rep. 914 (K.B. 1730) (interpreting a statute in a bankruptcy case); *R. v. White*, 20 Howell's State Trials 1376, 1377 (K.B. 1746) (interpreting a statute in an impressment case); *Gardener's Case*, 79 Eng. Rep. 1048 (K.B. 1601) (ordering release base upon prisoner's submission that his possession of a handgun was justified due to his status as a deputy sheriff); *Good's Case*, 96 Eng. Rep. 137 (K.B. 1760) (finding petitioner was legally exempt from military service based on his submission of an affidavit showing he was a freeholder).

28. *Bushell's Case*, 124 Eng. Rep. 1006 (C.P. 1670).

29. Sir Edward Coke, *The Second Part of the Institutes of the Laws of England*, 5th ed. (London: E & R. Brooke, 1797), 43.

30. William Blackstone, *Commentaries on the Laws of England*, vol. 3, 133; Sharpe, *The Law of Habeas Corpus*, 19.

31. *Opinion on the Writ of Habeas Corpus*, 107 Eng. Rep. 29, 43 (H.L. 1758) (opinion of Wilmot, J.); *Ex parte Beeching*, 107 Eng. Rep. 1010 (K.B. 1825). Courts did, however, inquire

whether prisoners should be bailed in advance of trial. See, for example, *R. v. Greenwood*, 93 Eng. Rep. 1086 (K.B. 1739) (reviewing affidavits asserting prisoner was not at place of robbery); *Farington's Case*, 84 Eng. Rep. 1227 (K.B. 1682) (granting bail based on affidavits "showing good reason for it").

32. *INS v. St. Cyr*, 533 U.S. 289, 301 (2001); Note, "Developments in the Law—Federal Habeas Corpus," 83 *Harvard Law Review* 1038, 1238 (1970) .

33. Sharpe, *The Law of Habeas Corpus*, 115–16.

34. *R. v. Schiever*, 97 Eng. Rep. 551 (K.B. 1759).

35. *Case of Three Spanish Sailors*, 96 Eng. Rep. 775 (C.P. 1779).

36. Halliday and White, "The Suspension Clause," 585–86.

37. *Bourn's Case*, 79 Eng. Rep. 465 (K.B. 1619) (writ issued to Cinque Ports town of Dover); *Jobson's Case*, 82 Eng. Rep. 325 (K.B. 1626) (writ issued to Durham, a County Palatine).

38. *R. v. Salmon*, 84 Eng. Rep. 282 (K.B. 1669) (writ issued to Channel Island of Jersey); *R. v. Overton*, 82 Eng. Rep. 1173 (K.B. 1668) (writ issued to Jersey).

39. William Blackstone, *Commentaries on the Laws of England*, vol. 3, 131 (italics added).

40. Leonard Woods Labaree, ed., *Royal Instructions to British Colonial Governors* (New York: D. Appleton Century, 1935), vol. 1, 334–38 (Crown instructions to the governors of Barbados, the Bahamas, and St. John in the West Indies, Nova Scotia, and Quebec).

41. Halliday and White, "The Suspension Clause," 586–87.

42. *R. v. Cowle*, 97 Eng. Rep. 587, 599 (K.B. 1759). The "King's dominions" were not restricted only to "sovereign territories" but encompassed areas over which the Crown exercised de facto control. See *Sir Matthew Hale's The Prerogative of the King* 19; *Oxford English Dictionary*, 2d ed., 1989; Halliday and White, "The Suspension Clause," 633.

43. *Ex parte Mwenya*, 1 Q.B. 241, 303 (C.A. 1960).

44. *R. v. Cowle*, 97 Eng. Rep at 600.

45. A. B. Keith, *A Constitutional History of India, 1600–1935* (1969), 24–25.

46. P. J. Marshall, "The British in Asia: Trade to Dominion, 1700–1765," in *The Oxford History of the British Empire*, vol. 2, ed. P. J. Marshall (Oxford: Oxford University Press, 1998/99), 487, 503.

47. Charter Act, 53 Geo. 3, c. 155, § XCV (1813); H. H. Dodwell, ed., *British India, 1497–1858*, vol. 4 of *The Cambridge History of the British Empire* (Cambridge: Cambridge University Press, 1929), 595, 605.

48. Nasser Hussain, *The Jurisprudence of Emergency: Colonialism and the Rule of Law* (Ann Arbor: University of Michigan Press, 2003), 81 (writ issued in 1775 on behalf of revenue collector imprisoned by East India Company over issue of late payments); B. N. Pandey, *The Introduction of English Law into India: The Career of Elijah Impey in Bengal, 1774–1783* (Bombay: Asia Publishing House, 1967), 151 (writ issued in 1777 on behalf of Indian arrested and confined without trial in Bengal).

49. Hussain, *The Jurisprudence of Emergency*, 81 and 164, n. 36 (citing Chief Justice Impey to the Lord Chancellor, "Observations on the Administration of Justice in Bengal" (September 20, 1776) (British Museum Add. MS. 16,265, fol. 235)); Brief of Legal Historians, *Boumediene v. Bush*, at 13–14 (citing *Cumall a Deen Ally Khan v. Charles Goring*, BL Add. MSS 38,400, folio 84 (Sup. Ct. Calcutta 1775) (opinion of Chambers, J.)).

50. Brief of Legal Historians, *Boumediene v. Bush*, at 15; Halliday and White, "The Suspension Clause," 663–67.

51. Duker, *A Constitutional History of Habeas Corpus*, 42.

52. *Proceedings in Parliament against Edward Earl of Clarendon, Lord High Chancellor of England, for Treason, and Other High Crimes and Misdemeanors: 15 and 19 Charles II. A.D. 1663–67*, 6 Howells State Trials 291, 330, 396 (1668).

53. 31 Car. 2, c.2, §§ 11–12 (1679).

54. Francis Paschal, "The Constitution and Habeas Corpus," *Duke Law Journal* 605, 608 (1970); Milton Cantor, "The Writ of Habeas Corpus: Early American Origins and Development," in *Freedom and Reform: Essays in Honor of Henry Steele Commager*, ed. Harold M. Hyman and Leonard W. Levy (New York: Harper & Row, 1967), 55, 74; Rollin C. Hurd, *A Treatise on the Right of Personal Liberty, and on the Writ of Habeas Corpus*, 2d ed. (Albany, NY: W. C. Little & Co., Law Booksellers, 1876), 101–2.

55. Daniel J. Meador, *Habeas Corpus and Magna Carta: Dualism of Power and Liberty* (Charlottesville: University of Virginia Press, 1966), 24. See also Jack N. Rakove, *Original Meanings: Politics and Ideas in the Making of the Constitution* (New York: Knopf, 1997), 290–93; Louis Henkin: "Rights: American and Human," 79 *Columbia Law Review* 405, 408–9 (1979).

56. *The Federalist* no. 84, ed. Clinton Rossiter (New York: New American Library, 1961), 512.

57. Duker, *A Constitutional History of Habeas Corpus*, 115; A. H. Carpenter, "Habeas Corpus in the Colonies," 8 *American Historical Review* 18, 21, 26 (1902).

58. *The Declaration of Independence*, paras. 12, 18 (1776).

59. See, for example, 17 Geo. 3, c. 9 (1777). See generally Halliday and White, "The Suspension Clause," 645–51.

60. Paschal, "The Constitution and Habeas Corpus," 608. See also Gerald L. Neuman, "Habeas Corpus and the Suspension Clause after *INS v. St. Cyr*," 33 *Columbia Human Rights Law Review* 555, 566 (2002).

61. Max Farrand, *The Records of the Federal Convention of 1787*, vol. 2 (New Haven, CT: Yale University Press, 1911), 341, 438; Duker, *A Constitutional History of Habeas Corpus*, 127–28.

62. The clause provides in full: "The privilege of the Writ of Habeas Corpus shall not be suspended, unless when in Cases of Rebellion or Invasion the public Safety may require it." U.S. Const., art. I, § 9, cl. 2.

63. Zechariah Chafee Jr., "The Most Important Human Right in the Constitution," 32 *Boston University Law Review* 143, 143 (1952).

64. David L. Shapiro, "Habeas Corpus, Suspension, and Detention: Another View," 59 *Notre Dame Law Review* 59, 64 (2006).

65. Eric M. Freedman, *Habeas Corpus: Rethinking the Great Writ of Liberty* (New York: New York University Press, 2001), 20–21; "Developments in the Law—Federal Habeas Corpus," 1265; Paschal, "The Constitution and Habeas Corpus," 623–24.

66. As Marshall explained, "If at any time the public safety should require the suspension of the powers vested by this act in the courts of the United States, it is for the legislature to say so." *Ex parte Bollman*, 8 U.S. (4 Cranch) 75, 101 (1807). See also Joseph Story, *Commentaries on the Constitution of the United States* § 1342 (Boston: Hilliard, Gray & Co., 1833).

67. Judiciary Act of 1789, ch. 20, § 14, 1 Stat. 73, 82. The present version of the act is codified at 28 U.S.C. § 2241.

68. *Marbury v. Madison*, 5 U.S. (1 Cranch) 137 (1803). In *Marbury*, Marshall interpreted another section of the Judiciary Act of 1789 as empowering the Court to issue writs of mandamus and then struck down that section for expanding the Court's original jurisdiction beyond the limits of Article III of the Constitution. Article III vests original jurisdiction in the Supreme Court "in all cases affecting ambassadors, other public ministers and consuls, and those in which a state shall be party, the Supreme Court shall have original jurisdiction." U.S. Const., art. III, § 2.

69. *Bollman*, 8 U.S. (4 Cranch) at 100–101. For a discussion of the relationship between Marshall's decisions in *Marbury* and *Bollman*, see Paschal, "The Constitution and Habeas Corpus," 626–28; Freedman, *Habeas Corpus: Rethinking the Great Writ of Liberty*, 20–35. For a discussion of "original" habeas petitions, see Dallin H. Oaks, "The 'Original' Writ of Habeas Corpus in the Supreme Court,' *Supreme Court Review* 153 (1962).

70. *Bollman*, 8 U.S. (4 Cranch) at 125–37.

71. Ibid., 95. The Suspension Clause is not the only example of constitutional guarantees that rely on legislative action for their implementation. See Neuman, "Habeas Corpus and the Suspension Clause," 581 (citing "Enumeration" clause of article I and "Compensation" clause of articles II and III).

72. As Professor Eric Freedman explains, the suggestion that Congress could suspend the writ by doing nothing "would certainly have come as a shock to all of the debaters over the Suspension Clause." Freedman, *Habeas Corpus: Rethinking the Great Writ of Liberty*, 26.

73. *St. Cyr*, 533 U.S. at 304 n. 24. See also *Jones .v Cunningham*, 371 U.S. 236, 238 (1963) (the habeas statute "implements the constitutional command that the writ of habeas corpus be made available").

74. Duker, *A Constitutional History of Habeas Corpus*, 126–56; Rex Collings, "Habeas Corpus for Convicts—Constitutional Right or Legislative Grace?" 40 *California Law Review* 335, 340 (1952).

75. *Ableman v. Booth*, 62 U.S. (21 How.) 506 (1858); *Tarble's Case*, 80 U.S. (13 Wall.) 397 (1872).

76. Gerald L. Neuman, "Habeas Corpus, Executive Detention, and the Removal of Aliens," 98 *Columbia Law Review* 961, 975 (1998); Paschal, "The Constitution and Habeas Corpus," 607.

77. The current version of the habeas statute is the "direct ancestor" of the 1789 Judiciary Act. See *Felker v. Turpin*, 518 U.S. 651, 659–60, n. 1 (1996).

78. Act of March 2, 1833, ch. 57, §§ 3, 7, 4 Stat. 632, 633–34.

79. Act of August 29, 1842, ch. 257, 5 Stat. 539.

80. Act of February 5, 1867, ch. 28, § 1, 14 Stat. 385.

81. See, for example, Antiterrorism and Effective Death Penalty Act, Pub. L. No. 104-32, 110 Stat. 1214 (1996).

82. *Hamdi v. Rumsfeld*, 542 U.S. 507, 525 (2004) (plurality opinion).

83. See David J. Barron and Martin S. Lederman, "The Commander in Chief at the Lowest Ebb—A Constitutional History," 121 *Harvard Law Review* 941, 997 (2008).

84. Daniel Farber, *Lincoln's Constitution* (Chicago: University of Chicago Press, 2003), 16–17.

85. *Ex parte Merryman*, 17 F. Cas. 144 (C.C.D. Md. 1861) (No. 9487) (Taney, C.J.); Jeffrey D. Jackson, "The Power to Suspend Habeas Corpus: An Answer from the Arguments Surrounding *Ex Parte Merryman*," 34 *University of Baltimore Law Review* 11, 15–24 (2004).

86. "Message to Congress in Special Session," July 4, 1861, reprinted in *The Collected Works of Abraham Lincoln*, vol. 4, ed. Roy P. Basler (New Brunswick, NJ: Rutgers University Press, 1953), 430–31.

87. Act of March 3, 1863, ch. 81, § 1, 12 Stat. 755. See also Stephen I. Vladeck, Note: "The Detention Power," 22 *Yale Law & Policy Review* 153, 162 (2004).

88. Steven R. Shapiro, "The Role of the Courts in the War against Terrorism: A Preliminary Assessment," 29 *WTR Fletcher F. World Aff.* 103, 104 (2005); Mark E. Neely Jr., *The Fate of Liberty: Abraham Lincoln and Civil Liberties* (Oxford: Oxford University Press, 2001), 20–23, 113–31.

89. Lou Falkner Williams, *The Great South Carolina Ku Klux Klan Trials, 1871–1872* (Athens: University of Georgia Press, 1996), 46; Amanda L. Tyler, "Is Suspension a Political Question?" 59 *Stanford Law Review* 333, 345–46 (2006).

90. Act of July 1, 1902, ch. 1369, § 5, 32 Stat. 691, 692.

91. *Fisher v. Baker*, 203 U.S. 174, 179–80 (1906).

92. Hawaiian Organic Act, ch. 339, § 67, 31 Stat. 153 (1900).

93. *Duncan v. Kahanamoku*, 327 U.S. 304, 307–8, 313, n. 5 (1946); Tyler, "Is Suspension a Political Question?" 346–47.

94. *United States v. Villato*, 28 F. Cas. 377 (No. 16,622) (C. C. Pa. 1797); *Commonwealth v. Holloway*, 1 Serg. & Rawle 392, 1815 WL 1249 (Pa. 1815); *Ex parte D'Olivera*, 7 F. Cas. 853 (No. 3,967) (C. C. Mass. 1813). Historical evidence suggests the writ was available to noncitizens during the colonial era as well. See James Oldham and Michael J. Wishnie, "The Historical Scope of Habeas Corpus & *INS v. St. Cyr*," 16 *Georgetown Immigration Law Journal* 485, 496–500 (2002).

95. Neuman, "Habeas Corpus, Executive Detention, and the Removal of Aliens," 989–92.

96. *United States v. Villato*.

97. *Ex parte D'Olivera*, 7 F. Cas. 853 (No. 3,967) (C.C.D. Mass. 1813). Justice Story, however, directed that the prisoners be discharged by delivery to their ship as an act of comity.

98. Act of July 6, 1798, ch. 66, 1 Stat. 577.

99. Gerald L. Neuman and Charles F. Hobson, "John Marshall and the Enemy Alien: A Case Missing from the Canon," 9 *Green Bag 2d* 39 (2005). State courts similarly entertained habeas petitions on behalf of foreign nationals during wartime. See, for example, *Lockington's Case*, Bright (N.P.) 269 (Pa. 1813) (reviewing claim of British citizen detained under Alien Enemies Act of 1798 but denying relief).

100. Steven I. Vladeck, "Enemy Aliens, Enemy Property, and Access to the Courts," 11 *Lewis & Clark Law Review* 963, 970–79 (2007); Brief *Amici Curiae* Professors of Constitutional Law and Federal Jurisdiction, *Al-Marri v. Wright*, No. 06-7427 (4th Cir. 2006), 13–17.

101. *Ludecke v. Watkins*, 335 U.S. 160 (1948).

102. *In re Jung Ah Lung*, 25 F. 141, 142 (D. Cal. 1885), *aff'd sub nom. United States v. Jung Ah Lung*, 124 U.S. 621 (1888).

103. Courts, for example, examined whether those decisions conformed to statutory and procedural requirements, and had some evidentiary support. Neuman, "Habeas Corpus, Executive Detention, and the Removal of Aliens," 1007–16; *Heikkila v. Barber*, 345 U.S. 229 (1953) (summarizing prior decisions).

104. *Gegiow v. Uhl*, 239 U.S. 3 (1915) ("public charge" provision); *Kessler v. Strecker*, 307 U.S. 22 (1939) (ideological deportation provision).

105. *Yamataya v. Fisher*, 189 U.S. 86 (1903).

106. The "plenary power" doctrine was first articulated in the late nineteenth century to give Congress sweeping authority to define the terms and conditions under which aliens could enter and remain in the United States. See Stephen H. Legomsky, "Immigration Law and the Principle of Plenary Congressional Power," *Supreme Court Review* 255, 256 (1984).

107. *St. Cyr*, 533 U.S. at 314.

108. Ibid., 309–14.

109. And, in another important habeas corpus case decided three days later, the Court rejected the government's contention that the executive could detain foreign nationals indefinitely if it were unable to remove them from the United States. *Zadvydas v. Davis*, 533 U.S. 678 (2001).

110. *In re Stacy*, 10 Johns 328, 334 (N.Y. Sup. Ct. 1813).

111. For other early examples, see *Wilson v. Izard*, 30 F. Cas. 131 (C.C.D.N.Y. 1815) (No. 17,810) (considering the habeas corpus petition of British subjects who had previously enlisted in the U.S. army); Brief *Amici Curiae* Professors of Constitutional Law and Federal Jurisdiction, *Al-Marri v. Wright*, at 16.

112. See, for example, *Matter of Peters*, M-1215 (D.W. Tenn. December 31, 1827) (examining whether prisoner "enlisted . . . when he was wholly incapable of transacting business or understanding it by reason of intoxication," thus invalidating the legal basis for commitment), cited in Freedman, *Habeas Corpus: Rethinking the Great Writ of Liberty*, 28 and 166, n. 56; *United States v. Irvine*, M-1184, roll 1 (C.C.D. Ga. May 8, 1815) (examining whether enlistment was based on the necessary parental consent), cited in Freedman, *Habeas Corpus: Rethinking the Great Writ of Liberty*, 165, n. 55; *State v. Clark*, 2 Del. Cas. 578, 580–81 (Del. Ch. 1820) (examining whether soldier was intoxicated at time of enlistment and rendering enlistment invalid).

113. For a relatively early, but influential expression of this view, see *Dynes v. Hoover*, 61 U.S. (20 How.) 65 (1858), and *Ex parte Reed*, 100 U.S. 13 (1879).

114. *Loving v. United States*, 517 U.S. 748 (1996); *Weiss v. United States*, 510 U.S. 163 (1994); *Burns v. Wilson*, 346 U.S. 137, 144–45 (1953) (plurality opinion) (noting the "peculiar relationship" between civil and military law); Neuman, "Habeas Corpus, Executive Detention, and the Removal of Aliens," 1042.

115. *Givens v. Zerbst*, 255 U.S. 11, 19 (1915). See also, for example, *McClaughry v. Deming*, 186 U.S. 49 (1902) (court-martial composed of regular army officers lacked jurisdiction under governing statute to try officer of volunteer army); *In re Grimley*, 137 U.S. 147 (1890) (examining whether solider had been under the proper age when he enlisted).

116. A plurality of the Supreme Court, for example, suggested this more expanded role when it said that judges could consider whether a defendant's claims had received "fair consideration" by a court-martial. *Burns*, 346 U.S. at 144–45.

117. Richard H. Fallon Jr. and Daniel J. Meltzer, "Habeas Corpus Jurisdiction, Substantive Rights, and the War on Terror," 120 *Harvard Law Review* 2029, 2099–2100 (2007).

118. *Ex parte Milligan*, 71 U.S. (4 Wall.) 2, 6–7 (1866) (statement of the case). Ibid., 140 (Chase, C.J., concurring).

119. Ibid., 6–7, 121, 130 (italics in original).

120. Ibid., 120–22, 130.

121. Ibid. 120–21.

122. Ibid., 135–36 (Chase, C.J., concurring).

123. *Reid v. Covert*, 354 U.S. 1, 30 (1957) (plurality opinion).

124. Edward S. Corwin, *Total War and the Constitution* (New York: Knopf, 1947), 117.

125. At the time, a criminal conviction for sabotage carried a maximum thirty-year sentence. See Daniel J. Danelski, "The Saboteurs' Case," *Journal of Supreme Court History* 1, 61, 65–66 (1996).

126. Executive Order No. 9185, 7 Fed. Reg. 5103, "Appointment of a Military Commission," July 2, 1942.

127. Francis Biddle, *In Brief Authority* (New York: Doubleday, 1962), 331.

128. Danelski, "The Saboteurs' Case," 71.

129. *Ex parte Quirin*, 63 S. Ct. 1 (1942).

130. *Ex parte Quirin*, 317 U.S. 1 (1942); Danelski, "The Saboteurs' Case," 71–72.

131. *Yamashita v. Styer*, 327 U.S. 1 (1946).

132. Danelski, "The Saboteurs' Case," 80; Louis Fisher, *Nazi Saboteurs on Trial: A Military Tribunal and American Law* (Lawrence: University Press of Kansas, 2003), 119–21. For another excellent account, see Pierce O'Donnell, *In Time of War: Hitler's Terrorist Attack on America* (New York: New Press, 2005).

133. Danelski, "The Saboteurs' Case," 72–73.

134. Steven B. Ives Jr., "Vengeance Did Not Deliver Justice," *Washington Post*, December 30, 2001.

135. Richard L. Lael, *The Yamashita Precedent: War Crimes and Command Responsibility* (Wilmington, DE: Scholarly Resources, 1982), 81; *Yamashita*, 327 U.S. at 33 (Murphy, J., dissenting).

136. Lael, *The Yamashita Precedent*, 80–81; Ives, "Vengeance Did Not Deliver Justice."

137. *Yamashita*, 327 U.S. at 27–28 (Murphy, J., dissenting).

138. Ibid., 61 (Rutledge, J., dissenting).

139. *Quirin*, 317 U.S. at 19.

140. *Yamashita*, 327 U.S. at 9.

141. *Johnson v. Eisentrager*, 339 U.S. 763 (1950).

142. *Eisentrager v. Forrestal*, unpublished opinion (D.D.C. October 6, 1948), reprinted in Transcript of Record at 16–17; *Johnson v. Eisentrager*, 339 U.S. 763 (1950) (No. 306).

143. *Ahrens v. Clark*, 335 U.S. 188 (1948).

144. Ibid., 193, n. 4.

145. Ibid., 195 (Rutledge, J., dissenting).

146. *Eisentrager v. Forrestal*, 174 F.2d 961, 963 (D.C. Cir. 1949).

147. Ibid., 965.

148. *Johnson v. Eisentrager*, 339 U.S. at 769.

149. Ibid., 771.

150. Ibid., 778–79.

151. See Timothy Endicott, "Habeas Corpus and Guantánamo Bay: A View from Abroad," 54 *American Journal of Jurisprudence* 1 (2009).

152. *Johnson v. Eisentrager*, 339 U.S. at 795 (Black, J., dissenting).

153. Ibid., 798.

154. *Ex parte Burford*, 7 U.S. (3 Cranch) 448, 452 (1806).

155. For a general overview of the tribunal, see Arnold C. Brackman, *The Other Nuremberg: The Untold Story of the Tokyo War Crimes Trials* (New York: Morrow, 1987); Tim Maga, *Judgment at Tokyo: The Japanese War Crimes Trials* (Lexington: University Press of Kentucky, 2001).

156. Hirota was the only civilian sentenced to death by the Tokyo tribunal. See Steven I. Vladeck, "Deconstructing *Hirota*: Habeas Corpus, Citizenship, and Article III," 95 *Georgetown Law Journal* 1497, 1499–1500 (2007).

157. The petition thus invoked the Supreme Court's so-called original jurisdiction under the 1789 Judiciary Act. The Court had previously considered "original" habeas petitions challenging action by military commissions. See, for example, *Ex parte Yerger*, 75 U.S. (8 Wall.) 85 (1869).

158. When the Court denied the first habeas petitions in 1946—before its decision in *Ahrens*—it noted that the prisoners could refile in the appropriate district court. See *Ex parte Betz*, 329 U.S. 672 (1946).

159. In May 1948, for example, the Court had refused to hear petitions brought on behalf of seventy-four German soldiers convicted at a war crimes trial at Dachau. *Everett ex rel. Bersin v. Truman*, 334 U.S. 824 (1948).

160. Vladeck, "Deconstructing *Hirota*," 1500–1501.

161. *Hirota v. MacArthur*, 338 U.S. 197, 198 (1948).

162. Vladeck, "Deconstructing *Hirota*," 1515–16.

163. Charles Fairman, "Some New Problems of the Constitution Following the Flag," 1 *Stanford Law Review* 587, 597–600 (1949); Vladeck, "Deconstructing *Hirota*," 1524–25.

CHAPTER 6

1. J. Andrew Kent, "A Textual and Historical Case against a Global Constitution," 95 *Georgetown Law Journal* 463, 488–89 (2007) .

2. Louis Henkin, *Constitutionalism, Democracy and Foreign Affairs* (New York: Columbia University Press, 1990), 99–100.

3. Joseph Gales, ed., *Annals of Congress*, vol. 1 (1834) (statement of Rep. Madison), 449.

4. U.S. Constitution, 5th and 6th amends.

5. Sarah H. Cleveland, "Our International Constitution," 31 *Yale Journal of International Law* 1, 35 (2006).

6. Alien Friends Act, ch. 58, § 1, 1 Stat. 570, 570-571 (1798).

7. Sedition Act, ch. 74, 1 Stat. 596 (1798).

8. *Annals of Congress* vol. 8 (1798), 2008 (statement of Rep. Harrison Gray Otis); *Annals of Congress*, vol. 8 (1798), 1984–85 (statement of Rep. William Gordon); Gerald L. Neuman, *Strangers to the Constitution: Immigrants, Borders, and Fundamental Law* (Princeton, NJ: Princeton University Press, 1996), 54–56.

9. Neuman, *Strangers to the Constitution*, 53.

10. *Annals of Congress* vol. 8 (1798), 2012 (statement of Rep. Edward Livingston).

11. Madison's Report on the Virginia Resolutions, reprinted in *The Debates in the Several State Conventions on the Adoption of the Federal Constitution*, ed. Jonathan Elliot, vol. 4 (1836), 556.

12. Ibid.

13. *Yick Wo v. Hopkins*, 118 U.S. 356 (1886).

14. *Wong Wing v. United States*, 163 U.S. 228 (1896).

15. See, for example, *Bridges v. Wixon*, 326 U.S. 135 (1945) (First Amendment); *INS v. Lopez-Mendoza*, 468 U.S. 1032 (1984) (Fourth Amendment); *Russian Volunteer Fleet v. United States*, 282 U.S. 481 (1931) (just compensation clause).

16. Gerald L. Neuman, "Closing the Guantanamo Loophole," 50 *Loyola Law Review* 1, 8 (2004).

17. Neuman, *Strangers to the Constitution*, 73–74. Senator Daniel Webster offered a different vision of this approach, rooted in membership in the Union rather than the states (78–79).

18. *Loughborough v. Blake*, 18 U.S. (5 Wheat.) 317, 319 (1820). In *Lougherborough*, the Court upheld Congress's power to impose a direct tax on the District of Columbia but required that any duties, imposts, and excises be uniform, as the Constitution requires. U.S. Constitution, art. I, § 8.

19. See, for example, *United States v. Dawson*, 56 U.S. (15 How.) 467 (1854) (applying venue requirements of article 3, section 2); *Webster v. Reed*, 52 U.S. (11 How.) 437 (1851) (applying Seventh Amendment's guarantee of a jury trial in civil cases); Neuman, "Closing the Guantanamo Loophole," 8.

20. *Loughborough*, 18 U.S. (5 Wheat.) at 319.

21. 60 U.S. (19 How.) 393 (1857). Benjamin Curtis's dissenting opinion agreed that the Constitution covered territories but rejected the Court's conclusion that due process required the protection of slavery. Ibid., 624–27 (Curtis, J., dissenting).

22. *In re Ross*, 140 U.S. 453, 464 (1891).

23. *Neely v. Henkel*, 180 U.S. 109, 122 (1901).

24. John Heffner, Note: "Between Assimilation and Revolt: A Third Option for Hawaii as a Model for Minorities World-Wide," 35 *Texas International Law Journal* 591, 595–96 (2002); Gavan Daws, *Shoal of Time: A History of the Hawaiian Islands* (Honolulu: University of Hawaii Press, 1974), 271–80.

25. Julius W. Pratt, *America's Colonial Experiment* (New York: Prentice-Hall, 1950), 68; Gary Lawson and Guy Seidman, *The Constitution of Empire* (New Haven, CT: Yale University Press, 2004), 11.

26. *Downes v. Bidwell*, 182 U.S. 244 (1901).

27. Ibid., 251.

28. Ibid., 287.

29. Ibid., 378, 380 (Harlan, J., dissenting).

30. Ibid., 293 (White, J., concurring).

31. Ibid., 291.

32. See *Balzac v. Porto Rico*, 258 U.S. 298 (1922) (Sixth Amendment right to jury trial inapplicable in Puerto Rico); *Ocampo v. United States*, 234 U.S. 91 (1914) (Fifth Amendment grand jury provision inapplicable in Philippines); *Dorr v. United States*, 195 U.S. 138 (1904) (jury trial provision inapplicable in Philippines); *Hawaii v. Mankichi*, 190 U.S. 197 (1903) (grand jury and jury trial provisions inapplicable in Hawaii); see also *Downes v. Bidwell* (revenue clauses of Constitution inapplicable to Puerto Rico).

33. Christina Duffy Burnett, "American Expansion and Territorial Deannexation," 72 *University of Chicago Law Review* 797 (2005).

34. *Balzac v. Porto Rico*.

35. Gerald L. Neuman, "Whose Constitution?" 100 *Yale Law Journal* 909, 965 (1991).

36. *Reid v. Covert*, 354 U.S. 1 (1957).

37. Ibid., 5–6 (plurality opinion).

38. Ibid., 9.

39. Ibid, 6.

40. Ibid., 12.

41. Ibid., 74 (Harlan, J., concurring).

42. Neuman, *Strangers to the Constitution*, 93.

43. *Kinsella v. United States ex rel. Singleton*, 361 U.S. 234 (1960) (civilian dependents for noncapital crimes); *Grisham v. Hagan*, 361 U.S. 278 (1960) *Grisham v. Hagan*, 361 U.S. 278 (1960) (civilian employees of the armed forces accused of capital crimes); *McElroy v. Guagliardo*, 361 U.S. 281 (1960) (civilian employees of the armed forces accused of noncapital crimes).

44. See, for example, *Ramirez de Arellano v. Weinberger*, 745 F.2d 1500 (ruling that a U.S. citizen could bring claim against the military under the Due Process Clause for using his farm in Honduras to train Salvadorian soldiers), *vacated and remanded as moot*, 471 U.S. 1113 (1985); *Berlin Democratic Club v. Rumsfeld*, 410 F. Supp. 144 (D.D.C. 1976) (ruling that the First, Fourth, and Sixth Amendments applied to U.S. citizens in Germany based on allegedly illegal intelligence gathering).

45. Isthmian Canal Convention, November 18, 1903, U.S.-Panama, art. 2, 33 Stat. 2235.

46. Ibid., art. 3.

47. Panama Canal Treaty of 1977, September 7, 1977, U.S.-Panama, 33 U.S.T. 39, T.I.A.S. No. 10030.

48. Act of August 24, 1912, ch. 390, §§ 8–9, 37 Stat. 560, 565–66 (1912).

49. Neuman, "Closing the Guantanamo Loophole," 18.

50. Ibid., 18–19.

51. *Canal Zone v. Castillo L. (Lopez)*, 568 F.2d 405, 407–11 (5th Cir. 1978) (evaluating a provision of the Canal Zone Code outlawing vagrancy under the federal Constitution's due process standard); *Raven v. Panama Canal Co.*, 583 F.2d 169, 171 (5th Cir. 1978) (subjecting the exclusion of Panamanian employees of the Canal Zone from the protections of the federal Privacy Act to review under the equal protection clause of the U.S. Constitution but rejecting the claim on the merits).

52. *Canal Zone v. Scott*, 502 F.2d 566, 568 (5th Cir. 1974).

53. Trusteeship Agreement for the Former Japanese Mandated Islands, July 18, 1947, art. 3, T.I.A.S. No. 1665, 8 U.N.T.S. 189.

54. Neuman, "Closing the Guantanamo Loophole," 23–24.

55. Ibid., 24–25.

56. *Ralpho v. Bell*, 569 F.2d 607, 618–19 (D.C. Cir. 1977).

57. Ibid. (internal quotation marks omitted).

58. *Juda v. United States*, 6 Cl. Ct. 441 (1981).

59. See Harold Hongju Koh, "America's Offshore Refugee Camps," 29 *Richmond Law Review* 139–43, 153–55 (1994); Brandt Goldstein, *Storming the Court: How a Band of Yale Law Students Sued the President—And Won* (New York: Scribner, 2005).

60. *Haitian Refugee Ctr. v. Baker*, 949 F.2d 1109 (11th Cir. 1991); *Haitian Refugee Ctr. v. Baker*, 953 F.2d 1498 (11th Cir. 1992).

61. *Cuban-American Bar Ass'n v. Christopher*, 43 F.3d 1412, 1430 (11th Cir. 1995).

62. *Haitian Ctrs. Council, Inc. v. McNary*, 969 F.2d 1326, 1342–43 (2d Cir. 1992) (italics omitted), *vacated as moot*, 509 U.S. 918 (1993).

63. *Sale v. Haitian Ctrs. Council, Inc.*, 509 U.S. 155 (1993).

64. *Haitian Ctrs. Council, Inc. v. Sale*, 823 F. Supp. 1028, 1042 (E.D.N.Y. 1993).

65. Compare *United States v. Toscanino*, 500 F.2d 267 (2d Cir. 1974) (ruling that the Constitution's protection against unreasonable searches and seizures and guarantee of

due process applied to the FBI's alleged abduction and torture of a suspected Italian drug smuggler in Uruguay), with Neuman, "Whose Constitution?" 970–71 (discussing cases). Also, two courts of appeals rejected challenges to arrests and seizure of foreign nationals outside the United States after assuming, but not actually deciding, that the Constitution applied. See *Sami v. United States*, 617 F.2d 755 (D.C. Cir. 1979) (rejecting claim of wrongful arrest by Germany based on information provided by the United States); *United States v. Rubies*, 612 F.2d 397 (9th Cir. 1979) (finding that the search of alien's vessel interdicted on high seas was reasonable).

66. *United States v. Verdugo-Urquidez*, 494 U.S. 259 (1990).

67. Ibid., 262–63.

68. Rehnquist also suggested that the Fourth Amendment did not apply to aliens inside the United States without a sufficient connection to the country to make them part of the national community because the amendment's text referred to "the right of the people," a connection that Rehnquist said Verdugo-Urquidez lacked, since he had been brought to the United States involuntarily. *Verdugo-Urquidez*, 494 U.S. at 271. But Justice Kennedy, who provided the necessary fifth vote for the Court's ruling, explicitly rejected that suggestion.

69. *Verdugo-Urquidez*, 494 U.S. at 273.

70. Ibid., 275 (citation and internal quotation marks omitted).

71. Ibid.

72. Ibid., 282–84 (Brennan, J., dissenting).

73. Ibid., 284.

74. Ibid., 285–86. Justice Harry Blackmun adopted a similar approach in his separate dissenting opinion in *Verdugo-Urquidez* but differed from Brennan in arguing that the Fourth Amendment's extraterritorial protections should be limited to "unreasonable searches and seizures," not the amendment's separate warrant requirement, at least with respect to noncitizens (297–98), (Blackmun, J., dissenting).

75. Ibid., 275–78 (Kennedy, J., concurring).

76. For a discussion of Kennedy's approach, see Neuman, *Strangers to the Constitution*, 8.

CHAPTER 7

1. *Rasul v. Bush*, 542 U.S. 466 (2004).

2. *Hamdi v. Rumsfeld*, 542 U.S. 507 (2004); *Rumsfeld v. Padilla*, 542 U.S. 426 (2004).

3. Transcript of Oral Argument, April 28, 2004, *Hamdi v. Rumsfeld*, 542 U.S. 507 (2004), 2004 WL 1066082 at *41.

4. The United States released the two British citizens, Shafiq Rasul and Asif Iqbal, before the Supreme Court decided their case.

5. *Johnson v. Eisentrager*, 339 U.S. 763 (1950).

6. The point was made by Justice David Souter. See Transcript of Oral Argument, *Rasul v. Bush*, 542 U.S. 466 (2004), 2004 WL 943637, at *43.

7. *Eisentrager*, 339 U.S. at 778.

8. Ibid., 789–90.

9. *Ahrens v. Clark*, 335 U.S. 188 (1948).

10. *Braden v. 30th Judicial Circuit Court of Kentucky*, 410 U.S. 484 (1973).

11. Ibid., 494–95.

12. *Burns v. Wilson*, 346 U.S. 137 (1953) (court-martial of U.S. soldiers in Guam); *United States ex rel. Toth v. Quarles*, 350 U.S. 11 (1950) (court-martial of U.S. soldier arrested in Pittsburgh after his discharge from the military and then taken to Korea to stand trial for acts committed while previously in military service there).

13. *Rasul*, 542 U.S. at 478–79.

14. Ibid., 478.

15. Ibid., 497–98 (Scalia, J., dissenting).

16. Ibid., 486–87 (Kennedy, J., concurring).

17. Ibid, 486.

18. Ibid., 487.

19. 542 U.S. 507 (2004).

20. Ibid., 511–12 (plurality opinion)

21. Ibid., 512–13.

22. *Hamdi v. Rumsfeld*, 243 F. Supp. 2d 527, 535 (E.D. Va. 2002).

23. *Hamdi v. Rumsfeld*, 316 F.3d 450 (4th Cir. 2003).

24. Ibid., 465–66.

25. *Hamdi v. Rumsfeld*, 337 F.3d 335, 344 (4th Cir. 2003) (Wilkinson, J., concurring in the denial of rehearing en banc).

26. Ibid., 357 (Traxler, J., concurring in the denial of rehearing en banc).

27. Ibid., 371–73 (Motz, J., dissenting from the denial of rehearing en banc).

28. *Hamdi v. Rumsfeld*, 542 U.S. at 516 (plurality opinion) (internal quotation marks omitted).

29. Ibid., 519–21.

30. Ibid., 536.

31. Ibid., 533, 539.

32. Ibid., 534.

33. Ibid., 538–39.

34. Ibid., 547–48 (Souter, J., concurring in part, dissenting in part, and concurring in the judgment). See also 18 U.S.C. § 4001(a).

35. *Hamdi*, 542 U.S. at 547–48 (Souter, J., concurring in part, dissenting in part, and concurring in the judgment).

36. Ibid., 548–51.

37. Ibid., 554–69 (Scalia, J., dissenting).

38. Ibid., 524 (plurality opinion).

39. Scalia did leave open the possibility that his opinion might apply to noncitizens arrested and detained in the United States who did not fall within the narrow definition of "enemy alien."

40. *Hamdi*, 542 U.S. at 579–99 (Thomas, J. dissenting).

41. Ibid., 583.

42. *Padilla*, 542 U.S. at 447, n. 16; ibid., 453 (Kennedy, J., concurring).

43. See *Al-Marri v. Rumsfeld*, 360 F.3d 707 (7th Cir.) *cert. denied*, 543 U.S. 809 (2004).

44. *Padilla*, 542 U.S. at 465 (Stevens, J., dissenting).

45. Ibid.

46. While it is uncertain how the Court would have decided the merits, it appears that at least five justices disapproved of Padilla's military detention. In a footnote in his dissent, Justice Stevens indicated that Padilla's military detention as an "enemy combatant" was

illegal. *Padilla*, 542 U.S. at 464, n. 8. Four justices (Stevens, Scalia, Souter, and Ginsburg) believed that Hamdi's military detention was illegal, even though Hamdi, on the facts alleged, presented a stronger case for military detention than Padilla, since Hamdi was seized on a foreign battlefield carrying a weapon during combat against U.S. and allied forces there. Although Breyer had joined O'Connor's opinion in *Hamdi* accepting the possibility of military detention in a battlefield case like Hamdi's, he joined Stevens's dissent in *Padilla*, suggesting that he too believed that the president could not subject to indefinite military detention an American arrested in a civilian setting in the United States. This suggests that at a minimum five justices (Stevens, Scalia, Souter, Ginsburg, and Breyer) would have invalidated Padilla's continued detention as an "enemy combatant," even on the facts alleged.

CHAPTER 8

1. Order, *Hamdi v. Rumsfeld*, Civil Action no. 2:02cv439 (E.D. Va. October 5, 2004) (Under Seal Until Friday, October 8, 2004, at 12:00 pm EST); "Man held as enemy combatant to be freed soon," CNN.Com, September 23, 2004.

2. *Yaser Esam Hamdi v Donald Rumsfeld*, Settlement Agreement, September 17, 2004; Joel Brinkley and Eric Lichtblau, "Held 3 Years by U.S., Saudi Goes Home," *International Herald Tribune*, October 13, 2004; Jerry Markon, "Hamdi Returned to Saudi Arabia; U.S. Citizen's Detention as Enemy Combatant Sparked Fierce Debate," *Washington Post*, October 12, 2004.

3. Memorandum for the Secretary of the Navy, Order Establishing Combatant Status Review Tribunal, July 7, 2004 (CSRT Order).

4. See Memorandum, "Implementation of Combatant Status Review Tribunal Procedures for Enemy Combatants Detained at Guantanamo Bay Naval Base, Cuba," July 29, 2004, encl. 1. para. G (11); "A Government Lawyer's Take on Gtmo: Interview with Captain Pat McCarthy," NPR (*Fresh Air*), November 1, 2007.

5. Mark Denbeaux and Joshua Denbeaux, *No-Hearing Hearings: An Analysis of the Government's Combatant Status Review Tribunals at Guantánamo* (Newark, NJ: Seton Hall Law School, 2006), 14–18.

6. Ibid., 1, 19, 25–33; Michael Melia, "Enemies Reunite at Guantanamo," *Associated Press*, September 11, 2007.

7. Geri L. Dreiling, "Changing the Ground Rules: DOJ Proposes New Limits on Lawyer Access to Detainees," *ABA Journal & Report*, November 3, 2006.

8. See *Miller v. Fenton*, 474 U.S. 104, 109 (1985). See also *Rochin v. California*, 342 U.S. 165, 173 (1952). Coerced confessions are thus inadmissible in criminal trials, regardless of their purported reliability. See *Rogers v. Richmond*, 365 U.S. 534, 540–41 (1961).

9. See *Jackson v. Denno*, 378 U.S. 368, 385–86 (1964); *Spano v. New York*, 360 U.S. 315, 320 (1959).

10. U.S. Department of the Army, *U.S. Army Field Manual 34–52: Intelligence Interrogation*, 1–8 (1992).

11. Eighteen percent of detainees alleged they had made statements under torture. Denbeaux and Denbeaux, *No-Hearing Hearings* 24, 36.

12. Human Rights Watch, *Guantanamo: The Road to Abu Ghraib* 17 (2004).

13. Department of Defense, news release, June 12, 2005.

14. James Risen, *State of War: The Secret History of the CIA and the Bush Administration* (New York: Free Press, 2006), 33; Baher Azmy, "Executive Detention, *Boumediene*, and the New Common Law of Habeas," 95 *Iowa Law Review* 445, 478 (2010).

15. Brief of Respondents at 20–21, 27, *Hamdi v. Rumsfeld*, 542 U.S. 507 (No. 03-6696).

16. CSRT Order, para. a.

17. "Prepared Remarks of Attorney General Alberto R. Gonzales at the U.S. Air Force Academy regarding Civil Liberties and the War on Terrorism," November 20, 2006; White House, "Press Gaggle with Scott McClellan and Faryar Shirzad," July 6, 2005.

18. Mark Denbeaux et al., *The Empty Battlefield and the Thirteenth Criterion* (Newark, NJ: Seton Hall Law School, 2007). This report does not consider the fourteen "high-value detainees" transferred to Guantanamo from CIA "black sites" in September 2006.

19. Mark Denbeaux et al., *The Meaning of 'Battlefield': An Analysis of the Government's Representations of 'Battlefield' Capture and 'Recidivism' of the Guantánamo Detainees* (Newark, NJ: Seton Hall Law School, 2007), 9–10.

20. Ibid. In fact, only a small percentage of the former prisoners who the Defense Department says have "returned to the battlefield" actually engaged in hostile activities following their release from Guantánamo (1–2, 5, 18).

21. *Parhat v. Gates*, 532 F.3d 834, 848–49 (D.C. Cir. 2008) (quoting Lewis Carroll, *The Hunting of the Snark* 3 [1876]).

22. Denbeaux and Denbeaux, *No-Hearing Hearings*, 10–11.

23. News transcript, Defense Department Special Briefing on Combatant Status Review Tribunals, March 29, 2005.

24. Ibid.; Denbeaux and Denbeaux, *No-Hearing Hearings* 37–40.

25. Order, Administrative Review Procedures for Enemy Combatants in the Control of the Department of Defense at Guantánamo Naval Base, Cuba, May 11, 2004, at 1–2.

26. Farah Stockman, "Some Cleared Guantanamo Inmates Stay in Custody," *Boston Globe*, November 19, 2007.

27. *Al Odah v. United States*, 346 F. Supp. 2d 1, 5, (D.D.C. 2004).

28. Ibid., 10.

29. Tim Golden, "Naming Names at Gtmo," *New York Times*, October 21, 2007.

30. *Al Odah*, 346 F. Supp. 2d at 6–7. See also *Harris v. Nelson*, 394 U.S. 286, 298 (1969).

31. "Lawyer to Visit Guantanamo Pair," *BBC News*, August 31, 2004. Previously, only the handful of Guantánamo detainees designated for trial by military commission had been able to meet with a lawyer, and those detainees had met only with military, not civilian, counsel.

32. For a collection of these accounts, see Mark Denbeaux and Jonathan Hafetz, eds., *The Guantánamo Lawyers: Inside a Prison Outside the Law* (New York: New York University Press, 2009).

33. See Murat Kurnaz, *Five Years of My Life: An Innocent Man in Guantanamo* (New York: Palgrave Macmillan, 2008); Moazzam Begg, *Enemy Combatant: My Imprisonment at Guantanamo, Bagram, and Kandahar* (New York: New Press, 2007).

34. See Carol Rosenberg, "U.N. Fact-finders Reject Pentagon Offer to Tour Guantanamo," *Miami Herald*, November 18, 2005. The ICRC visited the detainees, but its reports were supposed to remain confidential, to be shared only with the detaining power, pursuant to ICRC policy.

35. *In re Guantanamo Detainee Cases*, 344 F. Supp. 2d 174 (D.D.C. 2004).

36. Ibid., 180. See also Brendan M. Driscoll, Note: "The Guantánamo Protective Order," 30 *Fordham International Law Journal* 873 (2007).

37. *Khalid v. Bush*, 355 F. Supp. 2d 311, 320–27 (D.D.C. 2005).

38. Ibid., 317–20.

39. Eleven early habeas cases, which had been assigned to various district judges, had been consolidated for decision by Judge Green on common issues, including the validity of the CSRT. Those cases originally included the habeas petitions before Judge Leon. But Judge Leon subsequently exercised his prerogative to have the cases originally assigned to him returned to him so he could decide all issues, including the common ones.

40. *In re Guantánamo Detainee Cases*, 355 F. Supp. 2d 464 (D.D.C. 2005).

41. Ibid., 458 (quoting *Ralpho v. Bell*, 569 F.2d 607, 618–19 (1977)); ibid., 463–64.

42. Ibid., 468–74.

43. Ibid., 469.

44. Ibid., 470–71.

45. Carol D. Leonnig, "Evidence of Innocence Rejected at Guantanamo," *Washington Post*, December 5, 2007, A1.

46. *In re Guantánamo Detainee Cases*, 355 F. Supp. 2d at 473–74; Joseph Margulies, *Guantánamo and the Abuse of Presidential Power* (New York: Simon & Schuster, 2006), 182–88.

47. See, for example, U.S. Department of State, "Country Reports on Human Rights Practices 2003: Egypt" (Washington, DC: U.S. Government Printing Office, 2004).

48. Raymond Bonner, "Australian's Long Path in the U.S. Anti-Terrorism Maze," *New York Times*, January 29, 2005.

49. *In re Guantanamo Detainee Cases*, 355 F. Supp. 2d 482 (D.D.C. 2005).

50. Judges would, however, continue to consider certain applications intended to maintain the status quo, including requests to maintain a detainee's access to counsel and to afford limited protection to detainees on life-threatening hunger strikes. See, for example, *Al-Joudi v. Bush*, 406 F. Supp. 2d 13 (D.D.C. 2005) (ordering that the government notify detainees' counsel within twenty-four hours if their clients were being forced-fed as a result of a hunger strike and provide counsel with access to those detainees' medical records).

51. Jonathan Mahler, "The Bush Administration vs. Salim Hamdan," *New York Times*, January 8, 2006.

52. Ibid.

53. Press release, "Department of Defense, President Determines Enemy Combatants Subject to His Military Order," July 3, 2003.

54. Because Hamdan had been designated for trial by military commission, the Bush administration gave him access to an attorney—access that other Guantánamo detainees who had not been charged or designated for trial were denied until after the Supreme Court's June 2004 decision in *Rasul*.

55. *Hamdan v. Rumsfeld*, 344 F. Supp. 2d 152, 155–56 (D.D.C. 2004).

56. U.S. Department of Defense, "Military Commission List of Charges for Salim Ahmed Hamdan," July 13, 2004.

57. Hamdan's case was transferred to the U.S. District Court for the District of Columbia from the Western District of Washington, where it was originally filed, following the Supreme Court's decision in *Rasul*.

58. *Hamdan*, 344 F. Supp. 2d at 161–62. The CSRT, Judge Robertson said, did not satisfy the requirements of a "competent tribunal" because it was not established to address a detainee's status under the Geneva Conventions but, rather, to determine whether the detainee had been properly classified as an "enemy combatant" for purposes of continued detention.

59. Ibid., 172.

60. *Hamdan v. Rumsfeld*, 415 F.3d 33 (D.C. Cir. 2005).

61. Ibid., 44 (Williams, J., concurring).

62. *Hamdan v. Rumsfeld*, 546 U.S. 1002 (2005).

63. Pub. L. No. 109-148, 119 Stat. 2680 (2005) (DTA).

64. *Ex parte McCardle*, 74 U.S. (7 Wall.) 506 (1868). The following year, the Court ruled that it had jurisdiction to hear a habeas challenge to a prospective trial by a military commission through that very avenue. See *Ex parte Yerger*, 75 U.S. (8 Wall.) 85 (1869). More than a century later, the Supreme Court again declined to read a legislative restriction as an absolute bar to the exercise of its appellate jurisdiction in habeas cases. See *Felker v. Turpin*, 518 U.S. 651, 661–62 (1996). See generally William W. Van Alstyne, "A Critical Guide to *Ex parte McCardle*," 15 *Arizona Law Review* 229 (1973).

65. DTA § 1005(e)(3).

66. See, for example, *Yamashita v. Styer*, 327 U.S. 1, 9 (1946); *Ex parte Quirin*, 317 U.S. 1, 25 (1942).

67. DTA § 1005(e)(3).

68. 151 Cong. Rec. S12777-02, S12800 (November 14, 2005) (statement of Sen. Graham).

69. *Quirin*, 317 U.S. 1; *Ex parte Milligan*, 71 U.S. (4 Wall.) 2 (1866).

70. 151 Cong. Rec. S12777-02, S12803 (November 15, 2005) (statement of Sen. Kyle); 151 Cong. Rec. S12777-02, S12799 (November 15, 2005) (statement of Sen. Graham); 151 Cong. Rec. S12752-01, S12755 (November 14, 2005) (statement of Sen. Graham).

71. Dan Eggen, "Senate Approves Plan to Limit Detainee Access to the Courts," *Washington Post*, December 11, 2005.

72. 151 Cong. Rec. S12777-02, S12802 (November 15, 2005) (statement of Sen. Levin).

73. DTA, § 1003(a).

74. Ibid., § 1005(b)(1).

75. Ibid., § 1003(d). The Fifth Amendment standard is derived from the Supreme Court's decision in *Rochin v. California*, 342 U.S. 165 (1952), in which the Supreme Court overturned a conviction after the police had ordered a doctor to forcibly pump a suspect's stomach to obtain narcotics.

76. Scott Shane et al., "Secret U.S. Endorsement of Severe Interrogations," *New York Times*, October 4, 2007.

77. George W. Bush, "President's Statement on Signing of H.R. 2863," December 30, 2005.

78. For a discussion of Bush's unprecedented use of signing statements, see Phillip J. Cooper, "George W. Bush, Edgar Allan Poe, and the Use and Abuse of Presidential Signing Statements," 35 *Presidential Studies Quarterly* 515 (2005).

79. Petition for Writ of Habeas Corpus, *Padilla v. Hanft*, No. 04 Civ. 2221 (D.S.C.), *filed* July 2, 2005.

80. *Padilla v. Hanft*, 389 F. Supp. 2d 678 (D.S.C. 2005).

81. *Padilla v. Hanft*, 423 F.3d 386, 389 (4th Cir. 2005).

82. Ibid., 391–92.

83. "Terror Suspect Charged," CNN.com, November 22, 2005.

84. Deborah Sontag, "In Padilla Wiretaps, Murky View of 'Jihad' Case," *New York Times*, January 4, 2007.

85. Douglas Jehl and Eric Lichtblau, "Shift on Suspect Is Linked to Role of Qaeda Figures," *New York Times*, November 24, 2005.

86. *Padilla v. Hanft*, 432 F.3d 582 (4th Cir. 2005).

87. Ibid., 584–87.

88. *Padilla v. Hanft*, 547 U.S. 1062 (2006).

89. Kirk Semple, "Padilla Sentenced to 17 Years in Prison," *New York Times*, January 22, 2008.

90. *Hamdan v. Rumsfeld*, 548 U.S. 557 (2006). Chief Justice John G. Roberts did not participate in the Supreme Court decision because he had served on the panel of the court of appeals that had decided the case before he was appointed to the Supreme Court.

91. *Hamdan v. Rumsfeld*, No. 05-184, Transcript of Oral Argument 57–58 (March 28, 2006).

92. *Hamdan*, 548 U.S. at 613–25 (finding that the commissions failed to satisfy UCMJ article 36(b)'s requirement that their rules be "uniform insofar as practicable").

93. Ibid., 613–16, 623–24.

94. Geneva Convention [III] Relative to the Treatment of Prisoners of War, art. 3, § 1(d), August 12, 1949, 6 U.S.T. 3316, 75 U.N.T.S. 135 (Third Geneva Convention).

95. *Hamdan*, 548 U.S. at 630–33. Four justices determined that the commissions also contradicted Common Article 3 because they denied the defendant the right to be present at trial, a judicial guarantee "recognized as indispensable by civilized peoples." Ibid., 633–34 (plurality opinion of Stevens, J.).

96. Ibid., 595–613 (plurality opinion of Stevens, J.).

97. Ibid., 593, n. 23.

98. Ibid. 635.

99. Third Geneva Convention, art. 3, § 1(c).

100. 18 U.S.C. § 2441.

101. Tim Golden, "The Ruling on Tribunals: The Prison; after Ruling, Uncertainty Hovers at Cuba Prison," *New York Times*, June 30, 2006, A1 (quoting Rear Admiral Harry B. Harris).

CHAPTER 9

1. "President Discusses Creation of Military Commissions to Try Suspected Terrorists," September 6, 2006.

2. Ibid.

3. Memorandum for John A. Rizzo, Acting General Counsel, Central Intelligence Agency, from Steven G. Bradbury, Acting Assistant Attorney General, Re: "Application of the Detainee Treatment Act to Conditions of Confinement at Central Intelligence Agency Detention Facilities," August 31, 2006; letter from Steven G. Bradbury to John A. Rizzo, August 31, 2006.

4. Executive Order 13440, "Interpretation of the Geneva Conventions Common Article 3 as Applied to a Program of Detention and Interrogation Operated by the Central Intelligence Agency," July 20, 2007; Joby Warrick, "U.S. Transfers Bin Laden Aid; CIA Moves

Former Translator to Guantanamo, Officials Say," *Washington Post*, March 15, 2008; "CIA Admits Waterboarding Inmates," *BBC News*, February 5, 2008; Richard Esposito and Brian Ross, "Coming in from the Cold: CIA Spy Calls Waterboarding Necessary but Torture," *ABC News*, December 10, 2007.

5. Pub. L. No. 109-366, 120 Stat. 2600 (2006).

6. Ibid. § 3, 120 Stat. 2625–30 (adding new 10 U.S.C. § 950v).

7. Ibid., § 3, 120 Stat. 2608–9, 2611–12 (adding new 10 U.S.C. §§ 949a and 949d).

8. Ibid., § 3, 120 Stat. 2615 (adding new 10 U.S.C. § 940j(d)).

9. Ibid, § 3, 120 Stat. 2607 (adding new 10 U.S.C. § 948r).

10. Ibid., § 3, 120 Stat. 2611–13 (adding new 10 U.S.C. § 949d).

11. Ibid. §§ 5, 6, 120 Stat. 2631, 2633.

12. Ibid., § 6, 120 Stat. 2632–35.

13. See Donna Mills, "England Memo Underscores Humane Policy on Treatment of Detainees," American Forces Press Service, July 11, 2006.

14. Executive Order 13440, "Interpretation of the Geneva Conventions Common Article 3"; David Cole, "Bush's Torture Ban is Full of Loopholes," Salon.com, July 23, 2007.

15. Memorandum for John A. Rizzo, Acting General Counsel, Central Intelligence Agency, from Steven G. Bradbury, Principal Deputy Assistant Attorney General, Re: "Application of the War Crimes Act, the Detainee Treatment Act, and Common Article 3 of the Geneva Conventions to Certain Techniques That May Be Used by the CIA in the Interrogation of High Value al Qaeda Detainees," July 20, 2007.

16. MCA, § 7(a), 120 Stat. 2635–36 (amending 28 U.S.C. § 2241).

17. Ibid., § 7(b), 120 Stat. 2636 (amending 28 U.S.C. § 2241).

18. 152 Congressional Record S10273 (September 26, 2006) (statement of Sen. Cornyn).

19. 152 Congressional Record S10269 (September 27, 2006) (statement of Sen. Kyl).

20. 152 Congressional Record S10403 (September 28, 2006) (statement of Sen. Sessions).

21. Statement of U.S. Senator Russ Feingold on the President Signing the Military Commissions Act, October, 17, 2006.

22. Editorial, "Rushing Off a Cliff," *New York Times*, September 28, 2006, A22; Daniel Michael, "The Military Commissions Act of 2006," 44 *Harvard Journal on Legislation* 473, 479–80 (2007).

23. Michael, "The Military Commissions Act of 2006," 480; Habeas Restoration Act, S. 4081, 109th Cong. (2006); Habeas Corpus Restoration Act of 2007, S.185, 110th Cong. (2007); Habeas Corpus Restoration Act of 2007, H.R.1416, 110th Cong. (2007); Military Commissions Habeas Corpus Restoration Act of 2007, H.R.267, 110th Cong. (2007); Restoring the Constitution Act of 2007, H.R. 1415, 110th Cong. (2007); Restoring the Constitution Act of 2007, S.576, 110th Cong. (2007).

24. John Yoo, "Congress to Courts: 'Get Out of the War on Terror,'" *Wall Street Journal*, October 19, 2006, A18.

25. James Dao, "A Nation Challenged: The Prisoners; Detainees Stage Protest at Base over a Turban," *New York Times*, March 1, 2002; Carol D. Leonnig, "More Join Guantanamo Hunger Strike; Detainees Demand Hearings, Allege Beatings by Guards," *Washington Post*, September 13, 2005; Neil A. Lewis, "Guantánamo Prisoners Go on Hunger Strike," *New York Times*, September 18, 2005; Jane Sutton, "75 Prisoners Join in Hunger Strike at U.S. Base at Guantanamo Bay," *Washington Post*, May 30, 2006; Tim Golden, "Tough U.S.

Steps in Hunger Strike at Camp in Cuba," *New York Times*, February 9, 2006; Center for Constitutional Rights, *The Guantanamo Prisoner Hunger Strikes and Protests: February 2002–August 2005* (September 2005). For a discussion of the medical ethics of force-feeding, see Sondra S. Crosby et al., "Hunger Strikes, Force-feeding, and Physicians' Responsibilities," 298 *Journal of American Medical Association* 563 (2007).

26. Scott Horton, "The Guantánamo 'Suicides': A Camp Delta Sergeant Blows the Whistle," *Harper's*, March 2010.

27. Josh White, "Death of Guantanamo Detainee Is Apparent Suicide, Military Says," *Washington Post*, May 31, 2007.

28. James Risen and Tim Golden, "3 Prisoners Commit Suicide at Guantánamo," *New York Times*, June 11, 2006; "Guantanamo Suicides 'a Good PR Move,'" *ABCNewsOnline*, June 12, 2006, available at http://www.abc.net.au/news/newsitems/200606/s1660550.htm (last visited July 8, 2010).

29. Jason Oddy, "Living with the Enemy," *Independent* (London), December 7, 2003.

30. From the beginning, the United Nations and international human rights organizations had criticized the United States for its detention and treatment of prisoners at Guantánamo. See, for example, "Red Cross Inspects US Prison," *BBC News*, January 18, 2002.

31. Josh White, "ICRC Chief Faults Rights Protections at Guantanamo," *Washington Post*, April 5, 2007.

32. Lizette Alvarez, "Rights Group Defends Chastising of U.S," *New York Times*, June 4, 2005.

33. "Top UK Judge Slams Camp Delta," *BBC News*, November 23, 2003.

34. Jeffrey Toobin, "Camp Justice," *New Yorker*, April 14, 2008.

35. Thom Shanker and David E. Sanger, "New to Job, Gates Argued for Closing Guantánamo," *New York Times*, March 23, 2007; Dianne Feinstein, Open Forum, "Close Guantanamo Now," *San Francisco Chronicle*, July 30, 2007.

36. *Boumediene v. Bush*, 476 F.3d 981 (D.C. Cir. 2007).

37. Ibid., 990–91.

38. Ibid., 991–92, n. 10.

39. Ibid., 992.

40. *Boumediene v. Bush*, 127 S. Ct. 1478, 1478 (2007) (statement of Stevens and Kennedy, JJ., respecting the denial of certiorari). Justices Breyer, Souter, and Ginsburg all voted to grant review (ibid., 1479) (Breyer, J., joined by Souter and Ginsburg, JJ., dissenting from the denial of certiorari).

41. Ibid. (statement of Stevens and Kennedy, JJ., respecting the denial of certiorari).

42. *Boumediene v. Bush*, 127 S. Ct. 3078 (2007).

43. Declaration of Stephen Abraham, Lieutenant Colonel, United States Army Reserve, June 15, 2007 (Abraham Declaration, June 15, 2007); Declaration of Stephen Abraham, Lieutenant Colonel, United States Army Reserve, November 9, 2007 (Abraham Declaration, November 9, 2007).

44. Declaration of William J. Teesdale, Esq., filed in *Hamad v. Bush,* No. 95-1009 (JDB) (D.D.C.) (Teesdale Declaration). The declaration was incorporated into the body of a sworn statement by an investigator for a public defender representing a Guantánamo detainee. The statement corroborated many of Abraham's assertions.

45. Abraham Declaration, November 9, 2007, ¶ 45.

46. Ibid, ¶ 47.

47. Ibid., ¶ 48.

48. Abraham Declaration, June 15, 2007, ¶ 22.

49. Teesdale Declaration, at 8.

50. Abraham Declaration, June 15, 2007, ¶ 23.

51. *Boumediene v. Bush*, 128 S. Ct. 2229 (2008).

52. Ibid., 2244.

53. Ibid., 2246.

54. Ibid., 2253.

55. Ibid., 2254–55 (italics added).

56. Ibid., 2255.

57. 354 U.S. 1 (1957).

58. *Boumediene*, 128 S. Ct. at 2257.

59. Ibid., 2259.

60. Ibid.

61. Ibid.

62. Ibid., 2261.

63. Ibid., 2262–64.

64. *United States v. Hayman*, 342 U.S. 205 (1952); see also *Swain v. Pressley*, 430 U.S. 372 (1977).

65. *Boumediene*, 128 S. Ct. at 2270.

66. Ibid., 2269.

67. Ibid., 2279 (Roberts, C.J., dissenting).

68. Ibid., 2280–83.

69. Ibid., 2303–7 (Scalia, J., dissenting).

70. Ibid., 2298.

71. Ibid. (opinion of the Court).

72. Ibid.

73. *Al-Maqaleh v. Gates*, 604 F. Supp. 2d 205 (D.D.C. 2009).

74. Ibid., 223–24.

75. Ibid., 209.

76. Ibid., 226-27.

77. Ibid., 229–30.

78. *Al-Maqaleh v. Gates*, 605 F.3d 84 (D.C. Cir. 2010).

79. Ibid., 95–96

80. Ibid., 96–98

81. Ibid., 98–99

82. See Constitution of Afghanistan, article 27.

83. *Munaf v. Geren*, 128 S. Ct. 2207 (2008).

84. *Hirota v. MacArthur*, 338 U.S. 197, 198–99 (1948).

85. *Munaf*, 128 S. Ct. at 2217.

86. Ibid., 2220.

87. Ibid., 2221 (quoting *The Schooner Exchange v. McFaddon*, 11 U.S. (7 Cranch) 116 (1812)).

88. Ibid., 2220.

89. Ibid., 2227; see also, for example, *Valentine v. United States ex rel. Neidecker*, 299 U.S. 5 (1936).

90. *Munaf*, 128 S. Ct. at 2227–28.

91. Ibid., 2226.

92. Ibid., 2226, n. 6. See Foreign Affairs Reform and Restructuring Act of 1998 (FARR Act), Pub. L. No. 105–227, div. G., 112 Stat. 2681. The Court, however, noted—incorrectly—that Munaf and Omar had failed to raise claims under the FARR Act in their habeas petitions and so declined to address the act's application to their cases. Both men had, in fact, raised claims under the act, which implements the Convention against Torture and prohibits transfers to likely torture, and subsequently filed amended habeas corpus petitions in the district court seeking relief on that basis.

93. *Munaf*, 128 S. Ct. at 2228 (Souter, J., concurring).

94. *Kiyemba v. Obama*, 561 F.3d 509 (D.C. Cir. 2009).

95. Ibid., 525–26 (Griffith, J., dissenting).

96. *Kiyemba v. Obama*, No. 09-581, 78 U.S.L.W. 3302 (March 22, 2010).

CHAPTER 10

1. David B. Rivkin Jr. and Lee A. Casey, Opinion: "Lawfare," *Wall St. Journal*, February 23, 2007.

2. *Olmstead v. United States*, 277 U.S. 438, 479 (1928) (Brandeis, J., dissenting).

3. Gerald L. Neuman, "The Extraterritorial Constitution after *Boumediene v. Bush*," 82 *Southern California Law Review* 259, 261 (2009).

4. David D. Cole, "Rights over Borders: Transnational Constitutionalism and Guantanamo Bay," 2008 *Cato Supreme Court Review* 47, 52 (2008).

5. For a discussion of the disciplining role judicial review has played in the immigration context, see Adam B. Cox, "Deference, Delegation, and Immigration Law," 74 *University of Chicago Law Review* 1671 (2007).

6. 339 U.S. 763 (1953).

7. Judiciary Act of 1789, ch. 20, § 14, 1 Stat. 73, 82. The current version of the habeas provision from the 1789 act is codified at 28 U.S.C. § 2241(a).

8. U.S. Const., art I, § 9, cl. 2.

9. Act of July 6, 1798, ch. 66, 1 Stat. 577.

10. *Demore v. Kim*, 538 U.S. 510 (2003); *INS v. St. Cyr*, 533 U.S. 289 (2001); *Ludecke v Watkins*, 335 U.S. 160 (1948).

11. Tung Yin, "The Impact of the 9/11 Attacks on National Security Law Casebooks," 19 *St. Thomas Law Review* 157, 182 (2006).

12. In more nuanced descriptions, the Bush administration described it as a war against al Qaeda, the Taliban, and "associated" groups.

13. U.S. Const., art. I, § 8.

14. U.S. Const., art. II, cl. 2.

15. See Geneva Convention Relative to the Treatment of Prisoners of War, August 12, 1949, 6 U.S.T. 3316, 75 U.N.T.S. 135 (Third Geneva Convention); Fourth Geneva Convention Relative to the Protection of Civilian Persons in Time of War, August 12, 1949, 6 U.S.T. 3516 , 75 U.N.T.S. 287 (Fourth Geneva Convention); Protocol Additional to the Geneva Conventions of 12 August 1949, and Relating to the Protection of Victims of International Armed Conflicts, June 8, 1977, 1125 U.N.T.S. 3 (Additional Protocol I). The Additional Protocol is a 1977 treaty intended to reflect subsequent developments in the

law of armed conflict. While the United States has not ratified the Additional Protocol, a number of its provisions, including article 75, which delineates fair-trial rights, are binding on the United States as customary international law.

16. U.S. Const., art. I, cl. 11.

17. U.S. Const., art. II, cl.2.

18. Michael Bahar, "As Necessity Creates the Rule: *Eisentrager, Boumediene,* and the Enemy—How Strategic Realities Can Constitutionally Require Greater Rights for Detainees in the Wars of the Twenty-first Century," 11 *University of Pennsylvania Journal Constitutional Law* 277, 282–83 (2009).

19. Ibid., 283–84; *Bas v. Tingy,* 4 U.S. (4 Dall.) 37, 40 (1800).

20. Francis Lieber, War Department, Adjutant General's Office, General Orders No. 100: Instructions for the Government of Armies of the United States in the Field, art. 20 (1863), in *Lieber's Code and the Law of War,* ed. Richard Shelly Hartigan (Chicago: Precedent 1983).

21. Bahar, "As Necessity Creates the Rule," 286–88.

22. Ibid., 285; *The Brig Amy Warwick (The Prize Cases),* 67 U.S. (2 Black) 635, 666–67 (1863).

23. See International Committee of the Red Cross, *Commentary: Additional Protocols of 8 June 1977 to the Geneva Conventions of 12 August 1949,* ed. Claude Pilloud et al. (Geneva: International Committee of the Red Cross, 1987), 1332; Gabor Rona, "An Appraisal of U.S. Practice Relating to 'Enemy Combatants,'" 10 *Yearbook of International Humanitarian Law* 241 (2007).

24. Additional Protocol I, articles 45(3), 75(7)(b); International Covenant on Civil and Political Rights, art. 9, G.A. Res. 2200A (XXI), U.N. GAOR, 21st Sess., Supp. No. 16 U.N. Doc. A/6316 (1966) (ICCPR); Rona, "An Appraisal of U.S. Practice," 240–43; Legality of the Threat or Use of Nuclear Weapons, Advisory Opinion, 1996 I.C.J. 240 (July 8). See also Sean D. Murphy, "Evolving Geneva Convention Paradigms in the 'War on Terrorism': Applying the Core Rules to the Release of Persons Deemed 'Unprivileged Combatants,'" 75 *George Washington Law Review* 1105, 1132–35 (2007).

25. See Third Geneva Convention, art. 118; Fourth Geneva Convention, arts. 132–35. Civilians interned under the Fourth Geneva Convention may continue to be held only for the duration of penal proceedings for offenses committed during the conflict and for any sentenced imposed following those proceedings or for the duration of any previously imposed sentence.

26. See Jelena Pejic, "Procedural Principles and Safeguards for Internment/Administrative Detention in Armed Conflict and Other Situations of Violence," 87 *International Review of the Red Cross* 375, 384–90 (2005).

27. Murphy, "Evolving Geneva Convention Paradigms," 1108–9; Richard R. Baxter, "So-Called 'Unprivileged Belligerency': Spies, Guerrillas, and Saboteurs," 28 *British Year Book of International Law* 324, 328 (1951); Jason Callen, "Unlawful Combatants and the Geneva Convention," 44 *Virginia Journal of International Law* 1025–26 (2004).

28. Francis Lieber, "Guerrilla Parties Considered with Reference to the Laws and Usages of War," (1861), reprinted in Hartigan, *Lieber's Code and the Law of War,* 45; Murphy, "Evolving Geneva Convention Paradigms," 1108–9.

29. Fourth Geneva Convention, art. 5. Unprivileged belligerency is not, however, a crime itself under international law.

30. David L. Franklin, "Enemy Combatants and the Jurisdictional Fact Doctrine," 29 *Cardozo Law Review* 1001, 1032 (2008).

31. Rosa Ehrenreich Brooks, "War Everywhere: Rights, National Security Law, and the Law of Armed Conflict in the Age of Terror," 153 *University of Pennsylvania Law Review* 675, 729 (2004).

32. Rona, "An Appraisal of U.S. Practice," 240.

33. See Public Committee against Torture in *Israel v. Israel* (2006), HCJ 769/02, 13 December 2006.

34. In May 2009, the ICRC issued a report suggesting that organized armed groups belonging to a party to the conflict could—like the members of a state's army—be legitimate targets of military action, thus broadening the traditional understanding about who could be targeted during hostilities. This standard, however, does not alter the international rules governing detention. See International Committee of the Red Cross, *Interpretive Guidance on the Notion of Direct Participation in Hostilities* (2009).

35. Derek Jinks, "The Declining Significance of POW Status," 45 *Harvard International Law Journal* 367, 406–9 (2004).

36. See, for example, *Ex Parte Milligan*, 71 U.S. (4 Wall.) 2 (1866).

37. U.S. Department of the Army, Enemy Prisoners of War, Retained Personnel, Civilian Internees and other Detainees, § 1-6e; ibid., § 2-1a(1)(d). See also Third Geneva Convention, art. 5.

38. Human Rights First, "Fixing Bagram: Strengthening Detention Reforms That Align with U.S. Strategic Priorities," November 2009, at 1–2. A U.S. habeas court should still, however, be able to review the transfer of detainees to Afghan custody to ensure that the transfer complies with applicable legal requirements, including the Convention against Torture.

39. Bahar, "As Necessity Creates the Rule," 278.

40. U.S. Army–Marine Corps, *Counterinsurgency Field Manual*, para. I-132 (Chicago: University of Chicago Press, 2007).

41. *Boumediene v. Bush*, 128 S. Ct. 2229, 2277 (2008).

CHAPTER 11

1. 28 U.S.C. § 2241(c).

2. Joanne Mariner, "We'll Make You See Death," Salon.com, June 4, 2008.

3. William Blackstone, *Commentaries on the Laws of England*, vol. 1 (1765), 131.

4. *Jones v. Cunningham*, 371 U.S. 236, 243 (1963); *Abu Ali v. Ashcroft*, 350 F. Supp. 2d 28, 45–51 (D.D.C. 2004).

5. Act of September 24, 1789, ch. 20, § 14, 1 Stat. 82 (currently codified at 28 U.S.C. § 2241 (c)(1)); *Abu Ali*, 350 F. Supp. 2d at 46.

6. Act of February 5, 1867, ch. 28, § 1, 14 Stat. 385 (currently codified at 28 U.S.C. § 2241 (c)(3)); *Abu Ali*, 350 F. Supp. 2d at 47–48. See also *Ex parte McCardle*, 73 U.S. (6 Wall.) 318, 325–26 (1867).

7. *Hensley v. Municipal Court*, 411 U.S. 345, 350 (1973).

8. *Justices of Boston Municipal Ct. v. Lydon*, 466 U.S. 294, 300 (1984); *Galaviz-Medina v. Wooten*, 27 F.3d 487, 492 (10th Cir. 1994).

9. *Braden v. 30th Judicial Circuit Court of Ky.*, 410 U.S. 484 (1973).

10. *Galaviz-Medina*, 27 F.3d at 493.

11. *Jones*, 371 U.S. at 242–43.

12. Ibid., 239; *United States v. Jung Ah Lung*, 124 U.S. 621, 626 (1888).

13. *Abu Ali*, 350 F. Supp. 2d at 47–49 (summarizing cases).

14. See Habeas Corpus Act of 1679, 31 Car. 2, c. 2.

15. International Covenant on Civil and Political Rights (ICCPR), art. 9, G.A. Res. 2200A (XXI), U.N. GAOR, 21st Sess., Supp. no. 16 U.N. Doc. A/6316 (1966).

16. U.N. Human Rights Comm., *General Comment no. 20*, ¶ 9, U.N. Doc., A/47/40 (1992), reprinted in *Compilation of General Comments and Recommendations Adopted by Human Rights Treaty Bodies*, at 31, U.N. Doc. HR1/GEN/1/Rev.1 (July 29, 1994).

17. Convention against Torture and Other Cruel, Inhuman or Degrading Treatment or Punishment arts. 2, 3, December 10, 1984, S. Treaty Doc. No. 100-20 (1988), 1465 U.N.T.S. 85.

18. U.S. Reservations, Declarations and Understandings, ICCPR, 138 Cong. Rec. S4781-01 (daily ed., April 2, 1992).

19. *Cornejo-Barreto v. Seifert*, 218 F.3d 1004 (9th Cir. 2000).

20. As the Supreme Court has explained, "An act of Congress ought never to be construed to violate the law of nations if any other possible construction remains." *Murray v. The Schooner Charming Betsy*, 6 U.S. (2 Cranch) 64, 118 (1804).

21. Foreign Affairs Reform and Restructuring Act of 1998, Pub. L. No. 105-277, § 2242, 112 Stat. 2681; Margaret L. Satterthwaite, "Rendered Meaningless: Extraordinary Rendition and the Rule of Law," 75 *George Washington Law Review* 1333, 1365–66 (2007).

22. Satterthwaite, "Rendered Meaningless," 1381–82; U.N. Human Rights Comm., *Concluding Observations of the Human Rights Committee: United States of America*, ¶ 16, U.N. Doc. CCPR/C/USA/CO/3/Rev.1 (December 18, 2006); U.N. Comm. against Torture, *Conclusions and Recommendations of the Committee against Torture: United States of America* ¶ 21, U.N. Doc. CAT/C/USA/CO/2 (May 18, 2006).

23. U.N. Comm. against Torture, *Conclusions and Recommendations* ¶ 21; Satterthwaite, "Rendered Meaningless," 1385.

24. Satterthwaite, "Rendered Meaningless," 1359–69.

25. Ibid., 1363–64; U.N. Human Rights Comm., *Communication No. R.12/52: Burgos v. Uruguay*, ¶ 12.3, at 176, Supp. No. 40, U.N. Doc. A/36/40 (1981).

26. J. Herman Burgers and Hans Danelius, *The United Nations Convention against Torture: A Handbook on the Convention against Torture and Other Cruel, Inhuman or Degrading Treatment or Punishment* (Boston: Martinus Nijoff, 1988), 126 (italics added).

27. *Ocalan v. Turkey*, 41 Eur. H.R. Rep. 985, 1018 (2005).

28. *Coard v. United States*, Case 10.591, Inter-Am. C.H.R., Report No.109/99, OEA/Ser.L./V/II.106, doc. 6 rev., ¶ 37 (1999).

29. *Abu Ali*, 350 F. Supp. 2d at 31–32.

30. Ibid., 32.

31. Ibid., 32–33.

32. Ibid., 37.

33. Ibid., 32–36.

34. Ibid., 36.

35. Ibid., 38–39.

36. Ibid., 67–69.

37. Although the trial court sentenced Abu Ali to thirty years in prison, the court of appeals ruled that the sentence should be life imprisonment. See *United States v. Abu Ali,* 528 F.3d 210 (4th Cir. 2008); David Stout, "American Is Sentenced to 30 Years in Terror Case," *New York Times,* March 30, 2006.

38. For a critique of the court's admission of these statements, see, for example, Jon Sawyer, "Abu Ali Case Shows U.S. Outsourcing Dirty Work, Some Say," *St. Louis Post-Dispatch,* December 4, 2005.

39. Human Rights Watch, "Ghost Prisoner: Two Years in Secret CIA Detention" (New York: Human Rights Watch, February 2007), 2–3.

40. I, along with Victor J. Rocco, represented Amir Meshal's family in its effort to secure his freedom from detention in the Horn of Africa. I also am one of the attorneys representing Meshal in a suit filed by the American Civil Liberties Union seeking damages against four U.S. officials for their role in Meshal's detention, rendition, and abusive interrogation. See *Meshal v. Higgenbotham et al.,* No. 09-2178 (D.D.C.) (EGS).

41. The four other detainees from Meshal's rendition flight from Kenya to Somalia, all of whom were British citizens, were handed over to U.K. authorities in Somalia and returned to England.

42. Paul Salopek, "Renditions Fuel Anger against U.S.," *Chicago Tribune,* December 4, 2008.

43. Ibid.

44. *Mallouk v. Bush et al.,* Petition for Writ of Habeas Corpus, No. 08-cv-2003 (D.D.C.) (JR) (dkt. no. 1); *Mallouk v. Obama et al.,* Petitioners' Response to Motion to Dismiss, No. 08-cv-2003 (D.D.C.) (JR) (dkt. no. 21); Jonathan S. Landay, "Did U.S. Push Detention of American without Charges," *McClatchy Newspapers,* November 17, 2008.

45. *Mallouk v. Obama,* Civ. No. 08-2003 (D.D.C.) (JR) (dkt. no. 28).

46. U.S. Embassy, Kabul, Afghanistan, "Detainee Transfers to Afghanistan," press release, August 4, 2005.

47. Tim Golden, "Foiling U.S. Plans, Prison Expands in Afghanistan," *New York Times,* January 18, 2008; "U.S. Eyes Afghan Jail for Some Gitmo Detainees," MSNBC.com, June 22, 2007.

48. Golden, "Foiling U.S. Plans."

49. Tim Golden and Eric Schmitt, "A Growing Afghan Prison Rivals Bleak Guantánamo," *New York Times,* February 26, 2006.

50. Human Rights First, "Arbitrary Justice: Trials of Bagram and Guantánamo Detainees in Afghanistan" (Washington, DC: Human Rights First, April 2008), ii, 3.

51. Ibid., 7.

52. Ibid., 5.

53. Ibid., iii, 2.

54. Information from Mr. Ahadullah Azimi ¶ 19, *Ruzatullah v. Gates,* No. 06-1707 (D.D.C.) (GK).

55. Joe Palazzolo, "The New Gitmo: The Latest Legal Showdown over Detainee Rights," *Legal Times,* November 2, 2007.

56. Compare *El-Masri v. Tenet,* 479 F.3d 296 (4th Cir. 2007) (upholding invocation of state secrets privilege and dismissing lawsuit by rendition victim Khaled El-Masri), with *Mohammed v. Jeppesen Dataplan,* 563 F.3d 992 (9th Cir. 2009) (rejecting invocation of state secrets privilege in a challenge brought by victims of the CIA rendition program), *pet'n for rehearing en banc granted,* 586 F.3d 1108 (9th Cir. 2009).

57. See *Harlow v. Fitzgerald*, 457 U.S. 800 (1982). This defense, for example, has been successfully invoked to bar damage suits by former Guantánamo detainees for abuses they suffered. See *Rasul v. Myers*, 563 F.3d 527 (D.C. Cir. 2009).

58. See, for example, *Saint Fort v. Ashcroft*, 329 F.3d 191, 202 (1st Cir. 2003); *Ogbudimkpa v. Ashcroft*, 342 F.3d 207, 220 (3d Cir. 2003); *Wang v. Ashcroft*, 320 F.3d 130, 141 n.16 (2d Cir. 2003).

59. The most infamous case involving the Japanese internments, *Korematsu v. United States*, 323 U.S. 214 (1944), was technically not a habeas corpus case but the direct appeal of a criminal conviction. However, the point holds: that court review alone—whether through habeas or some other means—does not ensure a correct or just outcome.

CHAPTER 12

1. *Al-Marri v. Wright*, 487 F.3d 160 (4th Cir. 2007).

2. *Al-Marri v. Pucciarelli*, 534 F.3d 213, 216–17 (4th Cir. 2008).

3. Ibid., 217–76 (Motz, J., concurring in part, dissenting in part).

4. Ibid., 231.

5. Ibid., 240–41, 248–49; see Uniting and Strengthening America by Providing Appropriate Tools Required to Intercept and Obstruct Terrorism Act of 2001, Pub. L. No. 107-56, 115 Stat. 272 (Patriot Act).

6. *Al-Marri v. Pucciarelli*, 534 F.3d at 252 (Motz, J., concurring in part, dissenting in part).

7. Ibid., 252–53.

8. Ibid., 293, 296 (Wilkinson, J., concurring in part, dissenting in part).

9. Ibid., 293.

10. Ibid., 319.

11. Ibid., 308–9.

12. Ibid., 308.

13. Transcript of Sentencing Proceedings at 33, *United States v. Ressam*, No. 99-cr-666 (W.D. Wash. July 27, 2005).

14. Hal Brenton and Sara Jean Green, "Ressam Judge Decries U.S. Tactics," *Seattle Times*, July 28, 2005.

15. See, for example, David B. Rivkin Jr. and Lee A. Casey, Op-ed: "Impunity for al-Qaeda: The Implications of a Bad Ruling on 'Unlawful Enemy Combatants,'" *Washington Post*, July 2, 2007.

16. Tom Malinowski, Op-ed: "When Terrorists Become 'Warriors,'" *Washington Post*, March 18, 2007.

17. U.S. Department of Defense, "Verbatim (Unclassified) Transcript of Combatant Status Review Tribunal Hearing for ISN 10024," at 23 (March 10, 2007).

18. "Reid: 'I Am at War with Your Country,'" CNN.com, January 31, 2003.

19. Wesley K. Clark and Kal Raustiala, Op-ed: "Why Terrorists Aren't Soldiers," *New York Times*, August 8, 2007.

20. Peter Finn, "Guantanamo Jury Sentences Bin Laden Aide to Life Term," *Washington Post*, November 4, 2008. Hicks was the dupe, Hamdan the driver, and al-Bahlul the default since he did not defend himself.

21. Military Commissions Act of 2006, Pub. L. No. 109-366, § 949b(a)(2)(C), 120 Stat. 2609 (2006).

22. Ruling on Motion to Dismiss (Unlawful Influence), *United States v. Hamdan*, May 9, 2008; Josh White, "From Chief Prosecutor to Critic at Guantanamo," *Washington Post*, April 29, 2008.

23. *Hamdan v. Rumsfeld*, 548 U.S. 557, 632–33 (2006).

24. Gabor Rona, "Military Commissions: The Golden Rule and the Laws of War," 31 *American Bar Association National Security Law Report* (July/October 2009).

25. Ruling on Motion to Dismiss (Unlawful Influence), *United States v. Hamdan*.

26. Ruling on Defense Motion to Suppress Out-of-Court Statements of the Accused to Afghan Authorities, *United States v. Jawad*, October 28, 2008.

27. Morris D. Davis, Op-ed: "AWOL Military Justice: Why the former Chief Prosecutor for the Office of Military Commissions Resigned His Post," *Los Angeles Times*, December 10, 2007.

28. Declaration of Lieutenant Colonel Darrel J. Vandeveld, para. 7, *United States v. Mohammed Jawad*, September 22, 2008; Stacy Sullivan, "Confessions of a Former Guantánamo Prosecutor: The Inside Story of a Military Lawyer Who Discovered Stunning Injustice at the Heart of the Bush Administration's Military Commissions," Salon.com, October 23, 2008.

29. William Glaberson, "Guantánamo Memo: In Detainee Trial, System Is Tested," *New York Times*, July 29, 2008.

30. Robert Chesney and Jack L. Goldsmith, "Terrorism and the Convergence of Criminal and Military Detention Models," 60 *Stanford Law Review* 1081, 1081 (2008).

31. Ibid., 1120.

32. Jack L. Goldsmith and Neal Katyal, Op-ed: "The Terrorists' Court," *New York Times*, July 11, 2007.

33. Kenneth Roth, "After Guantánamo: The Case against Preventive Detention," *Foreign Affairs*, May/June 2008, at 9, 12.

34. Andrew C. McCarthy and Alykhan Velshi, "We Need a National Security Court," *American Enterprise Institute for Public Policy Research* (2006).

35. Michael B. Mukasey, Op-ed: "Jose Padilla Makes Bad Law," *Wall Street Journal*, August 22, 2007.

36. McCarthy and Velshi, "We Need a National Security Court." For a similar proposal, see Amos N. Guiora and John T. Parry, Debate: "Light at the End of the Pipeline? Choosing a Forum for Suspected Terrorists," 156 *University of Pennsylvania Law Review* PENNumbra 356, 361 (2008) (position of Amos N. Guiora).

37. McCarthy and Velshi, "We Need a National Security Court," 36.

38. Benjamin Wittes, *Law and the Long War: The Future of Justice in the Age of Terror* (New York: Penguin, 2008).

39. Ibid., 128.

40. Ibid., 151–82.

41. Ibid., 124.

42. The Goldsmith-Katyal proposal is an exception, as it would apply to all persons, regardless of citizenship.

43. McCarthy and Velshi, "We Need a National Security Court," 13.

44. Wittes, *Law and the Long War*, 174.

45. Neal Katyal, "Equality in the War on Terror," 59 *Stanford Law Review* 1365 (2007); The Constitution Project, "A Critique of 'National Security Courts': A Report by the Constitution Project's Liberty and Security Committee and Coalition to Defend Checks and Balances," June 2008, at 3 and n. 6.

46. See David Cole, "Closing Guantánamo: The Problem of Preventive Detention," *Boston Review*, January/February 2009; David Cole, "Out of the Shadows: Preventive Detention, Suspected Terrorists, and War," 97 *California Law Review* 693 (2009).

47. Cole, "Out of the Shadows," 740.

48. Ibid., 711.

49. See, for example, McCarthy and Velshi, "We Need a National Security Court."

50. Richard B. Zabel and James J. Benjamin Jr., *In Pursuit of Justice: Prosecuting Terrorism Cases in the Federal Courts* (New York: Human Rights First, May 2008), 31.

51. Kelly Moore, Symposium: "The Role of Federal Criminal Prosecutions in the War on Terrorism," 11 *Lewis & Clark Law Review* 837, 838–39 (2007).

52. H.R. Rep. No. 104-383.

53. 18 U.S.C. § 2339A; Robert M. Chesney, "The Sleeper Scenario: Terrorism-Support Laws and the Demands of Prevention," 42 *Harvard Journal on Legislation* 1, 12 (2005).

54. The definition of material support was added in 1996. 18 U.S.C. § 2339A(b), as amended by Pub. L. No. 105-458, § 6603(b), (g), Pub. L. No. 107-56, § 805(a)(2), and Pub. L. No. 104-132, § 323.

55. 18 U.S.C. § 2339B.

56. 18 U.S.C. § 2339B(a)(1); *Holder v. Humanitarian Law Project*, 130 S. Ct. 2705 (2010).

57. 18 U.S.C. §§ 2339C, 2339D.

58. See generally Alexander J. Urbelis, "Rethinking Extraterritorial Prosecution in the War on Terror: Examining the Unintentional Yet Foreseeable Consequences of Extraterritorially Criminalizing the Provision of Material Support to Terrorists and Foreign Terrorist Organizations," 22 *Connecticut Journal of International Law* 313, 315-19 (2007).

59. Zabel and Benjamin, *In Pursuit of Justice*, 33.

60. Ibid., 33–38.

61. Ibid., 35.

62. Ibid., 36.

63. 18 U.S.C. § 2384.

64. *United States v. Rodriguez*, 803 F.2d 318, 320 (7th Cir. 1986).

65. *United States v. Rahman*, 189 F.3d 88 (2d Cir. 1999).

66. Zabel and Benjamin, *In Pursuit of Justice*, 55.

67. Ibid, 51–54.

68. U.S. Department of Justice, Counterterrorism Section, *Counterterrorism White Paper* 29 (2006).

69. 18 U.S.C. § 3142.

70. 8 U.S.C. § 1226. See also *Demore v. Kim*, 538 U.S. 510 (2003).

71. Pub. L. No. 96-456, 94 Stat. 2025, 2025-31 (1980) (codified at 18 U.S.C. app. 3) (CIPA).

72. Serrin Turner and Stephen J. Schulhofer, *The Secrecy Problem in Terrorism Trials* (New York: Brennan Center for Justice, New York University School of Law, 2005), 22–25.

73. Ibid., 19–20.

74. 18 U.S.C. app. § 6(c).

75. Turner and Schulhofer, *The Secrecy Problem in Terrorism Trials*, 20–22.

76. Ibid., 25–27; Ellen C. Yaroshefsky, "The Slow Erosion of the Adversary System: Article III Courts, FISA, CIPA, and Ethical Dilemmas," 5 *Cardozo Public Law Policy & Ethics Journal* 203, 205 (2006).

77. 18 U.S.C. app. § 4.

78. Turner and Schulhofer, *The Secrecy Problem in Terrorism Trials*, 25.

79. McCarthy and Velshi, "We Need a National Security Court"; Mukasey, "Jose Padilla Makes Bad Law."

80. Zabel and Benjamin, *In Pursuit of Justice*, 88.

81. Mukasey, "Jose Padilla Makes Bad Law." Mukasey mistakenly asserts that the phone records were introduced in Ramzi Yousef's trial for the 1993 World Trade Center bombing, rather than in the 1998 embassy bombings case.

82. Zabel and Benjamin, *In Pursuit of Justice*, 88–89.

83. Donald H. Rumsfeld and Paul Wolfowitz, Prepared Statement: U.S. Senate Armed Services Committee "Military Commissions" (December 12, 2001).

84. Spencer J. Crona and Neal A. Richardson, "Justice for War Criminals of Invisible Armies: A New Legal and Military Approach to Terrorism," 21 *Oklahoma City University Law Review* 349, 382 (1996).

85. Federal Rule of Evidence 902.

86. Federal Rule of Evidence 901(a).

87. Zabel and Benjamin, *In Pursuit of Justice*, 108; Adam Liptak, "Padilla Case Offers New Model of Terrorism Trial," *New York Times*, August 18, 2007.

88. Zabel and Benjamin, *In Pursuit of Justice*, 109.

89. Federal Rule of Evidence 804(b)(3) (exception for statement against interest); Federal Rule of Evidence 801(d)(2)(E) (exception for statement of co-conspirator).

90. See, for example, Guiora and Parry, Debate: "Light at the End of the Pipeline?" 359.

91. *United States v. Moussaoui*, No. CR. 01-455-A, 2002 WL 1987964 (E.D. Va. August 23, 2002).

92. One proposed reform would be to establish a permanent national security bar consisting of lawyers with the highest level of security clearance and to modify the rules for handling classified information. See Robert S. Litt and Wells C. Bennett, "Better Rules for Terrorism Trials," a working paper of the Series on Counterterrorism and American Statutory Law, a joint project of the Brookings Institution, the Georgetown University Law Center, and the Hoover Institution (May 2009).

93. William Glaberson, "Detainees, as Lawyers, Test System of Tribunals," *New York Times*, July 11, 2008.

94. *United States v. Moussaoui*, 382 F.3d 453 (4th Cir. 2004).

95. *Miranda v. Arizona*, 384 U.S. 436 (1966).

96. *Dickerson v. United States*, 530 U.S. 428, 443 (2000).

97. *United States v. Bin Laden*, 132 F. Supp. 2d 168 (S.D.N.Y. 2001) (applying *Miranda* when U.S. officials questioned a terrorism suspect apprehended and detained in Kenya); *United States v. Abu Ali*, 528 F.3d 210, 227-30 (4th Cir. 2008) (recognizing that *Miranda* applies to the questioning of detainees in foreign custody by U.S officials when those officials are sufficiently involved in the coordination and direction of the investigation such that it constitutes a "joint venture").

98. Zabel and Benjamin, *In Pursuit of Justice*, 103–5.

99. *Quarles v. New York*, 467 U.S. 649 (1984).

100. *In re Terrorist Bombings of U.S. Embassies in East Africa* (Fourth Amendment Challenges), 552 F.3d 157 (2d Cir. 2008); *In re Terrorist Bombings of U.S. Embassies in East Africa* (Fifth Amendment Challenges), 552 F.3d 177 (2d Cir. 2008). The defendants raised other issues as well. *In re Terrorist Bombings of U.S. Embassies in East Africa* 552 F.3d 93 (2d Cir. 2008).

101. Zabel and Benjamin, *In Pursuit of Justice*, 115–20.

102. U.S.S.G. § 3E1.1.

103. Ibid., § 5K1.1.

104. See, for example, ibid., § 3A1.4 (terrorism enhancement).

105. Moore, Symposium: "The Role of Federal Criminal Prosecutions," 847.

106. U.S. Department of Justice, "Preserving Life and Liberty: The Record of the U.S. Department of Justice, 2001–2005."

107. Zabel and Benjamin, *In Pursuit of Justice*, 118–19.

108. Deborah N. Pearlstein, "We're All Experts Now: A Security Case against Security Detention," 40 *Case Western Reserve Journal of International Law* 577, 584–85 (2009).

109. Moore, Symposium: "The Role of Federal Criminal Prosecutions," 848.

110. Daniel Benjamin and Steven Simon, *The Age of Sacred Terror: Radical Islam's War against America* (New York: Random House, 2003), xii–xiii.

111. Moore, "The Role of Federal Criminal Prosecutions," 847.

112. Roth, "After Guantánamo," 16.

113. Zabel and Benjamin, *In Pursuit of Justice*, 118.

114. Darius Rejali, Op-ed: "5 Myths about Torture and Truth," *Washington Post*, December 16, 2007.

115. Scott Shane, "Interrogations' Effectiveness May Prove Elusive," *New York Times*, April 22, 2009.

116. Daphne Eviatar, "OLC Torture Memos Were Based on Faulty Assumptions," *Washington Independent*, April 20, 2009.

117. Intelligence Science Board, *Educing Information: Interrogation: Science and Art; Foundations for the Future* (Washington, DC: National Defense Intelligence College Press, 2006); Scott Shane and Mark Mazzetti, "Advisers Fault Harsh Methods in Interrogation," *New York Times*, May 30, 2007.

118. Letter from David H. Petraeus to Soldiers, Sailors, Airmen, Marines, and Coast Guardsmen Serving in Multi-National Force–Iraq, May 10, 2007.

119. See Memorandum for John A. Rizzo, Senior Deputy General Counsel, Central Intelligence Agency, from Steven G. Bradbury, Principal Deputy Assistant Attorney General, Office of Legal Counsel, Re: "Application of United States Obligations under Article 16 of the Convention against Torture to Certain Techniques That May Be Used in the Interrogation of High Value al Qaeda Detainees," May 30, 2005 (May 30, 2005, OLC Convention against Torture Memo); David Johnston, "At a Secret Interrogation, Dispute Flared over Tactics," *New York Times*, September 10, 2006; James Risen, *State of War: The Secret History of the CIA and the Bush Administration* (New York: Free Press, 2006), 22–23; Ron Suskind, *The One Percent Doctrine: Deep inside America's Pursuit of Its Enemies since 9/11* (New York: Simon & Schuster, 2006), 115; Brian Ross and Richard Esposito, "Sources Tell ABC News Top al Qaeda Figures Held in Secret CIA Prisons," *ABC News*, December 5, 2005.

120. May 30, 2005, OLC Convention against Torture Memo, 37; Ali H. Soufan, Op-ed: "What Torture Never Told Us," *New York Times*, September 6, 2009.

121. Jane Mayer, *The Dark Side: The Inside Story of How the War on Terror Turned into a War on American Ideals* (New York: Doubleday, 2008), 156.

122. May 30, 2005, OLC Convention against Torture Memo, 31, n. 28; Spencer Ackerman, "James Mitchell Asked, 'Please Can I Torture Abu Zubaydah?'; Did Alberto Gonzales Say Yes?" *Washington Independent*, May 20, 2009.

123. Johnston, "At a Secret Interrogation"; Katherine Eban, "Rorschach and Awe," *Vanity Fair*, July 17, 2007. The FBI interrogations also were credited with providing the lead about Jose Padilla.

124. Mayer, *The Dark Side*, 155–56.

125. Peter Finn and Joby Warrick, "Detainee's Harsh Treatment Foiled No Plots; Waterboarding, Rough Interrogation of Abu Zubaida Produced False Leads, Officials Said," *Washington Post*, March 29, 2009; Scott Shane, "Divisions Arose on Rough Tactics for Qaeda Figure," *New York Times*, April 18, 2009.

126. Jason Leopold, "US Recants Claim on 'High Value' Detainee Abu Zubaydah," *Truthout*, March 30, 2010.

127. Finn and Warrick, "Detainee's Harsh Treatment Foiled No Plots."

128. Statement of Ali Soufan to the U.S. Senate Committee on the Judiciary, May 13, 2009; Bobby Ghosh, "After Waterboarding: How to Make Terrorists Talk," *Time*, June 8, 2009.

129. Matthew Alexander, *How to Break a Terrorist: The U.S. Interrogators Who Used Brains, Not Brutality, to Take Down the Deadliest Man in Iraq* (New York: Free Press, 2008).

130. Ghosh, "After Waterboarding."

131. Soufan, Op-ed: "What Torture Never Told Us."

132. Jane Mayer, "Outsourcing Torture," *New Yorker*, February 14, 2005.

133. Darius Rejali, *Torture and Democracy* (Princeton, NJ: Princeton University Press, 2007), 504; Mayer, *The Dark Side*, 105.

134. Mayer, *The Dark Side*, 105.

135. Ibid., 106.

136. Ibid.

137. Ibid., 135.

138. Stephen Grey, "CIA Rendition: The Smoking Gun Cable," *ABC News*, November 6, 2007; Michael Isikoff and Mark Hosenball, "Al-Libi's Tall Tales," *Newsweek*, November 10, 2005; Dana Priest, "Al Qaeda–Iraq Link Recanted," *Washington Post*, August 1, 2004.

139. Grey, "CIA Rendition: The Smoking Gun Cable."

140. Ibid.; Michael Isikoff and Mark Hosenball, "Terror Watch: Death in Libya," *Newsweek*, May 12, 2009.

141. Louise Richardson, *What Terrorists Want: Understanding the Enemy, Containing the Threat* (New York: Random House, 2006).

142. Lawrence Wright, *The Looming Tower: Al Qaeda and the Road to 9/11* (New York: Random House, 2006), 54–56.

143. Richardson, *What Terrorists Want*, 228–29.

144. "Guantanamo's Shadow," *Atlantic Monthly*, October 2007. See also Paula Reed Ward, "The Case against Torture; Ex-military Officers Take Argument to Presidential Hopefuls," *Pittsburgh Post-Gazette*, December 10, 2007; Matthew Alexander, Op-ed: "I'm Still Tortured by What I Saw in Iraq," *Washington Post*, November 30, 2008.

145. European Parliamentary Assembly, Committee on Legal Affairs and Human Rights, *Secret detentions and Illegal Transfers of Detainees Involving Council of Europe Member States: Second Report*, Doc. No. 11302 rev., para. 337 (June 11, 2007).

146. Josh Meyer, "U.S. Anti-Terror Role Criticized," *Los Angeles Times*, May 26, 2007.

147. John Burgess, "Court Frees Moroccan Convicted in 9/11 Case," *Washington Post*, April 8, 2004.

148. Meyer, "U.S. Anti-Terror Role Criticized."

149. National Commission on Terrorist Attacks upon the United States, *The 9/11 Commission Report* (2004), 379.

150. National Commission on Terrorist Attacks upon the United States, "Report on the Status of the 9/11 Commission Recommendations; Part III: Foreign Policy, Public Diplomacy, and Nonproliferation" (November 14, 2005), 8–9.

151. Senate Rep. No. 110-175, at 36 (2007) (Report of U.S. Senate Intelligence Committee for Intelligence Authorization Act for 2008).

CHAPTER 13

1. "Barack Obama's Inaugural Address," *New York Times*, January 20, 2009.

2. Executive Order, "Ensuring Lawful Interrogations," January 22, 2009.

3. Executive Order, "Review and Disposition of Individuals Detained at the Guantánamo Bay Naval Base and Closure of Detention Facilities," January 22, 2009.

4. Executive Order, "Review of Detention Policy Options," January 22, 2009.

5. *United States v. Al-Marri*, No. 99-CR-10030 (C.D. Ill. 2009).

6. *Al-Marri v. Spagone*, 129 S. Ct. 1545 (2009).

7. Carrie Johnson, "Judge Credits Time Served in Sentencing al-Qaeda Aide," *Washington Post*, October 30, 2009. The district judge gave al-Marri credit for the nearly six years he had spent in military custody as well as an additional reduction to reflect the harshness of his conditions during his first years of imprisonment at the navy brig.

8. See Respondents' Memorandum Regarding the Government's Detention Authority Relative to Detainees Held at Guantanamo Bay, *In re Guantanamo Bay Detainee Litigation*, Misc. No. 08-442 (D.D.C., filed March 13, 2009).

9. White House, Office of the Press Secretary, "Remarks by the President on National Security," May 21, 2009.

10. Ibid.

11. Ibid.

12. See *ACLU v. Dep't of Defense*, 543 F.3d 59 (2d Cir. 2008), *vacated and remanded by* 130 S. Ct. 777 (2009).

13. Memorandum for Heads of Executive Departments and Agencies; Memorandum for the Heads of Department Components, from the Attorney General, Re: "Policies and Procedures Governing Invocation of the State Secrets Privilege," September 23, 2009.

14. Charlie Savage, "Accused 9/11 Mastermind to Face Civilian Trial in N.Y.," *New York Times*, November 13, 2009.

15. National Defense Authorization Act for Fiscal Year 2010, Pub. L. No. 111-84, tit. XVIII, 123 Stat. 2191, 2572-2614 (2009). See also Jennifer K. Elsea, "Comparison of Rights in Military Commission Trials and Trials in Federal Criminal Court," Congressional Research Service, November 19, 2009.

16. Memorandum from the Detention Policy Task Forces to the Attorney General and the Secretary of Defense, July 20, 2009, Tab A ("Determination of Guantanamo Cases Referred for Prosecution").

17. *Gherebi v. Obama*, 609 F. Supp. 2d 43 (D.D.C. 2009).

18. *Hamlily v. Obama*, 616 F. Supp. 2d 63 (D.D.C. 2009) . The judge here did, however, find that "substantial support" was relevant to determining membership in al Qaeda, which would provide a basis for military detention.

19. *Al-Bihani v. Obama*, 590 F.3d 866, 871–72 (D.C. Cir. 2010).

20. William Glaberson, "Judge Declares Five Detainees Held Illegally," *New York Times*, November 21, 2008; William Glaberson, "Judge Opens First Habeas Corpus Hearing on Guantánamo Detainees," *New York Times*, November 6, 2008.

21. Transcript of Open Habeas Opinion Hearing, *Boumediene v. Bush*, Civ. No. 04-1166 (D.D.C.) (RJL), November 20, 2008, at 20.

22. Ibid., 28–29.

23. *Ahmed v. Obama*, 613 F. Supp. 2d 51 (D.D.C. 2009).

24. Ibid., 56.

25. Ibid.

26. Ibid., 57.

27. Ibid., 58.

28. Ibid., 64.

29. *Al Ginco v. Obama*, 626 F. Supp. 2d 123 (D.D.C. 2009).

30. Ibid., 127.

31. Ibid., 128–29.

32. Ibid.

33. Transcript of Hearing of July 16, 2009, at 6, *Al-Halmandy v. Obama* (Mohammed Jawad, ISN 900), No. 05-2385 (D.D.C.) (ESH). I represented Jawad in the habeas corpus challenge that secured his release, along with Jawad's military defense team.

34. Ibid., 7, 13.

35. Order of July 30, 2009, *Al-Halmandy v. Bush* (Mohammed Jawad, ISN 900), Civ. No. 05-2385 (D.D.C.) (ESH).

36. *Al Rabiah v. United States*, 658 F. Supp. 2d 11, 23 (D.D.C. 2009).

37. Ibid., 34.

38. Ibid., 32.

39. William Blackstone, *Commentaries on the Laws of England*, vol. 3 (1765–69), 133.

40. See, for example, *Al Ginco*, 626 F. Supp. 2d at 130; *Ahmed*, 613 F. Supp. 2d at 66. The order in Mohammed Jawad's case was an exception, directing the prisoner's release from Guantánamo.

41. Craig Whitlock, "82 Inmates Cleared but Still Held at Guantanamo," *Washington Post*, April 29, 2007, A1.

42. Edward Cody, "Ex-Detainee Describes Struggle for Exoneration; in France, Algerian Savors Normal Life," *Washington Post*, May 26, 2009.

43. *Parhat v. Gates*, 532 F.3d 834, 844 (D.C. Cir. 2008).

44. Transcript of Hearing, October 7, 2008, *Kiyemba v. Bush*, Civ. No. 05-1509 (D.D.C.) (RMU); William Glaberson, "In Blow to Bush, Judge Orders 17 Guantánamo Detainees Freed," *New York Times*, October 8, 2008.

45. *Kiyemba v. Obama*, 555 F.3d 1022 (D.C. Cir. 2009).

46. Erik Eckholm, "Out of Guantánamo, Uighurs Bask in Bermuda," *New York Times*, June 15, 2009; "Guantanamo Uighurs Sent to Palau," *BBC News*, October 31, 2009.

47. See Supplemental Appropriations Act of 2009, Pub. L. No. 111-32, 123 Stat. 1859, 1920–21 (2009).

48. *Kiyemba v. Obama*, 130 S. Ct. 1235 (2010).

49. Special Task Force on Interrogations and Transfer Policies Issues Its Recommendations to the President, U.S. Department of Justice, August 24, 2009.

50. *Kiyemba v. Obama*, 561 F.3d 509 (D.C. Cir. 2009), *cert. denied*, 78 U.S.L.W. 3302 (March 22, 2010).

51. Eric Schmitt, "U.S. to Expand Detainee Review in Afghan Prison," *New York Times*, September 13, 2009.

52. U.S. Department of Defense, Detainee Review Procedures at Bagram Theater Internment Facility (BTIF), Afghanistan, July 2, 2009.

53. Jonathan Horowitz, "New Detention Rules Show Promise and Problems," *Huffington Post*, April 20, 2010.

54. The Obama administration recently announced that some Bagram detainees would be charged and tried before Afghan judges in courts at the military base. While this represents a step forward, it is incomplete, as other detainees will continue to be held indefinitely without trial. In addition, early reports have raised questions about the fairness of the trials. See Heidi Vogt, "First Hearings Open for Afghans Detained by US," *Associated Press*, June 1, 2010.

55. Central Intelligence Agency, Inspector General, "Special Review: Counterterrorism Detention and Interrogation Activities (September 2001—October 2003)," May 7, 2004.

56. Ibid., 102.

57. Ibid., 42–43, 69–70.

58. Ibid., 42.

59. Ibid., 94.

60. R. Jeffrey Smith, "Two Administrations Drew Different Lessons from 2004 CIA Report," *Washington Post*, August 25, 2009; Scott Horton, No Comment, "Seven Points on the CIA Report," *Harper's*, August 25, 2009.

61. U.S. Department of Justice, "Statement of Attorney General Eric Holder Regarding a Preliminary Review into the Interrogation of Certain Detainees," August 24, 2009.

62. Carrie Johnson, Jerry Markon, and Julie Tate, "Inquiry into CIA Practices Narrows; Ex-Agency Directors Urge Administration to Drop Investigation," *Washington Post*, September 19, 2009.

63. Scott Shane and Benjamin Weiser, "U.S. Drops Plan for a 9/11 Trial in New York City," *New York Times*, January 30, 2010.

64. Matthew Alexander, Op-ed: "Torture's Loopholes," *New York Times*, January 21, 2010.

65. Alissa J. Rubin, "Afghans Detail Detention in 'Black Jail' at U.S. Base," *New York Times*, November 29, 2009.

66. Letter to Senators Patrick Leahy (D-VT) and Jeff Sessions (R-AL), from Ronald Weich, Assistant Attorney General, March 26, 2010.

67. Charlie Savage, "Bill Targets Citizenship of Terrorists' Allies," *New York Times*, May 6, 2010; David Cole, "Bar to Expatriate Those Who Support Terrorists More Symbol Than Substance," *Washington Post*, May 8, 2010.

68. Charlie Savage, "Holder Backs a Miranda Limit for Terrorism Suspects," *New York Times*, May 9, 2010.

Index

1951 UN Convention Relating to the Status of Refugees, 110
1998 U.S. Embassy bombings, 228

Abdulmutallab, Umar Farouk, 254–55
Abraham, Lt. Colonel Stephen, 157
Absconder Apprehension Initiative, 70
Abu Ghraib, 44, 63–66, 117, 142, 192, 234
Addington, David S., 12, 21, 27, 38
Administrative Review Board (ARB), 133, 157
Afghanistan, 12, 48; Afghanistan Human Rights Organization, 201; Afghan National Detention Facility (ANDF), 201; detentions in, 178 (*see also* Bagram Air Base; Geneva Conventions, 19, 36, 187; habeas corpus review for detainees captured in, 132, 166, 189; International Security Assistance Force, 189; mistreatment of detainees in, 44, 245; prisoners in, 28, 50, 201; U.S. invasion of, 15, 35
Agiza, Ahmed, 53–54
Ahmed, Ali, 244–45
Ahrens v. Clark, 96, 99, 119
Al-Bahlul, Ali Hamza, 211
Al-Ginco, Abdul Rahim, 37
Al-Kidd, Abdullah, 73
Al-Libi, Ibn al-Shaykh, 233–34
Al-Maqaleh v. Gates, 165–66, 167, 179
Al-Marri, Ali Saleh Kahlah, 73–78, 127, 205, 208, 219, 239
Al-Marri v. Pucciarelli, 187, 205–9, 239, 250
Al-Marri v. Wright, 205
Al-Nashiri, Abd al-Rahim, 252
Al-Odah v. United States, 117

al Qaeda, 11, 220, 259n1; application of Geneva Conventions to, 18–20, 21, 139, 184; detention of, 53, 218–19, 242; hunt for, 15, 52, 53. 119, 186; material support for, 185, 239; prosecution of, 16, 208, 218, 220
Al-Qahtani, Mohammed, 38, 39, 40, 132; torture of, 40, 42
Al-Rabiah, Fouad Mamoud, 247
Al-Rawi, Bisher, 34
Al-Shibh, Ramzi bin, 150
Al-Zarqawi, Abu Musab, 64, 233
Al-Zawahiri, Ayman, 234
Al-Zery, Muhammad, 53–54
Alexander, Matthew, 233
Ali, Ahmed Abu, 196–97, 200
Alien Enemies Act of 1798, 90, 96, 102, 153, 177
Alien Friends Act, 102, 104
Alito, Justice Samuel, 162
Allred, Captain Keith, 213
American Civil Liberties Union (ACLU), 42, 252
Amnesty International, 155
Arar, Maher, 54–55
Army Field Manual 34-52: Intelligence Interrogation, 39, 131, 238, 254
Army Regulation 190-8 (AR 190-8), 35–37, 78, 163
Ashcroft, John, 23, 47, 68, 75
Authorization for the Use of Military Force (AUMF), 11, 243; lower courts' interpretation of, 205–7, 243; Supreme Court's interpretation of, 123, 124–25, 126; U.S. government's interpretation of, 12, 220, 249

Bagram Air Base, 1, 254; conditions at, 49; differences from Guantanamo, 51, 179; habeas review for detentions at, 165–67, 189, 236; history of, 48–49, 50; mistreatment of detainees at, 39, 138, 245; under Obama administration, 251–52

Bail, denial of, 69–70, 222–23

Bail Reform Act of 1984, 222–23

Bates, Judge John D., 165–66, 196–97, 243

Beaver, Diane, 39

Behavioral Science Consultation Team (BSCT), 44

Bill of Rights, 68, 74, 106, 107, 108, 112, 125, 206, 207

Bin Laden, Osama, 11, 52, 224–25

Bismullah, Haji, 131

Black, Justice Hugo, 98, 106, 160

"black sites." See CIA

Blackstone, William, 82

Blair, Tony, 60

bond. See bail, denial

Bosnia, 34, 136, 145, 244

Boumediene, Lakhdar, 34, 248

Boumediene v. Bush, 5, 158–66, 169–71, 189, 197; effects of, 175–76, 188, 242, 243–44, 247–49; limitations of, 164–65, 171

Braden v. 30th Judicial Circuit Court of Kentucky, 119–20

Brandeis, Justice Louis, 175

Bremer, L. Paul. See Iraq

Brennan, Justice William J., Jr., 112

Breyer, Justice Stephen, 127, 146

Brosnahan, James, 14

Brown, Justice Henry Billings, 104

Brown, Senator Scott, 255

Bush, George, H. W., 51

Bush, George W.: authorization of CIA "black sites," 58; commander-in-chief power, 179; defense of interrogation policies, 25, 231–32; denial of process in Afghanistan, 187–88; DTA signing statement, 143–44; "enemy combatant" definition, 33–35, 47, 50 78, 15, 186; executive power, 26–27, 57; immigration detention after 9/11, 68–71; material witness detention after 9/11, 71–73; Military Commissions Act and, 153; national address of September 6, 2006, 150–51, 240; November 13, 2001 Order establishing military commissions, 16–18, 37; post-9/11 terrorism policy, 11–12, 14 ,18; result of, 236–37; scope of executive detention power, 187; steps to avoid judicial review, 27–28, 29–30, 133, 191, 255

Bybee, Jay S., 19, 21, 22, 25. See also Torture

Camp Bucca. See Iraq

Camp Cropper. See Iraq

Camp Delta, 31–33

Camp Nama. See Iraq

Camp No, 154

Camp X-Ray, 31, 40

Canada, 54

Cheney, Dick, 11, 23, 25, 27, 53, 212

Chertoff, Michael, 72

Chesney, Robert, 215

CIA, 19, 37, 53, 58; al Qaeda unit, 59; bin Laden unit, 52; 30, 48, 49; CIA Counter-Terrorism Center, 52; closure of secret prisons, 238, 254; interrogation of Abu Zubaydah, 22, 143–44, 232; Office of Inspector General report (2004), 252–53; rendition of terrorism suspects, 46–47, 51, 55–56, 235; secret prisons, 1, 22, 30, 39, 48, 49, 58, 59, 60, 150, 151, 153, 192; use of torture, 23, 38–39, 43, 233

Clark, Gen. Wesley, 211

classified evidence, 134, 202, 208, 244; legal procedures to protect, 216, 223–25; to conceal torture, 48, 72, 212; use in CSRT, 135, 137, 162; use of generally, 54, 70, 251

Classified Information Procedures Act (CIPA), 223–24, 227

Clement, Paul D., 117

Clinton, Bill, 12, 52

Cloonan, Jack, 233

Coalition Provisional Authority (CPA). See Iraq

Cole, David, 175, 218

Combatant Status Review Tribunal (CSRT), 130–45, 163; flaws, 130–35, 147, 156–58, 162, 230; procedures, 130–31
Committee against Torture, 195, 202
Common Article 3 of the Geneva Conventions. *See* Geneva Conventions
Consolidated Navy Brig in Charleston, South Carolina, 48, 74, 77, 205; conditions at, 76
constructive custody, 193, 196
Convention against Torture and other Cruel, Inhuman or Degrading Treatment or Punishment (CAT), 21, 56, 57, 143, 169, 194
Cooke, Judge Marcia G., 146
Coughenour, Judge John C., 209–10
criminal justice system, 211, 218; alternatives to, 214–20; applied to terrorism, 13, 147, 186, 209–11, 220–31, 236, 239–40; criticisms of, 208, 216–17, 220, 223, 224, 225, 229; intelligence-gathering value, 229–31

Dark Prison, 47, 245
Davis, Morris, 211, 213, 214
Defense Intelligence Agency (DIA), 75–76
Delahunty, Robert J., 18, 19
Department of Defense, 17; CSRTs and, 133, 157; torture policy, 24, 44, 212; use of extraordinary rendition, 6, 56, 202
Department of Homeland Security, 69, 202
Department of Interior, 108
Department of Justice, 25–26, 42, 153; criminal prosecution of terrorist suspects, 222, 230, 239; August 2006 memorandum re "Application of Detainee Treatment Act to Conditions of Confinement at CIA Detention Facilities," 151; Office of Legal Counsel (OLC), 12, 44; OLC September 25, 2001 memorandum (Yoo), 12; OLC October 23, 2001 memorandum (Yoo), 12–13; OLC December 28, 2001 memorandum (Yoo & Philbin), 29; OLC January, 9, 2002 memorandum (Yoo & Delahunty), 18–19. *See also* torture; torture memos

Detainee Treatment Act (DTA), 5, 140–44, 147, 149, 152–54, 156–58, 161, 162, 163, 177; Graham-Kyl-Levin Amendment to, 142, 147
Dilawar, 49
Dinh, Viet D., 36
diplomatic assurances, 57–58, 194, 251
Doumar, Judge Robert G., 122, 129
Downes v. Bidwell, 104
"Dred Scott case." See *Scott v. Sandford*
DuCastro's Case, 83
Dunlavey, Major General Michael, 37, 39

East India Company, 85
East Turkestan Islamic Movement (ETIM), 249
Edwards, Judge Harry T., 166
Egypt, 52, 53, 234; rendition to, 53, 55, 56, 137, 199, 233–34
El-Banna, Jamil, 34
El-Masri, Khaled, 58–59
Enemy Combatant Review Board (ECRB), 50
"enemy combatants," 18, 33, 61, 72–77, 175, 208, 218, 239, 243; access to U.S. courts, 141, 153, 179; in America, 68, 73, 144, 205; application of Geneva Conventions to, 57, 61; compared with "unprivileged belligerent," 186; contesting status as, 130, 133, 145–46; definition of, 34, 35, 50, 132, 136, 158, 163, 185–87, 206, 207; in Iraq, 170; president's authority to detain, 123, 125, 129; rights of, 148, 150
England, Gordon, 213
Ethiopia, secret jail in Addis Ababa, 199–200
European Court for Human Rights, 195
Ex parte Bollman, 86–88
Ex parte Milligan, 92–94, 141, 206
Ex parte Quirin, 94, 95, 100, 123, 141, 145, 182
extraordinary rendition, 48, 51–57, 60, 155, 192–94, 198, 203, 241; Bush administration defense of, 57; countries involved, 56; history of, 51–53; non-refoulement, 56

Federal Bureau of Investigation (FBI), 69, 72–73; concern about torture, 42, counterterrorism division, 69; interrogations, 40, 46, 232–33; use of proxy detention, 196, 199–200; use of material witness statute, 72; use of rendition, 51
Feingold, Senator Russ, 153
Field, Justice Stephen Johnson, 104
Fitzgerald, Patrick, 224
Five Knights (Darnel's) case, 81
Flanigan, Timothy E., 21
Foreign Affairs Reform and Restructuring Act, 169
Frankfurter, Justice Felix, 95, 107, 160
Fredman, Jonathan, 38–39
Freedom of Information Act (FOIA), 42, 136, 241, 252
Freeh, Louis J., 52
Fugitive Slave Act of 1850, 88

Gates, Robert M., 155
Geneva Conventions, 16, 20; application to "enemy combatants," 34, 57, 77, 118, 122, 139, 143, 163, 256; Common Article 3 of, 5, 16, 18 19, 139, 143, 147–48, 151, 152–53, 213, 238; enforceability by the courts, 135; Fourth Geneva Convention, 15, 62, 181, 186; habeas corpus and, 180, 182, 189; in Iraq, 61, 62, 65, 67, 139; secret prisons and, 150–51; Third Geneva convention, 15, 16, 35, 139, 181, 186; in the "war on terror," 18–19, 20, 26. *See also* International Humanitarian Law
ghost detainees, 58, 62, 192
Ginsberg, Justice Ruth Bader, 127, 146
Goldsmith, Jack, 25, 215, 216
Gonzales, Alberto R., 12, 19, 20, 33, 55, 145
Gordon, John A., 17
Graham, Senator Lindsey, 141, 142
Green, Judge Joyce Hens, 135–37
Guantanamo Bay, 33, 142, 151, 201, 212; application of international human rights instruments to, 143; application of U.S. Constitution to, 109–11, 134; conditions at, 154; death of detainees at, 154–55; December 28, 2001 OLC memo-

randum discussing, 29–30; detainee hunger strikes, 154; effect of DTA on, 140, 141, 144, 149; history of, 28, 31, 104; interrogations at, 41, 44, 132, 234, 247; jurisdictional issues surrounding, 29–30, 118–21, 127, 135, 230; Obama's decision to close, 3, 6, 238, 240, 251, 254; population of, 31, 34, 36, 37, 130, 132, 142, 151, 178, 205, 236, 248; positive effects of, 255–56; pressure to close, 155; Working Group Report for interrogations, 76

habeas corpus, writ of, 2, 29, 150, 161–62; application in wartime, 84, 91–93, 95–96, 124, 176–82, 188–90; application to detentions as part of a international force, 167–68; application to foreign nationals in the U.S., 96; application to foreign nationals outside the United States, 96–98, 100, 134 (see also *Boumediene v. Bush*)l application to Guantanamo, 118–21, 134, 147, 156, 158, 161; application to U.S. citizens held as enemy combatants, 121–26; avoidance of, 85, 130, 133, 135–37, 149, 160, 167, 170, 191–204; as a challenge to military commission process, 138–40; congressional attempts to restrict or eliminate, 2, 5, 151–56, 161, 257 (*see also* Detainee Treatment Act,Military Commissions Act; "in custody" requirement, 193–201; extraterritorial application of, 103–4, 112, 155, 177–78; failure to provide an adequate substitute for, 162–63, 182; history of, 81–85, 177; historical scope of, 83–84; history in America of, 86; history of jurisdictional stripping in the United States, 140; limitations based on citizenship, 177; limitations of, 191–204, 219, 257; remedies available under, 248–51, 257; role in preventing torture, 236; separation of powers and, 117, 159, 247–48; suspension of, 82–83, 89–90, 96, 124, 125–26, 147, 207
habeas corpus acts, 193; of 1641, 82; of 1679, 85; 1867 amendments, 193
Habib, Mamdouh, 137

Hague Conventions. *See* International Humanitarian Law
Haitian Refugees, 109–11
Hamdan, Naji, 200–201
Hamdan, Salim Ahmed, 137–39, 140, 147, 211, 212
Hamdan v. Rumsfeld, 5, 147–49, 150, 151, 152, 154
Hamdi v. Rumsfeld, 4, 121–26, 132, 162, 163, 189, 206, 207, 219, 243
Hamdi, Yaser, 77–78, 117, 121–26, 144; arrest, 77; release, 129
Hamiduva, Shakhrukh, 36
Hamilton, Alexander, 12, 26, 86
Harlan, Justice John Marshall, 105
Harlan, Justice John Marshall II, 107, 160
Harper's, 154
Harris, Rear Admiral Harry B., 33
Hartmann, Brig. Gen. Thomas W., 212
Haynes II, William J., 12, 18, 19, 38, 41, 213
hearsay evidence, and use of, 77, 122, 124, 130, 147, 162, 223, 242, 245
Heath, Attorney General Robert, 81
Henkin, Louis, 101
Henley, Colonel Stephen R., 213
Hicks, David, 211, 212
Hill, General James T., 40
Hirota v. MacArthur, 96, 98–99, 100, 168
Holder, Eric H., Jr., 241, 253
Hood, Major General Jay, 37
Hussein, Saddam. *See* Iraq
Huvelle, Judge Ellen S., 247

Ibrahim, Mohammed, 233
Idr, Mustafa Ait, 136
Immigration and Naturalization Service (INS), 54, 69. *See also* Department of Homeland Security
immigration law, 55, 177, 193, 202; history of, 90–91; use of for detention, 69–71
Immigration or Nationality Act, 110
In re Ross, 103–4, 106
INS v. St. Cyr, 91
Insular Cases, 104–6, 107, 109, 135, 156, 159–60
Inter-American Commission for Human Rights, 195

International Committee of the Red Cross (ICRC), 63, 185–86; criticism of U.S. actions, 42, 45, 49, 155; restricted access to detainees, 38, 39, 43, 58, 59, 63, 192
International Covenant on Civil and Political Rights (ICCPR), 56–57, 143, 194, 195; Human Rights Committee and, 56, 195
International Humanitarian Law, 15, 18, 125, 184, 186, 187; customary international law, 14, 124, 154, 181, 183, 186, 187; Hague Conventions, 15, 185. *See also* Geneva Conventions
International Military Tribunal for the Far East (IMTFE), 99, 168
Iraq, 5, 44, 55, 187; Bremer, Paul L., 60; Camp Bucca, 60; Camp Cropper, 60, 66; Camp Nama, 64; Coalition of the Willing, 60; Coalition Provisional Authority (CPA), 60; detentions in, 60–67, 167, 178; Hussein, Saddam, 60, 233, 234; invasion of, 25, 60, 234; Multi-National Force-Iraq (MNF-I), 60, 61, 167, 168; Task Force 6-26, 64; UN Security Counsel resolutions, 61

Jabour, Marwan, 59
Jackson, Justice Robert, 26, 29, 97, 98
Jacoby, Admiral Lowell E., 75
Jama'at-al-Tabliq, 136
Jandal, Abu, 232–33
Janko, Abdulrahim Abdul Razak, 246
Jawad, Mohammed, 213, 214, 246–47
Jefferson, Thomas, 86–87
Jessen, Bruce, 43, 44
Johnson Judge Sterling, Jr., 110–11
Johnson v. Eisentrager, 96–98, 100, 120, 121, 156, 160, 165, 168, 176, 182; compared with Guantanamo detainee cases, 118–19
Joint Task Force 170 memorandum, 76
Judge Advocate General Corps (JAG), 17, 39, 40, 138
Judiciary Act of 1789, 87, 88, 140

Katyal, Neal, 216
Kennedy, Justice Anthony M., 112, 121, 146, 156, 157, 159–62

Kenya, 199–200, 228
Kessler, Judge Gladys, 245
Khadr, Omar, 212
Kiyemba v. Bush, 249–50
Koh, Harold H., 25
Kollar-Kotelly, Judge Colleen, 134, 247
KUBARK Manual, 43
Kurnaz, Murat, 136
Kyl, Senator Jon, 141, 142

Lakawanna Six, 221, 230
Laws of War. *See* International Humanitarian Law
Leon, Judge Richard J., 135, 243–44, 246, 248
Lieber, Francis, 185
Lieberman, Senator Joe, 255
Lincoln, Abraham, 89
Lindh, John Walker, 13; detention and torture of, 14
Luban, David, 21
Lucenti, Brigadier General Martin, Jr., 37
Luttig, Judge Michael, 144–46

Maddox, Eric, 233
Madison, James, 26, 101–2, 106
Magna Carta, 81, 82
Malik, Mohammed Abdul, 199
Mansfield, Lord, 84
Marbury v. Madison, 87
Marshall, Chief Justice John, 87, 90, 98, 103
Marshall, Justice Thurgood, 112
material support laws, 221, 239
material witness statute, 71–73
Mayfield, Brandon, 72–73
McCain, Senator John, 142, 155
McCarthy, Andrew, 216–17
McFadden, Robert, 232
McKay, John, 209
McVeigh, Timothy, 217
Meshal, Amir Mohamed, 198–200
Meyers, General Richard B., 40
Micronesia, 108

military commissions, 17, 138–39, 152, 179, 218; alternatives to, 214–20, 226; Bush's order establishing, 16, 37; Convening Authority for 213; flaws in, 17, 147–48, 152, 211–14 (*see also* Military Commission Act of 2006 (MCA)); under Obama administration, 3, 238, 240, 241, 242; resistance to, 256; violation of Common Article 3 of the Geneva Conventions, 213
Military Commissions Act of 2006 (MCA), 5, 151–55, 156, 158, 177, 212
Miller, Major General Geoffrey D., 40, 45, 65
Miranda v. Arizona, 227
Miranda warnings, 227–29, 255
Mitchell, James, 43, 44, 232
Mobbs, Michael, 122; affidavit of 122, 124
Mohamed, Binyam, 46–47, 198
Mohammed, Khalid Sheikh (KSM), 145, 150, 151, 210, 232, 241, 254
Mora, Alberto J., 41
mosaic theory, 70, 245
Motz, Judge Diana Gribbon, 123, 206–7
Moussaoui, Zacarias, 13, 226–27
Mubahith, 196
Mueller, Robert S., 231
Muhamad, Faiz, 36
Mukasey, Michael B., 47, 216
Multi-National Force-Iraq (MNF-I). *See* Iraq
Munaf, Mohammad, 167, 169
Munaf v. Geren, 167–71
Murphy, Justice Frank, 95

National Security Court, 6, 215–18, 230, 236
National Security Entry-Exit Registration System, 70
NATO, 15
Navy Criminal Investigative Service (NCIS), 40, 42, 232
Neely v. Henkel, 104
Neuman, Gerald, 107, 175
New York Times, 23, 132, 153
Newman, Donna R., 47
Non-refoulement, 56–57, 140, 168–69, 194–95, 202, 203

Northern Alliance, 15, 28, 34, 77, 122, 246, 248
Nuremburg trials, 99

Obama, Barack, 3, 238, 253; administration, 6, 238–42, 250–51; Detention Policy Task Force, 238, 242, 251; executive orders, 238
O'Connor, Justice Sandra Day, 123–26
Office for Administrative Review of the Detention of Enemy Combatants (OAR-DEC), 157–58
Omar, Abu, 55–56, 195, 235
Omar, Shawqi, 167, 169
One Percent Doctrine, 25
Operation Enduring Freedom, 15
Osama Mustafa Hassan Nasr. *See* Omar, Abu

Padilla, Jose, 46, 47–48, 73–78, 117, 126–28, 144–45, 147, 208, 225, 232
Pakistan, 59
Panama Canal Zone, 108
Parhat, Hozaifa, 36
Parliamentary Assembly of the Council of Europe, 234–35
Patriot Act, 13, 206
PENTTBOM investigation, 69–71
Petraeus, General David H., 231
Posse Comitatus Act, 12
Powell, Colin L., 20, 23, 234
Philbin, Patrick F., 29–30
Philippines, 90
proxy detention, 193–94, 198, 200–202, 256

Qassem, Talaat Fouad, 52
Qatada, Abu, 34

Rahman, Sheikh Omar Abdel, 222, 224
Randolph, Judge A. Raymond, 156
Rasul v. Bush, 4, 117, 119–21, 126, 127, 130, 133, 135, 138, 140, 141, 147, 154, 156, 163, 166
Reagan, Ronald, 12, 27, 51
Rehnquist, Chief Justice William, 111–12, 127
Reid, Richard, 210–11, 255

Reid v. Covert, 106, 111, 112, 160
Ressam, Ahmed, 209
Rice, Condoleezza, 23, 57
Rizzo, John, 38
Roberts, Justice John, 146, 162–63
Robertson, Judge James, 139
Romig, Thomas J., 25
Ruhani, Gholam, 37
Rumsfeld, Donald, 23, 33, 35, 38, 40, 41, 75, 225
Rumsfeld v. Padilla, 4, 126–28, 187, 207, 219
Rutledge, Justice Wiley Blount, 95, 97

Salt Pit, 59
Sanchez, Lieutenant General Ricardo S., 62
Scalia, Justice Antonin, 120, 125, 162, 163–64
Scheuer, Michael, 52
Scott, General Winfield, 16–17
Scott v. Sandford, 103
secret evidence. *See* classified evidence
security detainees, 62, 64
Sedition Act of 1798, 102, 153
Seton Hall Law School, 34
Shahzad, Faisal, 255
"short shackling," 131
Somalia, 198–99
Soufan, Ali, 232
Souter, Justice David, 124, 127, 146, 147, 169
Spanish-American War, 104
Stevens, Justice John Paul, 125, 127–28, 146, 147–48, 156
Steyn, Lord, 155
Stone, Chief Justice Harlan Fiske, 95
Story, Justice Joseph, 90
Survival, Evasion, Resistance and Escape (SERE), 42, 44; reverse engineering of, 43, 62
Swartz, Bruce C., 42
Swift, Lt. Cmdr. Charles D., 138
Syria, 54

Taguba, Major General Antonio M., 63, 66
Taliban, 15; application of Geneva Conventions to, 18–20, 21; detention of, 119, 132, 219, 243

Task Force 6–26. See Iraq

Tatel, Judge David S., 166

Tenet, George, 23

Thomas, Justice Clarence, 126, 162

torture, 188, 190, 218, 237, 241; compensation for, 54–55, 153, 201–2, 241; cruel, inhuman, or degrading treatment (CID), 142–43, 144, 148, 152; development of, 42–45; effectiveness of, 231–36; "enhanced interrogation techniques," 22, 38–39, 40, 58, 142, 153, 212, 232, 240; use of evidence procured through, 131–32, 137, 143, 147, 152, 212, 213, 246, 247. *See also* torture memos

torture memos: criticisms of, 25; memorandum of August 1, 2002, on definition of torture (Yoo-Bybee), 21–22, 25; memorandum of August 1, 2002, for interrogation of Abu Zubaydah (Bybee), 22–23, 26, 241; memorandum of April 16, 2003 (Rumsfeld), 41; memorandum of January 25, 2002 (Gonzales), 20; memorandum of March 14, 2003 (Yoo), 24, 41, 65; OLC memoranda of May 2005, 26, 143

Uighurs, 36, 248–50. See also *Kiyemba v. Bush*

Uniform Code of Military Justice (UCMJ), 17, 24, 92, 138

unitary executive theory, 27, 57, 240

United Arab Emirates, 200–201

United Nations Security Council, 60–61, 100

United States Army-Marine Corps Counterinsurgency Manual, 190

United States Constitution, 69, 255–57; application to aliens in United States, 101–2, 160, 176; application to non-U.S. citizens abroad, 98, 107–13, 141, 156, 159, 160, 164, 288n65; application to U.S. citizens abroad, 103–7, 160, 164; Article I of, 87; Article II of, 12; Article III of, 87; Due Process Clause, 48, 110; federal habeas corpus jurisdiction, 88; Fifth Amendment, 106, 143; fair trial guaran-

tees, 207, 226; Fourth Amendment, 74, 111–12, 228, 229; separation of powers, 26, 154, 179, 181, 190, 249; Sixth Amendment, 106, 227; Suspension Clause, 86, 101, 156, 158, 161, 163, 164, 166, 176, 177, 194; Takings Clause, 109

United States Court of Appeals; District of Columbia Circuit, 109, 139, 140, 157, 166, 167, 170, 179, 249–50, 251; Eleventh Circuit, 110; Fourth Circuit, 122, 127, 144–45, 205, 208, 239; Second Circuit, 110

United States Supreme Court, 2, 154; habeas corpus detention rulings, 69, 90, 146, 157, 190, 194, 239, 250, 257; on court-stripping measures, 156, 161–64; on equal protection, 103; on extraterritorial application of Constitution, 2, 106–7, 110, 168, 179, 255–56; on Suspension Clause, 86, 164; enemy combatant decisions, 5, 117–28, 135, 138, 150

United States v. Verdugo-Urquidez, 111–12, 121

unlawful combatant. *See* "enemy combatants"

unprivileged belligerent, 183, 185, 186, 239

Urbina, Judge Ricardo M., 249

Vance, Donald, 66

Vandeveld, Lt. Colonel Darrel, 214

Walton, Judge Reggie B., 243

war crimes, 18, 210, 213, 242, 246, 252

War Crimes Act, 19, 20, 21, 148, 152, 153

War of 1812, 91

"war on terror," 57, 67; Geneva Conventions application to, 18, 139; duration of, 34, 119, 208; Obama and, 251, 254

waterboarding, 22, 24, 142, 151, 212, 232, 233

Wedgewood, Ruth, 25

White, Justice Edward Douglas, 105

White, Mary Jo, 72

Wilkinson III, Judge J. Harvey, 207–8

Williams, Judge Stephen, 139

Wittes, Benjamin, 216

Wolfowitz, Paul, 130, 132, 225
Woolsey, James R., 25
Working Group Report for Interrogations at Guantanamo, 76
World War II, 17, 90, 94, 99, 100, 108, 165, 168, 189, 219

Yamashita v. Styer, 94–95, 96, 100

Yoo, John, 12, 18, 19, 21, 24, 29–30, 41, 65, 228. *See also* Department of Justice; torture
Young, Judge Richard, 211
Yunis, Fawaz, 51

Zubaydah, Abu, 22, 43, 44, 46, 48, 145, 150, 231–32

About the Author

JONATHAN HAFETZ is Associate Professor of Law at Seton Hall University School of Law and has litigated leading habeas corpus detention cases. He is the coeditor (with Mark Denbeaux) of *The Guantánamo Lawyers: Inside a Prison Outside the Law* (New York University Press, 2009).